The Psychology of Crime

The Psychology of Crime

BY DAVID ABRAHAMSEN, M.D.

Columbia University Press New York 1960

For WINFRED OVERHOLSER, M.D.,

whose friendship and pioneering endeavors

have stimulated my work so much

Preface

Since my first book, *Crime and the Human Mind*, was published by Columbia University Press some sixteen years ago, we have experienced deep-seated changes in our society. Against a background of social unrest we have witnessed a sharp increase in the number of antisocial and criminal persons and in emotionally disturbed ones. It was therefore obvious that a new book in the field of criminal psychopathology with due consideration to the many sociological aspects had to be written.

The task has been arduous because in the intervening years new research in the field has been carried out by many investigators, including myself, and the findings have had to be sifted and evaluated. The book is therefore based upon research findings from both here and Europe. In particular it is drawn from my own research and teaching in the field of mental and social pathology at the Psychiatric Institute, Columbia University, as Consultant to the Department of Mental Hygiene in the State of New York, and at the Graduate Faculty of the New School of Social Research.

This book undertakes the task of studying the basic factors that are instrumental in bringing about criminal behavior and criminal careers. Since the causes, or what we believe to be the causes of crime are relative, this study runs the gamut of the complexity of human behavior. The book deals, as the title indicates, in the main with the mind of the criminal, his emotions and his behavior, as it expresses itself in his social environment. It is not enough just to understand his motivations for his antisocial and criminal behavior; we also have to keep in mind the constant intermeshing and interaction between his personality and environment. This intertwining has a crucial bearing upon the prevention of crime, and a vital relationship to medicine and sociology, to law and anthropology.)

True, although we leave still many problems unanswered concerning the control of crime, we may hope, with our concerted efforts, one day to be able to master this social disease. We, in the United States, as well as people elsewhere in the world, may then be able to look forward with some optimism to the day when many youngsters and adults alike will turn away from their criminal path toward constructive conduct.

Those of us who deal with the many unfortunates know through painful experience the pitfalls and disappointments we have to face in trying to rehabilitate them, whether they be emotionally disturbed persons or criminals, or both. By the same token we shall try to remember those offenders we were able to rehabilitate who, we know, will always remain grateful because they once more were given a chance upon which a safe future could be built.

I am glad to extend my thanks to my many assistants and associates who have previously been connected with my research work. I would also like to thank Joan McQuary and Dr. William Bridgwater of Columbia University Press for their stimulating interest, and my secretary, Mrs. Helen Bierman Morris, for her devoted and painstaking work on the manuscript; thanks also go to Mrs. Jeanne Coty Ringer for her many suggestions.

Last but not least, I would like to thank my wife, Lova, who has followed the development of this book with unending encouragement.

It is my hope that this book in general will be used by students in the fields of social pathology and criminal behavior, as well as

by lawyers, psychiatrists, educators, judges, psychiatric social workers, and personnel of law enforcement agencies. In the last analysis,
however, the purpose of any book is that it be meaningful and useful to people in all walks of life. I hope that this purpose will be
fulfilled.

May, 1960   DAVID ABRAHAMSEN, M.D.

Contents

xii   CONTENTS

The Psychology of Crime

Introduction

For many years I have studied various types of maladjusted individuals. Among them have been persons suffering from psychosomatic disorders, from neuroses or psychoses, and those who have transgressed the law. In delving into the minds of people who have committed crimes such as burglary, rape, or even murder, I have come to realize the necessity for a complete reorientation of our basic understanding of criminal behavior. The need for reorientation becomes essential when we realize that criminal law in the main has reflected the history of the emotional attitudes of men throughout the ages, as expressed through the evolution of society. However, while the riddle of crime is a riddle of society, it is also the riddle of the individual in all his infinite variations.

We may better realize what our attitudes toward the criminal are when we look at the development of the law. In primitive times people were bound together through blood relationship and through such common activities as the search for food and the building of fires to cook it. These common activities created a need for establishing customs, based largely on taboos, which were followed either through desire or fear.

In due time, according to Edward Westermarck, the customs

became law, and the law itself became an order to which all had to yield.[1] The exchange of services among members of the primitive community was the motivating force behind adherence to the law.[2] This principle of give-and-take was built upon emotional and social interchange, on which primitive society existed.

An infraction of the laws of taboo was considered a crime and brought automatic punishment. This attitude made an investigation of the crime and the criminal superfluous. Primitive society was not concerned with the motivation behind a criminal act; its only interest was to punish the culprit so that the people would obtain satisfaction for their vengeful feelings.

From time immemorial there have been two crimes—homicide and incest—which, with few exceptions, have been universally condemned by members of all societies. Incest had to be prohibited because, as stated by Malinowski, it too was incompatible with the basis of culture. We can deduce that since murder and incest were forbidden, these crimes were specifically singled out because of man's overwhelming tendencies in these directions. People in primitive societies, in order to protect themselves from those inclinations which they recognized as antisocial, raised barriers against them in the form of taboos. They were afraid of the evil powers which they believed were incorporated in these taboos in the same way they were afraid of witchcraft, which originated from the belief that the culprit could conjure evil spirits, but such a fear reflected also their own fears of committing criminal acts.

Since man in primitive society believed that his behavior was determined by fate or governed by divine guidance, there was no reason for him to find a motivation for his actions. Today, of course, we know that there is always some motivation behind criminal behavior. When we do not find it too readily, it does not mean that none exists; rather, it is simply more unconscious. These motivations, even if they stem only from superstitions, dreams, or legends, still act as powerful forces in precipitating criminal behavior.

It is not so surprising, then, that the enormous quantity of legal records and texts collected from the earliest days contains little information about the criminal himself. What stands out in sharp contrast to this distinct lack of understanding the offender is the strong reaction of the people to the culprit. There is hardly any aspect of human life in which a people's emotions and hostilities have been more forcefully expressed than in their attitude toward the man who has broken the law. When law-abiding citizens react mercilessly toward a criminal and his deed, it is not only because they want to see the law obeyed or because they want retribution, but also because the offender acts out antisocial impulses which so many people would like to act out but do not dare to because of fear of the consequences. Unconsciously they identify with the criminal because of their own latent antisocial tendencies and somehow vicariously demand and accept the punishment to relieve their own guilt feelings.

It is in the code of Hammurabi, fl. 2100 B.C., that we first encounter *lex talionis,* the principle of punishment which demands retaliation for the crime committed and is expressed in the old words, "an eye for an eye; a tooth for a tooth." This principle later appeared in the Mosaic law and has influenced Christianity and civil and criminal law up to our time. The demand for revenge expressed the self-preservation instinct within the group, which considered every infraction of the rules as a threat to its safety but which also expressed the unconscious desire of the group's vicarious need for punishment. Religious thoughts and fears about the fate of a man's soul have led to the belief that human justice should to some extent mirror the punishment or reward that he would receive in the after-life.

Unconcern with the fate of the criminal was a direct result of the belief in the depravity of man. Since the human being was considered evil by nature, it made no difference if he were sentenced to die for some trivial offense. The doctrine of freedom of the will implied that the criminal's free will produced his own antisocial or criminal behavior. Naturally, then, it seemed superfluous to inquire into any causes at all for the crime. According to this view the offender had perpetrated the crime because his own will had directed him toward accomplishing it. This belief bolstered the faith in retaliation as the guilding principle in punishing crime, and it also encouraged severe penalties. Even the philosopher

Emanuel Kant, who was considered to have a liberal mind, once said, "Before the earth perishes, the last thief should be hanged in the guts of the last murderer."

Despite Christ's statement "Let him who is without sin cast the first stone," it was not until the latter part of the eighteenth century that the question of more humane treatment of criminals first came under strong debate. Influenced by such contemporary humanitarian writers as Voltaire, Montesquieu, Condorcet, and Rousseau, Cesare Beccaria in 1764 violently protested against the cruel and inhuman punishment inflicted upon criminals and the arbitrary way in which sentences were imposed. He stated that any punishment should be the mildest permitted in a given case, that it should be in proportion to the crime, and that it should be determined by law.[3]

Faulty as this utilitarian doctrine of the Classical school might appear, it was embodied in the French Code of 1791, but in actual practice the Code became a compromise between Beccaria's ideas and the medieval system of penology. While it simplified the legal process and placed emphasis upon the crime by inflicting the same measure of punishment upon the first offender as upon the recidivist, it completely disregarded the personality of the criminal and failed to consider whether he was a minor, a mental defective, or a psychotic person.

The Neoclassical school asserted that not only should the degree of punishment be in proportion to the crime, but also it should be determined in accordance with the personality make-up of the criminal. Although such a view was put into the new revised French Code of 1810, in actual practice the criminal's personality was disregarded.

Since the new humanitarian ideas exerted influence only upon the punishment of the criminal, another concept was necessary to bring about a more realistic consideration of the offender. Such a view was hastened by scientific discoveries in the field of chemistry during the eighteenth century, carried out by such men as Lavoisier, Dalton, and Wohler. Their discoveries and those of others later on shook many old concepts about human behavior and the world. Scientific investigations opened new perspectives;

new fields were examined; new insight was achieved. This knowledge stimulated investigation of the intricacies of the human mind and the social relations of man. Although the search was basically directed toward sociological manifestations, it was later on turned toward man himself as part of the environment in which he lived. These ideas, partly stimulated by Philippe Pinel, "the liberator" of the insane, led Morel to state in 1857 that the criminal was a product of mental, physical, and moral introgression.

At this time a powerful idea appeared which gave quite a different characteristic not only to the conception of human life, but also to that of the criminal. It was Charles Darwin's theory of evolution, in which he held that physical and psychological functions gradually evolved through express adaptation to environment. As corollaries to this theory he contended that man was intimately connected with other animals and was motivated by the same biological drives. Here it must be said that the normal mind differs strongly from that of the animal, but both have in their basic structures and in their principal disposition mutual mental elements. These doctrines were destined to make a tremendous impression at a time when all seeking knowledge within the criminological field found themselves halted by a barrier of fixed and limited ideas. Darwin's theory impressed one of the most distinguished physicians and anthropologists in the criminological field, Cesare Lombroso (1836–1909), the founder of research in medical criminology. He tried to apply Darwin's biological theory to the criminal and to crime, as did Herbert Spencer by his scientific philosophy.[4] In a little pamphlet entitled *The Criminal in Relation to Anthropological Jurisprudence and Psychiatry*, published in 1876, Lombroso stated that the criminal behaved as he did because he was born so, and thus he did not act through free will but merely expressed his inner nature. Lombroso's pamphlet later grew to be a work of three volumes.

However much one disagrees with Lombroso's findings and conclusions, even his most ardent opponents must admit that he made the first attempt to establish a scientific criminal psychopathology. This is Lombroso's undying contribution. Among other things, his work gave rise to the idea that the study of psychiatry should be based upon medical experimental methods. Although his theory of the born criminal is not considered valid today, one must not forget the brilliant beginning which he made through his investigations of the scientific characteristics of the criminal and the causes of crime. His investigations consisted of measuring the skull and various other organs in post-mortem observation and of examining living criminals with regard to blood pressure, emotional reactions, hearing, taste, smell, and even handwriting. Thus Lombroso transferred the method of anthropological science to the field of psychiatry. In our time this type of anthropological study has been carried out upon criminals by Ernest A. Hooton [5] and by W. H. Sheldon,[6] thereby reviving the theory of predisposition to crime, which Lombroso envisioned.[7]

Here it must be pointed out that Lombroso and his followers claimed that there was an absolute correlation between bodily form and criminal behavior. However, as everyone acquainted with basic research knows, in order for such a conclusion to be valid, studies would have had to be made not only upon the criminal group, but also upon a noncriminal group as a control. The Lombrosian school did not take this into consideration, nor did it account for the fact that criminal behavior occurred in persons whose anatomical type differed from what they considered the criminal anatomical type. They also left unproved their theory that a particular anatomical type in itself would imply a certain kind of behavior.[8] Although Lombroso's data on anatomical characteristics of the criminal proved to be inaccurate and not at all conclusive, his description of the psychological traits which the criminal manifested (instability, impulsiveness, meagerly developed affections, vanity, lying, gambling, and lack of restraint) was more nearly correct.

When Lombroso launched his ideas, they were sharply criticized and caused heated debate. Because of new investigations and additional knowledge, he eventually began to modify them. It is a pity that the prominence given to his basic idea—the born criminal—obscured the fact that he was the first one to make a scientific attempt to classify criminals. Above all, however, he will be remembered for disproving the assumption that a criminal committed a criminal act because his will was free and so was unquestionably responsible for his act. Furthermore, by insisting that the personality of the offender be examined, he paved the way for the idea that the criminal was the cause and that the crime was the result. Lombroso realized that future research in criminology had to be built upon a new basis, for which he constructed the framework.[9] His ideas found fruitful soil in the minds of many conscientious sociologists, psychiatrists, lawyers. Not only did the criminal himself come under closer scrutiny, but also the entire prison system was placed in a new light.

In 1884 Enrico Ferri (1856–1929), a former pupil of Lombroso, in his *Homicide and Criminal Sociology* stressed sociological factors, such as industrial, economic, political, climatic and geographical conditions, and also such elements as the constitution of the family. He concluded that if people and their surroundings remained constant, crime would remain stable, regardless of methods of punishment used (the law of criminal saturation). Therefore he proposed preventive steps, both sociological and educational, such as better marriage and divorce laws, shorter working hours, and better education.

Closely related to Ferri's views were those of Raffaeli Garofalo (1852–1937), who considered criminal behavior from a psychological, rather than from a sociological or anatomical, viewpoint. He emphasized studying the criminal's personality and the circumstances under which the crime had been committed. The so-called French or Lyon school emphasized environmental or sociological elements in producing crime. The school was headed by A. Lacassagne (1843–1924), a specialist in forensic medicine.

It was but natural that the new ideas advanced by the Italian and French schools should spread and give impetus to new concepts of the criminal and his treatment. In Germany in 1880 the psychiatrist Emil Kraepelin published a pamphlet called *Die Abschaffung des Strafmasses,* which created a stir because it bore the motto *Pro Humanitate.* The result was the shelving of the policy of retaliation and the establishing of one aimed at improving the offender. The criminal was to be given an indeterminate sentence, not a fixed or flat one.

This new idea in penology was also adopted within the ranks of lawyers. In 1881 Professor Frantz von Liszt (one of the most illustrious figures in criminal law, as famous in his field as his cousin was in music) and Professor Adolph Dochow founded a periodical called *Zeitschrift für die Gesamte Strafrechtswissenschaft*, (*Periodical for Common Jurisprudence*). With youthful enthusiasm Liszt challenged the Classical philosophy of crime and its treatment. The main purpose of his school was to introduce a method of investigating the causes of crime which emphasized that crime should be examined as a social-ethical phenomenon and that punishment should be regarded accordingly.

Liszt, together with G. A. von Hamel, of Amsterdam, and Adolphe Prins, of Brussels, established on New Year's Eve, 1888, the International Association of Criminal Law (*L'Union Internationale de Droit Penal*). The association contended that crime and punishment should be considered as much from a sociological as from a judicial point of view. The psychiatrist Richard von Krafft-Ebing sharpened Liszt's awareness of the close relationship between psychology and psychiatry and criminal law.[10] Liszt maintained that the legislator who wants to get to the root of crime must know not only its exterior, but also its deeper layers. Without a scientifically founded etiology of crime, a rational philosophy of it is impossible.[11] His important text book on German criminal law first appeared in 1881 and later grew to be an invaluable work.[12] Widely distributed in translation, it made Liszt equally known outside of Germany. He may well be regarded as the founder of the German school of sociological criminology. (For a fuller development of criminal law, see Chapter XII.)

Some twenty years after Kraepelin's demand for reform of the criminal law, a young psychiatrist, Gustav Aschaffenburg of Cologne, who was to exert a tremendous influence upon the development of the philosophy of crime, came to the fore. He had gained valuable experience as a psychiatrist at a large penitentiary, and he collected considerable material as an expert in court cases. Aschaffenburg said there was no doubt that the new trend in criminal law was intimately connected with the advances being made in medicine and anthropology. In order to stimulate investigation and discussion of the causes of crime, in 1904 he founded a periodical on criminal psychology and criminal law reform. Publication was discontinued in 1936, when at the age of seventy, he was forced to leave Germany because of the Nazis. The last issue contained his article entitled "Ruckblick und Ausblick" ("Retrospect and Prospect"), in which he pointed out that the psychiatrist had to make a decisive contribution to the problem of crime. It is to be regretted that Aschaffenburg did not apply Freud's psychological findings to criminal behavior. If he had, the science of criminology would have been furthered immensely.

Charles Goring's book, *The English Convict,* covered extensive examinations of 3,000 English prisoners and a like number of normal people. Goring directed a devastating criticism against Lombroso's idea of the born criminal. "Our inevitable conclusion," he said, "might be that there is no such thing as a physical criminal type."

Thus we see that the Classical school, while emphasizing the rights and the liberties of the individual, maintained that the criminal be punished with an unvarying penalty; the Neoclassical school made the penal system flexible by excluding the child, the mental defective and psychotic from punishment; the Lombrosian school explained the criminal's behavior mainly by his anatomical, and to a lesser degree by his psychological, make-up, but it led to no specific changes in the penal code.

It is remarkable to see how one-sided the early criminological investigators were. They did not realize that many factors were involved in the causation of crime, and their limited view delayed progress in solving the sociological and psychiatric problems of society.

With the increase in crime and delinquency in the last thirty years, investigators have come to concentrate more and more upon the causation of crime. However, even in the United States, such investigation has been hampered because researchers do not basically interest themselves as much with the personality and behavior of the criminal as with isolating him from society. Thus they focus their attention upon imprisonment, which has naturally resulted in the development of our huge prison system, emphasizing custodial care rather than treatment and rehabilitation.

Yet as early as 1786 at a meeting of the American Philosophical Society, Benjamin Rush, "America's first psychiatrist," stated that when a criminal carried out a criminal act, it was accompanied by a certain state of mind, a statement which he reiterated in 1810 [13] in his lectures on the study of medical jurisprudence at the University of Pennsylvania. In 1838 Isaac Ray made a distinction between a criminal and an insane individual.[14]

It is a pity that for quite some time American criminology did not follow the path which Rush and Ray had opened. Almost fifty years lapsed before there was a renewed interest in criminal behavior among American psychiatrists. In 1886 Charles Mill, of Philadelphia, stated that since crime was in reality a violation of law, it was incorrect to build a theory of crime on an anatomical basis.[15] Further contributions were made by Hamilton Wey, a prison physican at Elmira Reformatory; [16] W. A. M'Corn, a prison physician at the Wisconsin State Prison (1896); and the psychologist George Dawson, who, in examining delinquent girls and boys from reform schools in Massachusetts, found that over 30 percent of the delinquent children had defective vision.[17] G. Frank Lydstone and Eugene Talbot carried out extensive investigations of the brains of murderers and other criminals at the Illinois State Penitentiary at Joliet. Their findings were published in 1891 and were later included in Lydstone's pamphlet, *The Diseases of Society* (1904), in which he pointed out that there was a correlation between a criminal's intelligence and his criminal ability, as well as the type of criminal he was. In a separate publication by Talbot, based on the same studies, he found the offender to be an irritable, frequently incorrigible, and stupid fellow.[18]

In 1900 August Drahms wrote about the American criminal from an anthropological and psychobiological viewpoint. In *The Criminal* he concluded that there was no such thing as a criminal type, even though in many instances he had discovered an imbalance of the autonomic nervous system, indicating a prevalence of a physical defect in the criminal. Equally important were G.

Stanley Hall's investigations, which brought out the fact that criminal children were of a neurotic character.[19]

In the last thirty years the American contribution to the science of criminology has come more and more to the fore. Partly responsible for this was the trial of Leopold and Loeb in 1924, when the defense counsel engaged several psychiatrists to examine the two young offenders. One of the psychiatrists was William A. White, superintendent of Saint Elizabeths Hospital in Washington, D.C., who, in addition to paving the way for a realistic understanding of the criminal, can be considered the dean of psychiatric criminology in the United States. The psychiatric findings brought out the conscious and unconscious sexual aspects of the case and helped the judge to arrive at a valid understanding of the defendants.

Since then a great deal of research has been done in the field of sex offenses by Karl Bowman in California and by me at Sing Sing Prison; at the Psychiatric Institute in New York City, and in the field of juvenile delinquency. William Healy and Augusta Bronner did research leading to a better understanding of delinquent behavior,[20] and there is no doubt that August Aichhorn, who applied psychoanalysis to delinquent children in order to help him understand their problems, provided much impetus for future work.[21] His child guidance clinic, established by Vienna's Psychoanalytic Society, became an institute for retraining and reeducating these children. In more recent years Sheldon and Eleanor Glueck have made extensive studies in which they have tried to establish a basis for predicting delinquent behavior.[22] And in New Jersey Ralph Brancale is the director of a diagnostic center designed especially for young offenders.

It is impossible to describe in detail all the contributions made to the field of criminology. In 1944 my book on the relationship between criminal behavior and the human mind was published.[23] After carrying out basic research in criminal behavior for many years and investigating the family situation as a fundamental source of crime, I found that family tension is the basic cause of such behavior and that there is a close relationship between psychosomatic disorders and crime. Then, of course, we must all pay tribute to such men as Winfred Overholser (Dr. White's most able successor at Saint Elizabeths Hospital, who has been very active in the realm of legal psychiatry), Gregory Zilboorg (who, with Dr. Overholser, established the Isaac Ray Lectures through the American Psychiatric Association, which is a reward to the most outstanding man in the field of criminology each year), Franz Alexander and Hugo Staub,[24] Manfred Guttmacher, Benjamin Karpman, Karl A. Menninger, and Bernard Glueck, not to mention those who have been very active in the sociological aspects of criminology, such as E. H. Sutherland, Thorsten Sellin, and Paul Tappan. In the field of prevention Austin MacCormick has been an ardent worker, and in England Edward Glover and Mellita Schmideberg, the latter now residing in the United States, have both carried out extensive work in the field of criminal psychopathology.[25]

Of course, Freud's contributions to general psychopathology were the greatest of all, particularly his idea that unconscious motivation is the drive for most of our actions. This has allowed the application of psychoanalysis to psychiatric criminology,[26] which has paved the way for a better understanding of the mind of the criminal and his act. Unfortunately, during his long and admirable career Freud did not find time to deal with criminal behavior specifically, since he put all of his energy into exploring the unconscious and its significance in individual psychopathology. But in spite of this as early as 1906 he wrote a paper discussing the theoretical and practical differences between the neurotic and the criminal,[27] and in 1915 he wrote about "criminality from a sense of guilt" in a chapter entitled "Some Character-Types Met with in Psycho-Analytic Work." [28]

As seen from this brief historical survey, criminology has now developed into a science with many ramifications, all of which are aimed at finding the causes of criminal behavior so that it can be counteracted and prevented realistically. Since much of the criminal's behavior expresses his aggressions and since mind and behavior are intimately connected, it is obvious that the psychoanalyst or psychiatrist, whose profession brings him into daily contact with the personality and behavior of man, must play a major part in solving the enigma of crime. Psychiatric examination is necessary because understanding the criminal requires an evaluation of his personality and of the emotional factors which contribute to his criminal act so that we can then direct our findings toward effective treatment.

But our approach cannot only be a psychiatric one. The field of criminology is complex and the causes of crime are manifold. We must not lose sight of sociological, anthropological, and biological factors when probing the depths of the human mind to ascertain the conscious and unconscious motivations of human behavior and especially those aspects which may lead man into crime.

CHAPTER I

Social Pathology and Crime

The fundamental desires and inclinations that motivate normal social conduct are the same ones that drive the offender into criminal acts. He differs from the law-abiding citizen chiefly in the means he chooses for the expression of his instinctual drives and in the object of his aggressions (society and its members). This difference is more a matter of degree than of kind, since basically the offender and the nonoffender are woven from the same cloth. Although their basic personality make-up is the same, both having social and antisocial, constructive and destructive traits, we can say here, as an introductory remark, that they both act and react differently to the stimuli in their personality make-up (hopes, wishes, fears, anxieties, and the like) and in the situation in which they find themselves.

For the purposes of this book I would like to make a distinction between an antisocial act and a crime. An antisocial act is one which is not socially acceptable but which may not necessarily constitute a crime. A crime is an antisocial act which is punishable by law.

In other words, an antisocial act is always involved when a crime is committed, but the reverse is not true; that is, a crime is not always involved when an antisocial act is committed. For example, an alcoholic may be antisocial but not a criminal, provided his actions do not harm society. Similarly, an habitual truant is antisocial but not a criminal unless during his truancy he commits a crime. Although an antisocial act by definition may seem more a psychiatric problem, a sociological element is still involved here, as it is in criminal behavior.

Since every person behaves and acts simultaneously as an individual and as a member of society, criminal behavior, as well as all other conduct, has two roots. However, society's construction and function make it possible to divide this further into the community and the family, with which the individual is in closer contact. We can therefore say that all human behavior really has four roots: 1) society at large, representing all law-enforcement bodies; 2) the community, with its subcultures; 3) the particular setup of the family; and 4) the individual himself. The first three influence the person through external pressures, which in turn produce an internal reaction in the individual himself. Among these four there is a complex and dynamic relationship, which becomes even more complicated when we have to deal with the intricate mechanism of the human mind.

To take the last point first, although we have a working concept of man's functioning, we still lack knowledge of the basic structure of the brain. It must be stated that psychiatry and psychoanalysis as sciences are very young compared with sociology, physiology, anthropology, and law. Yet they have made great strides in discovering many of the elements responsible for our behavior and have given us much more insight into the functioning of the human mind than other sciences. This is of course only to be expected, since it is the nature of psychiatry and psychoanalysis to probe the mind of man.

A human being is always a product of his personality and the situation in which he lives. In the same way that social behavior is a function of the personality, situation, culture, time, and geography, so also is crime.

A human being is never an isolated being, no matter how great an individualist he may be. He is intimately connected with his environment and can be understood only on the basis of this environment and his own personality. He is not only a center of action but also a center of reaction, both manifestations closely connected with his own field,[1] the field here meaning environment as a dynamic property. From the center of action impulses run to the periphery, which in turn transmits impulses back to the center. Since there is an incessant reciprocal interplay, there is an eternal contact so that the center—that is, man—creates a unit with his surroundings. A person forms a functional relationship with his environment, and the environment acts in a functional relationship to him. The result is that he is to a high degree tied to his own field. These elements, acting like the force of gravitation, consist of the conscious and unconscious emotions and the sociological and biological influences. An individual lives in his environment as if he were in a magnetic field. Many of his psychological qualities are the results of the field. We may be able to understand this better if we think of Buddhism from a cultural-psychological viewpoint as being a functional expression of the interaction between the Oriental personality and culture.

Every person lives in a socio-psycho-biological field and is influenced by all three forces. Man's comprehension of himself and his own situation we can call the psychological field.[2] Although he is influenced by his own judgment of the situation and circumstances under which he acts, he is consciously or unconsciously tied to his surroundings. What has been said for man in general applies equally to the specific case of the lawbreaker. His criminal act is directed according to his psychological make-up and his total situation. Although his mind is behind the act, many actions and reactions on the part of the perpetrator have taken place so that in a functional sense he constitutes a unit with his environment. If, for instance, a criminal pattern is present in his environment and the exposure is strong enough, it may affect his behavior and actions. This may take place without his being consciously aware of it, showing how intermingled his social field may be with that of his personality structure.

All activities, including criminal ones, must have nourishing soil in which to grow, and this soil we find within society, within the community, within the family, and within the offender himself.

In 1941 a little over 1½ million major crimes (according to FBI classification) were committed in the United States.[3] This number remained almost constant during World War II and until 1946, when it rose to about 1,700,000.[4] In 1952 the number of major crimes climbed above the 2 million mark;[5] in 1956 it was 2,563,150. The 1957 figure was higher than ever before—2,796,400; this was 9.1 percent above 1956 and 23.9 percent over the average for the previous five years.[6] In terms of volume alone (56.2 percent above the 1950 level), at the end of 1957 crime was rising four times as fast as the total population (up 13 percent since 1950),[7] and latest statistics for 1958 show that there has been a further increase of major crimes, up 8 percent over 1957. The increase was most pronounced in smaller cities and among juveniles, and New York, as usual, led the nation in seven categories of major infractions.[8] In 1950 it was estimated that a crime took place every 18 seconds; in 1957, one every 11.3 seconds. Thus we see how prevalent crime is in the United States and how much it has risen in the years after World War II.

It is only fair to mention that in other countries too, such as England, France, and Germany, there has been a marked increase in crime in the immediate postwar years. The Social Commission of the United Nations' Economic and Social Council reports that this increase took place mainly in the sphere of offenses against property. Canada, Australia, and certain South American republics were the exceptions. In most countries the increase was more marked among convicted women than among men. The rise was steeper among first offenders than among recidivists, and to a certain extent the increased volume of crime appeared to be due more to criminal activities of hitherto law-abiding citizens than to repeated offenses of recidivists.[9] In the Scandinavian countries there has been a general increase in crime, but it is far less than that reported in the United States.[10]

It is impossible to estimate how many billions of dollars crime costs the United States every year. Most of the cost is apparently due to the activities of organized crime syndicates. It has been estimated by the Federal Trade Commission that one racket, dealing with the sale of worthless securities, pocketed $25 billion in ten years. When Al Capone was at the height of his power, it was estimated that his income was about $30 million a year.

It is of course difficult for the average person to imagine how much a racketeer may earn a year. Some years ago I made an estimate of it. Let us consider how much even a "small-fry" racketeer earns on his slot machines. If he has two hundred machines, each averaging a take of $50 a week, his total for one week would be $10,000. Of this amount he receives half, that is, $5,000 a week, and the rest goes for expenses. Five thousand dollars a week comes to $260,000 a year—and this amount is only from slot machines.[11] Most of the income is never reported, and the government loses out on the taxes due.

However, the dishonesty involved is only part of the unhappiness and tragedy which crime brings in its wake. It is impossible to estimate the emotional and social degradation the criminal, his family, and his community suffer.

The crime rates for the United States, as mentioned above, are so high that the question of whether it is more lawless than other countries has been asked. Among other things, it has been stated that crime is a product of American culture.[12] But what is American culture? One salient factor stands out, and that is that life in the United States is basically complicated. Our country is very young and may be compared with an adolescent who feels he is powerful and at the same time is unsure of himself because he is still a child. Then there are many immigrants from many countries, and on the whole people here do not remain situated in any one location for any great length of time; they move from place to place rather frequently, thereby not establishing roots and without a feeling of permanence and stability. Also, because of this country's great size and heterogeneous population, resulting in various kinds of customs, habits, and living conditions in general, tension and unrest are bound to grow, and friction and violent reactions, often of a criminal nature, frequently follow. No group is immune to the effects of such sociological phenomena.

Another factor to consider is our enormous material resources, which are not found in similar abundance anywhere else in the world. These resources, of course, offer unusual opportunities, but they also create an unusually high degree of competition. There is little doubt that this keen competition is to a large extent instrumental in creating a climate of crime, particularly in the larger cities. On the other hand, our material resources have also become the stimulus for American wealth and success. This is borne out by history. One need only go back to the Age of Pericles in Athens or the Renaissance in Italy to see that these flourishing periods arose by and large as a result of great material wealth achieved under strenuous competitive conditions.[13] The same forces tending to work for destructive purposes can also work for constructive ones.

As we have seen, mainly because of the abundance of natural resources here and our primary concern with building our country, there has come to be an overemphasis on material things. Possibly, therefore, the human spirit in America has been compressed rather than expressed. It was Veblen who stated that the symbol of success in the United States is conspicuous consumption. Therefore, money is of immense importance in our culture. Although many people obtain their money honestly and thereby gain prestige, quite a few obtain it in a less honest manner and still gain the same prestige. However, I question whether greed for money and the material things it brings is the basic element which instigates criminal acts or whether it is not rather a lust for the power and success obtained through money which is often the driving force behind criminality.

There is no doubt that conspicuous consumption is dramatized and even glamorized by advertising and publicity, whose purpose is to stimulate unsatisfied desires and longings. The result is that our culture is one of competition, in which restless, dissatisfied, and competitive people are involved in an almost merciless struggle for "success." Then too, because of the many material resources here, the effect of technology upon our daily lives has possibly been far greater than in any other place. Mass production and division of labor have given many people a feeling of uselessness and therefore a heightened need for recognition. The craving for success becomes so intense for many people that life has little or no meaning beyond being "successful."

A person with an overpowerful drive for success is usually trying to fulfill some unsatisfied emotional need within himself. If he did not feel some void, his drive for success would not operate so continuously. This type of person feels insecure and therefore has to bolster his ego—his own self-esteem—in some way, which he can do only by external means because he lacks inner emotional resources. Thus even if he acquires a position of power, it is a hollow one; it is only something to cover up his basic feelings of failure. Therefore, while on the surface a power-ridden man may appear to be the most confident one in the world, his power is only a veneer, a compensation for his frustrated aggressions and anxieties. This is one of the reasons why he always has to have more power and more money so he can be more successful.

By real success I mean the courage to change obstacles into achievements, not through a need for external recognition but to make one feel happy and useful, regardless of how insignificant one's achievements may seem to others. When a person is genuinely successful, he is able to realize when he has done the best of which he is capable because he knows he has acted according to the best in himself. Therefore, he is fair and decent and does not begrudge others their accomplishments. Fame neither destroys nor changes his inner self. When a person is successful, he carries out his work because there is something within him which propels him to do it, and not because of any impression it will make on others or for credit he will receive. He just wants to know that the job is done and done well.

Genuine success, however, can only be achieved if a person has the qualifications and the endowment for achieving it and if his motivations are healthy. If he does not have these qualifications, he may be pushed aside, though frequently, because of his strong ambitions, he tries again to reach the top. The result is that new frustrations usually arise in him, and with frustrations come resentment and hostility. Many a man like this discovers "shortcuts" to getting ahead, often lawless ones. It is obvious that he may lose sight of himself and become so involved in his own ambitions, in his own drive for power, that he loses his sense of proportion between his abilities and his limitations and, what is more important, between what is right and what is wrong.

It seems then that American culture to some extent brings about an unrealistic attitude, which we find in so many criminals. They need not be psychotic. Sometimes this element of unreality is so hidden that we are not able at first glance to recognize it. Yet it is there and makes itself felt. The fact that most criminals believe they will never be caught is a revealing facet of this unrealistic attitude.

So far we have discussed the general pathological manifestation in society, and we must now mention the more specific ones which are related to the etiology of crime. It has been stated by Clifford R. Shaw and Henry D. McKay [14] that certain areas in a city acquire a high rate of delinquency through an end-product of processes in American city life over which, as yet, man has been able to exercise little control. Thus when cities have a high rate of crime, it is neither by chance nor by design. Shaw tries to prove this by presenting the geographical distribution and the correlations between rates of delinquency and indices of physical status, economic status, and population composition.

There is little doubt that deteriorated neighborhoods, housing congestion, unemployment, unsatisfactory economic and work conditions, poverty, and other factors of an economic nature play an important part in the origin of crime either directly or indirectly. When we add here the dislocation of people both socially and emotionally due to immigration or migration; unsatisfactory school conditions, with overcrowding, poor emotional relationships between teachers and pupils, lack of qualified personnel, and emotional problems of the students; poor recreational facilities, with insufficient organized group activities and insufficient play space in the form of parks and playgrounds; we see that such factors by their nature tend to increase criminal activities.

When we add also the pathological manifestations in the family in the form of imbalanced family patterns, with either a patriarchy or matriarchy; poor emotional structure of the family, resulting in family tension and broken homes due to separation or divorce; improper child rearing, with lack of discipline and guidance, and neglect by parents either because of lack of love or illness, poverty, or modern-day suburban living; we can better understand how antisocial and criminal activities are brought about.

We must not fail to include those pathological manifestations within an individual which might contribute to his becoming antisocial or even criminal, such as physical or mental illnesses, negative personality traits (excessive rebelliousness or conformity, undue hostility or excessive shyness), drug addiction, and alcoholism. Thus a man's crime can be considered an expression of his mental status and the situation in which he exists.

We may say then that the etiological factors causing crime and delinquency are emotional and social disorganization of the individual. Yet why does one person, who seemingly is exposed to the same factors as another, become criminal, and the other does not? Therefore, from an etiological viewpoint the mystery is that not everyone becomes a criminal in spite of the fact that he may be living in what is considered a criminal climate. On the other hand, we see a person becoming antisocial or criminal in spite of his having lived in good surroundings, those conducive to social conduct.

We may come nearer to a solution when we make an analogy between the criminal and a person suffering from tuberculosis. It is a long-established fact that we are all exposed to and infected with the tubercle bacillus; only a few of us, though, become afflicted with this disease. No one was able to give a satisfactory explanation of this phenomenon until it was found that the people who contracted tuberculosis were sensitive or allergic to the tubercle bacillus. Their bodies had become sensitized to the production of the bacteria. The degree of sensitivity depends upon the amount of exposure to the bacillus, the constitution of the individual, and his emotional resistance to becoming ill. I would like to stress, however, that there can be no tuberculosis without the tubercle bacillus.

Another example of a deep interrelationship between external factors and internal ones is the condition of hay fever. Hay fever cannot be contracted by anyone unless he is exposed to pollen. However, during the season when we are all exposed to pollen, most of us do not contract hay fever. The reason is that those who become afflicted with hay fever are sensitized to the pollen because of constitutional and emotional elements in themselves.

Thus in order for a person to be afflicted either with tuberculosis or hay fever, he has to be exposed to the exciting agents, which, however, can produce the particular illness only when he is sensitized to these agents. Three sets of factors are necessary, the first is environmental, the second, physiological or biological, and the third is psychological.

The same is true of antisocial or criminal behavior. Let it first be said that we all have criminal inclinations in us. That most of us are able to cope with these inclinations is due to our ability to suppress, repress, or rechannel them.

Dormant criminalistic traits within a person may become activated if he is exposed to an increasing degree (either in quantity or quality) of precipitating internal or external events (or a combination of both) which sensitize him or make him allergic to criminalistic influences. Yet the degree of strength of the precipitating events varies from person to person before resulting in a criminal act, depending upon the strength or weakness of his criminalistic traits, that is, how easily they are aroused and how easily the person becomes sensitized or allergic. (There is a basic difference, however, between contracting tuberculosis and committing a crime; in the latter a person's judgment is usually involved, at least to some extent.)

Certain persons may yield to criminalistic impulses more readily because of exposure to criminalistic influences, intermingled with one or more precipitating events, or because of a reaction formation resulting in the turning of criminalistic tendencies into manifest criminal acts. In both instances a mobilization of criminalistic tendencies occurs. The exposure hits certain personality traits that respond to the criminalistic stimulus in a positive way. A pattern of criminal behavior will then develop, practically in the same way as the individual develops a certain pattern of behavior or habits through exposure to other types of influences.

We may very well say that a quantitative replacement takes place between the person and his traits and the exposure. For example, strong criminalistic tendencies need little exposure to criminal influences; weak criminalistic tendencies need much exposure. That this is so is very much due to the fact that a human being represents a center of action and reaction, and as we have said before, in a functional sense he forms a unit with his environment.

All the elements which bring about crime are specific or vague strains and stresses in the person himself, in his situation, or in both, eliciting certain reactions in him which may eventually manifest themselves in a criminal act. To a higher or lower degree, depending upon the offender's personality make-up and particularly upon the development of his ego and superego (in lay terms called the conscience, which, however, is only the conscious part of the superego, most of which is unconscious), his emotional equilibrium will be disturbed by precipitating events. And the degree to which they disturb him both depends upon and determines the degree of his emotional adjustment. For example, after the stock market crashed in 1929, what made some commit suicide and others pick up the pieces and go on? In the main it was the degree of emotional adjustment achieved.

What are these factors which we call precipitating events? These elements, which provoke crime as well as neuroses, psychoses, and psychosomatic disorders, are often called traumata, but because this is a rather obscure term, they should be designated as "precipitating events" or "precipitating factors." Generally speaking, these factors are significant to the everyday adjustment of the person. Position among siblings (youngest, middle, oldest, or twin), being an only child, financial circumstances (wealth or poverty), sibling rivalry, broken homes, overprotective or neglectful parents, physical or mental illness—all these may act as precipitating factors. Then too there may be more immediate factors which can serve as precipitating events, such as the death of a loved member of the family, threatened financial, intellectual, emotional, or social security, geographical relocation, new situations (job, school, etc.), rise of anxiety or tension, homosexual panic, loss of prestige, or an alcoholic spree.

Depending upon the personality make-up, certain events may be precipitating factors for one person but not necessarily for another. The point is that what happens to an individual does not matter so much as how he reacts to that particular event. This reaction is directly related to the development of his ego and super-ego, a point which will be discussed in Chapter IV.

Just as a physical or mental disease is caused by various factors, so also is criminal behavior. These factors may be constitutional, predispositional, precipitating, psychological, physical, or a combination of several. When a person develops an emotional or physical illness or commits a criminal act, a selection or singling out of that particular manifestation has occurred.

Since an illness can be caused by these various factors, the disease can be considered a function of these factors. If A is the constitutional factor, B is the predispositional element, D is the precipitating factor, E is the psychological element, and G is the physical factor, we can say that the disease is a function of these factors. If "I" stands for illness and "F" for function, we may arrived at the following formula: $I = (F), A, B, D, E, G$.

In the same way, a criminal act can arise as a result of these various factors (A, B, D, E, G), and a crime can be a function of these elements. Thus if "C" stands for crime, we arrive at the following formula: $C = (F), A, B, D, E, G$.

Not every factor, however, needs to be present in order for a crime to take place. One person may commit such an act because at a certain stage he is predisposed to crime and because a precipitating factor mobilizes his antisocial tendencies. Another individual may require more such stimuli, for example, financial or intellectual deprivation, combined with hate or anxiety, followed by a precipitating event, may all be necessary to elicit a criminal act in him. The one essential factor is the precipitating event, which hits a person at the wrong time, for the transition of a potential offender into an actual one is always the result of such an event.

Frequently the precipitating events found in the immediate (family) or distant (society) environment appear to be more important than those found within the person himself because they can be more easily uncovered. This is not true, however. The inner elements are every bit as important as the external ones, and only in appreciating the importance of both, can we understand the etiology of criminal behavior. Unfortunately, too often we cannot readily detect the delicate and intricate mental reactions and processes which occur within the person, particularly the unconscious ones, which frequently lead people into criminal behavior. Then too in many cases a person's entire life has been a chain of precipitating events, which makes them difficult to detect. Thus we sometimes receive the impression that criminal behavior can develop without them, but further investigation undoubtedly reveals that these factors are always present, and their diversity can be seen from the following two cases.

In the first case a forty-five-year-old man who had never before been in trouble with the law was sentenced for larceny. He explained that he had to support his mother as well as an unemployed sister and a sick brother. When a prolonged illness left him unable to work and provide for his family, he resorted to stealing cars and selling them, until he was finally caught.

It is not hard to appreciate this man's difficult financial situation and his anxiety over being unable to work. But it is much less simple to understand the lengths to which he went in order to continue supporting his family. The explanation lay in his emotionally immature attachment to his mother, which, in a way, acted as a precipitating event.

His mother, a widow, had always relied on him as a pillar of strength, since he was the oldest and most capable of her children. And he had come to regard this as a form of approval which was extremely important to him. Thus illness and inability to work made him feel weak and in danger of falling out of favor with his mother. It was this feeling which blocked him from seeing his situation realistically and propelled him toward his crime. While his family made no offer to help when he became ill, neither did he seek their cooperation. Instead of asking them to reduce their standard of living and pressing his sister and perhaps even his mother into finding jobs, he felt compelled to continue carrying the entire burden himself. The fear of losing his mother's approval was far more threatening than the possibility of imprisonment.

The second is the case of a twenty-year-old boy whose criminality began with his flunking out of college. Instead of telling his parents, he used the rest of his tuition money as a down payment on a car which his parents had previously refused to buy him. Later, when he was unable to meet the installments on it, he forged his father's name to checks. When this was discovered, his father made restitution to save the family name and keep his son's reputation clean.

After some months the boy's father found him a job as a clerk in a friend's office, and there he met a young girl with whom he fell in love. At first she was rather unreceptive to him, and he felt rejected. But he was determined to succeed and kept buying her expensive gifts in order to make himself more attractive to her. When finally she became interested, his funds were depleted so he began stealing money from the company until his thefts were discovered and he was sent to a reformatory.

In my interviews with him he blamed the girl for being cold and interested in him only for what she could get out of him. When I pointed out that he had been unrealistic both in pursuing someone who was obviously not interested in him and in stealing in order to win her, he could not see my point. Because he had been spoiled and kept dependent by his parents, his emotional development had been stunted. He had grown egocentric, vain, and demanding. Unable to bear having his desires thwarted, he wanted immediate gratification of his every wish. And this need formed the inner precipitating factor that led him into crime.

From these two cases, we see that different elements, both in the individual and in his environment, contribute toward eliciting crime. We can say that criminal activities take place only under certain conditions and only after the person has been exposed to criminal activities or has indulged in criminalistic fantasies or thoughts for a long time. Only then does he become sensitized to criminalistic influences. This sensitization, however, depends upon definite biological, psychological, and sociological factors which act simultaneously to create a criminal. These elements work independently and dependently in him, each exerting a signal influence yet all interlocked and reacting with each other. Although frequently we find that predominantly psychological factors may produce criminal behavior in one person, while predominantly sociological factors may produce such behavior in another, these elements intermingle in a single causal process.

CHAPTER II

The Formula of Criminal Behavior

We must always keep in mind the multiple causative factors and their interplay in studying the etiology of criminal behavior. Among these factors one may be more contributory than another, according to the case, but no particular single element is ever the causation in all cases. Much previous research was focused upon specific individual factors which were always thought to be responsible for eliciting crime. But the truth is that any element can constitute a causative factor of crime, and yet this same factor in another constellation may bear not the slightest relation to the causation of crime. This is why it has been so difficult to uncover the causes of criminal activities and to find valid means of counteracting them.

Both sociological and psychological factors work upon each other and are interrelated. The first set of factors are present in the environment and influence the individual; the second set of factors are present within the personality and react toward the environment. It is obvious that there are innumerable ways in which these elements, which vary both qualitatively and quantitatively, can combine.

Based upon these considerations, we can formulate Law No. 1

in the science of criminology, which establishes a basis for the etiology of criminal activities:

Law No. 1

A multiplicity of causative factors go into the making of criminal behavior. Since these causative factors vary qualitatively and quantitatively with each case, the causation of criminal behavior is relative.

Although this law seems rather self-evident, there have been, and still are, many unfounded theories on the causes of criminal behavior.

Upon this law we can build a second one, which involves the psychological processes in the person when he performs a criminal act. They embody the predispositional and the constitutional factors which go into the making of man and his relationship to his social situation, his environment. In explaining the functioning of the human mind, we must therefore concern ourselves for a moment with the interrelationship between the person's constitution and his environment.

From our studies of the origin of human behavior and particularly of criminal activities and mental illnesses, we know that hereditary elements are affected by the environment and that environmental factors are influenced by heredity. While heredity endows a person with certain basic abilities, it is the environment which provides the opportunity for their development. Heredity determines what the person can do, whereas the environment determines what he does do. Under a given set of conditions a person will show certain characteristics due to inherited fundamentals. This means that certain inherited personality traits and features, as well as certain physical traits, create a predisposition in him and that the influences from the environment can work within that frame.

By predisposition we mean the individual's inherited propensities,[1] that is, his biologically inherited and determined inclinations to respond to certain stimuli with certain definite reactions. Predisposition, then, is an inherited potential, as opposed to qualities which are acquired. In our context we have to ask whether there exists a predisposition toward behavior which is considered criminal in our culture. Biological science today asserts that psychological potentialities may be inherited in the sense that they predispose toward certain behavior. It is noteworthy that in this connection the Expert Committee of the United Nations stated: "Crime is not inherited as such, but the individual biological endowments are vital behavior determinants." [2]

Although it has been said that when a person carries out any antisocial act, he is predisposed to antisocial behavior, such predisposition cannot be considered a criminal one unless there is a certain probability that a crime will be committed. However, when a person is basically equipped with poor traits, such as emotional instability, overpowerful drives, and an abundance of asocial feelings, environmental influences may easily elicit criminal behavior. Thus under a given set of conditions a certain number of people are born to crime, so to speak; that is their fate when particular constellations are fulfilled.[3]

Much research has been undertaken to determine whether hereditary or environmental elements are the more important in producing criminal activities. There was the investigation of the Juke family by Richard Dugdale in 1877 and of the Kallikaks in 1912 by Henry Goddard, who both claimed that criminal behavior was caused by hereditary traits. Then there was also Spaulding and Healy's research, in which they could not trace any direct inheritance of criminalistic tendencies. They claimed that if such inheritance existed, it might appear indirectly; that is, it might detour by way of certain mental conditions, such as feeble-mindedness or epilepsy, but this does not mean that any of these mental conditions inevitably bring about crime.[4] In *Varieties of Delinquent Youth*,[5] W. H. Sheldon gives predominance to constitutional factors as a cause of criminal behavior, while he minimizes the emotional relationships of the offender. Although his anthropometric analysis is more refined than that of Kraepelin, we might be nearer the truth if, instead of considering only the body as the constitution, we take a broader outlook and assume that there are three aspects of the constitution, as Stourzh-Anderle [6] suggests: 1) bodily or somatic; 2) psychosomatic; 3) psychological. This concept takes into consideration the emotional forces that are responsible for all human behavior, including the antisocial and criminal kind. It has long been my theory that criminal behavior expresses both emotional (which includes constitutional) and social disorganization.

The question of whether heredity or environment is the greater influence in causing crime is therefore an academic one. The frying of an egg might be considered analogous. We cannot say that the frying pan (environment) contributes any more or less to the final product than the properties of the egg itself. The two are interdependent. Thus instead of asking whether heredity or environment is the more important in producing a criminal, it would be a better approach to ask: What are the essential characteristics of the individual, and how do they act upon each other? Here we must consider such factors as physical make-up, intelligence, and feelings. Since each person is conditioned by exposure to environment and by emotional strivings, an adolescent, for example, with a high degree of intelligence who has a worth-while goal in life may veer on to a different path—even the road to crime—because he hates his parents or because he hates society. Thus we see that feelings (in this case hostility or resentment) as well as predominantly hereditary factors, play an important role in that they may stimulate criminal behavior when a person is exposed to certain situations. In each case, therefore, we must try to find out the psychobiological make-up of the person, how the bodily-emotional factors influence him, and what kind of environmental elements act upon him, instead of trying to find out whether heredity or environment has the greater influence.

Of course, the interrelationship between these elements must also be considered in order to find the etiological factors responsible for crime. Even if an obvious social situation instigates, or, so to say, invites, a person to commit a criminal act (opportunity makes the thief, his personality make-up plays an essential part in determining whether or not he yields to the temptation. This becomes clearer when we realize that certain inclinations, desires, and needs are usually satisfied when a person commits a crime (or, for that matter, any act). An understanding of the offender's personality and his childhood and adolescent development may therefore frequently be the key to understanding these facts. We find this especially true of those who are unable to adjust emotionally and socially and whose behavior is determined more by their inner urges creating conflicts than by environmental circumstances. Investigations of several thousands of cases by many researchers, including this writer, indicate this to be a fact in a large number of offenders.

There are three definite ways in which a person may be led into criminal activities:

1. When antisocial inclinations are exposed to criminal influences and are further stimulated by the impact of a precipitating event;

2. When there is a strong unconscious desire for punishment, owing to unconscious, deep-rooted guilt feelings, developed through past experiences (the offender obtains punishment by committing a crime);

3. As an indirect (or false) expression of aggressiveness. A person who feels emotionally weak and insecure may develop a defensive, aggressive emotional attitude as a cover-up. Expressing this aggression through protests and rebelliousness may lead him to commit antisocial or even criminal acts. Here too an unconscious need for punishment may be partially responsible for the action.

In one or more of these direct or indirect ways, antisocial inclinations are mobilized to such a degree that the person can no longer hold them back, and an antisocial or criminal act takes place.

However a person may be led into committing an antisocial act or a crime, his behavior is an acting out of his conscious or unconscious desires and fantasies. We frequently see similar "acting out," though perhaps to a lesser degree, in the offender's relationships with other people. The act which has made him an "offender" is usually the culminating one in a series of related actions in his past; that is, in acting out he repeats, without any emotional insight, his reactions to a previously traumatic (precipitating), but now unconscious, event. Apropos to this Eduardo

Weiss [7] states: "A man, for instance, repeats intense feelings of hostility towards his brothers and sisters by quarreling with his fellow workers."

In any event there is always a working relationship between the individual's personality make-up and his exposure to criminalistic influences or to factors which create strong emotional stress in his total environment. All other things being equal, the stronger the individual's antisocial tendencies and the stronger the exposure, the more likely it will be that a criminal act will be elicited. On the other hand, the less intense the antisocial inclinations and the exposure, the smaller the probability for the commission of a crime.

The way the relationship between the person and his social situation expresses itself can be understood better when we try to find out the nature of personality. Although I shall explain personality more fully later, it is important to say here that we are not born with a personality, or, in psychoanalytical terms, with an ego. It arises from the id, or instincts, which is completely unconscious, and develops throughout childhood, adolescence, and adulthood. In contact with both the instincts and the external world, the ego, or the personality, tests reality in the environmental situation. As an adult, the total individual expresses himself through his intellectual and emotional faculties and tendencies, which determine his behavior and characteristics. We can say that the personality, the only fully conscious part of a person, integrates his thinking, feeling, and acting, and represents him as a whole. It is the personality that makes each person unique.

To a large extent the ego is controlled by the superego (conscience, in lay terms), which is partly conscious and partly unconscious, and which, like the ego, is developed throughout childhood, adolescence, and adulthood. The two are always in conflict with each other, and the superego gives in only when its moral standards permit.

We must be aware that in all our behavior there is also a constant conflict between these two forces and our instinctual drives from the id, which are rooted in our biological needs and which constitute a force making itself felt whether we are awake or asleep. This is so because the mind is always working due to the fact that instincts possess constant energy. Although these instincts are unconscious, they frequently come into our consciousness as creations from our unconscious—in the form of dreams, for example—and influence our minds. Thus we see that the total personality (the id, the ego, and the superego) really is a dynamic unit—all components affecting each other and never at a standstill.

How does all of this influence criminal behavior? Since we are all born with instincts or drives, which are both social and antisocial in nature, all of us have antisocial inclinations within us, which we consciously or unconsciously try to resist. I recall reading what Goethe once said—that there was no existent crime the inclination toward which he could not trace within himself.

The question is: When are antisocial inclinations transformed into criminal acts? Two separate factors must be distinguished. The one is motivation; the other is the motor act. The first, partly conscious and partly unconscious, is intimately connected with the individual's personality make-up, while the latter, with a few significant exceptions, is conscious and is the physical carrying out of the act.

Motivation is by and large instinctual in nature, arising from our aggressive tendencies, which are linked to the sexual drive and the drive for survival. The fact that a person does not commit a crime is no indication that he does not possess antisocial tendencies. He may, instead, through suppression or repression, direct these tendencies against himself, resulting in emotional and physical illness, or he may sublimate them into healthier outlets. Aggression may often be expressed in the form of fantasies or dreams, during which a person kills or harms his loved ones or his enemies, though he never carries it out in real life. (Of course, not every dream of killing someone indicates unhealthy aggressiveness. For example, a man who dreams of killing his mother may be expressing his desire to end his dependency or to lessen his own femininity.) It is interesting that the fantasies of the neurotic or psychotic person, who may not commit any crimes, are often difficult to distinguish from those of the criminal.

Aggressive tendencies as such do not characterize criminals alone. These inclinations are present in every one of us. They are an integral part of our instinctual lives. When an instinct seeks expression, it produces a certain amount of tension, which has to be discharged. Thus aggression is inherent in our every thought and action and may appear in various forms, directly or indirectly, as primary aggression, constructive aggression, or destructive aggression.[8] Our main concern here is with constructive and destructive aggression.

Constructive aggression exists in many ways, from the simplest act of raising a window shade to let in more light, to doing a job or performing some art as a means of self-expression. Destructive aggression varies too, from a minor insult to murder. But aggression may meet with obstacles which interfere with its expression. The healthy reaction is to overcome the obstacle or to find another constructive outlet without too much anxiety. However, a person who expresses destructive aggressiveness will usually feel conscious or unconscious anxiety, frustration, hostility, and guilt because he knows it is wrong (although a timid or fearful person may experience such feelings even when expressing constructive aggressiveness). Frequently he tries to cover up his aggressiveness by disguising it with kindness, solicitousness, or friendliness to relieve the guilt he feels about his hostility.

All our tendencies—social, antisocial, or criminal—are linked to our needs and desires, which arise from our instincts (our libido, or life force) and which have been approved or disapproved by our ego and superego. Carrying out an antisocial or criminal act, then, depends upon how the ego and superego react to instinctual impulses. This reaction again depends upon the way these two personality elements have been conditioned by the environment and upon the situation to which the person is exposed.[9]

Those who have become more sensitized to criminal activities and emotional disturbances through having experienced emotional and social upsets develop a certain susceptibility to them. If such a person does not commit a criminal act, it is because he has resistance to it—a certain immunity, we might say—which varies with the individual. Where the immunity is weak, slight exposure to precipitating events may bring the person to succumb to criminal activities. Where a strong immunity exists, several or stronger precipitating events may elicit criminal activities. Only through the aid of a well-developed superego structure will this immunity be maintained sufficiently for the person to withstand criminalistic influences.

We see different degrees of immunity even in children. Most of them have at some time done things which could be considered antisocial (and sometimes criminal). Many children steal—pennies, apples, a piece of cake—or indulge in sex play or other acts which they know or feel are wrong. Usually they do these things when their parents are not around, no superego present. Children who do none of these things are usually overly timid, though sometimes they have developed enough conscience to resist such acts. Although these are very simple examples, showing antisocial and criminalistic inclinations being brought into action at an early stage of the child's development, the significant point is that it was the total situation which elicited the action.

In explaining the birth of a criminal act, we must thus consider three factors: criminalistic tendencies (T), the total situation (S), and the person's mental and emotional resistance to temptation (R).

We can now formulate Law No. 2 about criminal behavior—how a criminal act arises:

Law No. 2

A criminal act is the sum of a person's criminalistic tendencies plus his total situation, divided by the amount of his resistance.

This law can be put into a formula: $C = \dfrac{T + S}{R}$.

A person's criminalistic inclinations and his resistance to them may either result in an antisocial or criminal act or in socially approved behavior, depending upon which is the stronger of the two. All people have tendencies and counter-tendencies. A criminal act can take place only if the person's resistance is insufficient to withstand the pressures of his criminalistic tendencies and the situation. This mathematical formula is a concept which can be used in understanding criminal behavior.[10] In fact, it also applies to all types of human behavior. Thus if we substitute H (human behavior) for C (crime), we arrive at the same formula: $H = \dfrac{T + S}{R}$.

In looking at our formula for criminal behavior, we can well realize that there are limitless types of personality make-ups, innumerable situations, and many degrees of resistance. These variations are one more reason why we can maintain that the causes of crime are relative.

The situation upon which we shall concentrate in this book—the crime situation—is of great interest to us, since it determines to a large extent whether or not a criminal act will occur. It is difficult to list all factors that go into its making because the situation is related both to the personality of the individual and to his environment, but we can differentiate between an external and an internal criminal situation. √

The external criminal situation is the total environmental situation—all the stresses and strains which contribute to mobilizing a person's criminalistic tendencies; the internal criminal situation is the person's psychological state. However, the two are intimately linked, as we shall see by the following examples. The sight of a half-clad woman may be a sufficient environmental stress upon a rapist's particular psychological state to cause him to commit rape; an exhibitionist may be provoked to exhibit himself on noticing a woman's legs as she walks along the street; another offender might be tempted to steal on seeing a person being careless with money—for example, just leaving it around in a drawer. Often the environmental stress is much stronger, however; but the main point is how much of a strain it is on the person committing the crime. Whether the offender seeks out the situation himself (and to some extent a person "selects" his crime) or the situation comes to him by chance, so to say, it is his own reactions which bring the result. We *all* see women in some form of nudity at one time or another; we *all* see women's legs exposed constantly. Yet only those with tendencies toward sexual abnormality will react adversely. The same applies to the person inclined toward stealing.

Of course, we must not overlook those who follow criminalistic tendencies on a lesser level, for example, accepting more change than one is entitled to. The somewhat dishonest person does not give it back voluntarily but shrugs it off and feels pleased at "getting something for nothing." However, he would probably not deny it if the proprietor realized the error but would only be somewhat embarrassed, whereas the seasoned criminal would vehemently deny the error and keep the money.

The most difficult factor to determine is the amount of resistance a person may have to committing a crime in any given situation. Resistance arises from an emotional, intellectual, and social root, all three intimately connected with the superego formation and its relationship to the ego and the person's situation. When a person is generally fatigued or is suffering from an organic mental disease, it is understandable that his emotional and physical resistance will be lower. The dominating figure in resistance is the superego because it threatens the ego by commanding it to do only good deeds. Thus when a person commits a crime, he usually feels guilty, whereas he has a feeling of well-being when he carries out a good deed.

In this connection it is interesting to note that residues of the Oedipus-Electra stage (see Chapter IV) continue to live on in the supergo. We can therefore say that the degree of resistance to committing antisocial and criminal acts depends to a large extent upon how well the individual has resolved his unconscious incestuous desires, that is, upon the degree of his emotional maturity. However, although an unresolved Oedipus-Electra situation may appear to be the cause of criminal behavior in some cases, most often it is not the sole cause; usually both psychological and sociological factors in the person's total situation can more correctly be considered the true causes.

Because of the dominant position of the superego, there is hardly any person possessing only antisocial or criminal tendencies. The exceptions may be people who suffer from a deep-seated character disorder—so-called psychopaths (see Chapter VIII—such as we find in some profit murderers and gangsters. We all have a mixture of social and antisocial inclinations within us, and never do we find a person who has only pure thoughts and emotions. Every emotion has its counteremotion; every idea, its contrary one; every thought, its opposite. In some people this ambivalence of feelings and thoughts reaches such proportions that they sink into a state of morbid doubt, often to the point where they are unable to act. A person in such a state is trying to check his own aggressive and antisocial, perhaps even criminal, inclinations; he is trying to fend off his impulses toward aggression by suppressing or repressing them. We find this often in people who suffer from compulsive, obsessional behavior; their uncertainty and their difficulty in restraining themselves compels them to repetitious action (continual hand-washing, for example).

In contrast to those whose overly strong superego inhibits them from acting, there are others who commit antisocial and criminal acts impulsively. They act out their impulses on the spur of the moment, without forethought, because the development of their superego and ego has been stunted.

As I have stated before, criminal behavior can be produced in three different ways. The factor "T" contains not only the individual's direct aggressive inclinations but his indirect ones as well. Criminal behavior is not always the result of a direct breakthrough of aggressive inclinations. Indirect aggressiveness may also lead to criminal behavior. We find the highest degree of indirect aggression in those who turn their aggressions against themselves, such as the alcoholic and the person who commits suicide. A high degree of indirect aggressiveness is also found in the criminal who is led to commit a crime through strong unconscious guilt feelings which create a need for self-punishment. In these cases the guilt feelings form the motivating force, whereas in a direct breakthrough of aggressiveness hostility is the motivating element, and guilt follows the crime. Then, too, a high degree of indirect aggressiveness may be expressed in protest reactions, such as rebelliousness.

It may appear that the law $C = \dfrac{T + S}{R}$ does not cover indirect types of antisocial and criminal acts, but this is not the case. As I have said before, sometimes a crime is committed by a person who uses his aggressiveness as a defense mechanism (a cover-up for his real feelings). He shows aggressiveness in order to conceal his basically passive personality. Thus when he is faced with a threatening situation, he feels forced to prove that he is aggressive and does so either by protest, bullying, rebelliousness, or by an outright criminal act. Frequently such indirect aggressive attitudes are established in him in childhood, most probably at the oral stage. Behind most undue aggressiveness we find passivity, not only in the criminal, but also in the law-abiding citizen. It may be added too that aggressiveness is not always oral in nature; it may be anal, anal-sadistic, sexual, or a combination of all (see Chapter IV). The main point to remember is that aggressive impulses which are not accepted by the ego or superego and are not sublimated (channeled constructively) are suppressed or repressed. Those which are not suppressed or repressed successfully will break through, often resulting in a criminal act.

We can compare the course from criminal impulse to criminal act with the course of an illness. The conscious and unconscious emotional and mental processes act and react under criminalistic stimuli in the same way as the body acts when it is exposed for a prolonged period of time to an infection. The result is an illness of one sort or another. In the criminal the illness is defective behavior, directed against society, resulting from biological, psychological, or environmental defectiveness, and the crime indicates that there is a malformed relationship between the offender's inclinations, his situation, and his resistance.

Thus we have seen that only under certain circumstances will a person succumb to his antisocial tendencies: where instability exists within him (T and R), within his situation (S), or within both.

CHAPTER III

Family Tension

The family has been called the very basis of society. Family life, of such significance to adults, is of even greater importance to children because it is their first society. It is here that they receive their first experiences of living with others, and it is here that much of the foundation for later development and activities is laid. The family can bring out positive and constructive or negative and destructive traits, depending upon its inner atmosphere. To a large extent it determines whether we express love and affection or hostility and hatred. In fact, all adult attitudes and behavior, whether social or antisocial, are elicited by past experiences, and can be explained only in terms of them.

Because so much human activity can be explained by family background, it is necessary for us to investigate the role it plays in the world of criminal behavior. A four-year research project under my direction at Columbia University was conducted on known offenders and their families, children and adults. During the project we tried to find out the relationship between antisocial or criminal behavior and emotional attitudes as they arise in the family. We gave psychiatric interviews, examinations, and in some cases treatment to the offenders and their family members. Psychological tests given included the Rorschach (ink blot), the Thematic Apperception Test (picture interpretation), the Wechsler-Bellevue Test (intelligence), and a drawing test.

For control purposes we used an equal number of persons manifesting neurotic or psychotic conditions—but who were nondelinquent—and their families. We used no so-called normal persons in making the comparison because it was extremely difficult to get such people to volunteer for such a time-consuming experiment. Moreover, even if we had been able to group together persons usually considered normal, in the final analysis they might have turned out to be nothing of the kind.

The most significant finding was that those families which produced criminals showed a greater prevalence of unhealthy emotional conditions among the family members—that is, family tension—than did the families of the nondelinquent group. This family tension, manifested mainly through hostility, hatred, resentment, nagging, bickering, or psychosomatic disorders, engendered and maintained emotional disturbances in both children and parents alike.

At first all of the families emotionally resisted any deep examination, making it difficult to break through their defenses, but as time went on they became less defensive, and we could more readily discern some of the problems—how a parent dominated his children or how they dominated him, how a jealous child continually and unobtrusively teased her brother, how a mother unconsciously exhibited favoritism toward a particular child, and how one extremely demanding boy who rejected everyone acted the way he did because he himself felt rejected. Sometimes the emotional tension present within the family was quite subtle and only made itself felt as an undercurrent, yet nevertheless coloring the behavior of all its members and eliciting antisocial or criminal activities or emotional disturbances. However, in some families, as in Arnold's, whose story follows, the tension was extreme and quite apparent.

Arnold was an unwanted child, raised in a home in which his parents quarreled constantly and in which his drunken father often punished him severely for even the smallest lapse from good behavior. Arnold grew up feeling almost constant anger and resentment, and to complicate matters, when he was eight years old, a baby sister arrived on the scene, capturing all of his parents' attention. It seemed to Arnold that whatever little sympathy and warmth his mother had occasionally shown him now vanished completely. He felt more neglected and unloved than ever.

Shortly after the birth of his sister he started playing hooky from school, and when questioned, he told the authorities that he was afraid to attend classes because he was unable to prepare his homework amid all the arguments at home. His parents were furious with him for revealing such private matters, and this provided a new excuse for harsh punishments. Each time his father came home drunk, Arnold was the victim of another beating. While he resented his mother strongly for not protecting him at these times, his hostility toward his father grew limitless, and he was at a loss to cope with it. At the age of ten he ran away and roamed the streets with a gang of boys until he was picked up in another city by the police and returned to his parents.

As things progressed from bad to worse, Arnold grew frail and sickly. Then, when he was fifteen, his parents had a violent argument, during which his mother threatened to leave home. Still eager to win his mother's love, Arnold made the mistake of siding with her, and his father beat him and threw him out of the house. Arnold then began to steal cars, and continued to do so until he was put in prison at the age of eighteen.

As I have said before, we all have antisocial tendencies within us which can be stimulated and brought to the point of crime in many ways. In Arnold's case the steady quarreling between his mother and father, the harsh punishments inflicted on him for minor infractions, and his feeling of being unloved aroused and maintained his hostile feelings toward his parents and heightened his antisocial inclinations. Thus we can easily trace Arnold's criminal activities to his unwholesome family life.

Since the early years of a child's life are formative and impressionable, his emotional growth is easily stunted when there are frequent emotional outbursts in his home. Never sure about what is going to happen there and caught between trying to satisfy his own emotional needs and fitting into the actual pattern in which he lives, he loses his sense of belonging and becomes confused about his own identity—his role both as an individual and as a member of the family and of society.

A complicating factor for Arnold was his latent homosexuality. Although, like every boy, he had a strong need to identify with his father or some other male who might have been close to him, there was no such positive figure in his environment. Since his sister and mother elicited much less brutality from his father, unconsciously it seemed to Arnold that being a female was more desirable, and he felt safer emotionally in identifying with his mother. Yet at the same time he had contempt for her defenselessness during the many family disputes, and this feeling was reflected in his attitude toward himself and in his behavior.

Arnold unconsciously imitated the negative traits of his mother and father, and his behavior became both contradictory and unpredictable. Among his peers, where he felt more sure of himself, he was tough, hostile, and aggressive, pretending not to need any friends or affection. Before authority, however, he was more often submissive. For example, if a teacher reproached him in the classroom, he was easily offended and would withdraw and become meek. Hating this reaction in himself, however, he would then counter it with some hostile act to deny his passivity and dependence. This was precisely what happened after the argument with his father, when he stole the first car. He was rebelling against both his inner conflict and his actual environmental situation, in which he was not accepted. And each time there was a similar sequence of events, Arnold committed another theft, until he was caught.

We can see that for Arnold his family situation became traumatic in quality and degree. As a result of the tension in his home, Arnold lived through many severely unhappy and emotionally damaging experiences which made him immature. His reaction was to become hostile, fearful, and generally insecure. He was not given attention or care, and his own emotional needs and desires were never satisfied. This neglect—made more acute by the constant bickering and nagging in his home—plus his emotional immaturity constituted the basis for his antisocial and criminal behavior.

The presence of emotional tension also brings about emotional deprivation, which plays an important part in a person's life and is an essential factor in producing criminals and emotionally unhealthy individuals. As a matter of fact, behind all emotional difficulties, whether the result is a neurotic or a psychotic condition, a psychosomatic disorder, or antisocial or criminal behavior, a varying degree of emotional deprivation in childhood is always to be found. In criminal behavior, though, we find an exceedingly great amount of family tension as well as emotional deprivation. Again and again we have found that family tension breeds all kinds of emotional disorders. Basically it prevents children and their parents from realizing the best within themselves. Persistent nagging and bickering in the home causes children to tighten up with hostilities and resentment, eliciting innumerable disturbed behavior patterns. These may take a concealed form, as in overcompliance (a known cover-up for repressed or suppressed hostility and resentment), or may show up in open rebellion and defiance—toward parents and all authority.

In a family where strong emotional tension exists, the members are pitted against each other, and they have very little in common except for living under the same roof. They seldom have quiet discussions or interchange ideas of mutual interest; instead, they argue and fight with each other, reflecting their hostility and resentment and resulting in a weakening of family ties. In such families there is no unity, no cohesiveness; each member shifts for himself. They are like boarders in their own homes.

This tension, which brings in its wake a lack of family cohesiveness, is not confined to any specific socio-economic level. It is like a disease, attacking well-to-do, poverty-stricken, and middle-income homes alike and leveling them all to embittered and frustrated nests that breed more hostility and frustration. It grows out of emotional insecurity and gives rise to more and more emotional insecurity. Although Diana Addison was not the butt of outright cruelty as was Arnold, her case quite clearly reveals the

importance of a good emotional relationship between parent and
parent and between parent and child by showing what can happen
when this is lacking.

Diana was a fourteen-year-old girl who came from a well-to-do
home which was filled with tension and devoid of genuine love.
She came to the attention of the headmistress of the private school
she was attending when money began disappearing from the locker
rooms. For six months an investigation was quietly carried out, but
the culprit could not be found, until one day Diana was caught
with the money in hand. Her mother was called to the school, and
amid tears and whimpering Diana frankly admitted the thefts.
A short while later, after a serious quarrel with her mother, Diana
stayed locked in her room for two days, refusing to eat or go to
school. It was then that her parents decided they could no longer
cope with their child, and Mr. Addison brought her to see me.

Here too we can more readily understand the behavior when we
examine Diana's home situation. Mr. Addison, who was fifteen
years older than his wife, had thought a child would curb her
flightiness and give her a sense of responsibility. Mrs. Addison was
at first delighted with the idea of "a baby to play with," but once
she became pregnant, arguments began. She blamed her husband
for her discomfort and her distorted figure, which had once been
the envy of all the neighbors. He, on the other hand, felt that she
was rejecting the unborn child because it was his and because she
really wished to be attractive to younger men.

When Diana was born, she was surrounded by every luxury
her parents could provide. Although Mr. Addison was happy about
having a child, he was afraid to handle the infant, and his wife
complained that the "baby odor" made her ill. So a nurse was
retained for Diana while her mother resumed her social activities.
However, Mrs. Addison was so demanding of the nurses that they
were hired and fired in rapid succession, and finally, when Diana
was four, her mother was forced to assume the responsibility herself. Her own activities were now limited more than ever, and she
complained constantly. Although her husband looked forward to
seeing his daughter and playing with her in the evenings, his wife's

continual nagging and wish to take him on a round of parties grew increasingly unbearable. Gradually he remained away from home more and more, finding his club more restful than his wife.

Diana grew more tense every day. Her father's frequent absences and her mother's increasing short temper and self-preoccupation confused and frightened her. Often silent and withdrawn, at times Diana exploded in temper tantrums and destructiveness. During these outbursts Mrs. Addison could not cope with her and would threaten her with punishment from her father.

When Diana was six years old, she started bed-wetting, and her mother sought help from her family physician, who said this was not uncommon and would probably pass over shortly. About that time, because Mr. Addison was away from home a good deal on business, they decided that the child should be sent to an out-of-town boarding school. Here things grew worse. Diana's temper tantrums continued; she was sullen, uncooperative, lied a great deal, and was unable to get along with the other children. After a year her parents were compelled to take her out of that school and put her into a private one in the town where they lived. However, she began to steal money, even from their own servants. One evening when the Addisons became involved in a bitter quarrel about her stealing, Mr. Addison left the house. Diana did not see him again for three weeks, during which time she was more or less on her own or in the company of the servants.

And so the pattern continued, her parents constantly changing her schools and finally again sending her to one out of town. But Diana's behavior remained unchanged. She continued to steal and lie. When she was a little past thirteen, she had a date with a boy from a neighboring school and stayed away from her dormitory overnight. Appalled at her behavior, the school authorities expelled her, and her parents transferred her again to a private school in their home town.

Diana discovered that the situation between her parents had grown worse. They argued frequently and bitterly about matters which seemed to her rather trivial. At other times days went by without her parents saying a word to each other. Already feeling rejected by them, the climax came in her mother's refusal to buy her a new dress for the coming school dance. Diana flew into a rage, threatening not to go, and when Mrs. Addison slapped her, Diana hit her back. No sooner did her father return home that evening, than Diana related the whole story to him. A heated argument ensued between her parents, ending in a physical fight, which Diana witnessed. During the following two days she stayed in her room, refusing to eat or go to school, and it was at that time that her father consulted me.

Here was a young, good-looking girl, quite bright, but tense and obviously disturbed. Having been given every material comfort but none of the emotional ones, she was at the same time spoiled and yet grossly neglected. During the first interviews Diana gave me primarily "yes" or "no" answers, and it took a great deal of time to piece together her whole story. Her basic complaints were that her parents never cared about her and that she never could be heard because there were so many arguments between them or because they were too busy to listen. She resented and hated her mother and had deep contempt for her father, not only because she felt neither really cared about her, but also because of the disagreements, quarrels, and hostility between themselves.

All of Diana's feelings were quite unconscious when she first came for psychiatric treatment. She knew only that she was unhappy. Little by little, however, her real feelings about her hostility and rebelliousness came to the fore. Her stealing was an unconscious expression of her craving for attention. Her defiant attitude toward school and authority expressed her basic rebelliousness toward her parents. The emotional relationship between her parents and between them and her, with its strong undercurrent of tension, brought about an antisocial, criminalistic personality development in Diana, which could only be stopped through psychiatric treatment. This personality development was linked to a distortion of character, which will be discussed later.

In Diana's case, as in the case of many children who are reared by a succession of nurses or governesses, she was unable to form any healthy identification, for no one was close to her long enough for her to develop this emotional tie. The inconsistency in her upbringing, coupled with the existing family tension, confused and frightened her. She did not dare love anyone for fear that they too might soon vanish from the scene and leave her lonely and deserted.

Diana's parents are clear-cut examples of two people unable to fulfill their roles in creating a family climate free of emotional tension because of a lack of genuine love between them, which unfortunately not only made them unhappy, but also had serious repercussions on their child.

Even when family tension or pressures is so subtle that it is most difficult for anyone outside of the family to discern, it can be sensed in the atmosphere by the family members and can make children succumb more readily to antisocial or criminalistic inclinations. It is often difficult for even the experienced psychiatrist to detect without probing, however, because it can exist on an unconscious level and the family members may fail to realize its presence. But this does not mean that it is not sensed by them emotionally. On the surface everyone may be polite and kind to each other, but the very sterile quality of this atmosphere—that is, the substitution of tact for love and understanding—may produce even greater hostility within the home.

Nevin, a young boy of eleven, came from a middle-class home where the tension was so subtle that no one recognized it. Although he had been a sickly child, he had made excellent progress in school and caught up with children of his own age group. Then, quite suddenly, his marks started to drop, and he became truant. At first his mother thought that this was a disciplinary problem. When punishment brought no results, his parents came to me for psychiatric help. Both his father and mother appeared to get along well together, but they stressed this so much that I became suspicious and asked to see them individually. The father refused, supposedly because he had no time, but Nevin's mother came and started treatment. During one session she told me: "I don't understand my son's behavior. This can't be a question of his feeling neglected because Nevin was sick so much that I certainly gave him more than his share of love. He's the only boy and the oldest child, you know."

Whenever I asked her about her relationship with her husband, she either insisted that they got along beautifully, or she became evasive, talking about how well he provided for his family. It was a long time before she admitted that her husband and she had grown indifferent to each other and seldom discussed anything of real meaning between them. They were always polite and tactful, however, avoiding arguments so that Nevin and their other two children would not think anything was wrong between them and become upset. Although each one was active in his own group in the community, they rarely spent time with each other or went out together. She finally broke down in tears and admitted that their marriage had been completely unsuccessful, a failure almost from the very start. Basically she resented and even hated her husband because he seemed more concerned with the community and with keeping up appearances than he was with her or his family. When she made overtures to him, trying to suppress her hostility, he rebuffed them.

Her children therefore provided her with an outlet for the love she felt her husband rejected. When Nevin became ill, she felt more needed and wanted, and she lavished her affection upon him, spending a great deal of time tutoring him. When I suggested that her son and two daughters might have discovered that all was not well between her husband and herself, she assured me that her children had been very happy until this recent development in Nevin.

His parents' hostility was, however, the crux of Nevin's problem, although it took some time before his mother could accept the fact. Nevin had sensed that he was singled out as "different" from his two sisters. Even more important, he sensed that he was taking his father's place with his mother. Unconsciously it made him feel guilty, for while her attention pleased him, it made a demand on him which was too great a responsibility for his childish capacity. In becoming truant, he acted out his hostility toward both of his parents. Unconsciously he was rebelling against growing up, when the burden would become greater, and against feeling bound to his mother. He knew instinctively that failing in school would be a blow to her, since she had worked so hard to help him catch up, and it was also an unconscious expression of resentment toward his father, who had put him in this uncomfortable position by not taking his rightful role as a husband. Nevin also felt, somehow, that he was paying his "debt" to his sisters for having received a greater share of attention.

Although this deep emotional tension was not visible on the surface, it pervaded the entire home, and Nevin had felt it more than the others, for he sensed that beneath his parents' rationalized behavior he was not really loved but only served their neurotic needs. It was against this feeling—this lack of genuine love—that he had protested, by acting out his hostility toward them.

When there is subtle, although deep-seated, hostility and resentment between parents, they cannot work out their problems because their hostile feelings prevent them from discussing them impassionately or even at all. We saw this in Nevin's home. The situation is about the same where the hostility remains on the surface. Here too there cannot be a rational discussion about problems concerning the family members because the intensity of their hostile feelings prevents them from expressing themselves in a healthy way. They are anxious and crave attention and therefore try to do whatever they can in order to be heard. Frequently they scream at each other, which is often the only way of communication they know.

Whether the emotional tension is manifest or latent, however, the family equilibrium is unbalanced, and therefore, all of its members pull in different directions. Where the tension is subtle, the family setup may seem cohesive. Deep down, though, there is as much lack of cohesion as in a family with manifest tension. Either way family tension is a basic, serious factor not only in producing and maintaining antisocial or criminal activities, but also in being at the root of other disturbances.

As a matter of fact, the degree and type of emotional tension in a family largely determines the personalities of the children. It may also be a key to why one individual develops a neurosis, a psychosis, or a psychosomatic ailment while another develops into a criminal. To a great extent criminal activities are a reflection of a type of family tension which is quite different from that in the home of the neurotic or psychotic person. For example, when we study the type of emotional relationships and emotional tension of the delinquent and of the mentally ill person, we often find a distinct difference.

The psychotic or neurotic person usually has been raised in a family where tension has existed in a subdued form for a long period of time. There has most often been an overemphasis on moral standards of conduct so that the superego structure (or conscience) has reached too high a level of development. An overly developed conscience often leads these people into a submissive or suppressive, rather than an uninhibited, way of living. Since they are usually afraid to express themselves freely and therefore inhibit themselves, they often develop a neurosis, psychosis, or psychosomatic illness.

The atmosphere in the criminal's or delinquent's family, on the other hand, is quite different. Here we usually find a much weaker superego structure and much less inhibition. Emotional outbursts, physical violence, and heated arguments are more constant, intense, and acute, heightening the tension quite markedly. Here too, though, we find a great prevalence of psychosomatic disturbances (see Chapter V). In families with acute tension children usually come to feel isolated and displaced and have little or no incentive to identify themselves either with their parents or with acceptable standards of behavior. Frequently the emotional atmosphere in these homes is of such low quality as to engender only antisocial reactions in the offspring. Thus severe family tension can bring about a deformation of the character of the child, which makes him into an antisocial person and often a criminal. As a matter of fact, character deformation is the main characteristic of those who break the law, and the seriousness of the offense often varies according to the degree of the deformation.

All character formation, as we shall see later, is intimately bound to the ego and the instinctual forces of the child, although the individual character traits are to a high degree also molded by the emotional atmosphere in the home and the strength of the superego structure it creates.

There are three factors which influence the emotional growth of a child: 1) his inherent temperamental predisposition; 2) his biological and emotional development; 3) the emotional climate in his home. Antisocial and criminal activities can be produced when any or all of the above three factors are out of gear. The main result of interference with the normal development of these three elements is a stunting or arresting of the child's emotional growth so that he becomes egocentric, dependent, and hostile, which traits are invariably found to predominate in the criminal. He is therefore really a person with a pattern of childish emotional behavior.

We can understand this stunted development better when we realize that from birth on children are a composite of social and antisocial, constructive and destructive, traits, which must be healthily channeled. They are basically bundles of egocentricity and therefore demand every bit of attention they can possibly capture. Since they are a combination of extremes of behavior, disordered family life will stimulate the negative extremes and may in many cases bring out emotional disturbances, with or without criminal activities. We must remember that every child goes through a certain biological and emotional development during which negative feelings and traits, such as resentment, hostility, fear, aggressiveness, anxiety, and guilt arise. These thrive in a disturbing emotional home climate, while they can usually be minimized in a healthy one.

Of course, it is true, as Freud once said, "In our innermost soul we are children and remain so throughout most of our lives." None of us can ever hope to become so emotionally mature that we free ourselves completely from our childish emotions. What we can do is try to grow up and become as emotionally mature as possible. The criminal, however, is prevented from doing this because of his egocentric feelings. Unable to endure anxiety and lacking self-control, he must act out his impulses. One of the basic earmarks of any criminal is that he must have immediate gratification of his desires. We find this also to be true in children, particularly in the infant, who, when he does not get fed, screams. He is only concerned with himself, that is, with his own needs. He is demanding and has no consideration for the needs of others. The case is just the same in the antisocial and criminal individual. He, like a child, is dominated almost entirely by his emotions, consciously or unconsciously.

We can easily understand that a tense and pressured home atmosphere will block the maturation of childish feelings and constructive potentialities which the child may possess. In an atmosphere where insecurity produces more insecurity, antisocial tendencies will be made more acute, and a child reared in such a home often becomes sensitized to criminal activities. He starts to repress his painful memories about his early deprivations, but this repression results in free-floating hostile aggressiveness, usually tinged with anxiety and guilt. Since he has been hurt emotionally, he may try to strike back by acting out his hostilities.

We have often heard that broken homes and poor economic circumstances elicit antisocial and criminal activities. I do not deny this, but let us probe a little deeper to see what usually prevails or has prevailed in homes showing these socially pathological conditions and what is really the root and more basic cause of antisocial behavior, juvenile delinquency, adult criminality, and many emotional and mental disturbances. It is emotional dislocation, resulting in family tension, which in turn creates more emotional dislocation, thus forming a vicious circle.

Life cannot be meaningful to a child when the feelings of his parents fluctuate from love to hate and from security to insecurity. Such parents are not equipped either to be sensitive to the needs of their children or to meet them. And if a child is in any way sensitive and reacts adversely to this type of emotional atmosphere, he may very well be led into juvenile delinquency and an adult life of crime.

CHAPTER IV

Juvenile Delinquency

Every element that prevents children from developing in a healthy way both physically and emotionally tends to bring about a pattern of emotional disturbances, which is always at the root of antisocial or criminal behavior. Such behavior, when found in youngsters, is called juvenile delinquency. However, at the outset I would like the reader to know that when I use the term "delinquent," I do not mean it in a diagnostic sense. It is rather a legal and social description. Juvenile delinquency is a syndrome, not a clinical entity as such, and I use the term because it connotes one particular pattern of behavior, an antisocial one, which is considered by the law to be criminal and therefore punishable.

Juvenile delinquency, then, involves any criminal act against persons or property committed by a child. According to the law a child is responsible for his crime after the age of seven and is considered a juvenile until he is sixteen, seventeen, or eighteen. Nine states have the sixteen-year limit, sixteen states have the seventeen-year limit, and twenty-one states have the eighteen-year limit. The federal government has set the limit at eighteen, after which a person is considered an adult and subject to usual criminal procedures as they pertain to adults.

In the state of New York a person between seven and sixteen

years of age who commits a crime is considered a juvenile delinquent and is not subject to adult penalties. There is one exception
to this rule, however. If a fifteen-year-old commits a *capital* crime,
he may be subject to adult penalties, depending on the circumstances. In some states, such as New York, there is a special category
between the juvenile delinquent and the adult criminal called the
"youthful offender." In New York those between sixteen and nineteen years of age who commit a crime fall into this category. Among
its advantages are: the offender is not placed in the criminal category; he is treated separately and apart from the sessions of the
court reserved for adult trials; and he cannot be committed for
more than three years to any religious, charitable, or other reformative institution authorized by law to receive persons over the age of
sixteen. Furthermore, his record is sealed and not open to inspection, and his being a youthful offender is no disqualification for
public office or employment or any other privilege.[1] Similar laws
have been enacted in New Jersey and Califorinia.

It is alarming that today adolescents are committing the same
types of criminal activities as adults, whereas in former times the
type of crime changed as the person grew older. For example, young
people used to be involved in more youthful types of crime, such
as pranks or petty stealing, but today they are committing the same
vicious crimes as adult criminals—murder, robbery, rape, burglary,
vandalism, and automobile thefts, not to mention such minor
crimes as purse snatching, petty thievery, destruction of property,
and disorderly conduct (particularly in connection with gang mem-
bership and gang fights). Recently 67.7 percent of all arrests of
young offenders was for automobile thefts, their most prevalent
crime. Adolescents under eighteen years of age represented 53.1
percent of all arrests for crimes against property.[2] In addition to
car thefts, other types of thefts and burglary, larceny, and robbery
are considered the most usual types of crimes committed by adolescents.

Even though now the young offender seems to have become an
all-around criminal, there is one crime he usually does not commit
—forgery—which requires a great deal of skill and which usually
is committed only by adults. This type of fraud requires more plan-

ning and deliberation than, for example, stealing a car or breaking into a house. The latter crimes are more frequently of the impulsive type, which is more in keeping with the nature of the teen-ager. And just as in the adult offender, the type of crime committed by the juvenile transgressor reflects his personality make-up.

However, not only have the types of crimes changed, but there has been a tremendous and disturbing increase in the number of crimes carried out by young people today. From 1948 to 1957 cases of juvenile delinquency increased five times as fast as the population of the ten-to-seventeen-year-old age group,[3] and in 1958, while the overall number of arrests rose only .3 of 1 percent over 1957 figures, among those under eighteen years of age the increase was 6.7 percent.[4] Arrests of boys and girls under eighteen were 750,000 for 1958.[5] In the state of New York it was reported that arrests in the nineteen- and twenty-year-old age group were 23.8 percent higher in 1957 than for the same age group in 1956.[6] It is estimated that 1,000,000 will be arrested each year by 1962 unless methods are devised to reverse the trend.[7]

The increase in crime seems to be spreading horizontally across our nation, as well as vertically. For instance, a report by John Beckmann [8] indicates an increase in 1957 of 22 percent of crimes committed by young people in rural areas. Although the increase of crime in general was more pronounced in smaller cities than in larger ones according to latest statistics, let us take a look at our youth crime in a large city, such as New York. In 1957 more than 11,000 persons under twenty-one years of age were arrested for major offenses, which is about 10 percent more than in 1956.[9] The following figures released by Police Commissioner Stephen P. Kennedy on April 22, 1958 show the increase of arrests of juvenile delinquents and youths under twenty-one years of age for the six-year period 1952 to 1957, inclusive:

Year	Under 16 Years	16 to 20 Years	Total
1952	4,081	10,345	14,426
1953	4,804	10,773	15,577
1954	6,012	12,471	18,483
1955	6,578	12,359	18,937
1956	8,714	13,928	22,642
1957	9,886	15,317	25,203
	40,075	75,193	115,268

The increase of juvenile delinquency is not restricted to the United States. It has occurred in many countries throughout the world. It is a major problem in England today just as it is in America. Commander George Hatherill, of London's Scotland Yard, points out that 75 percent of indictable crimes in England are charged to persons under twenty-one years of age.[10] It is reflected by the big increase in the number of youths sent to prison or reform schools. In fact, indictable crimes by youths of eighteen or nineteen indicated a rise of 60 percent in 1956 compared with 1938.[11]

Italy too is being plagued by a flare-up of teen-age hooliganism. This comes from a country which has had one of the lowest juvenile delinquency rates in the world. Almost every day more violence seems to be breaking out. The youths wear loud shirts and blue jeans or white jeans. This wave of hooliganism is particularly alarming in Milan and in other cities of the prosperous north. Many of these boys come from respectable families. It is interesting that in the cities of the poor south, where family bonds are still tight and crime is still a serious thing that is committed for honor, not for play, youngsters seem best behaved.[12] A generation seems to be growing up in northern Italy, however, which feels the need of traditional family protection, but is in conflict with its parents because they are slow to understand the changing society in which they live.[13]

It is interesting to note that according to a report published for the United Nations Conference on Juvenile Crime in London 1960, juvenile crime has now declined in Italy as well as in Belgium, Switzerland, and Canada. It has, however, had a rapid rise in England, Wales, South Africa, Australia, New Zealand, East Germany, West Germany, Austria, Greece, Yugoslavia, France, Sweden, and Finland.

In France there was an immediate increase of juvenile delinquency just after the war, but between 1949 and 1952 juvenile crime dropped by 50 percent, and since that time there has not been any significant change. In Paris, with a population of nearly three million people, only thirty policemen and fifty policewomen are needed to cope with juvenile delinquency. No organized juvenile gangs exist. It is estimated that between 80 and 90 percent of the youngsters in France who get into trouble with the police are products of broken, or otherwise abnormal, homes, and the most common contributing factor is alcoholism on the part of the parents. In my own opinion, this low delinquency rate may very well be due to the strong family ties in France and its emphasis on the arts, hard work, and physical exercise, rather than economic competitiveness.

The Scandinavian countries, which ordinarily have a low crime rate, have reported an increase in juvenile delinquency, which was especially prevalent shortly after the war, when organized gangs came into existence. However, these gangs seem to have disintegrated now, although Sweden still reports a high rate of car thefts by young people.

This rise in auto thefts generally has gained world-wide attention. As mentioned before, they have been on the increase in the United States (68 percent of the arrests for auto thefts have been committed by juveniles sixteen years old or younger). In England auto thefts are considered to be a striking new form of crime, while in France, according to the above-mentioned U.N. report, it has been stated that cars, and particularly motorcycles, seem to come under semi-collective ownership in the eyes of the young. Sweden, as well as Belgium, has reported a corresponding rise in auto thefts by youngsters. The report indicates that even the relative scarcity of autos seems to provide little hindrance. Thailand has noted that bicycle thefts have been increasing.

Reports from the Soviet Union about the presence of juvenile delinquency are contradictory. One report, as recent as April, 1958, indicates that there was none. The reason for these contradictory reports may be that the Soviet Union would like to appear in the best possible light and is therefore not releasing accurate reports on the presence of juvenile crime. This may be substantiated by the fact that more than twenty years ago the Soviet Union saw a need to lower the age of responsibility for serious crimes to twelve in order to combat the delinquency problem, and it still remains at twelve today. I believe that the sociological and psychological reasons for juvenile delinquency there are by and large the same as in the capitalistic countries, including a keen competition for material wealth.

The causes of the overwhelming problem of juvenile delinquency are complex. By and large they are the same as those that give rise to the adult criminal and stem from mental pathology, in its broadest sense, and from social pathology. Although most juvenile delinquents do not suffer either from a well-defined psychiatric condition or a neurological one,[14] many of them are neurotic, suffer from phobias, show compulsive behavior patterns, or appear to be rigid in their behavior. Some are mentally defective; some show signs of the beginnings of a psychosis; others may show vague symptoms of a character disorder. All of them, however, are emotionally undeveloped. One difference between the adult criminal and the juvenile delinquent is that adults, to a great extent, can choose their environment, while children usually are dependent upon adults. Of course, even adults cannot control the state of the world or the economic conditions within their country—individually, anyway. But a child is restricted environmentally even in minor things. The fulfillment of his desire to go to a movie, for instance, depends upon his parents, as does his attending a good school or living in a nondelinquent area. Thus deprivations of any type, or unfavorable conditions, depending upon their character and the child's reactions to them, may be causes of juvenile delinquency.

Still what has been said here does not explain the great rise of juvenile delinquency and its changed character, which may very well be rooted in the social changes that have taken place in our society during the past fifty years. Although it is difficult to estimate the consequences of two world wars and the constant tension among nations, we certainly know that these factors do not increase the well-being of any person.

Progressive education and its companion, permissiveness, have been blamed unqualifiedly for the rise of juvenile delinquency by some who forget that old-style formal education had become too rigid and that it was necessary to foster individuality, within reason, in order to enhance the healthy emotional development of the child. However, Freud's basic idea that much in us that is now suppressed or repressed should be released was misinterpreted to mean that any suppression is bad. The concept of freedom with responsibility has thus been replaced by the unhealthy advocation of freedom without limit. This change of policies took place at a time when much of our concern was directed toward the needs of the child.

As other causative factors in the rise of juvenile delinquency we should consider the important sociological developments which have taken place in the last one hundred years, such as increased industrialization and our current trend toward surburban life,[15] both in their own ways tending to separate parents from children for longer periods of time than before and to make people migrate from the tremendously isolated, yet closely knit, farm life (where there were better chances to establish and develop roots and identities) to large cities (where we often find two working parents or one parent with a night job) or suburbs (where fathers often leave early in the morning and return late at night, mothers busy themselves outside the home, and servants rear the children).

Although these sociological changes are important in themselves, their resultant emotional effects are of even greater significance. A parent's frequent absence from home often leads to the most subtle forms of family tension. In many families today the father plays only a perfunctory role, mostly that of a provider, without taking an emotional part in his family's life. His role in the American home has become so minimized that frequently little attention is paid to him. Consciously or unconsciously his wife and children feel his absence in that they miss a man upon whom they can depend for guidance, leadership, and understanding. In addition the children have no male figure with whom to identify, which produces emotional insecurities in them and brings about tension and unbalanced family life.

Of course, in earlier times also there were fathers who could not take too active a part in the upbringing and the emotional rearing of their children. But families were less separated by physical distances, and the father's role could easily be filled by an uncle or grandfather. With a boy in particular, when there is no authoritative figure in the family with whom he can identify, such lack tends to show up in his later life, especially in adolescence, during which period he will identify with any strong figure in his environment. In fact, this is one of the main reasons why gangs have sprung up among juveniles today; the gang leader becomes the strong figure with whom the others can identify.

When there is a lack of identification between parents and children, they all live in different worlds, having very little in common with each other. They do not communicate with or belong to each other. They are each a separate unit, one generation having little or nothing to do with the other. As a matter of fact, parents frequently do not know what their children are doing, and children are not told what their parents are doing. Basically the family life becomes one where parents and children live without any fundamental common purpose, which is essential for a child's sense of belonging. The character of young people is undoubtedly linked to the kind of identification youngsters have with the older generation.

Lack of identification with older family members may explain the sharp increase in juvenile delinquency in Western countries, since those countries whose culture is imbued with respect for their elders do not show such an alarming rate. It is significant in this respect that criminal activities are rather low among the Chinese and the Jewish people, where there are strong family ties.

With uprooted community life and shattered family ties comes a deterioration of feeling between the individual and his family members and between him and his social environment. Furthermore, with today's emphasis on the importance of the individual and his fight for his own independence in general has come, in great measure, a looser family organization. In addition, the Boy and Girl Scouts, the sports team, the school class, and, in some cases, the gang, have to a large extent replaced parental authority—particularly the father's. The result is not only a weakening of the emotional ties among the various members, but also diminished regard and respect for the older members of the family, especially for parents and grandparents, who once played a significant role as social authorities.[16] This lack of respect breeds a feeling of irresponsibility toward adults in general. All these emotional attitudes, resulting in a sharp increase of juvenile antisocial and criminal activities and their changed nature, may also account in part for the increased number of character disorders among youngsters today.

As a matter of fact, it has been observed by psychoanalysts and psychiatrists that the problems of psychoanalysis today have changed with the altered personality structure.[17] In general it can be said that while previously the individual's superego was supported by definite standards of moral ethics and values, these standards have now become unstable and relative, so that religious and other moral authoritarian forces have lost their grip upon him. He has consequently come to rely more upon the standards of his fellow men or, in the case of a child, upon the standards set up by his classmates or friends, than upon the ancient commandments or unwritten laws. The loss of the elders' authority and the diminished power of moral and social authority bring about rebelliousness, loss of ideals, and lack of goals in the youngsters. Thus while psychiatrists and psychoanalysts previously treated many patients suffering from neuroses as a result of repression, today they find more patients are suffering from character disorders, reflecting a distorted ego and superego structure leading to acting out.

The large and heterogeneous population of the United States may be still another factor in the high rate of juvenile delinquency here. With so large a number of people from so many varied backgrounds, there is a greater possibility of more deviations from the kind of behavior recognized as normal. When the social and emotional dislocations of the family, the often poor neighborhoods, the unsatisfactory economic and work conditions, and the general drive for success are added to this, we can see that the soil is fertile for the growth of antisocial and criminal activities.

Although both sociologically and psychologically determined factors go into the making of a criminal act, it is difficult to say which causative factor is the more important. Even though we know that any act, social or antisocial, is a result of the emotional and mental state of the individual, we still must take the situation into consideration. The psychodynamics of an antisocial or criminal act (including juvenile delinquency) are therefore not only the psychodynamics of the person but also of the situation as we can readily see from our formula $C = \dfrac{T + S}{R}$.

The main characteristic of the juvenile delinquent is that he acts out his inner conflicts. Emotionally immature, he is unable to withstand pain and discomfort or to postpone immediate gratification of his desires. Consequently, any pressures from his environment make him feel anxious. His anxiety has to be discharged in some way, and, again because of emotional immaturity, the delinquent gains relief by acting out his impulses. This acting out is more understandable when we realize the inner tensions of even the normal adolescent. This is the time when he is bursting with a feeling of power and must find an outlet for his excess energy. Also it is a twilight period, when he is neither a child nor an adult. Actually he wants to be a little bit of both, and his struggles between childish wishes and needs—a feeling of dependence and insistence upon immediate gratification of his needs—and adult strivings, such as the wish to break away and become independent, create conflicts within him, resulting in confusion about his own role or status. For the juvenile delinquent, whose emotional foundation is already weak, the turmoil of adolescence is considerably more intense, and if he should feel neglected or unloved, he has an even stronger need to establish his identity and make people notice him.

The baffling point is that even if the juvenile delinquent acts out his impulses because of his own anxiety and discomfort, most frequently he carries out his aggressive act in a masochistic way. We see this in the case of Walter, a fourteen-year-old boy who had had chronic enuresis (bed-wetting) since early childhood. Despite his high intelligence, his grades in school were usually poor, and he was often truant. Given to overeating, frequently he stole money from other children in his class, using it mostly to buy candy, which he would tauntingly eat in front of them. His mother was a widow who disciplined him inconsistently and unintelligently. Although quite strict with her son, she felt guilty after punishing him because "poor Walter had no father to teach him," and she would follow up every punishment with rewards of candy or ice cream.

Walter's father had contributed a great deal to an unstable and otherwise unsatisfactory home life. All during his marriage he was involved with other women, and when Walter was only ten, his father was killed in an accident, the details of which are unclear. Both Walter and his mother remembered him as a selfish, unpredictable tyrant, who laid down strict laws in the household with complete disregard for anyone else's needs. Although a wealthy businessman, he was quite erratic in the way he spent money. At times he would splurge lavishly on his family, and at other times he would squander most of his money on women. When he died, he left his family practically nothing except the house in which they lived, and Walter's mother's greatest fear was that her son would turn out to be a "ne'er-do-well like his father."

Accounts of Walter's childhood disclosed that from the age of two he had been spiteful and difficult to manage. When he was about four, he locked himself in the bathroom several times, and once the handyman had to be called to break open the door because no amount of persuasion could get Walter to come out. His mother was shocked to learn that he had been masturbating in the bathroom and she punished him severely. It was about this time that his enuresis began, and Walter's mother became even more distraught. One day the boy went berserk and tore the house apart; when his mother returned home that afternoon, she found a frightened maid, who refused to stay with the child any more.

As Walter grew older, his stealing continued—usually from the five-and-ten-cent stores and most often "something that looked good to eat." His dishonesty came out in other ways too. Even when he had the price of admission to the movies, he would try to sneak in because it was more of a thrill that way. Many times after these escapades he would relate the incidents to his mother, knowing full well that she would punish him but getting a certain satisfaction from the attention it brought. At twelve Walter was reported truant from school for two weeks, and the case came to the attention of the school psychologist. His mother was extremely upset when they advised her of it. She explained to the school that she had little time for her child because she had to work to support him, but she promised to punish him for his truancy.

When the psychologist tried to explain that Walter needed attention instead, she shrugged her shoulders and said that a boy should grow up standing on his own two feet.

It was obvious that she had little insight into herself or her son. She knew only that "lack of discipline made his father the way he was, and if Walter were just disciplined, then everything would be all right." Unfortunately, it did not turn out that way; the more he was punished, the more defiant and spiteful he became. When he was fourteen and his truancy continued, the school recommended psychiatric treatment and referred him to me.

Walter was quite a nice-looking, strapping adolescent, although a good deal overweight. He munched candy throughout his first interview and was extremely sensitive and reticent, except to say that he was "fed up" at home and had had "his fill" of school too. "Nobody *really* cares what I do anyway as long as it doesn't give *them* any extra trouble," he told me rather pointedly. In later sessions he admitted that he felt unwanted and expressed a great deal of hostility toward his mother, finally blurting out that he hated her.

It was difficult to obtain a complete story of Walter's early childhood, particularly because his mother was hostile to the boy's receiving treatment and was even more defensive than her son. Little by little, however, the picture unfolded, and it became clear that Walter's mother and father had never gotten along well together. They had grown bitter and hateful toward each other, quarreling incessantly over the father's wastefulness and infidelity. But since the wife felt totally rejected by her husband, she had never admitted to him that secretly she had really admired some of his traits—his manliness, his unusual business acumen, and his magnanimity when he was in a good mood. When Walter was born, though she had wished for a girl, she saw an opportunity to shape and mold her son into the kind of man she felt her husband might have been were it not for his faults.

Thus she cherished great aspirations for Walter and never hesitated to show her disappointment when he was not perfect. She felt his every act reflecting upon herself. Almost from the start Walter knew instinctively how to get around her when he wanted something and how to irritate her when he felt hostile. And he usually made the most of it.

Her demands for perfection in him centered mainly around his cleanliness and his achievements at school. For example, she was extremely proud of his having been toilet-trained at the age of twenty months and completely chagrined over his bed-wetting again at four. When he got good marks in school, she was delighted and gave him anything he wanted, but when he failed even the smallest test, she was furious and rejected him completely, often punishing him severely. Walter grew to expect the same perfection of her and resented her fiercely when he found it lacking.

The inconsistency in her attitudes at times brought Walter immediate gratification of his needs and at other times created violent frustrations and anxieties in him because they were not satisfied. And the more resentful he felt, the more he enjoyed provoking his mother into punishing him, sometimes even to the extent of frightening her with wild tales of his misdoings. Once he told her a lurid, but untrue, story of how he had murdered one of his classmates. Thus he had developed toward her the same mixed— ambivalent—feelings of love and hate and the same alternatingly sadistic-masochistic attitudes which she displayed toward him.

One characteristic of the juvenile delinquent is that, generally speaking, he is much more demanding than the nondelinquent because consciously or unconsciously he feels deprived—regardless of whether such deprivation is actual or imagined. As a matter of fact, emotional deprivation, which most often stems from family tension, is an important cause of juvenile delinquency, much more so than any other kind of deprivation, whether it be educational, cultural, intellectual, social, or even economic, and is much more prevalent in a family with delinquent members than in one without them. Thus we see that it is a vicious circle. Emotional deprivation stems from family tension, which tends to create delinquents, who in turn create more family tension.

Before we can better understand how antisocial and criminal behavior patterns and emotional disturbances originate and develop by following the psychological and biological development of the child, we must first have a clear understanding of our instincts. Instincts, with which we are all born and which are both social and asocial, are often called by the Latin terms "id" or "libido." Because our instincts are rooted in the chemical-physical (biological) processes and state of our bodies, they are endowed with energy. An instinct can therefore be defined as a physical and emotional need which makes a demand upon the mind. Thus our instincts constitute a force within us which makes itself felt whether we are awake or asleep.

We can understand the course these instincts follow when we think of a simple physical need such as hunger, which may be considered part of the instinct for survival. Satisfying this urge requires a specific action, which when carried out brings relaxation, while frustration of it creates tension.

If an instinct is not gratified in its original form, it may change its direction and be released through healthy sublimation or be repressed and appear in various disguises. The latter happens most often with our sexual instinct because of the culture in which we live. But not every psychological phenomenon is sexual; there are other instincts which can also be thwarted, such as aggressiveness (e.g., striking back when attacked), which may also be an expression of the instinct for survival.[18] Because our instincts can be constructive or destructive, in effect all of our laws have been established in order to curb and control the destructive drives in our instinctual lives. A psychologically healthy person is one who has learned to rechannel these destructive impulses into healthy, constructive outlets so that they do not remain constantly unsatisfied and yet are not expressed in a harmful way.

Since today we are able to measure energy—by metabolic rate, electroencephalography, and electrocardiography, for example— we may very well say that physiological energy is involved in all of our functions, including those of the brain. The energy responsible for all our psychic activities cannot therefore be described either as sexual or general but must rather be described as physiological in nature.[19]

At birth every child is a bundle of unconscious emotions, of instincts which are polymorphic and sexual (manifested through sucking). If an infant does not receive food, he cries, and when he has other biological urges, such as the urge to urinate, he satisfies them without any concern. He acts automatically. His nervous and anatomical systems control his emotions and actions.

The child thus wants immediate satisfaction. He cannot postpone his desires; he must have them fulfilled immediately because this is more important to him than anything else; it determines how he feels. The chief characteristic of any child, and for that matter, of immature adults, is the need to have wishes fulfilled at once. The reason for this is that desires are basically connected with biological needs, which, if satisfied, give pleasure, and if unsatisfied, lead to pain. In fact, we may say that human behavior in general rotates around this important principle—the pleasure-and-pain principle.

Inability to postpone satisfaction indicates a serious defect in the character of a person, which, incidentally, is an earmark of the criminal, indicating the deep-seated pathological nature of the majority of offenders' minds. When we consider the psychological development of the child, we can better understand how such a character defect may arise.

The psychological and sexual development of the child have been dealt with so extensively by so many writers that much of the material is already familiar. Only a few brief paragraphs in the nature of a review will be necessary here. As most readers know, we divide the preadult sexual life of the child into three periods— the infantile period (consisting of the oral, anal, and genital phases), the latency period, and the puberty period.

The first stage of childhood is called the oral phase because the child's feelings center around food and nursing—the area of the mouth. He sucks the breast, the bottle, his thumb, and sometimes he just sucks nothing; he babbles away and puts everything into his mouth. This oral activity gives him a great deal of pleasure, which is partly sexual in nature.

The infant unconsciously associates the oral pleasure of taking food with love and security. Later, being held and fondled, particularly while being fed, adds to his feeling of security. Immediate gratification therefore unconsciously comes to mean pleasure or love, while postponement signifies rejection or pain. Consequently, if he is weaned too abruptly or denied normal satisfaction through his mouth, he feels it as a loss of love. He wants it back and may go on wanting it back for the rest of his life.[20] On the other hand, if his oral period is prolonged and he grows too accustomed to receiving oral satisfaction or things associated with oral satisfaction, he becomes spoiled and immature and does not normally grow into the next phase of development. Mishandling the oral drive lays the foundation for dependency and passivity, and excessive passivity is often behind antisocial and criminal aggressions. As we saw in the case of Walter, he seemed to be controlled by an excessive need for oral satisfaction in the form of eating. Since his eating was also a disguised need for love, he could not postpone satisfying his impulses and would resort to stealing money from his classmates to buy candy or sweets from the five-and-ten-cent stores. Thus we see how important it is to deal properly with the oral phase of the infant in order to avoid emotional disturbance and antisocial or criminal types of behavior.

Pleasurable oral eroticism similar to that experienced by infants is maintained in the adult in normal forms—kissing, smoking, drinking—and also in deviant ones. A person who is orally oriented—either because of overindulgence or deprivation associated with oral satisfaction—will be inclined toward excessive drinking, smoking, talking, or eating. These excesses have their roots in the latter part of the oral phase—the cannibalistic part, where the person wants to devour everything. We find oral-sadistic fixation in adult pathological cases, such as in sadistic sex offenders or in vampires. Their frustrations call forth oral-sadistic fantasies, which have to be satisfied even in a deviated way.

From the oral stage the child passes on to his anal phase, which lasts from approximately the time he is one to about two-and-a-half or three years of age. This is the time when he is being toilet trained and becomes aware of experiencing pleasure through the anus. Rigid toilet training tends to make him stubborn, formal, sadistic, and often suspicious; he may often refuse to "part with his product," knowing well that his holding back will upset his mother. Indifferent toilet training, on the other hand, may make him sloppy, careless, phlegmatic, and unresponsive to healthy stimuli.

Walter was toilet trained when very young, and the signs he showed of being sadistic and cruel were due to his being fixated at the anal level. He used to come in dirty at an age when most children keep fairly clean—a regression to his anal stage. It expressed his unconscious wish to play with his feces, which is normal for the child in the anal phase, since he wants to see what he has "produced." Walter's persistent bed-wetting was an unconscious substitute for masturbation, and it might very well have started in part as a way of showing hostility toward his mother because she did not permit him enough of the erotic pleasure a child normally derives from defecating. During his anal stage, as happens so often with children, the feces became for Walter the object of love and hate. Unconsciously he associated his need for love from his mother with his need for pleasure in defecating. Thus he began unconsciously to love and hate his mother practically in the same way that he began to love and hate his feces. We therefore see that Walter was fixated at or had regressed to both the oral and anal stages.

During the anal stage the child is faced with more problems. Because of his developing ego, he suddenly becomes aware that he is hemmed in by all sorts of restrictions. At every turn he hears "no" and "don't," making him angry and resentful. Similarly, indulgence will also create frustrations in the child because in indulging him, the parent is actually attempting to dominate him by making him dependent, which the youngster resents and hates. He goes through an emotional revolution. His superego has just begun to form, and he experiences guilt feelings. If too many restrictions or too frequent punishments are imposed upon him or if his freedom is too limited, he may become negativistic, rebellious, aggressive, hostile, fearful, or criminal, or he may become submissive, compliant, or perhaps even "crushed," all depending upon his innate reaction tendencies.

However a certain amount of negativism is normal during the anal phase. A child will often say "no" when he means "yes" just for the sake of saying "no." Then again he may say "no" for no reason. This reminds me of the two-year-old girl who walked a whole block to her grandmother's house, rang the bell, and before her startled grandmother could speak said "No," and then ran back home.

In view of the frustrations a child may experience during the first years of his life, a great deal of resentment and hostility will arise in him. These will be maintained and heightened as he meets new frustrations and may increase when he enters the genital stage, which normally lasts from about the third to the sixth year. While previously he sought pleasure through his mouth and anus, he now becomes more aware of his sexual feelings and seeks pleasure through his genitals. At this stage a boy unconsciously develops intense love for his mother and hostility toward his father, who stands in his way—the Oedipus situation. For a girl the situation is reversed. She loves her father and wants her mother out of the way—the Electra situation. But the child still needs love from both parents, and so his hostility engenders feelings of fear and guilt. In time and with proper handling normal children overcome their hostile feelings and identify themselves with their parents, especially with the parent of the same sex. Generally speaking, however, if these hostilities continue, they constitute a basis for future illnesses and antisocial or criminal behavior, depending upon the way the individual copes with his hostility.

In Walter's case he hated his father, the Authority, and therefore could not identify himself with any law or order. Since society is also law and order, a child may extend his lack of identification with his parents to a lack of identification with society and thus also direct his hostility toward the latter. This is what Walter did. In committing antisocial acts, he was not only rebelling against the law, but also unconsciously spiting his parents, who had arbitrarily laid down the law to him in the past. Such a pattern is quite frequently found in the reactions of offenders.

In the latency period, which lasts from the sixth or seventh year until puberty, while sexual phenomena do not disappear altogether, they seem to be temporarily halted. In this respect it is interesting to note that not all cultures have this period. The reason our society has a latency period may be that we have strong authoritarian forces at work which are opposed to the gratification of sexual desires. These same repressing forces have been instrumental in bringing about shame and disgust connected with sexual life.

Next comes the final preadult phase, puberty, which a girl enters at approximately the age of twelve and a boy at thirteen. It starts with the manifestation of secondary sexual characteristics, such as breasts in a girl, facial hair in a boy, and pubic hair in both sexes. A girl starts to menstruate at this time, and a boy undergoes a change of voice. It is the stage just preceding our adult sexual life and is especially difficult for the adolescent because it is a time when he finds it difficult to cope with his emotions and feelings. He is neither a child nor an adult and really wants to be a little bit of both.

In Walter's case, as in many others, we can see how the blending of personality traits and the situation, together constituting elements of symbiosis, brought about antisocial and criminal behavior. Such behavior never starts suddenly in any child but is rather a carry-over of predispositional or potential traits which are precipitated by a conducive environment.

The psychopathology of the juvenile delinquent and of the emotionally disturbed nondelinquent is manifold because each youngster goes through the same psychological development, although each one experiences it differently. Both may be said to be fixated at one or more stages of their development. Some, being orally oriented, strive for immediate satisfaction through the mouth; some, feeling sexually inadequate, strive for omnipotence. Others are anal-sadistic, cruel, and suspicious. Some show marked signs of poor superego development, while still others show a strong mother fixation. Despite this varied psychopathology and the varied situations, we are able to see the interrelationship between antisocial or criminal behavior and emotional disturbances and also to understand the various *early signs* of juvenile delinquency.

While negativism, rebelliousness, fearfulness, and hostility are natural to the early development of a child, in many cases these feelings persist far longer than they should, bringing about unhealthy emotional reactions and symptoms of disturbance which

vary in degree from child to child. The overtly rebellious youngster exhibits a general attitude of defiance, undue aggressiveness,
and even truancy. He will usually show other signs too, such as
temper tantrums, resentment, hatred, and excesssive bullying, and
often commits acts of revenge, ranging from petty stealing, lying,
and jealous aggressiveness to arson, sexual attacks, or homicide.
But another child may feel equally rebellious and hostile and yet
be afraid to express his feelings directly. He may instead become
unduly shy, fearful, sensitive, and anxious. Sometimes he may
even manifest so-called exemplary behavior, and seem a "model"
child. Another child may become moody and depressed, bite his
nails, revert to bed-wetting, develop psychosomatic symptoms, or
have continual fatigue, recurrent colds, headaches, or stomach
upsets. He may be prone to accidents.

At the present time we do not know of any signs of potential
delinquency that may not also be symptoms of an emotional disturbance, which may not necessarily lead to antisocial or criminal
behavior. Singly these early symptoms of delinquency may not
be significant, but in combination and duration, they are very important. Rebelliousness, for instance, can be healthy if kept within
certain limits, but if spite, defiance, and rebelliousness go on day
after day and month after month, then antisocial or criminal activities may occur. However, there is one exception to this rule;
there is one sign which, even appearing by itself, is an ominous
danger signal, and that is habitual truancy. I do not mean an occasional day or two of hooky-playing a year, but rather persistent
absence from school without a legitimate excuse. When we examine the records of adult offenders, we find childhood truancy
the most common phenomenon in the great majority of them.

It has been estimated that about 90,000 children are absent
from New York City's public schools every day and that of these
children about 2,000 are reported to the Bureau of Attendance
for investigation each day; 600 of the 2,000 are found to be illegally
absent. These children withdraw from school for many reasons.
They may have a reading disability or poor eyesight or hearing.
They may not be doing well in school and fear bringing home a bad
report card. There are those who are afraid of their teachers or

the principal. Then again they may feel inferior to the other children, either because they feel they are not as bright, as good-looking, or as well-dressed. These children suffer from obvious emotional problems, which, by the way, often lead to psychosomatic illnesses, and require immediate attention. However, habitual truancy occurs also as the result of rebelliousness or spite and in these cases it is frequently a forerunner to criminal activities. Needless to say, these youngsters need help too.

The type of symptoms manifested may indicate the type of criminal activities the young person carries out. For instance, if he shows persistent enuresis, which may indicate a disturbance of his character, he may have a preference for committing arson. This tendency toward fire-setting, which is associated with urethral eroticism, consciously or unconsciously expresses a sexual desire. As we saw in Walter's case, his enuresis began when he stopped masturbating, the one manifestation substituting, so to say, for the other. It is significant that a high incidence of enuresis is found among criminals. Sheldon and Eleanor Glueck disclosed in their studies that 28.2 percent of 500 juvenile delinquents showed persistent enuresis compared with 13.2 percent of nondelinquent young persons, who were used as controls.[21]

When we consider the overwhelming number of traumatic experiences that go into the making of a juvenile delinquent, it is understandable that his ability to distinguish between fantasy and reality may in many cases be impaired. His environment and his life situation have become distorted for him. While the "normal" child by and large uses his intelligence and feelings to rate any situation with which he is faced, the juvenile delinquent is unable to do so. His childhood experiences and reactions have given him a picture, a mental impression, of his environment, which is built mainly upon his wishes, desires, and fears. He sees his family, his friends, his schoolteachers, in fact, his entire situation, through his own emotions. His impressions are colored; he sees and perceives external reality not the way it truly is but the way he has been conditioned to see and perceive it. Because of his lack of ego development and the constant unconscious presence of his traumatic experiences, his memory also suffers, and he is unable to integrate new experiences.

This lack of reality is partially the reason that the juvenile delinquent blames his crimes upon the situation or circumstances, which he claims really forced him to carry out his deed. He tells you that he committed the crime because the victim provoked him or because the situation incited him to do it. Although at times there may be some truth in his reasons, he always projects the origin of his criminalistic impulses to sources other than himself. He acts with an almost schizophrenic-like mechanism. Although his ego is far from integrated, it functions well in the sense that it allows him to receive pleasure from acting out his impulses without feeling guilty. The part of his ego which is somehow split off from the rest of his personality might be called his "criminal ego."

A lack of integrated ego development is closely related to a defective superego, commonly found in the juvenile delinquent. The defective ego and superego are in large measure intimately linked to a lack of healthy identification with parental figures and to the type of the individual's own ego-identity. We can understand the poor functioning of the superego in the juvenile delinquent when we follow its development.

Let us first remember that from the time a child is small, he is taught by his parents that it is wrong to hate or resent, that it is also wrong even to possess sexual desires. Therefore, he (his ego) frequently has to reject impulses from the id, many of which are asocial or antisocial and often wild and untamed. Thus the child must fight his biological desires, which he tries to keep within the limits set by society. But these impulses from his id seek to express themselves. They pound his ego and try to weaken it, but the ego does not give in easily.

The part of his mind, the force within him, which tries or compels him to control his impulses is called the superego. It stems from the ego and is partly conscious and partly unconscious. It is the police, judge, or conscience within us and is often stronger than the ego, never permitting any compromises. As the child grows up, little by little he accepts his parents' dictates. If he does not obey, he is often punished and made to feel guilty and ashamed. In the course of his growing up, his parents' restrictions and rules of behavior—and the punishments for breaking them—gradually become an automatic, though unconscious, part of his own psychic apparatus. After a while he inhibits his "forbidden" desires automatically; that is, he represses and even "forgets" about them. While in early childhood the rules and regulations set down by his parents acted as an external pressure upon him to obey, thereby creating a conflict between him and his parents, this same pressure is eventually incorporated within the child and forms part of his ego—his superego. Now the conflict is within himself, between his ego and superego. Normally these conflicts resolve themselves if the child is allowed enough healthy ego formation without excessive restriction. Then, as he grows older, his behavior is also influenced and modified by the standards of society and the community, be they religious, ethical, legal, or other social forces.

The superego influences the individual according to its strength or weakness, the strength or weakness of the ego, and their interrelationship. The superego censures not only a forbidden act which a person has committed, but also his mere desire to carry it out, so that even unconscious fantasies or thoughts of committing such acts may give rise to a sense of guilt. Thus the superego becomes an intermediary between the id impulses and the ego. It acts as a defense, a restraining force against the antisocial desires which otherwise would reach the ego and possibly destroy it. By understanding this mechanism, we can see that a child who has developed a sufficiently healthy superego structure will be able to cope with his antisocial tendencies and sublimate them constructively. An unhealthy superego will eventually elicit antisocial or criminal activities or varying degrees of emotional disturbance.

If the criminal act of the juvenile or adult delinquent were only a matter of an unhealthy superego, understanding the mechanism of his crime would be rather simple. But many children who have been raised in a good environment and have had the opportunity to learn and to adopt social values have become criminals, while, on the other hand, there are many youngsters who have been raised in a delinquent climate, with poor ethical standards, and yet have been able to grow up to be responsible citizens.

We find part of the explanation of antisocial and criminal behavior in the fact that in the delinquent there is none of the merging between the ego and superego that normally takes place while a child is growing up. (Of course, there must be a certain degree of independence between the two also.) This natural blending may be hampered in the growing process when strong, powerful, instinctual forces pound the ego and deter its merging with the superego, whereas it is aided when the child is able to identify himself with his parents. Where a poor family relationship exists and a child cannot do so, as we saw in Walter's case, there is an undeveloped superego formation which is related to a malformed ego. Walter's malformed ego was rooted in his fixation at or regression to the oral and anal levels.

It is interesting that most delinquent children feel they have been deprived by their parents. In many instances this feeling is justified, for they have never received the love, affection, and economic and social security to which they are entitled. However, in some cases it is not justified at all, particularly with regard to economic and social security. No matter how much the delinquent child receives, he feels that he should have received more because the adult world "owes" it to him. As a matter of fact, very often delinquent youngsters have been brought up with a combination of severe deprivations and overindulgence.

We must remember that the growth of a child takes place in stages, with varying degrees of pace. If, during the development period, specific strains in the environment hit him, preventing him from developing fully in a normal direction, that special phase of development, such as oral, anal, or Oedipal stage, will be distorted or prolonged. His state of mind and the situation at a particular time determine the pattern of etiological factors which make a juvenile delinquent. These factors start at birth and find their final release through the individual's reaction, or process, to his social situation. Thus both a distorted or prolonged development and a process together are responsible for bringing about antisocial or criminal activities in the youngster. Such activities are probably more prevalent where there is acute family tension, with emotional outbursts.

Therefore, when an individual shows criminalistic tendencies in his teens, it is not because he suddenly becomes delinquent at that time, but because he has been suffering from a character deformation since childhood which was more or less hidden and so unnoticed earlier. A long process has gone on before a youngster commits any delinquent acts, and it is the quality of the character structure that determines whether conscious and unconscious conflicts, stresses, and strains from the environment will result in delinquent, rather than in neurotic, symptom formation.

By character I mean the personality structure of a person which determines his behavior—the way he carries out or does not carry out his actions. A person may have an aggressive or a passive character, to give some examples. He will accordingly solve his situational problems either by carrying out his actions in an aggressively constructive way or by conforming to the situation, that is, by passively submitting to it. Thus character presents the dominant set of one's feelings, emotional attitudes, and functions—total personality—which determine behavior, be it social or antisocial.

The formation of character starts from birth and develops in one definite direction according to the child's instinctual forces and his environment. However, his emotions, which dictate his evaluations, vary constantly, and therefore, his evaluations change according to his feelings. In this respect a child has an unstable character in that he changes his feelings from day to day. We find the same unstable character when he becomes an adolescent, although then he acts in a more definite way. In spite of this variance in behavior, he still retains certain fundamental trends which give his attitudes and actions a certain pattern. In fact, even when he becomes an adult, his basic style of behavior and his feelings are the same—his character remaining definite.

As I have said before, character deformation frequently occurs in a child who has been brought up without a reasonable amount of gratification—who has experienced deprivations—particularly of an emotional and biological nature. The crucial point, however, is not how much he has been deprived in reality but how much he feels he has been deprived. Therefore, we also find a disturbed character in a youngster who appears to have had his needs satisfied. Very often too we find a disturbed character formation in a child who is alternately deprived or gratified (usually in extreme form) according to the whim of his parents.

Depending upon the environment and the development of the character, juvenile delinquents constitute many groups, such as the momentary or accidental juvenile delinquents, who becomes involved in crime more through environment and association than through a basic personality disturbance, and the neurotic type of delinquent who, suffering from unconscious guilt feelings and the consequent need to appease his superego by punishing himself, carries out a crime to obtain this punishment. We have a third type, the youngster who suffers from a character disorder; a fourth one, the genuine psychopath; and a fifth, the child suffering from a psychotic condition. A sixth, though more rare, type of juvenile delinquent is the youngster who has had encephalitis, which may cause a personality distortion that is basically a character disorder.

Mainly because of the juvenile delinquent's character, regardless of the cause, he finds satisfaction of instinctual desires invariably more important than satisfaction gained from his object relationships. This is one basic reason he gives in to the immediate gratification of his id impulses. When he is frustrated, he becomes aggressive and anxious. He therefore has to discharge this accumulated anxiety impulsively in action. He discharges his aggressions by acting them out almost with a disassociated or split ego (his criminal ego), whereby his instinctual drives take the lead and he does not feel guilty.

Saying that the delinquent has a tendency to act out his antisocial impulses is in everyday language only saying that he is inclined toward antisocial or criminal behavior. The faulty formation of his character, responsible for this acting out, makes us see the necessity for handling practically all offenders with firmness when giving them psychiatric treatment.

Keeping in mind the great variety of pathological factors present in the juvenile delinquent and in his family, we can say that there are four basic causes of juvenile crime: 1) abnormal family relationships; 2) social disorganization or derangement; 3) individual mental and emotional pathology; and 4) organic conditions of the brain or endocrinological conditions in the body.

In comparing the emotional and mental qualities of the juvenile delinquent with the nondelinquent, we find that the delinquent is more aggressive, assertive, and defiant; he is more resentful and hostile and therefore has more difficulties in submitting to authority and law. When such a child is pressured into submissiveness by his parents, his emotional relationship with them becomes more strained and damaged, setting up a vicious circle. Basically the persistent juvenile delinquent has a deformed character structure, a deformation usually absent in the nondelinquent. This is a finding with which all experienced psychoanalysts agree and is in some measure reflected in the statistics brought out by Sheldon and Eleanor Glueck's study, where 36 out of 500 offenders were found to be psychopathic (indicating the presence of a character disturbance) in contrast to the nondelinquent, where only two were found to be psychopathic.[22]

Practically all juvenile delinquents present a picture of being oral-aggressive, behind which there is a great deal of oral passivity and dependency, coupled with masochistic colorings. Although Sheldon and Eleanor Glueck have found in their studies that a higher percentage of nondelinquents than delinquents show masochistic traits,[23] often in the form of self-punishment, self-humiliation, submissiveness, and asceticism, it is my opinion that these traits are more prevalent in delinquents than in nondelinquents but that they exist on a more unconscious level in the delinquents and therefore are not easily detected and do not show up in statistics.

The young delinquent also shows a marked destructive trend, in which is ingrained a great deal of cruelty and sadism; his capacity for self-control is much lower than that of the average or the neurotic child. His intelligence is about the same as that of the nondelinquent, although he is less methodical in his reasoning.

In both delinquent and nondelinquent groups we find a great many inner conflicts, but statistics show that more exist among delinquents.[24] However, again I question the validity of evaluating unconscious psychological phenomena on a statistical basis. It would certainly seem to be a fair assumption that emotionally disturbed nondelinquent persons have as many conflicts as delinquent persons. The difference lies in the way the conflicts are expressed and solved.

As pointed out earlier, the juvenile delinquent is characterized to a high degree by his poor emotional relationship with his family. This is confirmed by the Gluecks, who also report in their study that conflicts between son and father and between son and mother were more frequent in the delinquent than in the nondelinquent group. It is significant also that a poor relationship existed more frequently between son and mother, a finding with which I am in accord and which can be explained in many cases as an unsolved Oedipal situation. This, of course, is important not only in trying to establish the etiology of crime, but also in remedying criminal behavior. We can take credence in these statistical data because although much of the emotional relationship between family members may be unconscious, usually a person is aware of whether he loves, hates, or resents someone.

Above all, delinquent children show a great lack of realism, their school attainments are definitely lower, and, by and large, they have more difficulty in adjusting themselves to the demands of society. As I have said before, truancy is prevalent among them.

Statistically there is a valid difference between the delinquent and nondelinquent as to the extent and nature of the emotional and mental pathology involved. The Gluecks found that of the delinquents 51.4 percent and of the nondelinquents 44.3 percent were mentally abnormal.[25] Drs. Healy and Bronner found that in comparing a small group of delinquent children with their nondelinquent siblings, 91 percent of the delinquents and only 13 percent of the nondelinquents had deep emotional disturbances.[26]

We might better understand the prevalence of such mental pathology in delinquents if we consider its presence today in the general population. It has been estimated that: 1) about 17 million people in the United States are suffering from some mental illness or personality disturbance; 2) in the state of New York, one out of every ten children born each year will at some time during their lives suffer from a mental illness severe enough to require hospitalization; 3) throughout the country on any day of the year there are about 750,000 patients in mental hospitals.[27] Each year about 500,000 new patients are admitted to mental hospitals.[28] At least 380,000 people—children included—are seen a year in psychiatric clinics.[29]

When we compare these figures with those of 1930, for instance, we see that at that time the admission rate per year was 75,000, and only 300,000 persons were confined to mental hospitals at any one time.[30] The increase of emotional and mental disturbances is much greater than can be accounted for by the increase in the population.

Of course our better diagnostic procedures and the increased awareness of people about mental illnesses may in part be responsible for the higher statistics, yet, in spite of this, there seems to be an actual increase, which by necessity reflects itself in the greater number of juvenile delinquents. The question, however, is not only the presence of mental or emotional abnormality in the juvenile delinquent, but also how much bearing this abnormality has upon his antisocial or criminal behavior. The answer is obvious, since emotional disturbance is invariably at the root of mental abnormality, and we know that the emotionally disturbed child, who has conflicts and frustrations, will more easily show his antisocial or criminal tendencies than the one who is free from these disturbances.

We find emotional disturbances very frequently expressed in serious types of crimes committed either by the delinquent singly or as a member of a gang. In the past ten years street gangs have become characteristic of many urban communities in the United States, particularly in the larger cities. Since they have become a threatening problem to the community, especially to those youths who want to live normal and law-abiding lives, we must look more closely at this social phenomenon, which has been spreading like an infection.

Gangs are composed mainly of disturbed, upset, "shook-up" teen-agers and are an expression of dissatisfied and emotionally disturbed youths living in an emotionally and socially deranged family and social situation. It has been estimated that New York City alone has between 75 and 100 street gangs bearing such names as the "Egyptians," "Cobras," "Comaches," "Tiny Tims," "Silver-Arrows," "Dragons," "Stonekillers," "Daggers," "Scorpions," "Chaplains," and "Bishops." The latter two, by the way, are deadly enemies.

The gangs have the structure of an organization; they are controlled by leaders, usually a president, vice-president, war counselor, and a gunsmith or armorer, and they consist of boys from ten to twenty-two years of age, often being divided into "Diapers," "Juniors," and "Seniors." Frequently girls, the "Debs," are gang members who serve the purpose of carrying weapons to the "rumble" (gang fight). They provide alibis for the boys and usually are willing sex partners, but they also create conflicts between the gang members because of increased competition and jealousies.

A gang rules a certain territory, that is, a few streets or a park, in an almost feudal fashion and guards its territory jealously. While the president of the gang is concerned with strategy, the war counselor is concerned with tactics, such as collecting information about other gangs, planning fights, etc. None of the gangs permit any member of any other gang to enter its territory, each of the members knowing exactly where the borders are. Members assemble after school at gang headquarters, usually a candy store, while some members remain on the lookout for strange youngsters invading their territory. Although most of the boys join the gang voluntarily, many of them are forced to do so, since in this subculture being a nonmember (a "coolie") means being ostracized.

To enforce control of their domain, gang members are armed. They secure their weapons either through illegal channels, or they make them themselves. "Zip" guns, cap guns, and other various homemade guns are used as lethal weapons. Some gangs prefer knives or radio aerials, the latter of which are broken off from cars and are used as spears to penetrate the abdomen or as whips to slash the face of a boy. Frequently the weapons have been bought through advertisements in comic books. Some gangs use "Molotov cocktails," a fire bomb made out of a bottle filled with gasoline and a burning rag. These weapons and the fact that the gang members are drunk, "high," or "doped up" before they go into a fight with a rival gang make their battles vicious and often deadly, bringing them to the attention of the police and the public.

Although gangs vigilantly patrol their territory every afternoon and evening, Friday night is their night of celebration. On that evening they have parties, or, more accurately, drunken brawls, which more often than not end up in cruel fights. Summer evenings, when there is no school, are the best time for their parties, for scurrying into territories that belong to other gangs, and for getting into battles.

Members live in their own little confined world, even creating a unique language of terse, expressive, and tough expressions understood only by gangs themselves. The following is a list of terms used by teen-age gangs in New York City:

Term	Meaning
A fair one	A fair fight between gangs or gang members, fought in some accordance with rules.
A "win"	When the other side runs from the scene.
Balling	A good time.
Bop	To fight.
Bopping Club	A fighting gang.
Burn	A shooting affray between two gangs.
Busted	Getting arrested.
Cheesy	Traitorous.
Cool	An uneasy armistice.
Coolie	Nongang boy.
Debs	Girl affiliates of gang boys.
Diddley bop	First-class gang fighter.
Drop a dime	Give me a dime.
Duke	To fight (with fists).
Gig	A party.
Go down	To attack another gang, to declare war.
Heart	Courage.
Hooked	Seriously addicted to narcotics on a daily basis.
Jap	To ambush or attack an individual.
Jitterbug	To fight.
Junkie	A narcotic addict.
Mambo room	A neighborhood candy store.

Term	Meaning
Meet	A meeting, usually of gang chiefs.
Piece	Any kind of firearm.
Pot	Narcotics.
Punk out	Display cowardice.
Rank	To insult (usually profanity concerning a boy's mother).
Rep	Reputation, usually fighting reputation.
Rumble	Gang fight.
Sand sock	A sock filled with sand used as a blackjack.
Shack date	A sexually obliging girl.
Shin battle	Intragang practice or test-of-mettle fight among gang members.
Shuffle	To engage in a fist fight.
Smoking pot	Smoking marijuana.
Snag	To attack an individual.
Sneaky Pete	Cheap wine.
Sound	Talk.
Spike	Needle for injecting narcotics.
Steel	Knives used in fighting.
Stenjer	Alpine-style hat with narrow brim.
Swing with a gang	To be a gang member.
The old woman	A club member's steady girl friend.
The works	Full kit for narcotics, including syringe.
Tight	Friendly, as between gangs.
To sound	To joke or needle.
Tracks	Needle marks on skin.
Turf	A gang's own territory.

From where do the children come who constitute these gangs? Generally they are from areas considered to be delinquent or slum neighborhoods with exceedingly poor economic conditions. The members are white or colored, some gangs even being interracial. Occasionally gangs are formed among youngsters from well-to-do neighborhoods, but the bulk of tough gangs are found in slum areas where there are severe deprivations of all kinds. Although some of the members have religious affiliations, they practically never attend religious services. Unless deliberately stirring up a "rumble," a gang member rarely leaves the streets that define his gang's territory unless accompanied by someone else, usually another gang member, for fear of being attacked. Members have few thoughts about the future, and most of them seem to lack ambition other than being good members of the gang, that is, being able to fight for the gang, which requires undying loyalty. Their life is a world of hatred and aggression, of hostility and cruelty, a world which they themselves have created in part, but which also expresses what they see around them. These youngsters have absorbed much of the tension, hostility, fears, and anxieties from the adult world and have distorted them further. In a sense they are rebelling against adults, who, they feel, "owe them something"—the emotional security of which they have been deprived, not only in their own homes, but also in our culture and society.[31]

Because of this deprivation, these youngsters seek out each other in a desperate search for security. In a gang they seem to gain a feeling of belonging, which they have been unable to achieve anywhere else. Here too they have a chance to achieve status, according to the feats they perform for the benefit of the gang. This brings them recognition. Thus we see that they are fighting for their own little niche in life and are unable to see the futility of the means they choose.

That they are invariably tough, defiant, and spiteful indicates their emotional insecurity, hostility, and fearfulness, since the aggressive qualities act as shields for their inner insecurity. They find little or no guidance in the concepts of ethical and religious values which adults have created. One insidious danger of such gang development is the repercussion it has on children with tolerable home situations, who may join gangs, even reluctantly, for fear of being considered "sissies." Another is that when many of the members come of age, they continue their criminal behavior in other capacities. Often some of them find their way into organized crime.[32]

Gang members are generally proud of their long records of criminal behavior, which to them are a sign of glory. When many of them are not in a detention home, reformatory, or prison, they are on probation. Most of them dislike school intensely, and their attendance is sporadic; the percentage of those unable to read is shockingly high. Many of them have working parents and so have no supervision when they return from school. The housing conditions under which they live are abominable—often railroad flats with a family of ten living in four or five rooms.

Thus we see that a combination of factors is responsible for the creation and sprouting of juvenile delinquency. There are those within the individual himself and those within his environment, but perhaps most important of all is the way a person reacts to the elements in his environment.

CHAPTER V

Psychosomatic Disorders and Crime

Earlier we have noted the prevalence of psychosomatic disorders among emotionally disturbed persons and especially among criminals. This should not be difficult to understand when we realize that there is an intimate relationship between man's mind and body—his psyche and his soma. A dichotomy of them cannot be made, for even the slightest emotion, whether it be conscious or unconscious, influences the biological processes of the body, and every biological process, healthy or diseased, influences the mind. In fact, the functioning of the mind depends upon the physiological and chemical processes of the body, the external situation, and the interchange of the emotions with biochemical processes. This close relationship between the functioning of mind and body, psychosomatics—or as I have suggested in my book *Who Are the Guilty?* psychobiotics—is greatly affected by the inner conflicts of a person. We thus define a psychosomatic disorder as a disturbance of bodily functions closely related to emotional conflicts, which are frequently of an unconscious nature.

However, even though body and mind function as a unit, they can be examined individually, and in fact, they often must be, for each one requires different tools for its investigation. Feelings and intellect cannot be examined with a microscope, nor can we measure blood pressure through a friendly talk with a patient. But this must not deter us from studying the individual as a whole. The psychosomatic concept is one we can use with great advantage in our diagnosis, treatment, and prognosis of illnesses.

Since psychoanalysis basically deals with the study and treatment of emotional and mental disturbances chiefly through the study of unconscious emotions and their effects on human behavior, the psychoanalyst is in the unique position of being best able to observe and determine the relationship between feelings and disease, as well as between feelings and antisocial and criminal behavior. When he observes headaches, sinus conditions, diarrhea, asthma, or general fatigue arising in the midst of an inner conflict involving the feelings of the individual and when he observes their disappearance once that conflict is resolved, he must surmise that there is a connection between the manifestations he sees and the emotions. Although he frequently cannot support his conclusions with specific proof, it does not detract from their value, and although his observations may, of necessity, be in crude form until they become scientifically verified, it does not mean that they are false.

The idea of mind and body being interrelated in their functions stems from Hippocrates; however, the new aspect of psychosomatic conditions is that they are often connected with unconscious emotions, a discovery resulting from Freud's investigations into the unconscious mind. The whole concept of psychosomatic conditions thus becomes wider and deeper and provides us with a rational explanation of the causes of many ailments.

It has long been a theory of mine that psychosomatic disturbances, such as a peptic ulcer, colitis, asthma, migraine, hypertension, rheumatoid arthritis, eczema, etc., might be related to criminal activities as well as to emotional and mental disturbances. During my research project at Columbia University between 1944 and 1948, we investigated this. The project was also designed to find out what in particular makes one individual receptive to criminal behavior and another not.

We began by studying 150 persons: children, adolescents, adults, and their families. One group consisted of those who had manifested antisocial and criminal behavior, with or without emotional disturbances, and their families. For comparison and control purposes we examined those who were not antisocial or criminal but who had manifested neurotic or psychotic conditions, and members of their families. Therefore, not only were the principals involved examined and sometimes given psychiatric treatment, but also in many cases their parents and siblings were followed up as far as possible. The cases were referred to us from courts, public and private schools, the Jewish Board of Guardians, and the Psychiatric Institute in New York City. Many of those who showed antisocial or criminal behavior were children who had been brought to the attention of the courts for stealing, truancy, arson, etc. In some cases the child was hospitalized in the children's ward at the Psychiatric Institute.

The psychiatric examination of the delinquents, their family members, the control patients, and their families was carried out by the method of associative anamnesis, a technique outlined by Dr. Felix Deutsch when he examined the psychosomatic factors at work in a patient's illness.[1] By this method our subjects were asked to describe their lives and experiences and were permitted to talk freely about whatever came into their minds. Whenever a point touching upon their emotional attitudes was brought up, a relevant question was put to them, and this would elicit new free associations. By following the emotional stream of a person, rather than adhering to a rigid listing of data, we were able to elicit facts about medical histories, personalities, and emotional attitudes, relationships, and impressions through a person's feelings, which, after all, are the basis for his attitude and behavior. However, this type of examination can only be carried out if the subject has a positive attitude toward the examiner, that is, if the emotional relationship between them—the transference—is positive. The results obtained from this technique proved to be quite fruitful and allowed us to form very significant conclusions.

In addition, as mentioned in Chapter III, we administered standard psychological tests to each group. By this means it was possible for us to evaluate the psychological personality make-ups and the emotional attitudes and feelings of the principals and their families as well. (As far as I know, this is the first time comprehensive psychological tests were carried out on families of subjects.) Then, of course, we also gave physical examinations to our subjects, including X-rays and basal metabolisms. However, the latter test was frequently difficult to carry out because the subjects were anxious or fearful; some even refused to undergo it.

To further substantiate the results, we had psychiatric social workers interview each delinquent and control patient, their school teachers, and members of their families, which included parents or foster parents, who were sometimes examined in their homes. Our research thus utilized the teamwork of the psychiatrist, psychologist, and psychiatric social worker—all examining the same case, as is done by child guidance units.

The results of our project [2] revealed the following: 1) 55 percent of the delinquent group and 45 percent of the control group had disturbances of the gastrointestinal tract of a psychosomatic nature; 2) 17 percent of the delinquent group and 5 percent of the control group manifested skin eruptions of psychosomatic origin; 3) 20 percent of the delinquent group and 8 percent of the control group suffered from disturbances of the skeletal-muscular system of a psychosomatic nature; 4) 20 percent of the delinquent group and 10 percent of the control group were prone to accidents. (The prevalence of disturbances of the gastrointestinal tract among both groups may indicate that this tract is the system, more than any other, through which the emotions are most frequently expressed.)

All delinquents had suffered from bodily disorders of a psychosomatic nature at one or more times during their lives, either during childhood, adolescence, or adulthood. (There were two exceptions to this finding—two homosexual adolescents who denied ever having had any bodily diseases that could be interpreted as being of a psychosomatic type. However, these two subjects were extremely antagonistic and uncooperative, often refusing to give information about themselves, and in view of this, we feel their answers should be disregarded.)

While many of the control patients showed manifestations of

psychosomatic disorders, they did not seem to be so deep-seated or so prevalent as they were in the delinquent group. Also this type of disorder was constantly found in one or more members of the offenders' families—in the mother, father, or siblings—in contrast to the control patients' families, where psychosomatic disturbances did not show up so frequently.

It is interesting that twice as many offenders as nonoffenders whom we examined were prone to accidents. Most were children who had frequently been truant from school or who had stolen and who were of the blundering type, "happening" into or "daring" themselves into accidents. Accident proneness expresses a mechanism of self-punishment and may very well be due to guilt feelings and also to the fact that a great majority of these children had parents or grandparents who themselves were prone to accidents, which would predispose the children to expose themselves to similar situations because of identification with the grownups.[3]

Although the number of offenders and control patients investigated was small, the statistics still give considerable evidence of the predominance of psychosomatic disorders in offenders and in members of their families over the control patients. A word of caution, however. Although psychosomatic disturbances can almost always be found at some time during the lives of criminals or those who commit antisocial acts, there is no causal relationship between them; that is, psychosomatic disturbances in and of themselves do not cause crime. There are many who suffer from asthma, migraine, and any of innumerable other psychosomatic ailments who are not criminals and who probably never will be.

Psychosomatic disorders were frequently found in those from homes in which family tension was openly expressed in the form of hostility, violent arguments, sibling rivalry, rebelliousness, or hatred. These psychosomatic disturbances were usually also coupled with a history of overindulgence or overprotection. In the beginning of the study many of the youngsters revealed only undue rebelliousness or aggressiveness, but later we discovered that psychosomatic disturbances had been present. Frequently, however, the emotional and physical manifestations went hand-in-hand and were immediately apparent. The presence of both the emotional and psychosomatic conditions provided us with the opportunity to investigate the relationship between emotional attitudes and antisocial and criminal activities.

Sometimes psychosomatic disorders occurred as substitutes for antisocial manifestations.[4] A case in point is fourteen-year-old Mike, who came under study in our research project when he was hospitalized for rheumatic fever. Formerly a delinquent child with a long record of truancy, his antisocial activities had suddenly stopped—and just as suddenly he had suffered his first attack of rheumatic fever.

The father had deserted the family when Mike was only eight, leaving his mother an embittered woman who went to work to support her two sons—Mike and a younger boy of six. She eked out a living by working long hours, which meant the boys were alone a great deal and had to fend for themselves. When she was at home, she was constantly complaining and was very irritable with Mike, yet at the same time showed a great deal of favoritism to his brother because "he was the 'baby.' "

Mike felt unhappy and neglected, and when bullying his brother only increased his mother's sympathy for the younger boy, Mike resorted to stealing, lying, and truancy in a frantic effort to gain attention. But only when he became seriously ill did he really achieve his purpose. His mother was so upset by his sickness that she left her job to take care of him, and for a time Mike was happy because he could have her all to himself while his brother was at school. Once well and back in school, however, Mike again felt deprived of attention and immediately resumed his antisocial activities. When his purpose, which was unconscious, was not achieved, he became ill again and this time was hospitalized in an institution for rehabilitation.

After a year of psychiatric treatment in the institution, Mike improved considerably and was sent home for a week-end. He was hardly there one day when his high fever, headaches, and heart symptoms recurred. He was returned to the hospital, where his symptoms disappeared within a few days. After six months another trial stay at home was attempted, but again he became ill with the same symptoms and again was returned to the institution, where, as before, he became well almost immediately.

Careful studies of the situations under which Mike's symptoms arose and subsided revealed that his ailment was a desperate, though unconscious, attempt to fulfill his hunger for love, which was lacking in his home. It was also an unconscious substitute for his antisocial behavior, which had failed to bring him the satisfaction he sought. Our conclusions were further confirmed by the fact that each time he was about to be released from the institution, he broke several minor rules, consciously or unconsciously hoping that he would be forbidden to leave. It was his way of saying that he did not want to go home. By the time he was seventeen, when he was inducted into the Navy, he showed not a single trace of having had rheumatic fever. The vicious cycle had finally been broken—after prolonged psychoanalytic treatment.

Mike's psychosomatic disorder was a substitute for his delinquent manifestations. But underlying these manifestations was family tension, and imbedded in that was his anxiety, both of which had been instrumental in producing his psychosomatic disturbances and his delinquent activities. Anxiety is the device through which bodily disorders and behavior disorders are produced. When Mike could not satisfy his basic, natural needs in a normal way, he became insecure and anxious, which led to his truancy and thefts because he could not endure his state of anxiety and had to discharge the tension in some way. While another person may have done so through neurotic or psychotic behavior, Mike chose an impulsive form of release—that of acting out his insecurity and hostility in antisocial and criminal activities. This acting out was increased during his frequent arguments with his mother, which often resulted in violence between them.

It is also important to understand that Mike felt lonely and neglected at a time when he most needed a stable adult who could help him develop a healthy superego structure. He had a poor relationship with his mother, and there was no father around with whom he could communicate and who would understand him and give him the ego support he needed.

Above all, when Mike's stealing came to a climax, he was in his puberty, a period of development usually more difficult for a boy than perhaps any other, and a time for Mike when he felt afraid of being overwhelmed by his mother. On the one hand, he wanted to get away from her, to be independent, while on the other hand, he wanted to stay close to her, to be protected and receive attention. Even though he undoubtedly had strong feelings of hatred for her, he could not kill her outright—or, for that matter, himself, as a way out. Instead he unconsciously chose a slow killing of himself by becoming severely ill.

Although Mike showed some neurotic symptoms, they were overshadowed by his antisocial and criminal activities and his psychosomatic ailment. Since they were an excellent means for him to accomplish his aims, he fundamentally did not need to develop a neurotic condition. As a child he had always been given to steady complaining, thereby trying to stay as close as possible to his mother. Even attending school, though only a temporary separation from her, represented rejection to him. When his truancy and other delinquent behavior did not bring him enough satisfaction, and incidentally into closer contact with his mother, he developed rheumatic fever, which kept him home and compelled her to stay with him.

During psychoanalysis he was gradually able to see his own emotional difficulties—his narcissism, his ambivalent feelings toward his mother, and his conflict between being a child and a growing adolescent. He came to understand that because he was unable to cope with his anxieties, he discharged them in an impulsive way, through antisocial behavior, which was an indirect method of rebelling against his mother, since he could not rebel against her in a direct manner, partly because of guilt feelings. But since he apparently must have been afraid that his acting-out impulses might overwhelm his ego, particularly in a stress situation (all of this was unconscious), and since he did not receive sufficient satisfaction from his antisocial behavior (his anxieties were not dispelled sufficiently), he unconsciously diverted part of his emotional energy into psychosomatic channels; his anxieties infiltrated into his bodily structure.

Mike could not modify his impulses so his ego became weak, his sense of reality somewhat distorted, and the formation of his superego disturbed. In this transformation his libido or energy was involved. At one time his psychic energy produced a psychosomatic disorder; at another time it resulted in an antisocial act —all occurring through a qualitative replacement of his libido. The bodily disorder and criminal activity reflected Mike's emotional state, which was rooted in an antisocial development of his character. This character deformation was responsible for Mike's becoming receptive to criminal behavior, which we find in many cases, as we shall see.

It is interesting that not only did Mike substitute a psychosomatic disturbance for antisocial behavior, but so also did some of the other offenders we examined. For example, some did not manifest any psychosomatic symptoms until they served time in prison. Apparently a qualitative substitution took place—the psychosomatic disturbance being substituted for the criminal act, that is, the person's libido alternating, as did Mike's. One basic cause for the appearance of a psychosomatic disturbance, as we saw in these cases, is a character distortion.

A psychosomatic condition, an antisocial or criminal act, or a psychological disturbance each represents a particular aspect of a more fundamental disturbance, which may well be rooted in the character make-up of the individual. I have mentioned that before a person can commit a crime, he must be susceptible to it. The presence of psychosomatic disorders can to some extent determine the degree of susceptibility to, although it is not a cause of, antisocial or criminal behavior. We find a distorted character structure with extreme manifestations of psychosomatic disorders in many criminals. It is my considered opinion that the presence of psychosomatic disturbances in a juvenile delinquent or in an adult criminal is a new device of his to cope with his libido. He does not know how to handle that energy, and he has to discharge it the way his distorted ego sees fit. In general those individuals who frequently manifest psychosomatic symptoms in order to defend themselves against emotional difficulties show that a character deformation is involved. We found this to be true in the following case.

Al was a thirty-five-year-old man who for many years had been involved in embezzlement. He had already been arrested many times but always succeeded in obtaining suspended sentences. A look at his background shows that he was the second of three children, whose father had left them when Al was three and whose mother had to take care of the family. She was a slovenly, dependent, nagging, and sickly woman, often having to be supported by a public agency and often quarreling with her neighbors, usually because of imaginary insults. As we pieced her story together, we learned that she had always complained of headaches, colds, and stomach upsets and that her numerous medical examinations revealed no organic defects. Al's siblings manifested psychosomatic problems too. His older sister, who had an enormous appetite, of which his mother was very proud, was considerably overweight, and Al too had to be put on a diet when he was only twelve years old because he was 15 pounds overweight. His younger brother had always been a sickly child, suffering from respiratory illnesses with "choking," for which he had been hospitalized many times. He was shy and retiring.

Al was described as a bright child, who was well-liked by the other children. He was bottle-fed, began to talk when he was one year old, and was also walking quite well at the same age. When he was four, he began to wet his bed, and he was severely punished for it by his mother. At six she caught him masturbating and was very much disturbed. Even though her minister told her to go easy on the child, she did not heed his advice, but punished him again. About that time some of her household money began to disappear, and she suspected that Al had taken it, which he denied, however. In the meantime he was making rapid progress in school, even skipping one grade.

When he was twelve, Al and a friend worked out a scheme whereby they talked some of their classmates into giving them money for "investment" in some "fabulous venture." When it became clear that there would be no returns, the other children realized they had been swindled and attacked Al and his friend. The two boys were called before the principal. Al's explanation was unsatisfactory, and the parents of the cheated boys brought charges against him. He was taken to Children's Court, where his mother staunchly defended him, and he was permitted to return to school.

Years later, when Al was referred to our research project for treatment, he had already carried out numerous antisocial and criminal activities during adolescence and adulthood. When we met him, he was a short, stocky individual, a little over five feet tall and weighing 180 pounds, being 50 pounds overweight. His criminal activities consisted of taking money from women to whom he promised high returns. Since he invariably became sexually involved with them, they were reluctant to denounce him to the police, and it was only after he had swindled one woman out of a large sum of money, after having promised to marry her and then reneging, that he was brought to the attention of the authorities, apprehended, and given a suspended sentence upon the condition that he seek psychiatric treatment.

During the first few interviews he expressed a great deal of scorn for the woman who had brought charges against him. However, as treatment progressed, he came to see that this feeling was in reality contempt for his mother for not having taken proper care of him, particularly because he felt she had never given him enough to eat. Food to him—as to any child—represented love. As an adult, when he did not get a sufficient amount of food, he resorted to fraudulent means to get money to buy it. Frequently during the interviews he could be seen munching candy or biscuits, which he always carried in his pockets. Personalitywise, he was passive and dependent, and after a while it became clear to us that it was his strong oral drive which was at the root of his disturbance. It was the basis of his psychosomatic disorder (overweight) and his criminal activities, for he would go to great lengths to satisfy his need for love (food). In a way he had become a parasite, living upon others and expecting their support, an unconscious desire to be taken care of by his mother, who he felt had neglected him. This also explains why his victims were women; he was unconsciously taking revenge upon his own mother.

It is interesting to see how Al's siblings developed in the meantime. While his sister was merely overweight without much mental pathology, his brother, who never married, continued to develop psychosomatic symptoms and became an emotional and social misfit. Neither showed any criminal behavior, however, in contrast to Al, whose life's pattern was strongly criminalistic.

As a result of a poorly integrated personality structure, with resultant ego-malfunctioning and psychosomatic symptoms, Al's disturbed character formation made him sensitive and receptive to antisocial and criminal behavior. Without a distorted character formation, in all probability, a person will not commit a crime. Thus Al can be considered as having been in a state of latent delinquency, until his deformed character became an intricate part of his ego, and then he began to commit his crimes.[5]

However, when a person develops a psychosomatic condition based upon a character distortion, the distortion may not go so far as to change him into an antisocial person or into an offender. It very often rather serves as a defense against his antisocial and criminal tendencies, as well as against neurotic and psychotic conditions, and may very well be a means to which he has resorted in trying to handle a difficult situation.

Whether a person's outlet is antisocial or criminal behavior or whether it is a neurotic, psychotic, or psychosomatic condition depends upon his personality make-up and his previous experiences, precipitating events, and his reactions to them. Since all actions involve conscious and unconscious emotions, in every action there is an emotional matrix, which lays the basis for an emotional pattern of behavior, distinct for each individual. Whether his behavior is social or antisocial depends upon the type of his inner conflict and more particularly upon the way he tries to solve it. The means by which he attempts this solution are grounded in his conscious and unconscious forces, mostly the latter.

Not only does a person act and react in his own typical fashion to his external situation, but he also acts and reacts in his own typical fashion to his bodily needs. People react to stimuli in their environment on the basis of their psychobiological functional organism, and because of this no two people react exactly the same to the same stimuli. We see this phenomenon quite clearly when one member of a family becomes exceedingly neurotic, while another one, for example, develops a psychosomatic illness, such as colitis or a peptic ulcer, although both live in the same life situation. In a family I examined recently, one sister had developed headaches, which made her withdraw from people; her brother was prone to accidents; a younger brother, for many years a gambler, had been in constant conflict with the police; and the father suffered from phobias, which made it impossible for him to work.

Such findings are in accord with similar ones from my research project at Columbia University. A typical case in our study was that of an adolescent who was sent to a reformatory for having stolen several cars. His older brother suffered from schizophrenia and had to be hospitalized, while his younger sister, who had for many years manifested symptoms of recurrent "colds" and "bronchitis" without any organic basis, was finally helped by psychoanalysis.

Of course, I do not mean to say that just because two people happen to live in the same home, the external stimuli are exactly the same for both of them. While a person's reaction is a strong determining factor in the outlet he chooses, very often the external situation is not identical, as in Mike's case, where his brother seemed to be the favorite child.

However, in these cases, as in all others, we find that it is the previous personality make-up which determines to a large extent how a person reacts to a certain situation. If he has been emotionally disturbed in his childhood or early youth, he may become more anxious and more upset if confronted with a situation with which he cannot cope. These upsets may lead to or accentuate psychosomatic disturbances or antisocial or criminal behavior. Keeping this in mind, the previous personality also determines how maladjusted the person in question will be when afflicted with a bodily disease.[6] As the reaction to an illness depends upon what the personality was before the onset, so also the offender's reaction to his antisocial or criminal act is dependent upon his personality traits before he committed the act.[7]

Although sometimes an emotional or mental illness may be due to the immediate effect of some causative agent, it is usually the result of a chain of developmental factors and processes within the personality make-up. The same view of illness—that is, that it is caused by both development and reaction, or process—must also be held of certain sociological manifestations, such as war and criminal behavior. Since we know that satisfaction or frustration of biological needs during development influences personality reactions, we may safely say that a person who has been so deprived would be more apt to veer from the normal than one who has not.

We conclude that when a person commits a crime, both psychological and physical factors intermingle. Antisocial and criminal behavior, as well as a neurosis, psychosis, or psychosomatic condition, although different in their manifestations, are all expressions of human behavior, reflecting the different ways in which a person tries to cope with his problem and his situation. A psychosomatic condition, being an expression of both bodily and psychological maladjustment, is the result of a faulty development and reaction which has taken place at an early stage in the life of the person and which is related to a deformation of his character.

Returning to the relationship between psychosomatic disturbances and antisocial and criminal behavior, we can say that their mutual origin is to be found in the person's character. When disturbances of bodily or emotional functions, or of behavior, occur, they are related to the distorted character of the individual.

This being the case, we can very well understand that the criminal's psychobiological processes result from a personality reaction which can be compared to the reaction found in an illness. The formula $C = \dfrac{T + S}{R}$ (described in Chapter II) confirms this view.

We are now better able to understand a person's social and

antisocial behavior. Our research on the relationship between psychosomatic disorders and antisocial and criminal activities enables us to bridge the gap between these psychobiological, antisocial, and criminal activities, which previously we were not able to do because the sociologist was concerned only with manifestations in society, while the physician was preoccupied with his patient's body or mind. The result was that each was inclined to lose sight of the interrelationship between man and society. Only by having developed the psychobiological concept and finding the common denominator (character distortion) for crime and psychosomatic disturbances, could we have discovered the link between antisocial and criminal activities and man himself. This common denominator for human and social pathology, plus others we may find through future research, will enable the sociologically oriented psychoanalyst and the psychobiologically oriented sociologist to create a valid basis for understanding human behavior in both its social and antisocial manifestations.

CHAPTER VI

The Offender and the Emotionally
Disturbed Nonoffender

On the surface it would seem that the offender and the emotionally disturbed nonoffender are very much alike. However, when we penetrate their individual personality make-ups, their patterns of reaction, their emotional relationship to their environment, and the quality and degree of tension existing in their respective families, the differences as well as the similarities between them become more clear.

We can see the difference in the family backgrounds when we recall that the neurotic or psychotic person most often has been raised in an environment where although there was family tension, there were also ethical standards which brought about some development of his superego. In fact, such a person tends to have so strongly a developed superego structure that it leads him into a suppressive, rather than an uninhibited, way of life. This is one reason he may become neurotic, psychotic, or manifest psychosomatic disorders rather than exhibit antisocial or criminal behavior.

Generally speaking, then, we can say that a person becomes

neurotic, psychotic, or manifests a psychosomatic disorder because he has difficulty in expressing his feelings, particularly his hostile or antisocial ones. The unhealthy emotional, mental, or physical symptoms a person manifests is to some extent the price he has to pay for being unable to express his feelings, be they conscious or unconscious. In such cases either his superego is too strong for him, his ego too weak, or both.

A general characteristic both of people who are generally disturbed and of people who commit crimes is that they possess to an overwhelming degree abnormal emotional affects. The difference is that the criminal gives in to his feelings because of the often severe emotional and social pathology in his early life. The criminal acts out his criminalistic aggressions, with the result that he frequently gets locked up. This is in contrast to an individual suffering from an emotional or mental illness, who turns his hostile feelings toward himself and thereby locks himself up.

In mental or emotional conditions and in criminal behavior the same layers of feelings are active, but they move to a different degree, and they work in different constellations. Before we can go further into the mechanisms through which criminal activities are carried out, it is necessary to mention the most frequent forms of emotional disturbance and mental illness: neurosis and psychosis.

A neurosis is an emotional disturbance which arises from a conflict because the ego and superego find it difficult to deal with the impulses from the id. The products of the neurotic conflict are anxieties, inhibitions, perversions, repressions, and psychosomatic conditions. If the ego is unable to withstand the conflict between itself and the id impulses and becomes engulfed, it loses its balance and begins to disintegrate. This disintegration is called a psychosis.

The basic difference between a neurotic and a psychotic person is that the former is in touch with reality, while the latter's relationship with reality is broken. A neurosis differs from all other emotional and mental conditions in that the functioning of the individual is disturbed but still maintained to a varying degree of success. In a neurosis, the ego—that is, the coordinating center of the personality (of which the superego is a part)—is disturbed, while in a somatic illness one or more organs are diseased.

An outstanding feature in the development of a neurosis is that the individual's experiences from early childhood on have been repressed. Its incapacitating symptoms are varied and manifold, such as anxieties, guilt feelings, fears, hysterical paralyses, impotence, and frigidity. Most people having these symptoms and those showing even other pronounced neurotic traits are able to check their antisocial tendencies, although some of them have to raise extensive barriers or defenses against their hostile, or even criminal, inclinations, as is often the case with obsessive-compulsory individuals.

On the other hand, the psychotic person is unable to communicate with other people. He too, though, is afraid to express his feelings, since he has always suppressed or repressed them. He has therefore withdrawn and has turned away to a large extent from all real human contact. If there is any contact, it is only superficial and is of little, if any, emotional significance to him. Since his contact with the world is brittle, his tie with the world—reality —may break, and he is preoccupied only with himself. He becomes a victim of a psychosis, most often of a schizophrenic type —i.e., a splitting of the personality, dissociation, and emotional detachment. Being unable to identify himself, he is without a sense of reality.

His schizophrenic condition can go so far that he does not know who he is or what his name is. Basically this lack of identification can be so pronounced as to make it impossible for him to identify himself as a man or a woman. One male patient whom I knew insisted that he was a Mrs. Smith and that he was the "mother" of his children. Such a person, completely absorbed and preoccupied with himself, frequently is shy and most often is without friends. He becomes more and more withdrawn until finally he is completely narcissistic. Not all psychotic persons, however, are schizophrenics. There are also manic-depressives and those suffering from paranoia.

Both the average law-abiding citizen and the offender have fantasies and dreams, which they try to make come true. However, while the relatively normal person tries to do it in a realistic and methodical way and the neurotic or psychotic in a devious way, the offender does it haphazardly, without thinking of the reality of the situation and without regard for anyone but himself.

When a criminal acts out his antisocial aggressions, he does so because of his basic antisocial desires and fantasies, which, if left unsatisfied, would plague him. Because he cannot stand discomfort, he must act them out in an antisocial way, thereby committing a crime. Curiously enough, since the criminal is able to rid himself of his emotional tension by giving way to his desires, in a certain sense he could be called "normal" rather than "abnormal" in contrast to the neurotic or psychotic person who is too inhibited to obtain any release for his aggressions and prefers the safety of a fantasy instead.

The presence of abnormal psychological traits in a criminal stimulates our curiosity about the criminogenic factors within him which are responsible for his behavior. Only by careful examination of each individual can we find out the complex relationship between his criminal traits and his emotionally or mentally disturbed condition. We have previously mentioned the mental mechanism which takes place when a crime is committed. In differentiating between normal and abnormal traits in a person who commits a crime, we must find out how much of what is ingrained in his mentally abnormal traits is antisocial. When we remember the often complicated relationship between the criminal and his situation, we see the difficulties in unraveling the antisocial inclinations.

When I talk here about mental abnormality or mental illness, it presupposes or implies that the condition deviates from the normal or average mental condition. It is questionable, though, whether deviations can be considered diseases. We have previously mentioned the parallel between a mental disease and criminal behavior, both being a personality reaction. Although abnormality frequently connotes a pathological process, we cannot make this distinction, since a mental abnormality (as well as a physical one) may very well be the result of a process or a development or both.

Neurotic, psychotic, or psychosomatic conditions or character disorders are all predisposing factors toward criminal behavior. When we examine youngsters who have been truants or who have been in trouble with the police for thefts or disorderly conduct, we frequently find an intimate relationship between their anti-social or criminal manifestations and their emotional and mental conflicts. We also find this intimate relationship in the neurotic person who commits a crime because of unconscious guilt feelings which make him crave punishment. The criminogenic factors in arson and kleptomania too are undoubtedly allied to the emotional or mental abnormality of the offender, having their roots in the sensation of a thrill, which is sexual in nature. We also see the relationship between criminality and mental abnormality in some mentally defective persons where character disturbances may be responsible for their antisocial or criminal activities and in some individuals suffering from organic brain conditions, such as encephalitis, which often produce personality defects at times leading to crime. Then too there are criminogenic factors involved in certain types of psychotic conditions, such as schizophrenia where violent, aggressive criminal acts are committed.

Differentiating characteristics between emotionally or mentally abnormal persons and criminals is extremely difficult, particularly when we deal with an offender who manifests neurotic traits without being legally insane. By the same token, the similarities between these two conditions are also difficult to describe. Yet in spite of all these difficulties, I have reached some definite conclusions and for many years have instructed my students about the following psychodynamic criteria characteristic of the neurotic individual and those characteristic of the offender.

DIFFERENCES BETWEEN THE NEUROTIC INDIVIDUAL AND THE CRIMINAL

1. While the neurotic individual manifests an inner conflict through emotional and physical symptoms which he most frequently turns against himself, the criminal most often turns his aggressions against society. The offender tries to satisfy his criminal inclinations, even if only symbolically, and will usually not

denounce them, in contrast to the neurotic person, who frequently feels guilty.

2. The neurotic person suffers from his inner conflicts, inflicted upon him mainly by himself. The criminal apparently does not suffer from an inner conflict, since he convinces himself that all of his difficulties with the law stem from his environment. One reason for this lack of suffering, as mentioned earlier, is that the criminal is usually incapable of enduring anxiety. Therefore, he cannot allow himself to feel uncomfortable to the point of suffering and so has to transform his anxiety feelings into criminal activities by acting them out. His inability to withstand much anxiety and his feeling that he does not need help make treatment very difficult.

3. The neurotic person satisfies his desires mainly through his fantasies, while the offender discharges his anxiety-tinged desires through criminal actions. One main characteristic of the neurotic and the psychotic person is, as a matter of fact, that they are satisfied by their fantasies, a substitute satisfaction. The neurotic person holds on to his hostile or antisocial fantasies and is preoccupied with them, while the offender elaborates on them and finally carries them out.

4. Connected with the different reactions to the fantasies on the part of the neurotic and criminal individuals are their projections. While the neurotic person accepts his impulses and desires, projecting them as his own, the criminal denies this relationship and blames his environmental situation—parents, bad companions, the victim—for his criminal act.

5. While the neurotic person most frequently has a capacity for transference (a positive emotional relationship), be it inside or outside of the treatment situation, the criminal by and large lacks this capacity.

6. The neurotic person usually has a strongly developed superego, the best example being the obsessive-compulsory type. Their overdeveloped superego makes them greatly inhibited and at the same time checks their instinctual drives. This is in contrast to the criminal, whose superego, because of a faulty development,

is inadequate to cope with his id impulses, which therefore overwhelm him. Even in those neurotic criminals who commit crimes because of strong guilt feelings, which might indicate a strongly developed superego, their superego is rather hypertrophic, lacunar, or hollow because it has been hammered at incessantly by their unconscious impulses.

7. Intimately connected with the inadequate development and functioning of the criminal's superego is the development and functioning of his ego. Since his ego is weak, his character formation is faulty, leading to the formation of an antisocial character. While the neurotic person has a great deal of awareness of himself, a tendency to observe or study himself, and is able to perceive reality, the criminal lacks these inclinations and abilities. Instead he is more preoccupied with the other person, the object, and sees him in the light of his own emotions. Since the criminal does not observe, study, or try to improve himself, new experiences, with the exception of adventures, are not of importance to him. He therefore has no need to incorporate these new experiences in his ego, and hence he does not develop any capacity to learn from them.

8. Closely connected with this lack of ego functioning is the curious way in which the offender expresses his oral-passivity and dependency, which he does not consciously understand or admit and which lies beneath his aggressive antisocial inclinations and actions. Thus his hostile and oral-aggressive attitude is a cover up for his passivity. He withdraws from the object (the person), turns against it, and finds himself in the strange position of considering it as an enemy, against whom he has to protect himself. Yet he still yearns for and has hopes of receiving something from the object. His oral-aggressiveness and oral-passivity alternate, for he cannot remain passive, and he manipulates to take whatever he can "by hook or by crook." The neurotic person, too, is oral-passive and dependent, but he is able to admit its existence, although he dislikes and resents this passive relationship and dependency. Like the criminal, he often tries to cover it up by oral aggressions, about which he feels guilty. Unlike the criminal, he does not turn

against the object (the person). The oral fixation of the neurotic person is overwhelming, regardless of other fixations, because of his stunted psychobiological development.

9. With the particular development of the superego and ego, especially the ego's connection with the strong oral orientation, the character of the criminal becomes deformed; an antisocial character is developed. In fact, when we characterize an offender, we usually think of him as having a weak character. This is in contrast to the neurotic person, whose character by and large is normal or whose superego is overdeveloped. The criminal thus differs from the neurotic nonoffender in that the former has a distorted character, while the latter either does not, or it is very slight. This distortion is due primarily to the type of person he identifies with —his ego identity. He usually lives in a home where the tension is severe, the outbursts loud and frequent, and the emotional deprivations strong. Because he sometimes identifies with a member of his family, he has not learned to inhibit his criminal instincts, which are within us all. However, quite often, because he does not love or admire his family and feels emotionally deprived by them, he is not able to identify at all with them. In such a case, because of his own rebelliousness, he often identifies with some nonconstructive element in his environment, usually a friend with antisocial tendencies, a criminal hero, or the like. On the other hand, the neurotic nonoffender has found another outlet. Whereas he lives with family tension too, it is often of a subtle nature. The members of his family have learned to inhibit their inner feelings and tendencies, and because he identifies with them, he too inhibits these feelings. While his identification also is an unhealthy one and has its repercussions, it is usually not criminalistic (with the exception of the neurotic criminal, who commits a crime to elicit punishment for his guilt feelings).

10. Then, too, the emotional deprivations of the criminal are more severe in actuality or he feels them to be more severe than does the neurotic, particularly where punishments or threats of them have been alternating with overindulgence and gratification. We find this particularly true of offenders who commit rather serious types of crimes, and very often among sex offenders. Dur-

ing our research on sex offenders at Sing Sing Prison, we examined a young man named Jim, who was reared by alcoholic parents who constantly and violently argued and fought with each other and where the emotional deprivation was very strong. I quote from the report:

"He has no memory of his earliest years. But the records of the social service agencies are loaded with details about him.

"When a social worker first visited his home, the mother threatened to use her small baby as a weapon with which to strike the visitor. This baby was Case J.B. Thenceforth child caring agency visits were frequent, on complaint of the neighbors. Both parents were alcoholics, given to violent brawls. When J.B. was eleven months old, his father was sent to the workhouse for kicking his pregnant wife in the stomach. The children were taken to an orphanage. Soon afterwards the mother died of alcoholism.

"The baby was later returned to his grandfather, who was a brawling drunkard like the baby's parents. Then he dwelt with his father who lived with a succession of women. It was recorded, when he was four, that he had witnessed his father's sexual relations with two different women.

"His earliest memories, confirmed by documents, are of the continued beatings his father gave him. He ran away several times, and was beaten soundly when brought home. He remembers that he was always running away and never knew where he was running. From the age of twelve to sixteen he lived in an orphanage and an institution for juvenile delinquents, from both of which he ran away numerous times, to live by petty crime.

"At thirteen he had sexual relations with a girl in the orphanage, but even before this he had begun the practice of sodomizing younger boys.

"At sixteen, on request of his custodians, he was sent on to a State School for delinquents with a maximum term of three years. A year later he was released on parole.

"He had been at liberty a month when a policeman picked him up for trying to persuade a little girl to go into a cellar with him. Then he confessed that a few days prior to that he had taken the five-year-old daughter of an acquaintance of his into a basement and had sexually abused her. Probably he had committed offenses against other little girls and boys. He said he saw nothing wrong with this. He had no pangs of conscience about that type of act. He was sentenced in 1940 to serve from five to ten years in prison." [1]

As a result of his early deprivations, the extreme emotional tension in his family, and the lack of a healthy identification, Jim's ego and superego formation became distorted, resulting in a deformed character development, which climaxed in criminal activities.

11. Criminals seem to suffer more from psychosomatic conditions than noncriminals. Also there is a higher incidence of psychosomatic disturbances in the family members of the criminal than in the neurotic or psychotic nonoffender's family.

SIMILARITIES BETWEEN THE NEUROTIC INDIVIDUAL
AND THE CRIMINAL

1. The neurotic person and the criminal both suffer from conflicts which most frequently are unconscious and which arise because of their inability to withstand the demands of their instinctual drives and of society.

2. The inner conflict brings out neurotic symptoms or antisocial manifestations, which stem from irrational emotional attitudes. The neurotic person always exhibits this affect-determined irrational attitude, and it shows up also in the majority of criminals.

3. There is always a symbolic meaning behind the actions of the neurotic person, and very often the offender's actions too have such a meaning. For example, a neurotic patient may develop paralysis of his leg, which turns out to be caused by an unconscious conflict, stimulated by a frustrated love affair. His paralyzed leg may unconsciously symbolize his feeling of loss of power, that is, a loss of his virility, or, in other words, the loss of his male organ. By the same token, an individual may commit as serious a crime as murder because the person he kills represents his father or brother, for example, whom he unconsciously wished to kill.

The Oedipus legend is a little more complicated. Oedipus actually killed his father while consciously believing he had killed a stranger. However, unconsciously it was his father he had always wished to kill, which he unwittingly accomplished.

4. In their psychosexual development both the neurotic and the criminal have become emotionally fixated at a pregenital level.

5. Because of this fixation or regression, both the neurotic person and the offender are usually strongly narcissistic. They are both engrossed in their own emotions, problems, and conflicts and show little real interest in their environment or the world around them. Since the neurotic person is preoccupied with his desires, wishes, fears, fantasies, hopes, and dreams, which he cannot make come true in reality, he is to a large extent asocial. The criminal is also asocial, as well as antisocial, in that he carries out his crimes without consideration of anyone but himself. Often he is completely unaware of the pain or injury he may inflict upon his victim.

6. Both the neurotic and the criminal have a basic need to trust yet are distrustful. But they express it differently. The neurotic distrusts and deeply hopes he will be proven wrong. The delinquent distrusts and is afraid he may be proven wrong.[2]

7. All neurotic persons have feelings of guilt, which are also present in many types of criminals, such as the neurotic and the psychotic criminal.

8. Both the neurotic individual and the criminal need one or more precipitating events in order to produce neurotic symptoms or criminal activities, respectively. The presence of these precipitating events, by the way, is also necessary in producing psychotic or psychosomatic conditions. Frequently, however, these events are of an internal psychological nature, as shown in the following case.

A twenty-five-year-old man who was under the influence of alcohol was propositioned in a bar by a homosexual. The young man became anxious and frightened, very much due to his own unconscious homosexual feelings, and therefore left the bar hurriedly. Shortly thereafter he accosted a woman, whom he raped, chiefly because he unconsciously wanted to assert his masculinity.

The stimulus came originally from himself, although he thought it came from the homosexual man. Even though the precipitating event arose from an outside stimulus, that stimulus provoked the young man's own doubts about his masculinity, resulting in his definite desire to prove that he was masculine, which motivated the rape. A well-adjusted person would have rejected the proposition from the homosexual without becoming frightened or feeling compelling need to show that he was masculine.

This is an extreme example, perhaps, but how many of us have not seen two men fighting in a bar or a cocktail lounge, only to find out later that it was caused by a homosexual who propositioned another man?

The above-mentioned similarities between a neurotic person and a criminal further show the difficulty of distinguishing between the personality of the criminal and of the neurotic or the otherwise emotionally disturbed person. It is also a difficult task to predict when an emotional disturbance will give vent to itself in the form of a neurosis, a psychosis, or a psychosomatic disorder and when it will lead to criminal behavior. This is particularly true with juveniles in cases where antisocial behavior is frequently interspersed with emotional and mental disturbances.

We shall be better able to see the various criminogenic factors at work when we scrutinize offenders from the viewpoint of classification.

CHAPTER VII

The Classification of Criminals

A method for classifying offenders has to be based upon personal psychiatric-psychological factors, situational environmental factors, and a combination of both psychological and situational elements. Besides the personality-involvement in every criminal act and the presence of a certain situation or set of circumstances, one thing that must be taken into consideration when classifying any offender is the history of his criminal behavior. A person who commits only a single crime differs in personality make-up from one who repeats a criminal act several times or commits various crimes. The classification must reflect this, and the history of the offender's antisocial and criminal behavior will indicate whether he should be labeled an acute (momentary) or a chronic (habitual) offender.

Any classification, be it of plants, animals, or human beings, is to some extent artificial because there will always be individual characteristics or a set of characteristics which can properly be placed in more than one group. In our own attempt at classification, dealing as we often do with emotionally and mentally abnormal offenders, it is frequently difficult to distinguish between a criminal who is neurotic and one who suffers from a character disorder. Yet in spite of the shortcomings inherent in classification, we must attempt to categorize offenders if we are going to be successful in dealing with them. If we can classify them in a rational way, we can diagnose their characteristics, treat them, and predict their future behavior. However, such classification means that we will have to examine carefully each criminal to be able to find the characteristic and predominant traits that will tell us in which particular category he belongs.

One way of classifying offenders is to divide them according to those who commit crimes which are primarily directed against society (manifest criminals, such as gangsters), and those who commit crimes which primarily express their inner conflicts (symptomatic or reactive criminals, such as the kleptomaniac, pyromaniac, sex offender, and a certain type of murderer—on the whole, individuals suffering from a neurotic or psychotic condition or from a character disturbance).[1] However, the drawback to such a classification is that the overwhelming majority of all offenders manifest inner conflicts.

In trying to arrive at a system of classification in the field of criminology, we are faced with two problems—classifying the crimes and classifying the criminals. The first classification is a legal one, having its origin in criminal law. The law differentiates between crimes committed against the person (that is, crimes of violence, such as assault, murder, or sexual attacks), those committed against property (burglary or robbery), and crimes against the State. The law thus attempts to classify the criminal according to his act. This legally and sociologically colored method of classification is imperfect and unrealistic in the great majority of cases because an offender may very easily fit into two or all three of the categories. For example, he may kill and commit a burglary, thus committing crimes against person *and* property.

Theories of classification have been many. Lombroso expounded a type of classification based upon different criminal types. He divided criminals into: 1) the born criminal; 2) the epileptic criminal; 3) the criminal of irresistible passion; 4) the insane and the feeble-minded criminal, including those of border-line mentality; and 5) the occasional criminal. The last group was subdivided

into the pseudocriminal, the criminaloid, and the persistent offender of nonabnormal type.

Enrico Ferri divided criminals into occasional offenders and habitual offenders. To the first group belonged those whose criminal acts were due to external circumstances and who were driven to commit crimes because of a special passion. To the second group belonged those who were obviously insane or mentally defective, those mental deviates with inborn criminal tendencies (the so-called psychopaths), and persistent early offenders whose criminal behavior was caused by environmental elements.[2]

Franz von Liszt criticized the classification based upon the motivation of the criminal and instead followed a penological and sociological viewpoint, distinguishing between momentary offenders and corrigible and incorrigible permanent offenders.[3] Although this classification is clear-cut, it neglects to include offenders who are legally insane and is therefore incomplete and inaccurate. In order to avoid such a pitfall, Charles Goring classified criminals into physical, mental, and moral types.[4]

An interesting method of classification was proposed by Ernst Kretschmer,[5] who was the first to try to correlate the physical appearance of a person with his mental condition. Kretschmer's constitutional classification is based upon the study of people as psychobiological, or mental-physiological, entities. He established three types: the athletic, the asthenic-schizothymic-leptosomic, and the pyknic. He stated that there exists a clear biological connection between mental disposition toward schizophrenia and the asthenic-schizothymic-leptosomic and the athletic body builds and also between mental disposition toward a manic-depressive condition and the pyknic body type. His theory was applied to the classification of criminals, noting in particular that offenders who committed serious crimes were of the asthenic-schizothymic-leptosomic body build, while those offenders who committed less serious crimes had a pyknic body build.

While Kretschmer's idea of constitution is limited to a person's hereditary qualities, Olof Kinberg[6] includes a person's reactions if they are the result of his predisposition or of his environment.

Kinberg, in collaboration with Sjöbring,[7] gives a psychological classification wherein psychobiological correlation is not so predominant as in Kretschmer's hypothesis. This classification, which has advantages over that of Kretschmer, is, nevertheless, in the words of Hurwitz "open to substantial critical objections particularly as to the too vague definition of the marks differentiating the types and because no attempts have been made to control exactly the alleged correspondence with the actual facts." [8]

Classification of criminals can only be valid on an etiological basis. To classify according to the crime committed is untenable because the cause or causes of the crime are interrelated with the perpetrator and his environmental situation. Therefore, we can classify an offender only if we see the seriousness of his crime in relation to his personality make-up. This is as true for the momentary offender as for the habitual one, even though the frequency of the commission of the crime must also be considered, since it reflects the degree of inclination toward crime and of abnormality present in the offender. Such classification, however, presupposes that criminals be carefully examined, particularly to determine how much of the ego participated in the criminal act.

Recalling my discussion earlier of the formation of antisocial character, it is worth while mentioning here a classification of juvenile delinquents set up by Kate Friedlander, who divided them according to their antisocial character formation, organic disturbances, and psychotic ego disturbances.[9]

Burt,[10] Healy,[11] and Alexander and Staub [12] have tried to classify offenders according to etiological factors, but the difficulty here lies in determining exactly what the causes are. Generally speaking, there is no single cause or set of causes that cannot be considered as reasons both for criminal behavior and for disturbed mental conditions, or, to put it positively, the same cause or set of causes can lead either to criminality or to a disturbed mental condition. A valid classification of criminals can only be established when we consider the causative factors together with the personality make-up of the offender. These two elements are frequently so intimately tied to each other that we cannot consider them separately.

In each case we examine, therefore, we must ask: How far do mentally abnormal conditions present indicate the presence of criminological elements responsible for the criminal act? But we must remember that nothing is ever clear-cut. A person who is slightly neurotic may very well carry out a crime without being considered mentally abnormal. The borderline between normal and abnormal is at times so fine that nobody really can say where it is.

To ascertain the causative factors responsible for criminal activities in the offender, we must examine each person individually and give each case individual consideration. Sometimes an offender manifests signs of a character disturbance and yet still may have anxieties and feelings of guilt. Or, on the surface he may show signs indicating a neurosis, while deep within he may have a character deformation, which will put him into another group altogether. Another criminal may appear to be suffering from an anxiety hysteria, which may very well cover up a schizophrenic condition. The latter condition will place him in the psychotic classification, and not the neurotic one.

Another important point to consider is whether or not a criminal's aggressive drive, which has become antisocial, is the product of his distorted emotional and mental condition. Only a careful examination of the criminal, including his psychobiological development and his own personality reaction, will determine the causative factors responsible for his crime and his place in the classification system.

A system of classification which is methodologically sound has to be limited in scope. The purpose of the formation of categories in criminology is to determine how to deal with the offender in a rational way, be it by the court, the district attorney, the prison official, the probation officer, or the psychiatrist. An operational approach is therefore necessary,[13] which must take into consideration the offender's environmental background, immediate situation, and personality make-up. The classification will therefore have to be based on both sociological and psychological elements.

One factor reflecting both of these elements is the frequency and time factor, that is, whether the offender has committed only one crime or is a recidivist and the span of time over which he has committed his criminal acts. This factor is also applicable to medicine. For example, a cough which is the result of a cold and which does not recur too often or last for more than a short time is an acute condition and one which does not require great concern. However, a cough that recurs often or lasts for a long time may in reality be a chronic condition, such as tuberculosis.

The division of physical and mental diseases into acute and chronic ones gives us an excellent picture of the degree of severity of the illness. This division can also be used to great advantage in classifying offenders because it connotes at once the degree of criminal involvement of the personality of the perpetrator. Therefore, offenders can be divided into two groups—acute, or momentary, offenders and chronic, or habitual, offenders.

However, in designating a criminal as acute or chronic, we must take into consideration the seriousness of the crime or crimes committed, as well as the frequency and time factor. Otherwise, an individual who commits one premeditated murder would be considered simply an acute criminal, while another individual who repeatedly commits harmless or nuisance thefts would be considered a chronic offender. Obviously, this is wrong because the first individual is more dangerous than the second,[14] even though the latter in all probability has a personality defect. Of course, this might very well be true of the murderer, too, and although a man who commits murder may not necessarily be psychotic, he might display emotional or mental symptoms. His personality make-up is involved too much with his act to put him into the category of an acute offender.

In the following chapter I shall discuss in more detail some of the important aspects and sidelights of these two classifications.

CHAPTER VIII

The Acute and the Chronic Offender

Acute, or momentary, offenders are those who commit crimes once or twice under circumstances that tempt them to succumb to their antisocial impulses. These criminal activities are transient and usually not serious in nature with little involvement of the personality. Acute offenders do not have outstanding antisocial traits and therefore may be considered "normal" criminals. When such a person is faced with a particular situation, he may yield to antisocial impulses, but after he has committed the crime, he is often filled with regret or repentance—which could be the reason his criminal activities cease. He is a *situational* offender. In other cases the offender is influenced by antisocial patterns in his environment—bad companions or a family relationship wherein a member manifests antisocial or criminal inclinations. Removed from this environment, he no longer commits crimes. He is an *associational* offender. Then there is a third type of acute offender —the *accidental* offender—whose crime happens by chance or mistake.

Acute offenders are not really criminals, since they usually do not show a persistent antisocial or criminal attitude and do not frequently transgress this law. When we speak of criminals, we rather have in mind the habitual offender. It is really he who makes up the main body of the criminal group. In our discussion of acute offenders we shall describe only the three clear-cut examples given here (but, of course, there is always a certain amount of overlapping between groups).

The situational offender is characterized by the fact that a particular situation arises which elicits his antisocial feelings and puts them into action. This is the type of person about whom it can be said "opportunity makes the thief." The hungry man who passes a bakery shop and steals a loaf of bread or the man without means who finds a bulging wallet and does not return it, even though he can contact the rightful owner, is a situational offender. He is not criminal as a rule but only as an exception and takes advantage of a particular situation to commit an offense which is indictable. The dire need and unusual temptation, however, act as leniency factors in fining or sentencing these offenders.

The associational offender is influenced by his immediate environment, wherein external circumstances may arise that mobilize his criminalistic tendencies. Frequently we find a person without any apparent criminal tendencies who gets involved in a criminal act as a result of associating with people who have criminal patterns within them. I remember a young man who was friendly with three boys who had criminal records. One day he went along with them "just for the ride" while they were going to hold up a store. After they had accomplished their purpose, his friends gave him some of the stolen money. A police chase ensued, and the young man was given a gun. In the heat of the chase the young man shot and wounded a policeman. They were all caught and arrested.

Accidental offenders, who comprise the third group, are people involved in criminal acts by chance or mistake. Careless driving or the thoughtless throwing away of a burning match may put an otherwise law-abiding man in a serious predicament.

Consider the hit-and-run driver, for example. He may simply be on the way home from a party where he had a good time and a few too many drinks. The tragic accident occurs; he has brought death to a fellow human being. Normally a responsible citizen, he "blows up" and loses his head completely. He knows he has done something wrong and now wants to avoid responsibility. (Particularly where the driver is intoxicated, his sense of responsibility is diminished.) He panics and runs away, thus compounding his crime.

But the hit-and-run driver may find himself in a serious situation even though he successfully escapes the police. His action in leaving the scene shows a great deal of immaturity and emotional instability. In the normal, ethical individual there would be tremendous guilt feelings which usually lead to depression. Other emotions—anxieties, hostilities, a sense of worthlessness, self-accusation—would add to this depression and might lead to an emotional or mental breakdown. Of course, such a reaction depends on the personality make-up of the driver.

The conscience-stricken driver can help relieve his anxieties and possibly avoid a breakdown by surrendering and telling his story to the police. Talking about it and voicing his regrets will help him somewhat, and may minimize the shock.

These acute, or occasional, offenders are usually not essentially dangerous, although many of them are potentially so because it is from these acute offenders that the chronic ones may develop. In any event it is the quantity and quality of antisocial character traits which decide to what degree the criminal is a momentary one. As soon as the situation which led the person into committing a crime has passed, his antisocial tendencies recede and stay latent in him. Depending upon his ego involvement in his crime and his ability to learn from previous situations, he may either commit another crime as a situation arises or he may learn to check his antisocial inclinations.

Among acute offenders we find many children who display behavior disorders or psychosomatic ailments caused by early emotional difficulties and reactions. Many of these children are truant. If they are gang members they may be constantly exposed to association with other youngsters who display antisocial and criminal traits, which may lead them to become persistent or chronic offenders.

As I have mentioned before, to some extent each person selects his own type of crime, depending upon his ego and instinctual development. Although the selection may also depend upon the circumstances, frequently the offender himself creates those circumstances, of which he later becomes a victim. For example, during a holdup a criminal may be frightened into firing a gun if he meets with resistance. Nevertheless, to a great extent the criminal himself created his own situation, that is, he put himself into a situation which might lead to killing. Perhaps he even had an unconscious desire to kill.

The criminal act a man chooses to carry out is typical of his own special characteristics, even though it is also colored by the situation. For example, a mental defective will usually commit a primitive or a simple offense, such as breaking a window and stealing some unimportant objects, whereas a person who is more intelligent usually carries out a crime requiring more thought. For example, he may embezzle funds, which involves intricate manipulations. Often the sex of the perpetrator determines to some extent the type of crime committed. Although both men and women are mixtures of masculine and feminine traits,[1] we find that there is a prevalence of certain types of crime for each sex. For example, as we will soon see, shop-lifting (especially when due to kleptomania), poisoning, infanticide, and extortion are much more characteristic of women than of men. Men, however, commit many more murders, robberies, and embezzlements.

Thus we see that both personality structure and environmental (situational) elements determine the type of crime a person may commit. To a very large extent, then, it is the person's emotional state which determines the outlet he chooses, whether it be in the form of antisocial or criminal behavior, a psychosomatic disorder, or a neurosis or psychosis.

When a person carries out a crime for the third time, we designate him as a chronic offender. As mentioned before, however, this designation depends upon the seriousness of the crime, which reflects the degree of personality involvement and maladjustment.

Chronic offenders are divided into the following subclasses: 1) neurotic offenders; 2) offenders with neurotic character disorders and genuine psychopathic offenders; and 3) psychotic and mentally defective offenders.

NEUROTIC OFFENDERS

The criminogenic pattern of the neurotic offender has been established by his neurotic condition. In this group belong people who carry out criminal acts as a result of obsessive-compulsory afflictions, such as kleptomania, pyromania, dipsomania, nymphomania, dromomania, homicidal mania, and gambling. In this group may also be included compulsive wandering, as observed in fugue cases, although the mechanism is different from that in an obsessive-compulsory neurosis. Many of these neurotic offenders also display psychosomatic disorders. We constantly find that their neuroses and their criminal behavior patterns are as closely connected as the neuroses and behavior patterns of the neurotic nonoffender. An obsessional neurosis often acts as a defense against a person's aggressive or antisocial impulses.

An obsession (a persistent and inescapable preoccupation with an idea or emotion) intrudes itself upon its victim without any external stimulus. A compulsion (the motor counterpart of the obsession) is an obsessive acting-out. All obsessive-compulsory persons are emotionally stunted, fixated, and from time to time dominated by irrational ideas, which they understand are unhealthy or wrong but which they cannot resist carrying out. They are driven into actions by unhealthy unconscious drives.

The outstanding example of this type of neurotic offender is the kleptomaniac, whose continual stealing is closely allied to his whole personality structure in the same way that a phobia or an obsession is linked to the personality structure of the neurotic nonoffender. The difference is that the neurotic nonoffender does not commit a crime against society and is often enough disturbed about his mental symptoms that he realizes he must have help. The kleptomaniac, pyromaniac, dipsomaniac, and the nymphomaniac do not usually seek help until they are compelled to do so by order of the law or by other external forces.

Obsessive-compulsory offenders are maladjusted basically because of strongly repressed sexual desires. Kleptomaniacs do not steal because they are hungry or in want; nor do pyromaniacs set fires because of revenge feelings or any wish for material gains. Both adhere to the principle of pleasure rather than that of profit and are basically related to certain types of sex offenders. The pyromaniac experiences a sexual thrill when he watches a fire he has set, and the kleptomaniac is sexually excited when he takes something he neither needs nor even desires. The thrill of arson and kleptomania originates from the unconscious sexual gratification which these offenders receive from their acts. They are the prototype of the obsessive-compulsory offender.

The majority of kleptomaniacs are women, and when we look into the psychology of kleptomania, we shall understand the reason. The following case is that of a twenty-year-old girl who was arrested for shoplifting. Her motivation for it, difficult for the layman to understand since she was well-dressed and her parents were financially well-off, will be clearer when we study her background.

Her parents had been very strict, not even permitting her to have dates. During the time she attended a finishing school, several books disappeared from the school library. She was suspected, but since the missing books were not found in her room, no charges were brought against her. She graduated and went to a large city in the Midwest, where she worked as an office girl in a department store. When they no longer needed her in that capacity, she was transferred to the stock room. Shortly thereafter it was discovered that several articles of merchandise had disappeared. She was suspected and questioned but denied taking anything. The following day the police searched her room and found her closets filled with dresses and lingerie stolen from the department store.

In her interviews with me she readily admitted stealing the clothes and also the earlier thefts of the books from the school library. Little by little she grew aware that at the moment she took the clothing and the books she became excited in a way that was almost like a sexual thrill. It was the act of stealing rather than the stolen articles themselves, which gave her pleasure and satisfaction. Being strongly repressed, her sexual desires had sought another expression; it manifested itself in kleptomania.

The usual kleptomaniac is a woman who emotionally has never been able to obtain sexual gratification in a normal way because of her penis envy and castration fear. Therefore, she has to find some other means, and in this case chooses stealing. To her the stolen object is symbolic of the penis, and she takes it in revenge because she does not have the male organ. By taking what she has always wanted, she receives a sexual thrill. This psychological factor explains the prevalence of kleptomania among women. Sometimes a woman is partly conscious of her desire and even has fantasies about taking the penis. Because she feels guilty about the fantasy, she unconsciously is driven to steal so that she can be caught, punished, and thus appease her guilt feelings.[2]

The majority of pyromaniacs are men, and they too have not been gratified sexually. They have repressed their sexual desires to the point of feeling impotent. Like habitual gamblers, they are basically narcissistic and self-preoccupied people, suffering from an impulse neurosis. Fire-setting is a substitute for a sexual thrill, and the devastating and destructive powers of fire reflect the intensity of the pyromaniac's sexual desires, as well as his sadism. Fire, which to the pyromaniac has a magical power, provides him with the love, affection, and potency he seeks but cannot obtain in a normal way.

It is interesting that many fire-setters suffer from, or have suffered from, enuresis and that during psychoanalysis their pyromania is found to be connected with urethral eroticism.

In a kleptomaniac, as in a pyromaniac, the desires of the id and the desires of the superego and the ego alternate between carrying out the impulses and receiving punishment for them. While such a person's superego tries to check his id impulses, they overwhelm him so that he has to act them out. Deeply ingrained in him is the unconscious "forbidden" sexual wish, normal sex relations. Thus both in kleptomania and pyromania, as well as in many other forms of antisocial or criminal activity, symbolic acts are involved.

Another type of obsessive-compulsory neurotic person who often engages in antisocial and even criminal activities is the gambler. Many times he loses so much money that he has to steal in order to cover his losses. Although many a gambler keeps within certain bounds, such as betting only on horse races, he may frequently expand to betting on the numbers or on anything else which has a thrill for him. Deep in his unconscious his search for some thrill is frequently a substitute for sexual excitement.

This was the case with John, who was forty years old and serving a prison term for grand larceny. He was the oldest of three children, the son of a well-to-do businessman who used to take many chances in business deals. As a child, John would have frequent temper tantrums when he did not get his own way. In college he had only one friend, and they kept pretty much to themselves, rarely having any dates with girls. They were suspected of being homosexuals, and because of this, his friend was asked to leave college. When John's father died suddenly, he too had to leave college, and he took a job as a salesman. When he was twenty-three, he married, quit his job, and started a small business of his own, which was successful at the outset.

At twenty-six John began to gamble heavily, spending a good deal of time at the horse races and losing money constantly. He would go to the office in the morning and then leave work early for the race track. After a while his business failed, and his wife divorced him. For a few years he stopped gambling and finally moved back with his wife without remarrying her.

He had hardly stayed with her a week when he started to bet on horses once more. "I tried to fight against it, but I felt driven by something inside me. I began to place $2 bets with a bookmaker, and I was lucky. In a few days I had won $30, and I forgot to fight against betting. I played only on Wednesdays because that was my lucky day. Then I lost two Wednesdays in a row, and I switched to Saturdays. One Saturday I won $200. I went home and told my wife about it because I wanted to be truthful with her. She bawled me out, and the next day I went out to the race track and started all over again. That day I lost every dollar, but it didn't matter to me; what really upset me was that I had lost my good luck. The following Sunday I borrowed some money and lost everything. Next day was a work day. I felt low and came in late. There were some big sales in the shop so I 'borrowed' a few hundred dollars. I made some excuse to leave and started for the race track. It was raining hard when I arrived at the track so there were no races. I thought of the money I had taken and felt so bad about it I hurried back as fast as possible to the store, which was already closed. Now I could not put the money back, and I would be discovered. I was trembling when I went to work the next morning, but nobody discovered that money was missing. Then I thought: Why should I give it back now? So I waited, which was a big mistake because I went out that evening and played numbers and lost every dollar. That week was a black one. I did not think of my home, only about the money that I had taken. The following Saturday I 'borrowed' some more because I had to play in order to win back what I had lost. But my luck was gone."

After he had continued to take money for the next three years, he finally was discovered and sent to prison. During those three years, however, he had seemed to be a very conscientious worker, never even taking a day off for a vacation, so when his embezzlement was discovered, everyone was shocked. When his fine work record—not a day's absence—was brought out in court, everyone realized that he had stayed in the shop all year round because he did not dare to let anyone else see his books.

Luck was of great importance to John, as it is to every gambler, because it means not only that he wins the game, but also that fate or God has permitted him to win. When John had told his wife that he had won $200, it was because he wanted her to know that he had had luck, not because he wanted to tell her the truth. In examining John's background, we found that the cause of his excitement was sexual in nature. As a child he had either masturbated by himself or had had someone else masturbate him, for which he felt guilty even in adulthood. He had to try to find some way to bring about forgiveness, which unconsciously he felt he received when he won at gambling. However, because of his guilt feelings connected with his masturbation, he had an unconscious desire to be punished, which he was when he lost at gambling.

When he stole money in order to cover up his losses, he put himself in a worse position, thereby punishing himself even more. The greatest fulfillment of his unconscious wish to be punished came when he was imprisoned.

One root of gambling is masturbation, as we saw in John's case. We can understand this better when we realize that the purpose of all play, including sex play, is to relax, to get rid of emotional tensions. Since these tendencies build up constantly in a child, he repeats his sex play over and over again whenever he likes. Masturbation thus is like playing for sexual excitement. We see the same parallel in gambling because here also there is excitement attached to it.

That a person uses his hands both in some types of gambling and in masturbation is another similarity. The close tie between gambling and hands is illustrated beautifully in a story by Stefan Zweig, "Twenty-Four Hours from the Life of a Woman," where the movements of a gambler's hands are described in detail; when a woman notices his hands at the gambling table, she falls in love with him. Having lost his money, he promises to leave town with her. Through several mishaps, she arrives too late at the station. In despair she returns to her hotel, walks into the casino, and stops suddenly because she sees her lover's hands at the table.

The idea of using the hands, however, does not fully explain the obsessive-compulsory gambler. To John, who was a passionate and ardent gambler, gambling meant that fate had to be provoked. When he gambled wildly, it was obvious that he could not win back all of the money he had lost. The gods therefore had to decide. When he began to win at first, he thought that this was a promise that he had been protected against any losses. He believed that he could force fate to do what it ought to do for him, that is, to make him win and thus grant forgiveness.

John was also completely unaware that his gambling expressed an attempt to come to terms with his father. When his father died, John felt deprived both emotionally and financially. He felt his father's death as a rejection, and it aroused his hostility. His feeling that destiny owed him something was really an idea which unconsciously was connected with the notion that it was his father who owed him a debt. By leaving a thing to fate, he was unconsciously letting his father decide the outcome, thus taking on the responsibility which John did not want to assume for himself. Because he felt his father's death as a rejection, he in turn unconsciously wished to reject his father. He felt guilty about this and so felt a need for punishment. In his later life he repeated the pattern of his attitude toward his father; whenever John had money, he had to reject it, which he did unconsciously by losing at gambling. He lost not only to punish himself, but also to ingratiate himself with fate, or in other words, with his father. He lost to repay for his feelings of hostility.

John's gambling thus had two roots: his masturbation and his relationship with his father. His behavior was obsessive-compulsory; he was suffering from an impulse neurosis.[3]

Although the kleptomaniac is the prototype of the neurotic criminal, we also find symptoms of a neurosis among sex offenders, murderers, embezzlers, and thieves. Behind their aggressive nature is oral dependency, a passivity which they try to deny by their antisocial aggressions. As stated before, this type of offender will act out his aggressions because he cannot endure anxiety, which causes him too much discomfort. The criminogenic element rooted in this neurotic behavior is evident in offenders belonging to this group.

To the group of neurotic offenders must also be added those who commit crimes mainly because of unconscious guilt feelings, which arise either because they have a desire to commit antisocial or criminal acts or because they imagine that they have committed them or some other act which they deeply feel was wrong. As a result of their deeply imbedded hostility and hatred and consequent feelings of guilt, they unconsciously want to be punished, a wish they fulfill by carrying out a crime. An unconscious desire for punishment is not only present among neurotic offenders, but also among nonoffenders manifesting neurotic or psychotic symptoms. Sometimes a strong need to be punished is quite conscious in the offender, but most frequently it is not.

We clearly see this wish for punishment when an offender unconsciously makes some foolish move, such as returning to the scene of his crime or leaving some clue which will lead to his detection. Such was the case with Leopold and Loeb, for instance, when in 1924 they killed a young boy. A pair of eyeglasses discovered at the scene of the crime which turned out to be Leopold's was one of the chief clues leading to the apprehension of the criminals. Leopold and Loeb were thus trapped by a seemingly minor detail. There is little doubt that unconsciously Leopold wanted to be caught so that he could be punished for his crime.

Guilt feelings related to early incidents in the lives of neurotic or psychotic offenders are found more often than is generally thought. The only type of criminal who does not seem to have any feelings of guilt is the genuine psychopathic offender. Feelings of guilt, then, seem to be a primary force in mobilizing antisocial inclinations and leading a person into criminal acts. When such feelings are pronounced, there is a strong indication that the person suffers from a neurotic or a psychotic condition of an obsessive-compulsory or pseudo-obsessive-compulsory type.

OFFENDERS WITH NEUROTIC CHARACTER DISORDERS AND GENUINE PSYCHOPATHIC OFFENDERS

Offenders suffering from character disorders or character disturbances do not show neurotic symptoms as such. Their actions and behavior as a whole, however, are substitutes for symptoms of a neurotic nature. Foremost among these substitutes is a strongly colored aggressive, antisocial attitude, which at times goes so far as to approximate irrational behavior. This aggression frequently expresses unconscious self-destructive tendencies through the destruction of others.

A person suffering from a neurotic character disorder is able to commit all types of antisocial or criminal activities. In this group we find the rapist, the murderer, the pathological liar and swindler, the marriage wrecker, the Don Juan, the imposter, the nymphomaniac, the drug addict, the homosexual, and the alcoholic. To this category also belongs the shiftless, irresponsible, lazy, migrating person—the hobo type—who associates with others of the same caliber and who roams around the country without any plan or purpose.

We find that the characters of these people have become distorted or deformed and because of this have developed in an asocial or antisocial direction to a greater extent than those of the acute and neurotic offenders mentioned previously. Persons suffering from character disorders express themselves in antisocial or criminal behavior far more than in neurotic symptoms and manifestations as such. Because their emotions, as well as their characters, are distorted and defective, we are justified in designating them as offenders suffering from neurotic character disorders.

A person manifesting a neurotic character disorder is neither psychotic nor mentally defective. Sometimes he may suffer from a conflict because of his abnormality, but most often society is the sufferer because he inflicts disturbance and damage upon it. At times we find a person of this type who is extremely gifted; he may be highly intelligent or very creative. But in most cases his negative traits far outweigh his positive ones. Thus we find among offenders persons with superior intelligence who carry out criminal acts with great skill and adeptness and usually with much eccentricity. Not all people with neurotic character disorders become antisocial or criminal, though. Frequently, however, they get into trouble with their families, rather than the law, since they foment a consistently unhappy relationship, particularly because they are aggressive, impulsive, and emotionally immature.

Offenders manifesting character disorders are often described as psychopathic personalities without further investigation. As we shall see, this is unscientific because most of the people designated as psychopaths can be placed in more clearly defined categories. In the course of about thirty years, I have examined several hundred offenders and nonoffenders who have been classified as psychopathic personalities and have found that many of these people suffered from schizophrenic or neurotic conditions. The majority, though, displayed a definite distortion of emotions and character, which compelled me to designate them as suffering from neurotic character disorders.

It was Wilhelm Reich who first pointed out that the psychopath was an "impulsive character" and designated him so in his book *Der Triebhafte Character* (*The Impulsive Character*), while it was Franz Alexander, guided by examples of Freud and Abraham, who first introduced the concept of the "neurotic character."

Many other terms besides the "psychopathic personality" have been used for these persons. Partridge [4] wants to designate them as "sociopaths," while Karpman states that psychopathy is a very specific mental disease, which he designates as "anethopathy." According to Karpman the outstanding trait in such a person's mental make-up is pronounced egocentricity, which is also reflected in his sexual behavior.

Different authors place psychopaths in different categories. Eugen Kahn goes so far as to list sixteen categories,[5] while D. K. Henderson [6] classifies the psychopath according to psychobiological principles, dividing them into predominantly aggressive, predominantly passive or inadequate, and predominantly creative categories. His basis for his classification is psychopathic behavior, and he thereby disregards emotional conflicts. Henderson defines the psychopath in the following way:

The term psychopathic state is the name we apply to those individuals who conform to a certain intellectual standard, sometimes high, sometimes approaching the realm of defect but yet not amounting to it, who throughout their lives or from a comparatively early stage, have exhibited disorders of conduct of an antisocial or asocial nature, usually of a recurrent or episodic type, which in many instances have proved difficult to influence by methods of social, penal or mental care and treatment, and for whom we have no adequate provision of a preventative or curative nature.[7]

English and Finch characterize psychopaths as sociopathic personalities. Such a person is "characterized primarily by the individual's conflict with the society and cultural milieu in which he lives. He frequently runs afoul of the law because he transgresses what society has laid down as rules of conformity." [8]

Michaels asserts that persistent enuresis may be related to a specific type of juvenile delinquency and psychopathic personality. He also states: "Just as persistent enuresis represents an inability to control a local, specific, vesical function, so in the psychopathic individual who is persistently enuretic in his early development, the general diffuse pattern of the inability to control impulses permeates his whole personality. The quick transmission of stimuli and the lessened inhibitory tendencies, each complementary to the other, might be considered in a neurophysiologic sense as a short-circuiting leading quickly to motor response, and in a characterological sense (from the psychoanalytic standpoint) as acting out, acting upon impulses." [9] It must be said that we quite often find enuresis in juvenile delinquents, but it is still an unsolved problem whether this condition can be correlated with the psychopathic personality.

My own view is that we must apply a psychodynamic view in order to understand the so-called psychopath, whom I prefer to designate as manifesting a neurotic character disorder. Like the juvenile delinquent, he has usually been raised in a family having poor emotional relationships, emotional deprivations (usually real, sometimes imagined), and inconsistent upbringing (alternating between rejection and overindulgence).

In addition to numerous frustrations to which he has been subjected, his family has usually migrated very frequently; thus he has been uprooted from his home, friends, and school many times. His poor emotional relationship with his parents, plus the lack of any other stable force in his environment with which he could identify, resulted in a faulty development of his ego and superego structure, which made it impossible for him to form an emotional tie, that is, an object relationship, with anyone.

As a matter of fact, he has developed more of an external superego than an internal one, as shown by his reaction to the law. If a criminal who manifests a neurotic character disorder feels any regret or remorse at all, it is because he has been caught, not because of the harm he has done to society.

Because his superego development has been spotty, he is driven into both social and antisocial actions as if by a compulsion. His actions are therefore immediate and impulsive, without much forethought, and are always viewed from his own narcissism. There are people who try to get what they want at any cost—

bribery, extortion, etc.—a way of life which is most apparent in those who suffer from the purest form of character disorder—the genuine psychopath. Thus we see again that both emotional deprivation and lack of proper identification are responsible for the disturbed and antisocial character of this type of offender too.

Among offenders suffering from neurotic character disorders and among genuine psychopaths, we find a greater proportion of neurologically abnormal findings than we do among nonoffenders, findings such as increased deep reflexes, vertigo, disturbances of vision, and involuntary movements (tremors, twitches, etc.). We also find that many of these people have suffered from organic brain conditions, such as chronic encephalitis lethargica or toxic encephalitis, from head lesions, such as fractures of the skull, or from epileptic seizures. We have also found that more of these offenders than people in the general population have experienced still other brain-damaging illnesses and accidents during their childhood.

Generally speaking, offenders suffering from neurotic character disorders manifest an emotional instability which is more pronounced than that in the average person. They also manifest it earlier in life, and the instability lasts for a longer period of time, long after the normal person reaches mental and social stability. The emotional instability of the person manifesting a neurotic character disorder or genuine psychopathy (which is a neurotic character disorder in its most pronounced and extreme form) starts in early childhood, reaches a peak in young adulthood (during puberty), and subsides when he reaches his late twenties or early thirties. The reason we rarely find offenders of these types in older age groups in society is that society has in most cases caught up with them and has placed them either in prisons or hospitals.

There have been several theories on the relationship between abnormal electroencephalographic tracings and criminal behavior. Daniel Silverman [10] did electroencephalographic studies on criminal psychopaths and found that 80 percent of his subjects had abnormal or borderline tracings. Interesting in this connection is an electroencephalographic study by Michaels, who found that fire-setting was the only antisocial trait which was associated in a positive manner with electroencephalographic abnormality. However, there was the highest correlation between enuresis (a neurotic trait) and abnormal encephalograms. Stealing was the antisocial trait most negatively associated with electroencephalographic abnormality.[11] Jenkins and Pacella [12] did similar studies on delinquent boys and found that there is not a high correlation between criminal behavior and abnormal electroencephalographic tracings but only between electroencephalographic abnormality and epilepsy or organic brain disease, both of which conditions may result in a tendency toward antisocial behavior.[13]

Even though it has sometimes been claimed by the complainant in a court case that because epilepsy is followed by amnesia, a crime was committed by an epileptic during a seizure but not remembered, it has been my experience that it is extremely rare for an epileptic person to commit a crime during a psychomotor seizure. Therefore, a *direct* relationship between epilepsy and criminality is further refuted. We are closer to the truth when we say that electroencephalographic tracings are related to the epileptic manifestations rather than to antisocial or criminal behavior. Gibbs, Bagchi, and Bloomberg concur with this when they state: "In a prison population that includes the 'criminal insane' and more especially persons with epilepsy and organic brain disease, a group might be found in whom antisocial behavior and electroencephalographic abnormality seemed to correlate, but this correlation would be illusory; the true correlation is with the epileptic organic factors and not with criminality or psychopathy." [14]

Besides the pronounced narcissism and pleasure seeking, reflecting infantile fixation, there are two other elements which give the criminal of the neurotic character type a special quality—his means of satisfying his sex drive and his indulgence in alcohol and narcotics.

Many alcoholic persons suffering from disturbed characters may commit crimes while intoxicated. Frequently the alcoholic criminal manifests a character disturbance, although, of course, alcoholism is often also found in those suffering from a neurosis or a psychosis, especially in the form of schizophrenia. Assault is the crime most frequently committed by alcoholic criminals, while in the total group of offenders crimes against property seem to be most prevalent.

Alcoholism is not a disease as such; it is rather a symptom in a personality that has been emotionally disturbed even before the person actually started to drink. The alcoholic has a conscious or unconscious longing for love and security, which makes him orally oriented and which, when unsatisfied, makes him dependent upon the effects of alcohol to satisfy his unfulfilled needs. Since these people are orally fixated, they seek alcohol as other people seek food to satisfy their needs. The alcoholic's drinking is rooted in the cannibalistic part of the oral period of his psychobiological development. Having been orally frustrated, which created his oral fixations, he turns from the frustrating mother, whom he resents or hates, to the father, which most frequently brings about manifest or latent homosexual inclinations in him. Therefore, when alcoholism is involved in an offender's criminal activities, there is reason to believe that homosexual tendencies, weak or strong, are at play too.

His homosexual feelings become a further source of disturbance to him. At times the homosexuality is overt and conscious, and because of guilt feelings connected with indulging in such practices or in order to carry out a homosexual act, the person often drinks to the point of intoxication. Many times he enters into a drunken stupor so that he does not even remember what he has done, which makes it bearable for him.

The fact that there is a great deal of alcoholism among criminals has been confirmed by Gray and Moore, who, in a study of the histories of 1,637 prisoners in the Massachusetts State Prison, found that 66.3 percent were regarded as alcoholics. It is also interesting to note that of these, 68.6 percent had alcoholic relatives, 62 percent had alcoholic parents, and 26.1 percent had alcoholic siblings.[15] (Hurwitz too agrees that alcoholism is a very frequent phenomenon among the family members of offenders who commit serious crimes.) [16] Of the alcoholic prisoners 34.8 percent claimed to have been intoxicated at the time of their crimes, which was supported by other evidence in 22.8 percent of the cases.[17]

Alcoholism is seen frequently not only in young people who are gang members, but also in those who commit their crimes individually.[18] There is little doubt that it plays a tremendous part in eliciting criminal acts because during intoxication the individual's resistance to criminogenic impulses is reduced.

It has been claimed that the presence of alcoholism is more important as a causative factor in the first-time offender—that is, the acute one—than in the chronic one. This does not seem to be the case, however, since the alcoholic person, whether a first-time offender or not, has personality traits within him which make him vulnerable to his own antisocial inclinations and to those causative environmental factors which bring about criminal behavior. Although one could say that criminalistic inclinations and alcoholism seem to develop independently of each other, they are really intertwined, whereby use and abuse of alcohol maintains and increases antisocial and criminal activities.

Closely allied to those offenders suffering from neurotic character disorders or genuine psychopathy and those who show inclinations toward alcoholism are those who are addicted to drugs. In the second interim report of 1958 issued by the New York State Joint Legislative Committee on Narcotics Study, it is reported that the Federal Bureau of Narcotics states that excluding cocaine and marijuana users, in New York State and northern New Jersey there were 17,563 narcotic addicts. Of this group 13,407 are male and 4,156 are female; 16,850 use heroin; 418, morphine; 46, opium; and 249, synthetics. It seems that these figures are conservative for the areas studied, since they represent only known addicts, but it is not representative of the whole country, as it has been estimated that 40 percent of the entire nation's addict population resides in New York City, which, of course, was included in this particular project. Nevertheless, the statistics are shocking.

They are especially shocking when we compare the figures with those of the British Isles, where latest statistics reveal that there were only 359 addicts out of a population of 50 million. Of these 359, 149 were reported as addicted to morphine, 74 to pethidine hydrochloride, 52 to heroin, and the balance to a miscellany of drugs.[19] Similarly, out of a prison population of about 40,000 inmates in 1954, there were only 24 addicts. As Larimore and Brill state: "It appears obvious that, by any available index, narcotic addiction is currently not a major problem in England. It is equally apparent that there is little crime associated with narcotics in England and that the British narcotic problem in England is almost exclusively one of medical addiction: that is, addiction occurring in susceptible individuals exposed to narcotic drugs as a result of medical treatment. In short, England's problem is one of medical addiction not criminal addiction, which is addiction supported by illicit supplies of narcotic drugs, while in the United States we have both, with the latter being a larger contributor to the problem." [20]

Although there has been considerable debate as to the relationship between criminal behavior and narcotic addiction, it is fair to state that a person who has become an addict must sooner or later embark upon antisocial or criminal activities to obtain the drug. However, since the drug addict most often suffers from a character disorder, which most frequently is antisocial, it is fair to believe that most drug addicts already had sharp criminalistic inclinations before they started their drug consumption.

The surprising fact about drug addiction is that it is found most frequently in young people. An estimate has been made showing that 70 percent of drug addicts are under thirty, and of those, about 15 percent are under twenty.

The drug addict tries to obtain some emotional fulfillment, which he has not previously been able to do, and this need is more pronounced than any other, including the sexual one. Drug addicts are extremely narcissistic. Since they have not established any object relationship, they do not care about other people, except those who can supply them with the drug. The drug for them is almost like food or affection is for normal people; therefore, it is a substitute satisfaction. After taking the drug, they feel an elation, which gives them a narcissistic gratification, but after the drug has worn off, new longings arise for it, and they must have another dose because their bodies have become conditioned to it.

Because their bodies need more of the drug, the dosage has to be increased. In a psychological sense they become reduced to the status of infants, who can only receive but never give. They regress to an extreme stage of passive orality, during which their only concern is to satisfy their need for the drug.

In view of the different degrees of antisocial development in the characters of persons, it is understandable that we find so many types committing crimes. It is therefore not surprising that these types of persons have been lumped together into one category— described as psychopaths. This term has been used so much that if a person's condition could not be diagnosed properly, he was called a psychopath. Such a description has hampered both diagnosis and treatment of many people who otherwise could have been helped if a proper diagnosis had been made.

For example, there has been one type of person in particular, the sex offender, who has been described very frequently as a "sexual psychopath." When we began to study sex offenders in Sing Sing Prison, we found that the majority of them who had been previously labeled "psychopath" were rather persons reflecting conditions of neuroses, psychoses, reactive alcoholism, and character disorders. This was determined after careful psychiatric-psychological examinations. Of the 102 sex offenders examined, 25 revealed distinct disturbances of the character. We finally had to discard the terms "psychopath" and "sexual psychopath." My personal conclusion is that the only type of offender who can be called "psychopath" is the genuine psychopathic offender.

The diagnosis of genuine psychopathy can only be reached after excluding all other psychiatric conditions. A genuine psychopath is exceedingly narcissistic and impulsive. He is neither neurotic, psychotic, nor mentally defective, and he shows a pronounced absence of feelings of guilt and anxiety. He has been unable to establish any emotional relationship with others and is asocial and amoral. Since he is orally fixated, he is infantile in his emotional and behavioral manifestations and shows a polymorphic kind of sexual behavior. He can be heterosexual, bisexual, or homosexual. He differs from the person with a character disorder in that he has not developed any superego structure, while the offender with a character disorder has developed some superego structure, however weak. The difference between the neurotic person and the genuine psychopath is that the former manifests his conflicts in the form of fears, guilt feelings, and anxieties, which are mostly internalized (as are the conflicts of the psychotic), while the conflicts of the genuine psychopathic person are externalized, manifested by consistent criminal behavior.

The strongly antisocial and criminal attitude and behavior of the genuine psychopath are understood when we realize his gross lack of identification and his extremely stunted psychobiological development. Therefore, we see the symptoms of his behavior very early in his life. As a young boy he is often cruel. His background is one of thievery, chronic lying, and trouble-making outside and in school (when he is not truant). Since he is extremely narcissistic, he only cares about his own needs, having no superego to guide him. Being unable to establish any object relationship, his emotions are shallow, and he always expects immediate satisfaction. He often shows rapid mood swings and is untrustworthy, sly, and cunning. This is the type of person who may become a leader of gangs or a profit murderer. He rarely commits suicide, since he is in love with himself. Because of his undeveloped emotions, he rather prides himself in his criminal behavior, even though it has done harm to society or to those in his immediate environment. He is therefore a dangerous man and must be kept within walls, whether this be a prison or a mental hospital.

PSYCHOTIC AND MENTALLY DEFECTIVE OFFENDERS

The personality structure of the psychotic or mentally defective offender is impaired to such an extent that he does not understand or appreciate his crime. Because his reasoning is defective, he is unable to understand (either emotionally or intellectually) that his criminal act was wrong. According to the law this type of person is not responsible for his crime.

The factor responsible for the impairment of the mind of such a criminal may either be functional, psychogenic, toxic, infectious, or degenerative, leading to a disintegration of the ego. Foremost in this group belong those offenders suffering from psychotic conditions of a schizophrenic nature. Other types of offenders in this class are mentally defective persons, individuals with head injuries manifesting post-traumatic personality changes, persons with cyclothymic or manic-depressive psychotic features, paretics, and what is rather rare, epileptic persons, who during a psychomotor epileptic attack may be considered to be out of touch with reality and therefore psychotic.

Space does not permit me to consider each type here. Since the schizophrenic offender is the most common one among all mentally ill criminals, some details of his personality make-up and his participation in crime will be given. Probably the reason schizophrenic offenders are most common is that schizophrenia is the most common psychotic condition within the general population.

The schizophrenic person develops from what has been described as the schizoid (shut-in) personality. He is narcissistic and incapsulated in his own egocentric world, an autism which is characterized by an unreal attitude. His thinking is autistic, a term Bleuler first introduced, although he later on preferred the term "dereistic," by which he meant a thinking away from the subject. In his autism he does a great deal of day-dreaming, with which he is completely preoccupied; his own thoughts become so much more real to him than reality that they cannot be changed without treatment. (In fact, many times even with treatment there is no cure.) He lives in his own fantasy world to such an extent that he is out of touch with his surroundings and therefore has difficulty in distinguishing between what is real and what is not.

The root of the schizophrenic's basic schizoid attitude lies in the conflicting thoughts and emotions found in his personality make-up. When we examine such a schizoid person, we see a great deal of contradiction between his thoughts and emotions, on the one hand, and his actions, on the other. He simultaneously wants to perform opposite acts. When his contradictions are pronounced, he is frequently unable to accomplish anything. He cannot work; he cannot carry out the simplest tasks. If these conflicts become more pronounced, they cause a mental split.

The crucial point in his life is when the connection between his ego and his environment is broken. That is the moment when his emotions seemingly disappear, ending in schizophrenia. Because there are so many transitions between the schizoid and the schizophrenic person, it is always important to know the time when a schizoid person enters into a psychosis, not only because of the offender's own mental condition, but also because of the great social implications involved.

Generally when we carefully examine the schizophrenic person, we find that his thinking is illogical and his inhibitions are weak or absent, and so he follows his id impulses. He is emotionally rigid and flat. The development of such a case can be shown by the following example of a twenty-three-year-old man named Franklin, who for three years before his arrest had stolen several cars.

From the time he was a child, Franklin had always kept to himself. He did not enjoy playing with other children, became unpopular, and withdrew from people even more. He was easily frightened and could not stand loud noises. His father, who was strong and outgoing, had no understanding of nor tolerance for his son's behavior and he forced him to participate in sports. Franklin tried to be athletic, but when he could not make the school team, his angry father threatened to put him in a boarding school. His mother, who was rather lenient, succeeded in preventing this, however. When his father discovered that Franklin was playing hooky, he hired a tutor for him to watch and instruct him. With great difficulty Franklin managed to get into college. There he remained aloof, had no dates, showed little or no interest in his studies, and was finally asked to leave because of his poor school record. After his expulsion from college, he got a job as an office clerk. Since his work record was spotty, he was fired. He got another job, which ended with the same result. He then busied himself at home with small chores, but did not take an active part in his family life; instead, he kept mostly to himself.

When he was arraigned in court for his thefts, his father put up the bail, and Franklin returned home. That same evening he held up and assaulted a man. However, during the fight Franklin was seriously injured and had to be hospitalized. The following day he was transferred to the psychiatric ward, where I examined him. He had no emotional insight into his behavior, stating that the holdup was only a joke. He appeared apathetic, rather than depressed, answered questions with only "yes" or "no," and admitted readily to the holdup and the car thefts. He had no complaints and seemed rather to like it on the ward, although he always remained by himself. One day he smashed a chair and became violent and hallucinatory. He was later transferred to a state hospital.

Franklin was schizoid, showing preoccupation with himself and with his fantasies, which centered around his becoming a great man. He was rather a "lone eagle," out of touch with his environment but yet able to keep up somewhat with what his father demanded of him. When he stole cars, it was an unconscious wish to hurt his father and also to show that he was a man of action. His antisocial and criminal activities expressed an approaching schizophrenic catastrophe, which had not been recognized before.

Although on the surface the schizophrenic person may appear to be normal and to lead a rather conventional life, deep within his feelings are flat and his sex life of little or no interest to him. He is emotionally fixated because of his unsolved Oedipus situation. Being childish in his feelings, he cannot accept adult life, including work, a good relationship with other people, and a mature sex life. When he fancies himself in love, however, he may become violent if his "beloved" gives her affection to somebody else. Because he lacks real sexual feelings and has no emotional understanding of them, he compensates for genuine sexual emotions in a pathological way by overemphasizing sex in the sense that he attributes everything to it. For example, if a woman should make some remark to him which is totally unrelated to sex, he might think, "Ah! She wants to go to bed with me." This "sexualising" may be why so many more schizophrenic persons manifest sexual aberrations, such as exhibitionism, homosexuality, peeping Tomism, etc., than do those suffering from other mental conditions.

A schizophrenic person may be able to receive impressions from his environment, but his ego is unable to test them; he cannot incorporate them into his own ego, and therefore, they do not affect his inner life. He is fixated at or has regressed to an early narcissistic period of his psychosexual development, which makes him live in a world where he himself is the center. The world around him is without reality, since he cannot test it with his feelings. To him this reality is only words, of no emotional significance.

We understand this maladaptation when we see how a person suffering from schizophrenia thinks. When a normal person thinks about a certain object, he attaches to it all of its various qualities, and has associations regarding it, while the schizophrenic individual focuses his thoughts only upon the word itself. He is concerned with the term and not the object as such. For example, when a normal person thinks of a chair, he thinks of a comfortable place in which to sit and rest, while the schizophrenic person only thinks of the chair as a chair without attaching any qualities to it.

A schizophrenic type of thinking is found in certain kinds of murder cases, those which unfortunately have been labeled "committed without comprehensive motivation." We often find that when an apparently normal person commits an unexplainable crime, behind this so-called normality lies mental abnormality and frequently schizophrenia, particularly when the crime is somehow bizarre. Such schizophrenic persons are often designated as "ambulatory schizophrenics" and can be very dangerous, for based upon my experience, a psychotic individual can commit any type of crime.

The bizarreness of the crime reflects the presence of hysterical traits in schizophrenic persons, which traits are often found in them whether or not they are criminal. When patients manifest supposedly hysterical symptoms and later become deteriorated, they suffer not from hysteria, but from schizophrenia, a point of which the examining psychiatrist or psychoanalyst must be aware. The truly hysterical person tries to call attention to himself so that he can be in the limelight. His behavior pattern is dramatic, eccentric, and theatrical; his attitude is one of pose, one of simulating an attitude. Since the behavior of the schizophrenic person may be criminal and dangerous, it is important that his condition be recognized so he can be taken care of properly.

Not infrequently do we find a criminal who manifests cyclothymic or manic-depressive psychotic traits. When such a criminal is depressed, which comes about as a result of his feeling guilty because of his hatred, he may commit a crime. After the crime has been committed, he often becomes elated, going into his manic state. The manic-depressive psychosis is characterized by a person's being uninhibited, elated, and cheerful during the manic stage, while in the following depressive stage he is depressed and feels hopeless. The duration of the stages, as well as the duration of the condition, varies from individual to individual. At times it may be difficult to differentiate between a schizophrenic condition and a manic-depressive one. In the former the offender's behavior is more bizarre, out of touch with reality, while in the latter the offender's behavior is more characterized by mood swings, from one hour to the next, one day to the next, one week to the next, or even longer.

Offenders may also show psychoses due to alcoholism, encephalitis, syphilis, or other organic factors, or they may be mentally deficient. The results of studies on the number of criminals who are mentally defective seem to vary according to different researchers and to the time when the studies were carried out. In 1928 Sutherland found that out of 350 criminals about 20 percent were feeble-minded. Bromberg and Thompson examined 9,958 prisoners at the Court of General Sessions, New York City, and found that about 2.4 percent were mentally deficient.[21] During the first fourteen years that the Briggs Law was in effect in Massachusetts, Overholser found that of 5,159 defendants examined 432 (8 percent) were reported as mentally defective, while 69 were reported to be insane, 100 diagnosed as presenting other mental abnormalities, such as borderline intelligence, epilepsy, drug addiction, or psychotic personalities, and 169 were considered as requiring further observation in mental hospitals.[22]

The mentally defective offender may commit a variety of crimes, such as theft, assault, arson, exhibitionism, rape, incest, homosexuality, cruelty toward animals, manslaughter, and murder, but usually it is a simple crime, for this type of offender has a limited mental capacity. He is unable to commit crimes requiring a high level of mental activity, such as embezzlement or swindling. Hurwitz reports that in an investigation of 272 mentally retarded persons conducted by Norvig and submitted to the Danish Forensic Medicine Council during the years 1933 and 1942 shows that offenses by such persons against property play a relatively smaller part than they do in the case of offenders with normal, or non-defective, intelligence, while sexual crimes play a slightly larger one. "The cases submitted to the Forensic Medicine Council show further that the criminality of the mentally retarded as a rule declares itself earlier than does that of normal criminals and that the percentage of recidivism in young mentally retarded persons is extremely high (of mentally retarded persons convicted for the first time before their twenty-first year, no less than 80 percent were reconvicted). This experience tallies with the general impression in practice in regard to the early criminality of mentally retarded persons and the poor effect of punishment." [23]

Categorically, these offenders have all been grouped together, mainly because they are considered to be legally irresponsible for their crimes. However, Bowman finds it highly questionable whether a group such as mental defectives exists as an entity.[24]

Although the classification of criminals given here has certain drawbacks, as does every other classification method, it is a fairly accurate guide for demarcating them and thereby determining what kind of treatment or what kind of rehabilitation program is necessary for each one in order to achieve the best results. When we know more about the psychopathology of the criminal and are better able to determine his interaction with his social situation, we may then be able to improve this classification.

CHAPTER IX

The Sex Offender

The sex offender has been the object of so much hatred and venom that it has been difficult to study him on a scientific and rational basis, one that is free of prejudice. It is only in our time, thanks to investigators of human sexual behavior such as Magnus Hirschfield, Richard von Krafft-Ebbing, Havelock Ellis, Sigmund Freud, and Alfred Kinsey, that we are able to view him more objectively than before. Besides the lack of knowledge about sexual conduct in human beings, there has been another reason for man's condemning view of the sex offender—these offenders have transgressed a law which to most people is sacred. Not only does the offender attack his victims sexually, sometimes causing their death, but, if they survive, in most cases he also leaves a deep emotional scar upon them.

We are dealing here with a type of offender who in all probability is the most emotionally and mentally disturbed of all criminals because his problem reaches to the roots of his most basic and primitive impulses.

The incidence of sex crimes is not easy to estimate, since not all sex offenders are apprehended. Furthermore, different studies show a discrepancy in the numbers of sex offenders, depending upon the source of their figures. For example, Frosch and Bromberg made a psychiatric study of 15,000 offenders at the Court of General Sessions in New York City between 1932 and 1935, and found that only 709 of them were indicted for sex offenses.[1] But we must remember that misdemeanors are not handled in this court, and many sex offenses, such as exhibitionism, are misdemeanors. In a later study of 250 known sex offenders carried out by Apfelberg, Sugar, and Pfeffer, it was found that only 32 percent had actually been charged with sex offenses.[2]

It has been estimated that in the state of New York alone about 600 sex offenses, including prostitution, take place every day. In 1957 45,787 people were arrested for major crimes in the state of New York. Of these, 1,755 were charged with rape, and 4,151 were charged with other sex offenses.[3] The Federal Bureau of Investigation's *Uniform Crime Reports* [4] indicate that the number of cases of rape in the United States in 1950 totaled 16,580. In 1956 the number had risen to 20,300, while in 1957 it was 21,080.[5] Although there has been some increase in the population, the Federal Bureau of Investigation states that if the crime increase corresponded to the population growth, the Part 1 crime rate (major crimes, which include rape) would remain 1,188 measured against each 100,000 inhabitants, and that is the same figure as that of 1950.[6] The number of rape offenses increased 3.8 percent in 1957, which is 13.9 percent above the average for the previous five years.

In England the number of sexual crimes has increased from 5,000 in 1938 to more than 13,000 in 1950. Other crimes of violence have similarly increased from 2,700 to 6,200 in the same period.[7]

The participation of Negroes in sex offenses is somewhat lower than their participation in other types of crimes. In this connection it is interesting to see that between 1940 and 1945, and also later, the rise in crimes committed by Negroes was much more moderate than the rise in crimes committed by whites. In some states, such as California, the incidence of sex crimes is lower for Negroes than for white persons. In my own study of 102 sex offenders at Sing Sing we do not have any figures, since we did not differentiate between whites and Negroes.

The question naturally arises as to whether there is such a thing as a criminal who commits *only* sex offenses. This is an important question because many studies indicate that sex offenders commit only crimes of a sexual nature. During my research project at Sing Sing Prison, which lasted from 1948 to 1952, we found that over one-third of the 102 sex offenders had also committed other types of crimes. One offender had committed as many as seventeen crimes of various types, and some of the sex offenders who had committed incest or rape had also previously been charged with or imprisoned for robbery, burglary, or theft.

Although, of course, robbery and rape are two different types of crimes, basically robbery may be considered symbolic of rape and vice versa. In some offenders' minds these two types of crime may be synonymous. I remember one man who used to follow women into their apartments and then tie them up without molesting them. Upon leaving the apartment, however, he would take some money so that the police would believe, if he were caught, that his motive was robbery. One time he actually held up a woman with a toy pistol, then followed her into her apartment and tied her up. Again, he did not molest her but only took some money. The use of the toy pistol, which symbolizes his male organ, indicates how much his sexual desires entered into this crime. It is interesting that this young boy was indicted and convicted for robbery and sentenced for from five to ten years, reflecting the court's opinion that it really was robbery and not a sexual offense. Our psychiatric-psychological examination revealed the true nature of this case.

A basic finding about many sex offenders, though the court records do not always reflect it, is that they repeat their sex offenses. Our own research at Sing Sing indicated that almost one-fifth of the offenders had committed some sort of sex offense prior to the one for which they had been apprehended, convicted, and sentenced. Some sex criminals continually repeat the *same* sex offenses; they are the exhibitionists, the pedophiles, and, most frequently, the homosexuals. However, one type of sex offense may lead to another. For example, a person who had merely exhibited himself for many years may eventually commit rape.

When we review cases of persons charged with and arrested for rape, we find that many of them are acquitted, their cases dismissed, or they are charged with other crimes instead. The following figures are from the New York State Department of Correction. In 1948, 1,219 persons were charged with and arrested for rape. Of these, 630 were acquitted or dismissed. Of the 589 who were convicted, 123 were convicted of rape, 152 were convicted of third-degree assault, 93 were adjudged youthful offenders, 70 were adjudged wayward minors, 65 were convicted of felonious assault, 60 were convicted of endangering the lives or the health of children (carnal abuse as a misdemeanor), 22 were convicted of miscellaneous offenses, and 4 were convicted of sex felonies other than rape. Of these same 589 convicted persons 263 were committed to institutions, 253 were placed on probation, 15 were only fined, and 58 were given suspended sentences. Of the 138 total cases convicted of rape (123 charged with and convicted of rape and 15 charged with other crimes but convicted of rape), 95 were committed to institutions, 28 were placed on probation, 11 were given suspended sentences, and 4 were only fined.[8]

One of the most obsolete concepts of the law is what it terms statutory rape. Sexual intercourse with a girl under a certain age —and the age of consent varies throughout the United States— is considered statutory rape (a felony), usually regardless of the circumstances. This is both unfair and contrary to what we know about biological development. For example, we know that after a girl has started her menses she is no longer a child but has entered sexual adulthood with sexual desires no less pronounced than those of boys of even an older age. It is therefore unscientific to specify an arbitrary age limit for consent to sexual intercourse. Rather, the law should take into consideration the sexual maturity of the girl and especially whether or not she induced the act or was a willing participant to it.

It is interesting that the law should be so one-sided as to consider sexual intercourse with a girl under a certain age as statutory rape, while it disregards older women who have sexual intercourse with boys under this same age. Many of these older women and many of the young girls who willingly have intercourse with men and then call it "rape" are more in need of psychiatric help than are the men who are then termed "sex offenders." It is true that it is much more difficult to determine rape by biological standards and the girl's willingness than by setting up an arbitrary age limit, but it is certainly a more logical and fairer criterion.

Notwithstanding the great rise in the number of sex offenses of all kinds, which at times may seem to the public to take the form of sex crime waves, more interesting is the relationship between the personality make-up of the offender and his sex crime. The greatest number of sex offenders are those who are impotent, old, or senile—men who indulge in sexual activities with children. Pedophilia, an abnormal sexual inclination toward children, is carried out by impotent men, usually older ones, while sexual assaults and statutory rape are committed by younger men.

Apfelberg and his associates, who examined 250 offenders, found among them psychopathic personalities, psychopathic personalities with pathological sexuality, alcoholics, schizoid personalities, neurotic traits, cerebral arteriosclerosis, senility, neurosyphilis, and postencephalitic Parkinsonism. Only 53 did not show any abnormalities of such a nature.[9] In Norway Scharffenberg examined over 600 prisoners sentenced for sex offenses and found that about 30 percent were mentally defective, which was about double the average for all prisoners.[10] In Germany Aschaffenburg examined 200 sex offenders over a period of three years and found cases of senile dementia, dementia due to hardening of the arteries, psychosis, dipsomania, and severe hysteria. Fourteen were idiots, 3 feeble-minded, and 9 epileptic. Nearly one-fourth belonged in an asylum for the insane, an institution for the mentally retarded, or a home for the aged, rather than in a prison. Only 45 could be pronounced unquestionably normal in other respects, and 12 of these 45 offenders had been prompted by drunkenness.[11]

Manfred S. Guttmacher reported on 172 sex offenders who had been examined psychologically and found that 11 percent were legally irresponsible because of their mental conditions. Seventeen percent of the group had had head injuries with unconsciousness severe enough to require treatment in hospitals, while 8 percent had I.Q.'s of below 50.[12] Although no data is given for the remainer of the group, the percentages given indicate the prevalance of mental disorders in sex offenders.

Our own research covered 102 sex offenders, including those committing rape, carnal abuse of children, sodomy, and incest. The cases were selected on the basis of their case histories and not necessarily on the basis of their convictions. All of these offenders were studied intensively by psychiatrists, psychologists, and psychiatric social workers. The offenders' life histories were checked with probation reports, school records, and social service case histories, and in many cases the prisoners' families were interviewed. All data of the cases was discussed at staff meetings. Every case was diagnosed, and treatment, recommendations, and prognosis were outlined.

Of the 102 sex offenders 44 had perpetrated crimes other than sex offenses, 22 had committed sex and other crimes previously, and 16 had committed sex offenses prior to those for which they had most recently been sentenced; only 20 had not committed any previous crime. Fifty-six of the offenders had been sentenced before.

As interesting as these statistics are, it is possibly more significant that all 102 men suffered from mental or emotional disorders, ranging from neurotic conditions and character disorders to psychoses. The question is whether these sex offenders suffered from psychotic conditions to a greater extent than does the general population of offenders. Before we decide, let us look at the diagnoses of the sex offenders we examined.

It must first be stated that the psychiatric-psychological examination of sex offenders with complicated personality make-ups is not easy and does not readily give definite clues as to their exact grouping. The difficulty in making a diagnostic interpretation is that our psychiatric classification has primarily been set up for patients treated at psychiatric institutions. In general our usual diagnostic procedures do not cover criminals, even though their traits may differ from the above type of patient. For instance, at a time when the term "psychopath" was introduced, it was mainly to cover persons who had committed crimes. Later on this concept was broadened to include difficult borderline diagnostic cases. In

our own research project we found that about 40 percent of the
sex offenders had been diagnosed by other psychiatrists as psychopaths, with or without psychoses, while we found that they either
suffered from character disorders, from neuroses, or from psychoses. During psychiatric treatment we were able to elicit material which guided us in arriving at a more accurate diagnosis.
The following are our results:

Simple schizophrenics	5
Paranoid schizophrenics	4
Catatonic schizophrenics	2
Pseudo-neurotic schizophrenics	1
Paranoid condition	1
Psychosis due to alcohol	2
Schizoid personality	1
Character disorder	23
Genuine psychopath	2
Reactive alcoholism	7
Psychoneurotic	19
Obsessive-compulsive neurosis	24
Anxiety state	10
Conversion hysteria	1

We examined another group of 42 sex offenders who were not
included in the group of 102. This second group was compared
with 31 nonsex offenders. The number of examined persons was
admittedly small, but the results were in agreement with those
of other studies, indicating that schizophrenic, paranoid, and
obsessive-compulsive conditions, as well as character disorders,
were more prevalent among sex offenders than among nonsex
offenders.

On the whole, our research project indicates that sex offenders
appear to suffer from various types of emotional and mental disorders, but there is a common denominator to be found among
them: they are all sexually deviated. As mentioned before (see
Chapter VIII), many neurotic offenders, such as kleptomaniacs
and arsonists, show that their criminal behavior is rooted in a
sexually distorted drive.

In going over the experiences of the 102 sex offenders, we found
that they all had been emotionally and physically insecure during
childhood. Their parents had, by and large, been unstable; many

of them had been strict and domineering, sometimes even cruel. At other times they had been overindulgent and overprotective. Frequently, as children, these offenders had been socially displaced, not having a place they could call home. Many of them had been in orphanages or had been cared for by unloving stepfathers or stepmothers, making a positive emotional relationship with grown-ups difficult.

Their disturbed emotional lives were also revealed in their frequent truancy from school (about 60 percent of them were truant or had been suspended from school as disciplinary problems, often because of poor supervision. Their deprivations were pronounced emotionally, economically, and socially. As they frequently were unable to identify themselves with adults, they were also therefore confused about their own sexual roles and had not been able to develop normal sexual concepts. In contrast to the popular belief that sex offenders are oversexed, we found them instead to be undersexed. They were emotionally fixated at a pregenital level and frequently reacted impulsively.

Although many of these sex offenders had been considered "bad" boys, it was surprising to see that 14 of them had been considered model children, and at least 32 seemed to have been "good" boys. They had submitted to authority without being able to assert themselves because of fear. When they later committed sex offenses or other types of offenses, it was to express their hostilities and rebellion against the authority of their parents.[13]

It is interesting that of the 102 offenders we studied, 67 showed alcoholism to some extent (19 to a minor degree, 13 to a moderate degree, and 35 to a severe degree), and over 50 percent—56—had been under the influence of alcohol when committing their crimes. One of these 56 was a fifty-three-year-old man named Otto, who had been in prison for eight years for pedophilia. His father had been brutal and an alcoholic; his mother an overworked drudge. At twelve Otto became an apprentice in a small town in Europe. He was treated as a "slave in bondage," working from early morning until late at night. He never had enough to eat and received only leftovers from the master's table. He had a small piece of

bread and some water for breakfast and a small plate of soup with
bread for the other two meals. His employer used to cut the meat
in the dark "because it had worms in it." Even up to the time of
the study, Otto could not eat lamb. The master constantly beat
him on the head, and if he took a piece of ham because he was
hungry, he would be beaten with a rope. He never earned any
money but was given a certificate when he completed his appren-
ticeship. He never had close friends among the boys with whom
he lived as an apprentice.

At seventeen he came to the United States with money bor-
rowed from his sister and went to work at his trade. Here his
social life was practically nonexistent. Although he began to have
sex relations with women at the age of nineteen, in his own
words, "You could count the women on your fingers." A few years
later he was convicted of second-degree rape. The records of the
case are missing, but Otto always claimed it was the girl's fault.

Shortly thereafter he married a woman eight years older than
himself and was surprised to discover that she had two children
who were in Europe. When she brought her daughters over to
the States to live with them, he left her and became a nomad,
working in various American cities. Years later, an alcoholic va-
grant, he returned to his wife after begging her to take him back.
He continued drinking a great deal, worked very little, and was
nothing but a burden to his family. When he was drunk, he became cruel and sadistic, frequently striking his wife or twisting
her arms. She told us that at bedtime he would "spit in my face
or spit on the walls and never fall asleep."

In speaking of his sexual perversions, she said: "Being a coward,
he didn't dare do it until he was drunk." Her young daughter
was forced to leave home and move in with an aunt in order to
avoid his advances. As he himself said, he felt that his lack of
potency "put me on the spot with young girls; couldn't help myself." At middle age he was sentenced to two years for impairing
the morals of a minor. When paroled, he returned home, again
depending upon his wife for support.

A few years later he committed the offense for which he was
incarcerated at the time of the study: It seems that one Thanks-

giving, when three little girls came to his tenement apartment begging for presents, he took them into his room, and for a few pennies forced them to submit to his abnormal sexual attentions. He said of his crime: "If they hadn't resisted, nothing would have happened," and he also stated that he never would have abused the children had he not been under the influence of alcohol. He spoke of himself in relation to sex as "Now I'm all gone—going back like before I was nineteen—bashful, afraid, no sex, getting old, and going back."

Otto is a person who is emotionally fixated and who can be considered to be a deteriorated alcoholic. He is sexually twisted and not suitable for psychiatric treatment. He is hostile and afraid and therefore prefers to be by himself because only then does he feel secure. He is fearful of adults, which is one reason why he sought out small girls to satisfy his sexual desires; they did not present a threat to him. All sex offenders who commit pedophilia have this in common; they are afraid of adults and therefore approach children, who give them a feeling of potency and superiority and allow their drive to be gratified. Unconsciously they have always felt like children and therefore identify themselves with them. They are usually passive people, whether it be conscious or unconscious.

Frequently those involved in pedophilia may be older people who are somewhat senile or demented; sometimes they are mentally defective or suffer from neurotic or psychotic conditions. Usually they are not violent, but at times, particularly if the child starts to cry while the offender is committing his sexual act, the offender may be frightened into killing him.

It is interesting to note that many of the sex offenders we examined had been brought up by mothers who were stern, cruel, or sadistic and who apparently made the boys insecure and fearful of women. Because sadistic aggressions were frequently common occurrences in their homes, these boys grew up with the idea that women had to be taken by force. It is interesting to see that when such men married, they often chose wives who were as aggressive and sadistic as their own mothers, as we discovered when we examined the wives of these offenders. Such selection reflects masochistic passive dependency.

Every person acts in accordance with his emotional make-up, whether he is choosing a job, becoming emotionally or physically ill, or committing a crime. In this respect each person is an active partner to his own act. In the same way that a man chooses to become a physician, lawyer, printer, cab driver or barber, a man may also become a criminal or sex offender, the selection depending partly upon his situation but more upon his personality make-up.

There is frequently also a certain relationship between a criminal and the victim he chooses and we find this the case when a man commits a sexual assault. The offender often creates the circumstances (of which he too becomes a victim), but the victim herself unconsciously also may tempt the offender. The conscious or unconscious biological and psychological attraction between man and woman does not exist only on the part of the offender toward the woman but also on her part toward him, which in many instances may to some extent be the impetus for his sexual attack. Often a women unconsciously wishes to be taken by force (consider the theft of the bride in Peer Gynt). We sometimes find this seductive inclination even in young girls, in their being flirtatious or seeking out rather dangerous or unusual spots where they can be picked up, thus exposing themselves more or less unconsciously to sexual attacks.

Because of the unconscious masochistic feelings a man may have (frequently masochism and sadism go hand in hand), it is not surprising that many sex offenders married women who, so to say, could satisfy these strivings. When we made our study, we investigated particularly the relationship between wives and their sex-offender husbands. One of my associates, Rose Palm, devoted much time to this special aspect. Psychiatric investigations were made and psychological tests, particularly the Rorschach, were administered.[14] All of these tests helped us to get invaluable information about the personality structures of people in close contact with the criminal, the emotional climate in which he was raised, and his relationship to members of his family. The examinations helped us to evaluate the pressures against which he had been or still was reacting and also threw new light on the psychological motives which led him to commit his offense or offenses. Family testing revealed, for instance, in one case, that the complaints of a young offender about erratic and hostile ways of his mother were realistic and justified. All of his life he had been exposed to and had rebelled against his mother's unreasonable behavior, which was psychotic and which had never been recognized as such by anyone in her environment. In another case the sex offender had been exposed to an unconsciously sadistic brother. "Family testing also helped us in rehabilitating the offender, as it rendered a picture of the resources in his immediate environment. In one instance we encouraged a young offender to establish a closer relationship with an older sister, tests revealing that she was the only stable member of his family."

We made a Rorschach study of the wives of eight offenders convicted of rape. Since the rapes had been committed while the offenders were married, the question arose as to whether certain factors in a given marriage had played a role in precipitating the crime. Although the number of cases is too small to warrant definite conclusions, these eight Rorschach records showed such amazing similarities that it is worth while to report them here. "These similarities were expressed specifically in the concept these women had of men and in the particular way they related to them: a way of relating which appeared deeply embedded and was patterned after the relationship they had with their father in early childhood. The image of the father, as it transpired in the Rorschachs, was the following: all records, without exception, reflected the image and the influence of a threatening and sexually aggressive father figure. . . . The presence in our subjects of fear of men was confirmed during subsequent interview sessions. They conveyed fear of being alone in their apartments lest they be raped, a fear of being followed on the streets, a fear of going out at night, a fear of colored men, or other fears of being attacked." It was interesting to see that all wives were loyal to their husbands despite cruel treatment and unfaithfulness, although there had been temporary separations. When asked in individual interviews why they always returned to their husbands, they stated that they were afraid of being killed or beaten by them if they did not or that they had feelings of guilt about abandoning their husbands. Some felt that only they could reform their erring husbands.

I quote further from the report:

"If at this point we try to apply our findings toward the understanding of the marital relationship, the picture would appear simple: the offender needs an outlet for his sexual aggression and finds a submissive partner who unconsciously invites sexual abuse and whose masochistic needs are being fulfilled. Yet these eight marriages failed, although to all appearances the needs of both partners were satisfied. One may ask why.

"The answer is that thus far we have considered only one side of the picture. Our Rorschachs revealed that the psychodynamics were far more complex and that the overt masochism and submissiveness of these women was a reaction to their strong underlying feelings of hostility against men. Their fear and guilt resulted from aggressive intents toward men, intents which were exemplified in such responses as: 'a tiger skinned,' . . . 'giants, their heads cut off,' . . . responses easily recognized as the symbolic expresssion of death wishes in general and castration wishes in particular."

To explain this latent aggressiveness, another factor was considered, the influence of these women's mothers. The report continues. "We distinguished two trends: in some records female figures were completely absent; this indicates that either our subjects had no female figure to identify with in early childhood or that they had ineffectual mothers. At any rate the women of this type had identified with their aggressive fathers and had thus incorporated aggressive and masculine trends in their own make-up.

"In the records of the second type, female figures were present, but they were all seen as aggressive persons who were 'pulling,' 'stamping,' 'mad-looking,' and whose attributes, such as 'pointed hats standing on top of their heads' and 'hair-dos piled up high,' symbolized them as phallic and masculine figures.

"The conclusion that our subjects had identified either with aggressive males or with phallic females was strengthened by other factors. All eight women gave an unusually high amount of responses symbolizing the male sex organ, a feature which is found in the records of people for whom potency is a factor of conscious or unconscious concern. Responses of this nature were 'caterpillars,' 'animals with elongated beaks,' 'snakes with their heads stuck out,' 'tree trunks,' and others.

"Our records furthermore revealed that our subjects were greatly preoccupied with thoughts about their own inadequate physical functioning. Many considered themselves 'headless,' 'not developed right,' etc. . . .

"On the basis of this material it was apparent that these women, under the surface of their masochistic submissiveness, showed a masculine and aggressive orientation. They tended to compete with men and to negate their femininity. There can be no doubt that they had latent homosexual inclinations. In this connection it is interesting that the husbands, who were given psychiatric treatment in Sing Sing Prison, expressed various complaints about the lack of sexual spontaneity of their wives. They complained of having to 'bribe' her, about their wife's habit of sleeping in her underwear, and generally about their frigidity. In some cases a prolonged period of sexual frustration preceded the offense.

"In drawing up a completed picture of the psychodynamics of our subject, the following emerges: We deal with the type of woman who, in her sexual attitude, stimulates aggression only to encounter it with rejection." Thus in another sense too the wives were similar to the rapists' mothers, as we shall see from the following:

"We found consistent indication of the fact that these rapists had been sexually overstimulated in childhood by their mothers or mother substitutes. In one case the offender was, at the age of twelve, introduced to sex practices by his mother. In another case, the mother was greatly concerned with her own physical functioning and would draw constant attention to her body; she also had her son take care of her when she was ill in bed. In a third case, the mother was described as 'overprotective,' with the implication that she petted her son a great deal and demanded constant physical contact.

"While, on the surface, it would seem that the offenders had been given a great deal of care and affection by their mothers, they actually had experienced constant frustration. In some cases this frustration resulted directly from the fact that they were constantly stimulated but not satisfied. In most cases, however, seductive behavior by the mother alternated with cruelty and harshness and a great deal of beatings. One of the offenders who seemed consciously aware of this dual trait in his mother put it as follows: 'My mother was like two people. Sometimes she was drunk, cruel, and the most abusive person alive, and yet at other times she was very sweet.' In one of our cases the mother was seductive to the point of actual incest; then pressed charges against her son and had him arrested."

The conclusions reached were that the wives of the sex offenders on the surface behaved toward men in a submissive and masochistic way but latently denied their femininity and showed an aggressive masculine orientation; they unconsciously invited sexual aggression, only to respond to it with coolness and rejection. They stimulated their husbands into attempts to prove themselves, attempts which necessarily ended in frustration and increased their husbands' own doubts about their masculinity. In doing so, the wives unknowingly continued the type of relationship the offender had had with his mother. There can be no doubt that the sexual frustration which the wives caused is one of the factors motivating the rape, which might be tentatively described as a displaced attempt to force a seductive but rejecting mother into submission.

The sex offender was not only exposed to his wife's masculine and competitive inclinations, but also, in a certain sense, was somehow "seduced" into committing the crime. It is interesting that we find seduction applicable to many other types of crimes as well as sex ones. Often we see many women swindlers or "con" men able to cheat honest people out of their money. These swindlers and "con" men seem to possess a certain seductive ability, which is fundamentally sexual in nature. In examining many of these victims, we find that they too had seduced or intrigued the swindler into continuing his swindling game. As a matter of fact, extortion and the willingness to be bribed are counterparts in the same way as sadism and masochism are present in the attacker and his victim, respectively, even though it is unconscious.

We often find this mechanism of seduction operating between mother and son and between father and daughter, whereby the result may be incest. In fact, it might be interesting to investigate whether or not an aggressor does not always unconsciously choose as his victim the type of person who once was close to him, be it in a heterosexual or homosexual relationship. When rape or incest occurs it is safe to say that either of these sex crimes is basically connected with an unsolved Oedipus or Electra complex.

The highest rate of incest is found among illiterate people. In our study we found that sex offenders who had committed incest had pronounced anal-sadistic traits. Those who had sex relations with their daughters often spoke about their desire to prevent their daughters from marrying, the obvious motivation being to keep their daughters for themselves. It was also significant that all the inmates we examined for incest kept away from other women apparently because they were not sexually attracted to them or because they felt that they themselves were impotent.

It was interesting to find that rapists had tried to avoid women of their own age as sex partners in normal sex relations. It was equally interesting to note the great discrepancy in age which usually existed between the rapists we examined and their victims. Those who did rape women of their own age were fundamentally more obsessive-compulsory than the others. When they committed crimes, however, it seemed that suddenly their obsessive-compulsory inclinations diminished for a short while, with apparently little sense of guilt. They differed from persons suffering from obsessive-compulsory neuroses, who, when they had committed crimes of which they themselves disapproved, later experienced feelings of guilt. Frequently we found that many of the criminals who had committed rape or incest did not realize they had done anything wrong, nor did they regret having committed their crimes or repent them. Their only regret was the consequence of being apprehended and convicted. As I have said before, such a personality trait reflects a deformed character development. Since these obsessive-compulsory offenders had a temporary release of their superego, a temporary lowering of the superego barriers, during which time the crimes were committed, one might suspect that this temporary release is really what is criminogenic in them, that is, they have a superego which is faultily constructed, functioning only at certain times.

Interesting also is the rapist's ability or inability to handle his impulses. Persons who had actually carried through rape displayed the greatest gap between their impulses and the control of them, while the offender who had only attempted rape but did not complete it manifested only a small disproportion between his emotions and his control. Those men who had used violence had weaker motor control than those who did not.

When we examined the intelligence of the 102 offenders, we found that it was equal to that of the average general population. Of course, it must be remembered that Sing Sing does not accept mentally defective criminals.

Of the 102 men, 9 had been in state civil hospitals or in Matteawan Hospital for the Criminally Insane prior to their incarceration at Sing Sing. Only 59 of the 102 sex offenders had been given even limited psychiatric-psychological examinations prior to their current convictions. The rest of the sex offenders had been sentenced without any psychiatric evaluation of their personality make-ups.

Although we find that exhibitionism and pedophilia are the most frequent sex offenses, the most important one is homosexuality because it very frequently brings about other serious crimes in its wake. As practiced between men, it may take place as mutual masturbation, pederasty (anal intercourse), or inter femora fellatio (oral intercourse). In women homosexuality (Lesbianism) is limited mostly to mutual masturbation and anal intercourse and is not often connected with other crimes.

There are three types of male homosexuals. The first is the active male, who plays the part of the male during sexual intercourse. The second is the passive male, who plays the part of the female during the sex act. The third type, and perhaps the most prevalent, is the one who can play either the part of the male or the female. We find the same pattern to be true in female homosexuals.

There has been much debate about the nature of homosexuality. It will be clearer to understand if we are aware of the fact that every human being has bisexual tendencies within him; each one of us is a mixture of male and female traits. Therefore, a trace of homosexuality, no matter how weak, exists in every person.

Homosexuality is based partly upon biological, that is, constitutional, tendencies and partly upon psychological ones. Sandor Ferenczi,[15] in describing the nosology of male homosexuality, which was later taken up by Felix Boehm,[16] states that there are two types of homosexuals, the active one, whom he designates the object homoerotic, and the passive one, whom he calls the subject homoerotic.

The object homosexual person is primarily attracted by strong or muscularly developed men, while he feels more like a friend toward, and yet is competitive with, women. He does not have any conflicts apparent in relation to his homosexuality and is more of the intuitive type. The subject homoerotic individual is narcissistically in love with himself and his penis and is fixated to that period of his life when the decisive turn to homosexuality occured. He usually loves adolescent boys and actively seeks them out because they represent himself at the time of his own adolescence.[17] It seems that this type has become homosexual due to an innate biological development which in its nature is an anomaly, an inclination toward homosexuality which has been reinforced by the environment. If such a constitutional inclination exists, environmental influences, such as a boy being brought up in feminine surroundings without a father figure with whom to identify, will most probably produce homosexuality.

Homosexuality is widespread. Alfred Kinsey, who examined 12,000 persons, estimated that at least 37 percent of the male population has had some homosexual experience between the beginning of adolescence and old age. This is more than one male in three of the persons that one may meet as he passes along a city street. Among the males who remain unmarried until the age of thirty-five, almost 50 percent have had homosexual experience between the beginning of adolescence and that age.[18]

The development of a boy into a homosexual is rather complex. It may occur through identification with his mother and fear of his father—an unresolved Oedipus situation. (In a girl the same takes place, except that she identifies with her father and is afraid of her mother.) The strong attachment of a son for his mother with resultant hatred of the father brings about an adoration and idealization of women, resulting in the adoption of increasingly feminine behavior. Because of his pronounced female identification, he may become an overt homosexual, although he may still be very much afraid of the men he chooses. However, consciously or unconsciously, he may be even more afraid of and hostile toward women and therefore not want to give himself to them. (Dependency usually breeds hostility, which may be concealed by adoration.)

A typical homosexual, although not always so, may be described thus: He is thin and has slender limbs; his cheeks are flushed, his face soft, and his appearance and manners pleasant. Hair on the chest, axilla, and pubes is scarce. He behaves like a girl, walks like a girl, and smiles like a girl. He may like to cook and sew. He may even seek out girls, but this is only because his friends do, for in reality he is not attracted to them. Instead, without perhaps in the beginning being aware of it, he is attracted to boys. In any event he may start to dress like a girl, perhaps take a girl's name, "marry" a man, and pose as "his wife."

It is a striking characteristic of homosexuals that they often recognize each other. It is as though there is a mutual sexual attraction between them. Although they may vary a great deal in appearance, there is no doubt that there are psychological features in their make-ups which bind them together. In this connection it is interesting to note that they never completely accept within their circle anyone who does not seek the same type of sexual satisfaction they do.

In the underlying mechanism of the homosexual, the ego obeys the pregenital sexual impulses and prompts them to enter into his consciousness, thus apparently accepting this abnormal sexual behavior as a natural one, although frequently accompanied by conscious or unconscious guilt feelings. Actually homosexual persons feel isolated, a feeling found in all types of sex offenders we examined.

Homosexual behavior must be differentiated from homsosexual leanings (conscious homosexual tendencies not carried out in action), which again should be differentiated from homosexual inclinations of an unconscious nature. There is probably no person who does not possess some unconscious homosexual tendencies. For this reason, latent perversion may be brought to the fore accidentally or under such circumstances as may be found in prisons or any other place where males or females are confined to the company of their own sex exclusively. Thus the homosexual inclination, no mater how unconscious it is, may become manifest in certain situations.[19]

We often find in male homosexuals those who have been at one time unusually fixated on a man and have later regressed to selecting men who remind them somehow of their original object. If a boy is brought up only in the company of males, he may develop distorted attachments, which can produce homosexual inclinations. Freud emphasized that the prevalence of male homosexuality in ancient Greece might have been caused by male slaves who raised the children.

Many homosexual men may have a longing for women. However, because these men usually have the idea that sex is "dirty" and because they have been fixated on their mothers, idolizing and adoring them, they unconsciously feel that women cannot be "touched" or "soiled." The stronger the identification between a boy and his mother, the more chance of his developing into a homosexual. Such an identification also depends upon the strength or weakness of the father. When the father is weak or when there is no father figure at all, the son may tend to develop homosexual tendencies to a varying degree.

Hormone investigations seem to indicate that estrogen (the female hormone) is more predominant among homosexual men than among normal males. This is a problem which requires special study and which would be outside the scope of this book. However, it is interesting to note that the male hormones are first formed of unknown substances, and part of these hormones are then transformed into the female one.

That homosexuality is a motivation in many antisocial and criminal acts is a fact not readily understood by the public. However, many cases, particularly murder and extortion cases, frequently show that homosexuality in some way, either directly or indirectly, was at the root of the crime. This was so in the famous Leopold-Loeb case described in the following chapter.

In the same way that homosexuality and pedophilia represent a fixation or a regression to an earlier stage of the psychosexual development of a person, so also does exhibitionism. The person who exhibits himself is basically narcissistic; that is, he is in love with himself. He suffers from feelings of castration, which he tries to counteract by showing his penis, his symbol of power. The exhibitionist repeats his crime over and over. He wants the spectators to react to his male organ as if he were saying to them, "I show you my penis so that you can be afraid of me." Basically the exhibitionist's tendencies stem from his relationship with his mother, who most often has been domineering and overprotective. Because of the threatening mother figure, he has become anxious to the point of feeling impotent and overwhelmed. He therefore has to compete with her, consciously or unconsciously, but in this competitive situation he also wants something in return, her affection and love. It is under these circumstances that he may exhibit himself, as if unconsciously he were saying to his mother, "I will show you what I have, and you show me what you have." Exhibitionists may suffer from different types of neurotic or psychotic conditions; some of them are mentally defective; others show traits of character disorders, which makes psychoanalysis very difficult.

Exhibitionism is closely allied to voyeurism, which is sexual pleasure obtained by looking at the genitals of another person. A voyeur is more commonly known as a "Peeping Tom," and his behavior may often take on a form of sadism (the feeling of wanting to hurt). In a way we may say that voyeurism is a kind of passivity. The voyeur only looks at the person but does not act. In the words of Fenichel:

"The fact that no sight can actually bring about the reassurance for which the patients are striving has several consequences for the structure of voyeurs: they either develop an attitude of insatiability—they have to look again and again, and to see more and more, with an ever-increasing intensity—or they displace their interest from the genitals either to forepleasure activities and pregenitality or generally to scenes that may better serve as reassurances than does actual genital observation.

"Because of the insatiability, the desire to look may acquire a more and more sadistic significance . . . peeping may from the beginning be a substitute for sadistic acting." [20]

Conditions closely allied to voyeurism, or scoptophilia, are fetishism, coprophilia, and coprophrasia. Fetishism is a fixation of sexual interest on a part of the body, as the foot, or on an article of clothing, such as a pair of panties or a brassiere. The fetish stands as a substitute for the loved person. Coprophilia is a condition in which a person becomes sexually excited by excretory organs. Coprophrasia is a disorder whose chief characteristics are the use of obscene language or the collection of pornographic literature. Usually exhibitionistic, coprophilic, and sadistic tendencies are combined in the person suffering from coprophrasia.

Another frequent sex offense is prostitution, the "oldest profession." Although its basis is primarily psychological, it is also economically and socially motivated. Even though practiced mostly by women, to a lesser extent it is practiced also by men. Many prostitutes are mentally defective or psychotic, but their most important characteristic is that they have regressed to an earlier infantile level; their psychosexual development has stopped, and they have become emotionally stunted.[21] Contrary to common belief, the majority of them are sexually frigid. They have usually had a disturbed relationship with their father and more often than not are searching to find love through their prostitution. Often there is a close association between the sexual delinquency of young women and the sexual immorality of their mothers.[22]

Several states—Michigan,[23] Massachusetts, Illinois, Florida, Indiana, and New Jersey—have given serious consideration to the handling of sex criminals. California also made a study of sex offenders, which was under the direction of Dr. Karl Bowman, of San Francisco, and a program for sexual psychopaths has been instituted in state mental hospitals there. It is divided into two phases: 1) commitment for a ninety-day observation period and 2) commitment for an indeterminate period of treatment. The first phase determines if the sex offender is a "sexual psychopath" as defined by law. If he is found to fall within this category and is likely to benefit from treatment, he is admitted to the hospital for an indeterminate length of time.

Daniel Lieberman and Benjamin Siegel write that they find that most sex offenders fall into the group of persons suffering from neurotic character disorders or neuroses, and it is gratifying to note their statement: "Our data indicate that intensive psychiatric treatment for the sex offender is justified." [24] I agree with them on both counts on the basis of my own sex offender study at Sing Sing.

In our project we divided the sex offenders into four groups according to their psychiatric-psychological make-ups and the degree of seriousness of their crimes. Since the 102 selected prisoners we studied are not a true cross-section of the sex-offender population in all prisons (because Sing Sing is a maximum security prison with offenders who have committed serious crimes), the first two of the following categories—"predisposition to violence" and "untreatable at present"—would have been in a much smaller proportion to the other two groups, had they been a true cross-section.

The classifications are as follows:

A. Offenders who are predisposed to crimes of violence, are likely to commit new attacks if released, and are not treatable by present known methods   18
B. Offenders who, because of personality make-up, age, or alcoholism,

are not suitable for treatment at present and who are likely after release to continue as a danger to public morals and to women and children   32

C. Offenders who, because of their treatability, could be placed in a treatment center with a good prospect of improvement before release   44

D. Offenders who, because of their treatability, could be released on parole and treated on an out-patient basis   8

The evaluation of the 18 men classified in Group A was based upon the following criteria:

Most of them manifested hostility, aggressiveness, and resentment, often combined with outward cruelty. In addition they showed emotional instability, which made it difficult for them to control their feelings. Their motor control was poor or slight so that their reactions were out of proportion to the stimulus. In several of them their personality traits presented a disorganization which appeared to be psychotic, though it was not actually so. Others in this group showed actual symptoms of psychosis, though often not severe enough for them to be retained in a mental hospital. However, taken in conjunction with their criminal records, these psychotic tendencies made it probable that they would be dangerous if released.

These psychiatric observations were supported by psychological tests, such as the Rorschach, the T.A.T. (Thematic Apperception Test), the Szondi test, a drawing test, and the sentence completion test, which were given independently. The examinations indicated that these men were so aggressive and hostile that they had to be confined under conditions of maximum security. Their maladjustments could not be treated by any methods known to psychiatry at that time or even at the present. If released, they would be a continuous, violent danger to other persons.

The 32 individuals classified in Group B were those who would present a continuing threat to public morals, and especially to small children, after they had served their sentences under the present law. This group comprised those who were chronic alcoholics, too old to be treated, or whose personality maladjustments were too deep-seated to indicate the probability of change at that time. A number of them showed symptoms of psychosis. They were not given to types of behavior that made it necessary to keep them within a maximum security prison, and yet they should not be released.

The men in this group did not show excessive explosiveness or brutality, but they were immature and solitary figures who were withdrawn emotionally and set in their habit patterns. All of them had committed previous crimes. Like those of the preceding group, they could not be successfully treated by any currently known method of therapy.

Those in the third group, Group C, "treatable as in-patients," represented a much more hopeful outlook than those of the preceding two groups. These were men whom psychoanalysis or psychoanalytically oriented psychotherapy could benefit, and we advised that treatment be given before they were released to the community. These offenders were mentally abnormal and conflicted; they functioned on an immature sexual level because they doubted their own masculinity and therefore expected rejection and failure. This group was able to develop emotional insight, although at the time they committed their crime they had very little of it. Such offenders would benefit very much from a hospital atmosphere in which therapists would supervise their environment according to their individual needs. This type of experiment in treating these sex offenders might lead to the establishment of a new kind of institution in which mentally maladjusted offenders of all types might be truly rehabilitated. In the words of the report: "This is the most hopeful idea to emerge from the present study."

The 8 people in Group D, "treatable as out-patients," had very much of the same personality make-ups as the treatable in-patients group, except that the Group D men were so integrated that they did not need constant supervision. They were men who demonstrated a genuine desire to improve, who had a certain belief in themselves, and who had enough motor control to be able to channel their impulses into work and other constructive activities when they were away from the therapist. They had a greater sense of responsibility than the men in the other groups, and they had a stronger urge to meet life realistically. With constant guidance from a therapist, in combination with regular parole supervision, these men should be able to keep out of trouble with the law.

Although we shall deal with the psychiatric treatment of offenders in a later chapter, it is important to mention here the recommendations which were made in connection with our study, particularly with regard to dealing with sex offenders in a more effective manner. As mentioned before, many of these offenders were predisposed to violence and therefore had to be kept away from society. Since many of them represented a danger to women and children and frequently repeated their crimes, I suggested that it should be mandatory that such an offender have a psychiatric and psychological examination before being sentenced by the court. If he were found to be dangerous and suffering from a serious emotional or mental disorder, with the exception of a psychosis or mental defect, he could be sentenced from one day to life and transferred to a prison for psychiatric treatment.

In the case the offender showed an emotional or mental disorder and was not found to be dangerous, or in case he was found to be psychotic or suffering from a mental defect, he should be given psychiatric treatment in a mental hospital. If hospitalization were not necessary, he should be given psychiatric treatment as an out-patient in a hospital. If he were found to be an alcoholic, senile, or more of a nuisance than a threat to public safety, then he should be sent to a farm colony.

In the words of the commission the following recommendation was suggested:

"The need exists for law to protect women and children from certain dangerous sex offenders who, under present law, are held in prison for limited periods and then must be released, regardless of whether there is any improvement of the mental or emotional condition which caused them to commit abnormal crimes against the person; therefore,

"We recommend legislation providing that when any offender be convicted of rape or sodomy involving the use of force or violence, or against small children, or convicted of felonious assault involving a sexual purpose, the Court after psychiatric examination of such offender may sentence such offender to serve an indeterminate sentence having a minimum of one day and a maximum of the duration of his natural life;

"We recommend further that, whenever an offender shall be sentenced to such a term of from one day to life, the law shall impose upon the Department of Mental Hygiene, the Department of Correction, and the Board of Parole the solemn duty of giving his case prompt and intensive study, to be followed where feasible by therapeutic treatment, to the end that such offender may be rehabilitated and released whenever it may appear that he is a good risk on parole. When serving under this form of sentence, it should be required that a prisoner receive thorough psychiatric examination not less than once every two years and consideration by the Parole Board."

This new law was designed to provide for the rehabilitation, treatment, and release of sex offenders who suffered from some form of mental or emotional abnormality and at the same time to provide for the continued care of those who clearly were still a danger to society. Such a law in the opinion of the commission "will be administered with due regard for the rights and welfare of the offenders as well as of society." [25] The law was approved unanimously by the New York legislature in March, 1950, and was signed by the then governor, Thomas E. Dewey. Up to 1957 there were 160 sex offenders in New York State who had been sentenced, according to the new law, from one day to life. They are kept in two maximum security prisons, where, however, only limited psychiatric help has been available.

As was pointed out by my research group and the commission, such a law requires the largest possible psychiatric facilities in order to implement it. The commission originally suggested that an institute for those manifesting criminal behavior be established where most of these and other cases could be treated, where psychiatric personnel could be trained, and where further research on criminals, including sex offenders, could take place. Unfortunately, this proposal was scrapped, which has seriously hampered the success of the law. In 1955 the research project on sex offenders at Sing Sing Prison was given up, the result being that the implementation of the law has come to a standstill, with many judges being reluctant to sentence an offender from one day to life. This is most unfortunate, since the law had been shaped in such a way as to try to deal realistically with sex offenders. The law—indeterminate sentence from one day to life, with psychiatric-psychological follow-up and consideration by the Parole Board not less than once every two years—is a revolutionary step. Only the future can tell whether there are enough wise and far-sighted people who will continue to work and fight in order to implement this law.

CHAPTER X

The Personality of the Murderer

People have always had an avid interest in murder. Death, ever mysterious—being beyond the experience of any living person—becomes even more mysterious when it occurs as the result of deliberate homicide. Then too, the law-abiding citizen may secretly admire the murderer, although he may publicly denounce him and demand his punishment, because the murderer carries out in reality what the law-abiding citizen only dares to dream about.

From a sociological and a purely humanitarian viewpoint, the high number of homicides in the United States is significant. In 1957, according to the Federal Bureau of Investigation, the number of murders and non-negligent manslaughters was 6,920.[1] Statistics indicate that by and large the homicide crime rate is higher in the larger cities than in the smaller ones. In 1941 there were 268 homicides in New York City and 228 in Chicago, 3.8 and 6.2 homicides per 100,000 of the population, respectively.[2] In 1957 there were 314 homicides in New York City and 296 in Chicago.[3]

The high incidence of murder in our country becomes more important when we compare it with the incidence of this crime in other lands. While the homicide rate in the United States in 1941 was 5.5 per 100,000 of the population [4] and in 1957, 5.1,[5] in England (including Wales), this rate was much lower—in 1941 being .10 per 100,000 of the population [6] and .31 in 1957.[7] In comparing English statistics with those of the United States, we find that England's murder rate has been one for every 300,000 of the population, while in the United States the rate has been one for about every 26,000 persons—approximately twelve times as high.

Also in sharp contrast to the United States are the Scandinavian countries, which have an exceptionally low incidence of homicide, even on a proportion-to-the-population basis. In Sweden, for example, during the year 1920 there was a total of 11 homicides and attempts at homicide. This already low figure declined to 4 in 1943 and to a mere 2 in 1947.[8] These figures correspond to data given for Norway and Denmark.

In comparing the number of homicides for different countries, we must remember that international statistics cannot always be comparable because each country has a different basis for determining a homicide. For example, some nations use death certificates to compile their statistics on homicide, while others use judicial statistics. The two do not necessarily correspond because an actual homicide may not be equivalent to a homicide in law. Notwithstanding this consideration, homicide is more prevalent in the United States than in other countries. We therefore must ask ourselves whether there are any general factors in our culture or in our social situation related to the psychiatric-psychological aspects of homicide which can be considered as contributory causes to the prevalence of murder here.

The general psychological and sociological background of murder is about the same as that of crime in general. Homicide has its psychological roots in the offender's aggressive and sexual tendencies, related to attack and defense. In a society such as ours, where assertion and competition are part of the culture, a person will frequently try to find any means of asserting himself against his environment. Such a competitive drive is a potent contributory factor in instigating criminal behavior in general and homicide in particular. The United States has been considered to be the foremost land of private enterprise, a fact which makes itself felt in all ways in which a person expresses himself. Here life follows a certain pattern which might be, to some degree at least, instrumental in bringing about conditions under which homicide is likely to take place, although, of course, there still remains a great deal of individual responsibility.

Another factor which may have contributed to the prevalence of homicide in America is the rapid development of the country, with the great rise of industry and agriculture, the steady influx of immigrants, and the migration of the population to newly opened territory. As was the case in other parts of the world where an industrial and agricultural expansion took place, many people did not adjust to this new form of life. They were under almost constant strain. Thus frictions and conflicts arose, which brought forth antisocial and criminal activities, including homicide.

The fact that much of the population of the United States is concentrated in large cities may be a contributing factor toward increasing the emotional tension in individuals and families which we know can be expressed in crime. In large cities people are frequently crowded together in great masses where they live, work, and seek pleasure—in housing developments, subways, factories, department stores, and on highways and beaches. Consequently, many are apt to feel "fenced in" or even overpowered, resulting in a greater inclination toward hostility, aggressiveness, and emotional tension.

Although the factors mentioned here may not be considered as intrinsic, they are, nevertheless, of some importance because these elements provide the background for many murders.

In this connection the relatively small country of Japan comes to mind, with its population of over 60 million people crowded into a small area and yet with a very low homicide rate. A possible explanation lies in the tremendously high rate of suicide among the Japanese people, which can be considered to be a form of indirect homicide, a substitute, where the perpetrator has turned his hostility against himself. Therefore, a fairer comparison would be the combined homicide and suicide rate for the two countries.

When we compare the homicide rate in various parts of the United States, we find that the lowest rate is in New England (1.4 per 100,000 inhabitants) and that the highest rate is in the East South Central states—Alabama, Kentucky, Mississippi, Tennessee —(12.6 per 100,000 inhabitants). In the mountainous states (Arizona, Montana, New Mexico, etc.), the rate is 4.7 per 100,000 of the population, while in the South Atlantic states (Florida, Georgia, North Carolina, and Virginia), the average rate is 10.2 per 100,000. The homicidal rate in the Pacific states (California, Oregon, and Washington) is 4.2 per 100,000, while the rate in the Middle Atlantic states (New Jersey, New York, and Pennsylvania) is 3.1 per 100,000.[9]

The prevalence of homicide in the South can be understood if we stop for a moment and think of the historical development of the Southern states. First, up to the period of and including the Civil War, economic life in Southern society was to a large extent dependent upon slavery. Violence and threats of violence were often expressed in daily life, among slaves themselves, as well as between master and slave, so that one might say that there developed a pattern of behavior where violence and individual disregard of the law prevailed. Second, the years after the war were filled with tension, chaos, and disorder, thus increasing the sources of aggressions, and, with the end of Reconstruction, the white elements that had resorted most openly to violence and murder as instruments of policy were put into control. Third, since this same period, the people of the South have been emotionally, socially, and economically frustrated, which, in addition to their Negro problem, could not but leave its mark upon their attitude and give rise to aggressions.

One manifestation which has boosted the homicide rate in the South in the past is lynching. If we look into the actual psychological background of lynching, we find that the action of the crowd is motivated by a common aim that has to be fulfilled. This goal may originate from hate and fear felt for the culprit or affection felt for his victim, both leading to a desire for retaliation and revenge. Since emotions are easily roused, even an accidental circumstance may be sufficient to release pent-up feelings and thus cause lynching. People forming a lynching party are dominated by a common purpose. Their individuality disappears, and their responsibility decreases, with the result that they lose self-control and act impulsively.[10] Here an element of mass-suggestion and mass-psychosis occurs. The thought of revenge is harbored with violence in "the animal" of the human being.

Since Negroes constitute a great proportion of the population of the South and since it seems that a high rate of murders are committed by Negroes, this may be a possible explanation of the South's high homicide rate. A study of 200 murderers by Cassity revealed that 34 percent of them were Negroes,[11] while the annual report for 1941 of the Federal Bureau of Investigation showed an even higher percentage.[12] In 1957, out of 2,007 criminal homicides in cities of over 2,500 in population, 761 were committed by whites and 1,225 by Negroes. Manslaughter by negligence, on the other hand, was committed by 973 white persons and by 254 Negroes.[13] Since Negroes constitute only about 10 percent of the total population, their participation in both of these types of crimes, as well as in most others, is greatly out of proportion to their numbers.

The prevalence of criminality among Negroes is perhaps an expression of a poor environmental situation and discouragement and frustration at being unable to gain a foothold within a society mastered by whites who discriminate against them.

Although the environmental background for murder varies within the country, the law is clear in determining what constitutes a homicide. It defines murder as the unlawful killing, with malice aforethought, expressed or implied, of a human being by a person of sound mind and memory and discretion. It further states that murder perpetrated by means of poison, torture, or any other kind of willful, deliberate, and premeditated means, or where the murderer lies in wait for his victim, is murder of the first degree, and that manslaughter is the unlawful killing of a human being without malice, either voluntarily after a sudden quarrel or in heat of passion, or involuntarily in the commission of an unlawful act not amounting to a felony.

Sometimes it is difficult to determine whether or not a homicide was planned. A criterion for determining this phase of the case is whether or not the murder was committed in secrecy. One so committed frequently demonstrates that it had been premeditated and planned and is therefore to be considered as murder of the first degree.

The penal codes of the states of the United States make three basic distinctions in law regarding homicide: 1) Excusable homicide—Committed by accident or misfortune or in the heat of passion or upon combat on sufficient provocation, when no advantage was taken or no dangerous weapon used, or if the killing was not done in a cruel manner; 2) Justifiable homicide—Committed by a public official or by a person acting by his consent as his aide or assistant; committed in defense of habitation or property, in the lawful suppression of riot or in the lawful preservation of peace; committed by accident or through misfortune, under threats or menace sufficient to show there were reasonable causes to believe the person's life would be endangered; 3) Felonious homicide—Committed willfully under such circumstances as to consider it punishable.

The last and most important point in reference to our consideration is that the law excuses a crime committed by an insane person, an idiot, or by a child under the age of fourteen years. The insanity issue may be raised in the time between the indictment and the sentencing of the offender. The statutes in the penal codes of all the states provide that an insane person cannot be tried, incarcerated, punished, or executed.

Often there is a difference of opinion between psychiatry and the court regarding the problem of mental and emotional abnormality, and sometimes there is even a difference of opinion among psychiatrists. In one of our states the following case is on record: A low-grade, feeble minded boy, who previously had been an inmate of a state school for mental defectives, together with an older boy had raped and killed a girl. He was put under observation in a mental hospital, and three psychiatrists rendered an opinion to the effect that the boy was mentally defective and incapable of distinguishing between right and wrong. The jury, however, gave more credence to the police officers who had arrested him and had testified that the boy was of normal mentality. The boy was convicted, sentenced to death, and executed.[14]

In order to make headway in criminology—to prevent crimes and treat criminals effectively so that eventually all of society, as well as the offenders, will benefit—we must determine the motivation behind the criminal act. How much more important it is to determine this about the murderer, in view of the enormity of his crime! The motivation for murder can be so disguised that only a thorough probing into the mind of the murderer will unravel it. Each murderer should be examined psychiatrically, for without an appreciation of the quality of the psychological features and the personality pattern, we will be unable to fathom the man behind the act and to correct his behavior.

From a broad viewpoint it will be found that the force which compels a person to commit homicide is a conscious or unconscious feeling of sexual, intellectual, social, or financial inadequacy, often caused by frequent frustrations. Even when there is an apparent conscious motive for a crime such as a desire to obtain money or a wish to get rid of a person, unconscious motivations can rarely, if ever, be ruled out. A murderer is so completely dominated by his inner forces that apparently no means is too foul for achieving his goal, as seen in the following case.

A twenty-five-year-old man who had impregnated a girl planned to kill her. He met her in an isolated place. While having intercourse with her, he hit her in the face with a stone, then threw her down a steep cliff to her death. The manner in which he killed her showed his desperate desire to get rid of her and expressed the inadequacy in his mental make-up. His immediate motive is obvious—he did not want his life complicated by a pregnant girl. The psychiatric examination which followed indicated fear of his father, who was well esteemed in their community, but this was only part of the explanation, since later on it became apparent that he had always been jealous of his younger sister, who he felt had taken the affections of his mother away from him. His killing of the girl whom he had impregnated was an unconscious killing of his own sister.

An apparently senseless or purposeless murder is in reality incited by strong, although unconscious, motivations. If we could study the personality thoroughly enough, we would be able to trace these types of motivations in the great majority of cases. In a surrogate murder, for instance, where the actual victim is only a substitute for the intended one, the unconscious motivation remains unknown to the criminal. An illustration of this type of murder was the case of a taxi driver who murdered a passenger because of the latter's resemblance to the driver's father, whom he hated but dared not kill because of his strong inhibitory mechanism. This type of murder occurs more frequently than is generally realized.[15]

The unconscious motivation, which is by far the major driving force in a homicide and of which the culprit is usually unaware, is one of the reasons why he is unable to give a logical explanation for his act. The public is surprised, the judge baffled, but justice has to be meted out to the perpetrator.

This strong unconscious motivation in homicide is perhaps best described by Dostoyevsky in his masterpiece, *Crime and Punishment*, where a need for self-punishment called forth by a strong unconscious sense of guilt, based upon real or imagined wrongdoings, is the main motivation. It is beyond doubt that Dostoyevsky has touched upon a common trait in the hearts of human beings—a sense of guilt—in his haunting story.

As the reader will recall, a poor student, Raskolnikov, murders an old women moneylender and her sister. He is an intelligent man who has ingratiated himself with them to secure himself financially. This seems to show that he is a realistic person, aware of the everyday problems of life, though perhaps not completely scrupulous. However, beneath the surface he has wild fantasies —imagining that he is a superman who has a right to kill the two "worthless" women and take their money. He continues to play with these thoughts until he becomes preoccupied with them. He finally kills the women, taking no precautions against detection and unconsciously revealing his own crime, as we shall see.

After the murder he returns home and goes to sleep. When he awakens the next day, he carelessly throws away the purse which he has stolen. A few days afterwards he behaves peculiarly, unconsciously trying to attract attention to himself because of his feelings of guilt. Taken to the police station on a triviality, he mentions the murder, trying to link himself with it and thus betraying himself. Later he revisits the scene of the crime, and the police become suspicious of him. However, since they do not seem to be taking action and he is not receiving the punishment he unconsciously craves, he confesses the murder after a fashion, making them even more suspicious. A few days later he unburdens himself to one of his women acquaintances. So strong are his feelings of guilt that he believes another man has overheard this confession and fears now that this person will betray him. In this fear he roams around the city and enters a bar, where he unexpectedly encounters his fancied accuser. By unconsciously coming face to face with the man whom he thinks would denounce him, we again see how Raskolnikov tries to get himself punished. When finally he makes a complete confession of the murder and is sent to Siberia, he goes readily and willingly, welcoming punishment and relieved of his sense of guilt.

Homicide committed even in a psychosis, no matter how motiveless it seems, may have been brought about by unconscious elements, which, if uncovered, would establish the link between the mind of the murderer and his crime. I remember a man manifesting schizophrenic symptoms who murdered his wife after fifteen years of marriage. His story was, in short, that as a child his mother had left him and his father for another man. When he played with other children, they would tease him about being motherless, which caused him to shy away from them. Gradually he became more and more introverted and seclusive. When he was fifteen years old, he fell in love with a girl who later jilted him, although he insisted that she "loved" him. Shortly thereafter he became depressed, developed suicidal thoughts, and felt rejected and deserted by everyone. His father was advised to take him abroad, where he remained for six months and recovered somewhat. He then returned home, attended high school, and entered the university, which he left after only one year because of financial difficulties. With his father's help he got a job but felt unhappy and unsuited for it. He was on the verge of quitting when a girl grew interested in him and urged him to remain. She later became his wife. Shortly thereafter, however, he became depressed and complained particularly about the fact that he could no longer attend his former club at the university, of which he had been an active member since he had left school. He refused to go to work, stayed in bed for days, would not eat, and drank only water because, as he said, his thoughts had to be pure. Sometimes his mind apparently became less clouded and less preoccupied, and he would then read books, particularly about religion and philosophy.

During his illness, while he was at home, there were considerable complaints from his place of business, and his wife requested that he obtain a leave of absence, which he did. However, he became abusive to her, and she left him, but when he threatened to kill himself, she returned home. After a while, he seemed to recover, and he returned to work, but then he became more and suspicious that she was going to leave him again. He became preoccupied and seclusive; then "all things went dark," and one evening he fatally shot his wife.

This murder is a symbolic one in that he had unconsciously identified his wife with his mother, by whom he had always felt rejected. His wife was a woman who, although interested in him, was domineering, which made him fear her. Because she too had once "deserted" him and because he was dependent upon her, he became even more fearful of the possibility of her leaving again. As he felt more and more threatened, the disturbance of his ego increased, leading him into a psychosis.[16] His psychotic condition was a preparatory step in annihilating his victim. He unconsciously used it as a means of killing his wife, which he might never have been able to do had he not been in such a state, a point which is discussed in general by Philip R. Lehrman.[17]

As implicit in the formula for crime, criminal tendencies are more easily elicited when emotional or mental abnormalities are present in the person's make-up. Criminal activities and mental pathology are like two plants that derive their nutrition from the same soil. The frequency of gross mental abnormalities in criminals supports this analogy. Emotional and mental disorders are prevalent to a high degree in murderers, more so than in the general population of nonoffenders.

The electroencephalogram seems to be a helpful procedure in deciding whether or not a criminal is normal or abnormal. As a matter of fact, it is interesting to see that in some studies investigators have tried to correlate abnormalities of the electroencephalogram with crimes committed without any apparent motivation. D. Stafford-Clark and F. H. Taylor examined sixty-four prisoners facing charges of murder and found that a significant correlation existed between electroencephalographic abnormality and these crimes. Such mental abnormality, although it was not specific, manifested itself in over 70 percent of prisoners whose crimes seemed to have been carried out without motives, but who were otherwise clinically sane and normal. [18] It is unlikely that the correlation between an abnormal electroencephalogram and apparently motiveless violence is purely coincidental. Therefore, when a person manifests a great many personality traits that are abnormal in character, the electroencephalogram may be a decisive means of determining the true pathological quality of the person's mental disorder. It would seem that the electroencephalogram may be helpful for court purposes in obtaining a better measure of the personality traits that determine the presence of a psychosis and hence the state of responsibility.

Even if the individual is not considered insane in the legal sense, the discovery of pathological features in his personality indicates an underlying pathological development or process. This is a point of paramount importance. The criterion of a murderer's "sanity" or "insanity" should be based not only upon the murderer himself or his crime, but also upon the *connection* between the two, that is, the relationship between his mind and the accomplished act, although this may be difficult to ascertain.

It is not enough to say that the connection between the murderer and his act is clear when the corpse is discovered and he has confessed. We must go further if we are to find a deeper and more intimate relationship. We must learn the history of his childhood and adolescence, the exact method and manner in which his crime was carried out, and his behavior before, during and after his act. Thus in cases where a murderer appears normal, we must inquire whether previous to, at, or following the time that the crime was committed his emotions, thoughts, and will were deviated from the normal line to such an extent that they were of a pathological quality. If they were, then we must ask whether the presence of these characteristics was the main force which caused the murder.

The following case shows how Tom, a forty-two-year-old man, seemingly without any abnormal traits became a murderer. The immediate circumstances leading up to the murder of his wife are these: although he had already given his wife a major share of his salary, she demanded the rest of it; Tom gave her the money, turned around, seized an ax, and killed her.

A superficial examination might lead one to believe that Tom killed his wife merely because he was driven into a sudden rage over money. His history, however, revealed the following:

He had had a poor relationship with his father, who was a strict disciplinarian and against whom he rarely dared to assert himself. When he was nineteen years old Tom and his father had a heated argument when Tom told him that he had to marry a girl because she was pregnant.

His marriage was unsuccessful. He and his wife quarreled most of the time. She was a restless, nagging woman, who was inconsiderate, slovenly, and irresponsible. Many times Tom would have to take care of their four children while his wife visited her family. She always seemed to have some member of her family living with them, and once her sister and three children moved in. Tom's house always seemed to be overcrowded, and life became intolerable for him. A "war of nerves" existed.

Matters were not helped when Tom heard rumors that his wife was associating with another man, but he could not prove it. In any event the relationship between them became steadily worse. She took all the money he earned, complained about everything he did, made him the scapegoat for each trivial thing that occurred in the home, and thus increased his uncertainty and feelings of inferiority.

In the last months before the murder, his earnings were meager, and in order to support his family, he worked in a factory at night and drove a cab in the daytime. He was exhausted when he came home. On the day of the murder his wife started her usual nagging, accusing him of not adequately supporting her and the children. When she finally asked for his entire salary, Tom handed it over and then he killed her.

In Tom's case the murder was the result of long-accumulated bitterness and passive rebellion of masochistic coloring, of which he was partly aware but which he never expressed adequately. His hatred for his wife, which was partly unconscious and which was tied in with his hatred for his father, led him into killing her. Cognizant of the situation, the judge stated that the man did not act from a criminal will in the usual sense but from a greatly harassed and tortured mind. For this reason Tom was treated with leniency and received a short sentence.

From the psychiatric point of view, however, it is too naive to say that this man was tortured to the breaking point so that he committed murder. This is only a part of the story. The fact that murder seemed the only solution to his troubles indicates a basic inadequacy in his personality. Not only was he unhappy living with his wife, but he was unable to express any of his hostility toward her in an acceptable manner or to break away from her. Also from a psychiatric point of view the judge's statement that Tom did not act from "a criminal will" is not clear, for there is no such scientific entity as "a criminal will." In all probability individuals do not exist who perpetrate criminal acts without having experienced some kind of inner conflict more or less connected with some development of hate in childhood resulting in feelings of guilt and anxiety or in a self-punishing mechanism such as that seen in the above case. It is by uncovering the unconscious that we are able to trace the motivations of antisocial or criminal activities. When a man kills a person, it is safe to say that the reason existed within him long before he actually committed the homicide. The same protracted development also takes place in suicide, as Dr. Karl A. Menninger has pointed out.[19]

Another case is that of a thirty-three-year-old man who was

charged with having committed six murders in the course of three months. Because of the intricate personality make-up of the person and also because the crimes caused a state-wide sensation in the state where they occurred, it is worth while to examine the details. When I interviewed him in jail, I learned the following:

He was the second child in a family of four children, consisting of two boys and two girls. His brother had been in a mental hospital since 1951 suffering from a psychosis. His father was an alcoholic with little earning capacity and at one time was committed to a state mental hospital for about six months. The offender had a childhood and adult history of stealing, truancy, being AWOL while in the National Guard, vagrancy, burglary, assault, robbery, and murder, having spent altogether about fifteen years in state reform schools, reformatories, and prisons.

His first murder was committed in conjunction with robbery and with the help of his brother, who later informed on him and testified against him at the trial. The offender was sentenced to death but was released in 1954, after fifty-two months in prison, because his brother became psychotic, thus invalidating his testimony. When asked about how he felt while in prison waiting to die, he said: "After a while it didn't bother me, but then it became rather monotonous. I never intended to shoot him, but I was scared when he came after me. I never felt too much about it, except when I came home in the evening. I suddenly got the shakes, and it lasted for about half an hour. But after that, it didn't bother me at all."

The offender married a girl whom he met through the Lonely Hearts Club, and they shared an apartment with her father and brother. The marriage was marred by constant interference from the in-laws and by his wife's lack of knowledge about sex and her fear of and contempt for it. During that period he had several unskilled-labor jobs and did some boxing.

Then followed his series of murders, all connected with robbery. In one month he killed two people, and in the next month he fatally shot three men. In the following month he killed another man and was finally arrested. According to his own words regarding his reaction to his murders: "It didn't bother me. I didn't have any reaction."

He used to daydream about having a big car or a nice house or of being with a certain woman. He had had much sexual experience and was attracted to older women, while he showed a great deal of hostility toward his wife.

When asked about his crimes and why he committed them, he stated very frankly: "When society kills another human being, they don't think it's wrong. They wanted to kill me. They look on killing as if they enjoy it. Even the taxpayers enjoy the killing of other people, and the ministers enjoy it; they watch the execution. If the majority thinks it is right to kill, why couldn't I do it?" Asked what he thought would be the outcome of the trial, he answered flatly: "I'd rather be dead instead of going to prison."

When asked whether he felt that people were against him, he denied it, but he added, "I could never get a good job because of my previous record." Questioned about his work, he stated that he could usually get about $15 a day when he was working with a moving company. However, when he moved to where his wife wanted to live, he earned only $40 a week and "Who could get along on that?"

He stated that he had confessed to the crimes for which he was charged but did so only because of his mother. "If it hadn't been for my mother, I wouldn't have admitted it. It was the other fellow who had the gun. I took the gun from him."

"Is there anything wrong with you?" I asked.

He replied: "There must be something wrong with me. Maybe I have no conscience. It's funny, though. These things don't bother me. I never was afraid."

"Do you have much feeling for your family?" I queried.

"I have feelings only for my mother. Mother is the only one who can make me feel like crying. She takes it very badly. I want to die instead of doing life in prison. My wife didn't want to move to the town where my mother lives, and I wanted to see my mother." I asked him whether he didn't return to his home town in order to carry out his crimes. He stated that it was exciting, but "I really wanted to see my mother."

I continued: "Why did you kill when you were going out bur-
glarizing?"

His retort: "I didn't want to be identified. I really wanted to
die rather than be in prison. I remember," he continued, "that
they were trying to pass a bill here against capital punishment.
I was sitting in prison at that time, and I prayed that they
wouldn't pass it." While he said these last words, he smiled wist-
fully.

The defendant's background showed that he grew up without
any control or guidance from his parents. He showed early signs
of emotional instability by stealing and playing hooky. His vocational history is that of an unskilled worker. However, he was
the type given very much to pleasure and showed very little endurance for work. He therefore went on long trips all over the
country, hitch-hiking. He was shiftless, like a hobo, and whatever he undertook was a failure.

He did not seem to have any interests, hobbies, or friends, and
his relationship to his family, except to his mother, had been
superficial. Apparently he had not indulged in alcohol or drugs.
His history of antisocial behavior appeared to begin from the age
of seven. Thus his behavior disorders, expressed in impulsiveness,
truancy, and stealing, showed up early.

The psychological examination revealed that the defendant was
oriented as to time and space. He appeared somewhat restless,
moody, and quiet but showed no anxieties. He seemed to welcome
the interview but showed little spontaneity in his answers and
was cautious in replying. At times there was disharmony between
his verbal and emotional expression, particularly when he talked
about his murders. His voice was well modulated, and there were
no speech abnormalities. He was alert and oriented. His recent
memory seemed good. There were no illusions present, and no
hallucinations could be ascertained. Although he admitted that
people had treated him fairly well, he resented that his record
had kept him from getting a good job. When he was told that he
himself had committed the crimes and no one else and that he
therefore had such a bad record, he still continued to say: "Well,
my bad record prevented me from getting a good job." On that

point he did not seem to have any emotional insight, nor did he seem to have any conscious feelings of guilt. His repeated statements that he wanted to die instead of being imprisoned might indicate that he unconsciously wanted to be severely punished. When asked about his crimes, particularly about his murders, he did not admit that he had done anything wrong.

In view of this distorted thinking it is obvious that the defendant was laboring under the delusion that he was permitted to kill, since in his own mind he strongly believed that society had that right. No obsessions or compulsions could be ascertained.

The conclusions drawn from the examination were that the defendant was an individual who had lived under very deprived emotional, intellectual, and financial conditions since his earliest childhood. Because he received little guidance at home, having a drunken father and a weak mother, he developed a strong anti-social pattern of behavior early in his life, which increased as time went by, culminating in the series of murders with which he was then charged. Two precipitating events to the senseless killings might have been his marriage, which seemed to have been a rather unhappy experience for him, and the fact that he sat in prison for fifty-two months, waiting to be executed. No doubt the latter, coupled with the fact that he had previously spent time in prison, reformatories, and state reform schools, all tending to develop in him an attitude of callousness and hopelessness, of unreality and paranoid reaction, had been an instrumental factor in leading him to murder. The crimes, whereby he shot the persons he had burglarized or robbed, can be understood because he unconsciously wished to die. By killing these people, he made certain that when caught he would receive the maximum penalty. This is the reason why he himself stated that he preferred to die rather than sit in prison.

Within himself he harbored strong resentment and hostility toward his father and brother, toward the latter particularly because he testified against him after his first murder. Because both his father and brother had been declared psychotic (the brother still being in a state hospital), the defendant consciously and unconsciously did not want to be in the same category and therefore preferred to be antisocial rather than mentally sick. In him were ingrained strong constitutional elements of a diseased mind, as indicated by his father's and brother's psychoses. He tried to hide his mental disturbance by not showing any remorse or feelings of guilt for his crimes. Then too, the fact that he felt strongly that society was against him anyhow tended to ameliorate his guilt feelings.

In view of his previous criminal history, his lack of reality, and his inability to distinguish between right and wrong, he had developed a system of delusions, which brought me to the conclusion that the defendant was suffering from a schizophrenic reaction, paranoid type. For this reason, and since he also had to be considered as dangerous, my recommendation was that he be transferred to a mental hospital. The jury found him guilty of murder in the first degree, and he was sentenced to death, but his case is still under appeal.

The cases mentioned above may show how difficult it is to decide whether a person is to be considered "legally sane" or not. It is safe to say that unconscious elements play an overwhelming part in homicide, and if uncovered, they will provide us with material enabling us to establish the dynamic connection between the killer's mind and his homicide. As the individual manifests his actual and potential traits in a certain pattern, so this very pattern is reflected in the homicide committed. Though circumstance and situation may give the murder a certain color, nevertheless, the motivation which brought it about lends it a certain character which makes it possible to a large extent not only to classify the killer, but also to distinguish between the different types of homicide.

All murderers may be considered to be chronic. Depending upon the extent of their inner conflicts, their homicide may be divided into the following two groups.

SYMPTOMATIC MURDER

In a symptomatic murder the murderer kills because of an inner conflict caused by hatred for a person during his childhood, which may be unconscious in nature. The homicide takes place because of the murderer's distorted sex drive or because of his aggressive drive. In this type of murderer we often find strong emotions of jealousy, which, by the way, is a powerful motivating force in murder. Many times, the background is frustrated love caused by a real or imagined triangle situation. The psychological mechanism behind such a homicide consciously starts with the murderer feeling that his self-esteem and prestige are injured. Because he believes that he has a right to possess a particular woman, he becomes exceedingly jealous if she seems to, or does, turn to someone else. The varying direction of homicidal jealousy may often give a hint as to the underlying personality conflict. A young man will more often kill the woman of the triangle because of the injury she has done his pride, but an older man usually kills the rival, particularly if the rival is a younger person, because he may feel sexually inadequate and impotent and therefore inferior to the other man, of which he may not even be consciously aware. By killing his partner or his rival, his self-esteem or feeling of potency are restored.

Often a man's conscious or unconscious love for his mother hampers or prevents a satisfactory union between his wife and himself. He pays more attention to his mother than to his wife, creating a feeling of jealousy in the latter that may lead to the wife's killing her mother-in-law. The reverse situation, in which a mother kills her daughter-in-law, also occurs. This type of crime is an expression of hatred and jealousy having its roots in the childhood Oedipus conflict of the woman involved.[20]

An example of a situation where murder was the result of jealousy due to a strong mother attachment was the case of a fifty-year-old teacher who killed an eighteen-year-old girl and then made an unsuccessful attempt at suicide. It seems that the girl and he lived in the same building. He loved her, but apparently she rejected his attentions. Later he discovered that she had a boy friend, and because he consciously or unconsciously believed that he possessed her and that she should always belong to him, in the same way as his mother had always been attached to him, he became extremely jealous. For fear of losing her, he murdered her.

This man had completely identified the girl with his mother, which he later came to realize. Losing the girl to him meant losing his mother, something he could not endure. Thus this too was a surrogate, or substitute, murder.

Although murders occur very frequently as the result of a holdup or robbery, they are connected more often than realized with some form of abnormal sex activity. For example, they may occur during a sex offense, such as rape, or as the result of one, such as homosexuality. A famous case of the latter was the murder of a young boy by Richard Loeb and Nathan Leopold in 1924.

The case is particularly significant because for the first time in the history of medical jurisprudence the court paved the way for a completely scientific investigation of the mental conditions of murderers. Only the most pertinent facts are given here.

Richard Loeb came from a highly intelligent and well-to-do family. His father's first cousin had developed a definite psychosis at eighteen years of age and was committed to the Elgin State Hospital. While Richard's grandfather had been quite abusive of his children and beat them severely, Richard's father was lenient. His mother, who was very active in club work, left most of Richard's upbringing to a very strict governess. In order to escape punishment, he lied. Because of the governess's rigid discipline and supervision he was far ahead in school and was later the youngest person to graduate from the University of Michigan. Richard and the governess were very attached to each other, and he identified himself with her very strongly. This, plus the way she brought him up, tended to make him effeminate. Later he admitted that when he left her care, at fifteen years of age, he "broke loose."

When only a young child, Richard began to steal money and "pick up" things in stores whenever the opportunity presented itself, taking them even if he did not need them. As he grew older, he filched liquor from a relative, began to steal cars, and also set fire to some shacks—all in becoming "hard-boiled," egocentric, and developing a moral callousness. Throughout his childhood and early adolescence he had a vivid imagination, often daydreaming of himself as the greatest criminal of the century.

Nathan Leopold's family was also well-to-do. His grandfather was an alert and intellectual man. On his father's side there had been two cases of psychosis of the paranoid type. His mother died of a kidney disease, and Nathan was raised by three consecutive governesses. He repeatedly had the same vivid fantasy, which started when he was five years old, in which he would alternately imagine himself as a king or a slave. He identified himself with the king but usually preferred to play the role of the slave. He made rapid progress in school, entering the University of Michigan at sixteen where he studied psychology, ornithology, and various languages—German, French, Russian, Greek, Latin, Spanish, and Sanskrit. He worshiped his mother's memory, his aunt, and the Madonna, which might account for his lack of interest in girls. In all probability he never had a true love affair.

Leopold was a highly gifted, narcissistic person, who during childhood and adolescence became fixated at a pregenital level. He repressed his feelings, especially his heterosexual ones, and, because of his particular mental endowment, concentrated on intellectual matters. Although on the surface he appeared cold and aloof, he was not devoid of emotions, but he could not find any outlet for them.

Loeb too was an intelligent, intellectual, and narcissistic person who seemed to have a cold nature. His personality was marked by the strict upbringing of his governess, by his strong attachment to her, by feelings of inferiority, and by an apparent lack of feelings of guilt. His psychosexual development not only seemed to have stopped at an infantile level, but also took an abnormal deviation. To a certain extent he apparently became sexually impotent, for which reason he boasted of having many affairs with girls.

Nathan Leopold and Richard Loeb met. If one is fatalistic, one can say that their meeting was not by chance. Nevertheless, it was their undoing.

Because of the many similarities between them—their peculiar upbringing, intellectual endowment, repression of sexual feelings, and vivid fantasies—a warm friendship developed, one whose basis was homosexual in nature. Leob, apparently the stronger, took the lead. Leopold regarded him as the more intelligent and practically idolized him. In fact, in time he became so drawn to Loeb that he became his slave, thus fitting Loeb into his slave-king fantasy.

He had vivid imaginings about sex, and it is probable also that his dreams were strongly sexual in content. These fantasies and desires were so powerful and yet so repressed that his sexual drive became twisted, leading to strong homoerotic tendencies, which we can see by his own words about Loeb: "I almost completely identified myself with him." Here we find a psychological identification, indicating the firm love relationship between the two. Their homosexual activity is substantiated by their reported sexual relations with each other, which even occurred in the presence of a fraternity brother, but Loeb's abnormal sexual development could hardly be satisfied by homosexual methods, and his distorted sex drive had to find another outlet.

The murder is not the only crime the boys committed together. In November, 1923, with the aid of Leopold, Loeb planned a return to Ann Arbor to rob his fraternity house. They succeeded in the robbery and drove back to Chicago without being detected.

Further proof of Leopold's subjection to Loeb may be seen by his frank admission that he participated in the murder as part of his friendship for, and to prove himself to, Loeb.

Loeb's inner conflict over his abnormal drives, and particularly his actual homosexual relationship with Leopold, depressed him to the point of wanting to commit suicide. As a matter of fact, we can say that the murder was an indirect form of suicide, a psychic killing of himself, so to speak, for he consciously or unconsciously expected his own death as a penalty for the crime.[21] This also reveals his wish for punishment, emanating from strong, unresolved feelings of guilt. That he desired a great deal of punishment is also evidenced by the fact that even as a young boy he imagined himself in jail; further, after his confession of the murder, he apparently went happily into the prison cell and felt gratified in being deprived of his liberty, so precious to the normal human being. Leopold apparently also behaved in this manner.

In view of their strong homoerotic tendencies and unconscious desire for self-punishment, it seems rather strange that during the trial the murder was called a "senseless, useless, purposeless, and motiveless act." To my mind the case clearly demonstrates the relationship between the murderers' personalities and their act. The fact that the boys undressed their victim from the waist down and did not bury him until many hours after the murder indicates a possibility that some sex acts might have taken place after the murder. The method of killing their victim and the burial reveal the unconscious sexual character of the crime. Loeb chose the tool; Leopold, the receptacle (the same roles they themselves played in their relationship with each other). Then acid was poured over the face and sex organs, showing confusion about their own sex and probably a desire to be a girl instead. Finally the body was dragged through the swamps, pushed into a dark tube (a cistern), and buried under a railway track—all psychiatric symbols bringing out their strong death wish.

Taking into consideration the dynamic connection between the murderers' make-ups and their act, the conclusion was reached that the crime was a product of two morbid and abnormal, though not psychotic, minds, although the greater responsibility for the crime was Loeb's. The main point was that they were considered dangerous to society and had to be removed from it, which was accomplished by their imprisonment.

In the last few years the incidence of murders committed by adolescents has increased. According to Warren Stearns many of these homicides have taken place with obscure motivations.[22] However, it is difficult to accept this explanation, and, in fact, it is probably more fitting to say that the motivations in the cases described by Mr. Stearns were quite obvious, though often unconscious. The adolescents appear to have been "model" boys, and "model" boys usually are more inhibited than the average adolescent. Their crimes seem to have been expressions of a sudden release of sexual forces. Unfortunately, the cases given do not permit a conclusion, since the histories of these juvenile murderers are incomplete. From my own experience with juvenile murderers, I have found that there always was a motivation, unconscious though it might have been.

Although it is difficult to differentiate between homicides

which are exclusively due to the sex drive and those which are exclusively due to the aggressive drive because these drives are so intertwined, we find that when a homicide takes place under the influence of alcohol, it is the aggressive drive which comes particularly to the fore.

There is no doubt that alcohol plays an important role in a large number of assaults. Sheldon and Eleanor Glueck found that 39.4 percent of men in reformatories had used alcohol to excess.[23] In Norway it was found that 90 percent of those who committed assaults were alcoholics, and 80 percent of the total were intoxicated at the time of the assault. Of those accused of negligent manslaughter 92 percent were found to be intoxicated. Of those who committed murder 60 percent were intoxicated.[24] In a study of 200 murderers Cassity found that alcohol was a precipitating factor in approximately 50 percent of the total number of cases.[25]

Alcohol as a contributive factor in a murder may be viewed from three angles: the perpetrator's usual tendencies and behavior, his behavior during a usual alcoholic spree, and his behavior at the time of the homicide. The fact that a murderer is intoxicated does not mean that the homicide is senseless. The tendencies were within the person all along; the alcohol probably merely served to release the inhibitions or whatever superego control might have existed otherwise. Also an alcoholic may show the same pattern of behavior at the time of his homicide as in previous sprees, the only difference being that in the latter instances his behavior was not so extreme.

Alcoholic intoxication may not be only a contributive factor but even a causative one in homicide, as shown in the following case. A twenty-year-old boy who was inebriated was brandishing a knife in front of his friend, who was also drunk. The boy lurched forward and by accident struck the friend between the upper vertebrae, cutting the spinal cord and causing immediate death. Had he been sober, in all probability no crime would have been committed.

It must be stressed that the importance of alcohol as a contributory or causative factor in a murderer differs for the one-time offender and the recidivist. A first offense, even one as serious as homicide, may be attributed to alcohol if it is found that the perpetrator was intoxicated at the time of the crime. Quite different is the situation for recidivists. Those with a previous criminal record who commit homicide while intoxicated probably would have murdered without being intoxicated, for they have a tendency to act out their aggressions.

Sometimes a case is complicated by the fact that the murderer suffers from such abnormalities as epilepsy, hyperinsulinism, or encephalitis lethargica, which may serve as his excuse for the homicide. However, each case can only be judged by its own merits. Frequently, for example, when an offender suffers from epilepsy, the claim is made that he committed the crime because he was epileptic. Before such a conclusion can be justified, it must be clearly established that epilepsy was the cause of the criminal act.

At times we find that a murder stems from a physical defect. It is an old axiom that a healthy mind can exist only in a healthy body. A diseased or deformed body may in the course of time affect an individual's behavior and result in criminal activity. In the *Iliad* Homer described a hunchback, Tersites, who because of his malformation and monstrosity was repulsive and who, in trying to assert himself, chose the methods of deceit and fraud. Famous in classical literature is Shakespeare's description of Richard III, whose hideous crimes were perpetrated in revenge for his being an ugly misfit. Shakespeare's conception of how a cripple's mental attitude can be affected by his bodily deformity is revealing:

> But I, that am not shap'd for sportive tricks,
> Nor made to court an amorous looking-glass;
> I, that am rudely stampt, and want love's majesty
> To strut before a wanton ambling nymph;
> I, that am curtail'd of this fair proportion,
> Cheated of feature by dissembling nature,
> Deform'd, unfinisht, sent before my time
> Into this breathing world, scarce half made up,
> And that so lamely and unfashionable
> That dogs bark at me, as I halt by them;—

Why, I, in this weak piping time of peace,
Have no delight to pass away the time,
Unless to see my shadow in the sun
And descant on my own deformity:
And therefore, since I cannot prove a lover,
To entertain these fair well-spoken days,
I am determined to prove a villain,
And hate the idle pleasures of these days.
Plots have I laid, inductions dangerous,
By drunken prophecies, libels, and dreams,
To set my brother Clarence and the king
In deadly hate the one against the other.   Act I, Scene 1

We may say that each bodily disease or bodily defect may tend to produce a change in the mental attitude of a person. This inclination may disappear when the disease vanishes, but it may also develop further, particularly in the case where the disease leads to a long-time or permanent physical defect. Here lies a psychosomatic problem.

When a homicide occurs as the result of a physical disease or deformity of the body, the dynamic connection between the murderer and his crime may be difficult to trace because of the complexity of the elements involved. But it is easier to ascertain such a connection if the perpetrator becomes consciously aware that his mental attitude is affected by his bodily disease or defect. Apropos of this is an interesting experiment conducted by Ackerson on about 2,000 boys and 1,000 girls with feelings of inferiority. It was found that actual physical, mental, and social inferiority did not give rise per se to inferiority attitudes. Rather one's keen awareness of such defects and subsequent feelings of inferiority are largely due to environmental factors.[26]

Whether or not a physically defective person turns to criminal acts may depend upon the degree of his bodily deformity. Also he is particularly inclined to commit sex crimes because he cannot readily secure a partner to fulfill these needs. Even if he does find one, he may be involved in difficulties due to his deformity.

It is my view that where an obvious bodily defect is present in a murderer, we usually find an immediate relationship between him and his act. Such a man will not readily speak about himself, but once induced to do so, he will reveal the extent to which his deformity has influenced his mind and produced a deviation from sound judgment, forming a basis for the dynamic connection between him and the homicide.

MANIFEST (ESSENTIAL) MURDER

In a manifest or essential murder the murderer directs his crime primarily against society. Such a murderer comes from that bracket of society which identifies itself with crime in general and homicide in particular. In this group are included two types: the profit murder and the murder with unrecognized motivations.

Persons who commit murder for profit act in accordance with their own special concept of life and the rules of society. As a result of this faulty concept, murder is condoned by their whole personality—by their ego and superego alike. The motive of personal gain is obviously present, as is seen in murder "rings."

Illustrative of such a murder "ring" was Murder Incorporated, a gang of racketeers, many of whom were professional murderers, who operated in the 1930s in Brooklyn.[27]

Interestingly enough, homicide was not the original purpose. Murder Incorporated started during the prohibition era, with its members distributing liquor; later its scope was broadened to include other illegal activities, such as prostitution, gambling, and extortion. It became a very powerful force by owning night clubs and gaining control of certain unions through the extortion of money. It was during that time that murder was incorporated as a "legitimate" way to deal with competitors or other troublesome persons. Murder Incorporated, which among criminals was called "The Combination," was organized in Brooklyn but had branches in Chicago, Detroit, and San Francisco. While Benjamin ("Bugsy") Siegel, later killed, was dictator on the West Coast, Charles ("Lucky") Luciano, later deported to Italy, and Louis ("Lepke") Buchalter, later electrocuted in Sing Sing, operated in New York. According to the April 1, 1951, issue of the New York *Times* and to the Kefauver Crime Investigating Committee, the leaders of Murder Incorporated were Joe Adonis, Abe ("Kid Twist") Reles, who died in 1941 after "falling" from a window, and Albert Anastasia, fatally shot while sitting in a barber chair.

It has been estimated that between that 1931 and 1940 Murder Incorporated killed 63 men in the New York area alone and that even more people were murdered by the gang members in Chicago, Detroit, and San Francisco. The victims were usually men whom the gangsters considered potential informers. The manner in which these people were killed was infamous. Some were buried alive in sand; some were killed with ice picks; others were burned alive. One was found at the bottom of a river with his feet encased in cement. Sometimes law-abiding citizens were the victims.

The breakup of this gang came in about 1941, when Reles was arrested and confronted with a gangster who was going to inform on him. Reles promised to tell all he knew about the gang if he himself were given leniency. Several theories exist about his death. Even though he was guarded day and night by six policemen while in custody, it is not certain whether he fell to his death or was pushed. It is thought that he may have been killed in order to eliminate the State's case against Anastasia.

Important as it is to uncover the operation of such a gang, it is more important, perhaps, to study the psychiatric-psychological make-ups of its members. Very likely most or all were at least antisocial. To what extent character disturbances or neurotic or psychotic conditions were present we do not know, since none of these men were examined psychiatrically, even when in jail or prison.

Under the classification "murder with unrecognized motivations" belong homicides in which the murderer is undetected and no obvious motivation can be seen, or in which the murder is surrounded by such a complexity of factors that the motivation cannot be determined.

From the psychiatric and criminological points of view, it is imperative that every person accused of murder or any other serious crime be psychiatrically examined by a qualified psychiatrist appointed by the state before the trial. (The details as to how this examination is carried out will be given later.) The purpose is to find the predominating features in the personality structure which made it possible to determine the psychodynamics of the personality forces, the course of events, and whether or not the person is psychotic. We must also keep in mind the projections, phobias, and compulsions which arise as a disguise in the criminal's unconscious defense reactions against the aggressions.

Psychiatrists are sometimes accused of "sentimentality" in regard to criminals because they do not make moral pronouncements. For example, when a murderer behaves in a peculiarly callous and unfeeling manner, the public feels that his crime is all the more heinous, but the psychiatrist sees this as a characteristic way of handling anxiety. The following cases illustrate the point. In one case a man killed his mother, put her body into a suitcase, and then went to a movie with his girl friend. In another, after having killed his girl friend by throwing her down a steep cliff, a man went to a stadium and played football. These murderers continued their activities as if nothing had happened, and when they were eventually caught and questioned, the lay examiner was puzzled and shocked by their apparent indifference.

The psychiatrist recognizes such behavior as a pathological means of relieving conscious and unconscious tension. This psychological technique of finding relief from feelings of guilt by repudiating responsibility for the criminal act is commonly seen in convicted murderers serving life sentences, in whom the motivation for concealment and self-preservation often plays a greater part than it did before they were apprehended. On the surface they appear to be no different from the other inmates, but actually they live in the past with all their past hopes and wishes. Their inner lives often take on the form of reality they knew outside of prison so that emotionally and mentally they continue to live as they did before the crime. By this rationalization, which approaches a self-deception, they obliterate the crime from their mind, thus easing the discomfort of incarceration. When this type of offender is examined psychiatrically, his defenses rise even further, thus creating even more rationalization. Such prisoners frequently offer the examiner transparent rationalizations concerning their motivations and acts, which are more in the nature of a true self-deception than a conscious self-protective measure.[28]

CHAPTER XI

Psychiatric-Psychological Examination of the Offender

In examining an offender, the psychiatrist and psychoanalyst are concerned with three problems: diagnosis, treatment, and prognosis. The approach should always be a broad one, that is, the offender should be observed and studied as a total personality—a socio-psycho-biological unit—and the results should be interpreted with this same broad outlook in mind.

Fortunately, of late there has been increasing recognition of the fact that a psychiatric-psychological examination of an offender is desirable if a proper disposition of his case is to be expected. Futhermore, our system of probation, parole, and indeterminate sentence, along with the rapid development of special courts for juveniles and psychiatric treatment and rehabilitation, clearly shows that we have made some progress.

Since the examiner's aim is to understand the criminal's behavior and his motivations, he must have a thorough knowledge of human behavior, based upon psychological insight, training, and experience. It cannot be too greatly emphasized that psychiatric and psychoanalytic practice is an art. Psychological insight can be acquired only after long and patient experience. As a painter elicits the peculiarities and characteristics of his subject more by intuition than by formal learning, so must the psychiatrist and psychoanalyst penetrate to the depths of the mind. In examining the criminal, this is doubly important and difficult, consequently requiring heightened keenness, perception, intuition, and experience. The psychiatrist who believes he can become an expert in psychiatric criminology merely by learning an outline would do well to recall that no human being is a "case" which can be fitted into a scheme but rather is a living entity comprising a definite and individual pattern of behavior characteristics.

Diagnosis includes discovering the relationship between the offender's mental make-up and his emotional and biological development during childhood and adolescence. It also involves ascertaining the relationship between his mental make-up and his crime, for herein lies the discovery of the causative factors which prompted his offense. Last but not least its purpose is to determine whether there is anything pathologically abnormal with the offender. Only when all of this is known can the psychiatrist and psychoanalyst hope to treat the criminal effectively.

However, there is an important difficulty, which was recognized over half a century ago by Charcot, when he exclaimed: "Normal or abnormal—I dare not say where is the border!" And he was right. Sometimes we see an apparently normal individual suddenly display criminal behavior of an aberrant nature and then just as suddenly resume his conventional character. Is this man normal or abnormal? Or think of an offender who has violent mental conflicts which at times threaten to split his personality but who apparently is still able to control his mental condition by his capacity for performing organized, logical actions. Is he normal or abnormal?

We are closer to a true understanding when we realize that so-called abnormal psychological manifestations are merely exaggerations or distortions of normal ones. Abnormal mental phenomena differ from the normal only in degree and not in kind in both criminals and noncriminals. When a person shows a disintegrated personality, it is easy to recognize that he is psychotic, but it may be difficult to determine the mental make-up if his personality traits are so masked that they render no explicit clue to his mental condition.

In the same way that logical thinking and social behavior have a meaning to the normal person, so does incoherency have a meaning to the psychotic person and criminal behavior and distorted reasoning a meaning to the offender. Thus if we have enough knowledge of the offender's background, his life situation, and his mental make-up, we are able to uncover his personality traits and arrive at an understanding of the way he thinks and feels about himself and society.

The variety of personality traits and the immense number of constellations they can form make it obvious that there can hardly be two individuals alike in their mental make-up. Any apparent similarity will most likely be superficial. Therefore, the psychiatric-psychological examination must be carried out with a view toward individualization. Failure to observe this point would only lead the examiner, consciously or unconsciously, to adopt a preconceived view of the offender's personality make-up and motivation for the crime, according to a similar case he has seen before, which would undoubtedly be wrong.

Under no circumstances is a snap diagnosis justified, even if the psychiatrist is forced to hurry through an examination or is pressured to give his opinion based upon an examination performed under unfavorable conditions. No psychiatrist, psychoanalyst, or any other physician should render his opinion before he is satisfied that the examination is complete. This is an essential point because the examiner must not only try to explain psychological phenomena but in many cases must also try to alleviate pathological mental conditions. If he is to alter the personality make-up of a patient or an offender, it is absolutely necessary that he know the personality structure in detail.

Psychiatry is a science comprised of approved concepts and laws which are based upon the idea that there are certain intellectual, emotional, and behavioral characteristics in the individual that follow a pattern and can be observed and recorded. Not all of an offender's patterns and reactions can be measured exactly, but they can all be observed and written down. The order of collected data may vary and the procedure may change in some details from case to case, but a certain standard has to be followed, varying only with the experience of the psychiatrist. Thus if the psychiatrist is familiar with the different aspects of examination, he may be able to estimate some facts without scrutinizing them meticulously, while other elements may demand careful exploration. If he is in doubt, all facts will have to be checked. The usual procedure during an examination is to take notes of the information given by the offender and also to record his own observations. However, the examiner should always inquire whether the offender objects to this procedure. If so, the information will have to be retained by the examiner and written down immediately after the examination has been completed.

Unfortunately, the extensiveness of the psychiatric examination depends not only upon the examiner himself, but also in a large measure upon the policy laid down by the different courts. This policy is determined by the law of the different states or by the reason for the examination. Sometimes the examiner may be called upon to give the result of an examination after only one interview with an offender in jail. In other instances the court will give him an opportunity to observe a case over a considerable period, but this is more often true only in larger cities.

It is well for the examiner to remember that he has no legal right whatsoever to propose to the court how an examination should be performed satisfactorily. However, if the examination was unsatisfactory because it was made under unfavorable conditions, he should point this out clearly in his testimony. Much of the handling of such a situation depends upon the examiner's discretion and versatility. Should the court allow him to choose the place for the examination, he may suggest the jail, prison, or hospital, or he may immediately propose his office if this has not been ruled out. It is necessary that he be asked by the proper authorities to perform his examination. As the situation now stands, the attorney for the defendant will frequently secure a psychiatrist to examine his client, who has perhaps already been examined by the district attorney's psychiatrist. The best arrangement would be for the psychiatrists in all court cases to be appointed by the state from a panel of qualified experts. This would provide competent examiners and also would prevent irrelevant factors from interfering with the findings. It would also provide a further safeguard for the public.

The question has been taken up by a commission appointed by Governor Harriman in 1957 in New York in connection with the drafting of a modern code for the definition of criminal insanity as used in New York courts. Some members, particularly Professor Herbert Wechsler of Columbia University and myself, have come to feel that court-appointed psychiatrists would be able to render an impartial opinion and would eliminate battles in the courts between psychiatrists of the opposing parties. At this writing the proposal has met with some resistance from other members of the commission who emphasize the "difficulties of the method which exerts compulsion on defendants to submit to an examination by a court-appointed expert involved in their guilt or innocence in the crime."

It should be noted that New York statutes now make full provision for a system whereby the court designates a psychiatrist to examine the defendant when insanity at the time of the charge and capacity to stand trial are at issue. However, the defendant also has a right to appoint his own psychiatrist. At the present time the subject of court-appointed psychiatric experts is still under study by the commission.

Since it is impossible to examine all offenders, which ones should be given psychiatric examinations? With a few exceptions, there are at present no rules regarding such procedures. As has been pointed out, in the course of a trial the court may have the defendant examined psychiatrically if there is any doubt regarding his mental condition. The Court of General Sessions in New York City requires that all offenders be given a psychiatric examination between trial and sentence, and if it is deemed necessary, a psychological one also. These reports, as well as probation reports, accompany the offender to the institution or prison. If the mental condition of the defendant necessitates psychiatric observation, he is placed in the Psychiatric Division of Bellevue Hospital for a period of from four to six weeks.

The fact that the psychiatric-psychological examination takes place between the trial and the sentencing is a serious drawback, for the mental status of the offender may be quite different then from what it was before the trial. The proper procedure would be, of course, to have the criminal examined before the trial.

As yet, a common rule for examining offenders has not been worked out for the different jurisdictions of the United States. Because of this, the type of offenders examined depends upon the psychological insight of the probation officers, the prosecuting attorney, or the court. Sometimes the court may be able to see some mental abnormality in the defendant which will necessitate psychiatric examination. In other cases the counsel for the defense will require that an examination be made.

There is no doubt that to a certain extent the type of crime expresses a certain personality make-up. This fact then should be utilized in the selection of those offenders who ought to be examined psychiatrically, as long as we do not have a rule that provides psychiatric examination for all offenders. In any event, of those offenders without obvious psychotic manifestations, there are two types who should be psychiatrically examined without exception. They are murderers and sex offenders, many of whom reveal pathological symptoms. In a great number of these, upon deeper examination, we find perversion, neurotic character disorders, borderline intelligence, senility, psychoses, and alcoholism.

How important a thorough examination of this nature is may be shown by a case to which the Danish State Attorney, Harald Petersen, has referred.[1] A laborer was charged with having killed his wife and one of their children, the apparent motive having been jealousy. He received good reports from family friends and from his employer, who said that he was normal in every respect. In fact, he worked for a big industrial concern, where he operated a crane, an occupation requiring a great deal of care and caution. He also managed to convey the impression of normality even at the trial. However, because of the cold-bloodedness of the homicide, he was given a psychiatric examination, which revealed that he was mentally retarded—a moron. He was transferred to a special institution for this type of offender.

In addition it would be most beneficial for offenders who commit other types of serious offenses to be psychiatrically examined. Their acts may have been due to some abnormality of the mind, and every effort should be made to prevent any recurrence.

Criminals past middle age should also be examined if the circumstances warrant it. There is no doubt that the bodily infirmities related to old age may cause difficult social conditions for a person because he is no longer able to compete with other men as he had previously. Since senility may be accompanied by a certain degree of intellectual deterioration, poor ability to concentrate, poor memory, and rigid and narrow-minded thoughts, which may be more pronounced than is readily surmised—all changes brought about, on the whole, by such physical ailments of old age as hardening of the arteries in the brain and senile alterations in the brain cells—it is understandable how an old person may react abnormally and therefore behave antisocially or criminally.

It is a must for the very young, as well as the old, to be psychiatrically examined for the sake of early rehabilitation and reeducation. The same applies to persons who commit their first crime at the age of thirty or forty because a sudden change of behavior at this age may reflect an abnormal mind. These examinations will uncover mental abnormality in a great many offenders who are not legally insane.

Before beginning an examination it is most important that the examiner secure and read in advance all data available about the offender from the police and court records. If the offender has previously been in a hospital or institution, a record should be obtained. Too often the psychiatrist starts examining the criminal knowing little or nothing about his crime or his earlier behavior. If the examiner is unaware of the offender's past history, he will in all probability plunge into questions which may upset the offender or make him resentful or hostile from the very start. However, if the examiner knows the salient facts in advance, it will in most cases be easier to establish an amicable and congenial atmosphere.

The examiner must try to put the offender at ease, gain his confidence, and acquaint himself with the offender's concepts. He should therefore start his interview by talking about other subjects. Then, after a few opening sentences, he must tell the offender the reason for the examination. Most offenders are suspicious of any type of examination, whether conducted by a medical doctor, a policeman, or anyone else. A murderer, or someone accused of another serious crime, will even more likely be on guard and distrustful of the examiner, who must therefore use insight, based on scientific study, in observing and recording the intellectual, emotional, and behavioral pattern. Very often murderers and other serious offenders rationalize their behavior, and they are more apt to do this if they are not told the reason for the questioning. This is particularly true if the sentence has already been imposed; the examiner is able to elicit only rationalizations which the offender believes are beneficial to himself.

Assuming that the psychiatrist has read all the available facts about the crime and the offender, he proceeds to obtain the case history. The best method of obtaining a psychiatric history is through free associative anamnesis. In this procedure the defendant is asked to describe his life and experiences and is permitted to talk freely about whatever comes to his mind. Whenever a point in his own emotional attitude is brought up, a relevant question may be put to him, which often elicits new free associations. It is well to remember that an offender or a patient may have given much thought to his life before being examined, and if he is permitted to tell his experiences in his own way, the psychiatrist may obtain new insight into his life situation and into the motivation for his crime. Such examination, however, presupposes that the offender has established a positive attitude toward the examiner, i.e., that a positive emotional relationship—transference—has been obtained.

Using the method of free associative anamnesis enables the examiner to obtain the facts about the offender's family and medical history, emotional attitudes and relationships, sexual experiences, and criminal history in an indirect, and often more illuminating, way. By following the emotional stream of the offender, the examiner is able to bring out the offender's feelings which, consciously or unconsciously, are the basis for his attitudes and antisocial behavior.

While the offender relates his story in his own words, the experienced psychiatrist is able to observe his behavior. He will take note of whether the defendant is uneasy, tense, or indifferent, whether or not he gives a rather prepared story in order to prove his innocence, and whether he reacts positively or negatively to the psychiatrist.

A further point which the examiner should try to observe is: What type of personality did the offender have before he committed his crime, and has his personality now changed? The answers may very well be revealed through the historical data, which should comprise the following:

1. Historical Data

1. Family History. Brief statement of age, number of siblings, structure of family situation, and emotional attitude of parents.

While taking the family history, the home situation should be explored. It is therefore well to corroborate evidence from the offender with that of his parents. Was the offender's birth normal or complicated? How was his mother's pregnancy? Was there much strain? Was the child planned or unwanted? What was his order of birth into the family (first-born, last-born, twin, etc.)? Was he breast-fed or bottle-fed? When did the offender start to walk and to talk? How and when was he weaned and toilet-trained? Was there harmony, or was there tension and emotional outbursts within the family? Were his parents authoritative toward the children? Were they strict, over-indulgent, or neglectful in bringing them up? What was his parents' attitude toward constructive groups, such as Boy Scouts, church, and kindred organizations? What was the family's attitude toward sex? What were his parents' reactions toward delinquent behavior? All these questions aim at ascertaining whether the offender became hostile or rebellious toward his parents and family, producing antisocial attitudes in him, and whether criminal habits were established within the home itself. The type of neighbourhood in which the offender was raised should then be considered. Was delinquency prevalent? What was the prevailing attitude toward the law and the police? This may indicate whether or not the home environment instilled law-abiding principles in the child.

2. *Development History*. Memories, behavior in childhood, school and adolescent periods, reactions to parents and family.

In the development history the examiner should try to find out the offender's personality reactions as a child to his total situation, to school, and to his parents and siblings, and also the character of his emotional adjustments. This part of the history should include such information as a chronological survey of the schools attended and the age when he started school (if later than usual, the reason should be recorded). Did he skip grades, or was he kept back? Did he leave school voluntarily, or was he expelled? Did he misbehave in class or was he a model child, both at home and at school? Was he a conformist, a follower rather than a leader? Did he show tendencies toward stealing or lying? Was he uncooperative, hostile, rebellious, negativistic, or truant? Any information about truancy should be given careful consideration because over 60 percent of all offenders start their criminal careers in this way. The truancy situation must therefore be investigated as to its start, its frequency, and its relation to the offender's home and school atmosphere, the possible influence of his companions, and his parents' reactions. His schoolteachers are a source of information about this and other types of misbehavior, but the knowledge gained has to be used with insight. The offender's behavior in school has considerable bearing upon the remedies to be recommended; consequently, the examiner should interview the schoolteachers or employ a psychiatric social worker for this specific purpose.

3. *Educational and Vocational History*. Record of higher education, if any, and experiences; positions held, statements about success or failure, reasons for leaving or changing jobs, etc.

The educational and vocational history follows logically upon the developmental history, clarifying the progress the offender was able to make with his education and later work and whether or not he chose a profession. If he did choose a profession, it is particularly significant, as it indicates a certain mental ability and endurance, which many offenders lack. It must also be determined whether the offender was a success or failure at the positions he held. For instance, did he increase his earnings and better his position, or did he have to take a less significant job for less money? To a large extent, this may depend not only upon his knowledge and ability but also upon his adaptability to a situation. Did he feel his work was what he really wanted to do, and was he happy in it or was his choice prompted more by his parents' wishes or rebellion against parental pressure? It is most important to elicit the offender's own feelings about whether he was a success or failure, regardless of environmental opinions.

4. *Social History.* Social contacts, friendships, social activities, indulgence in alcohol and drugs.

The social history should point out the offender's interests, hobbies, recreational and athletic activities, companions and his relationships to them, club life or other organized activities, cultural and political interests, religious affiliations, and so on. It is important to know whether the offender is gregarious or introverted, and whether he is able to establish friendships and maintain them. Does he indulge in alcohol or drugs? The examiner should particularly try to determine whether the offender was friendly and congenial up to a certain point in his life and then gradually or suddenly lost interest and became sullen, uncooperative, and involved in antisocial and criminal activities. If so, the examiner must attempt to discover the turning point in his life and the possible causes. Was it the death of a loved one, loss of a job, a marriage involving economic burdens, a mental or economic depression? This leads into consideration of his pre-criminal personality, which is covered in greater detail later.

5. *Medical History.* All diseases, their treatment, and results therefrom; general health condition, proneness to accidents, and particularly psychosomatic symptoms.

Closely connected with such changes are the alterations that may take place in the mind as a result of diseases, and these will be found in the offender's medical history. Birth trauma, even though slight, may have caused hyperirritability or personality change, including mobilization of criminalistic tendencies. Accidents which may have affected the brain capacity must be recorded. X-rays, if available, or a report from the physician who treated the offender should be reviewed by the examiner. All reactions resulting from nursing and toilet training should be noted. Change of behavior after such infectious diseases as encephalitis and influenza may take place, and for this reason the examiner should ask explicitly if there has been any prolonged fever of known or unknown origin or if there has been insomnia or drowsiness. Such behavior irregularities, seen mostly in children and comprising emotional irritability, overactivity, and impulsiveness, frequently manifest themselves in lying, stealing, truancy, assaults, sexual offenses, and sadism, which may make the examiner think the offender exhibits a serious emotional disturbance or even a character disorder.

Altered behavior, although of another type, may even result from a disease such as hypoglycemia. In one case a man was charged with physically assaulting a young woman. The woman stated that she was given a ride in a car by the accused, who fell asleep (apparently after previously having had five pints of beer) and upon waking attacked her with a monkey wrench. The prison psychiatrist stated that the attack was motiveless and that tests showed the accused to be suffering from hypoglycemia. He testified that at the time of the attack the man did not know what he was doing, that he acted as an automaton. The jury found him not guilty.[2]

In concluding the medical part of the examination, the offender should be asked if he has had any venereal disease and, if so, what treatment he received and the results. Here too any records available should be reviewed by the psychiatrist.

6. *Sexual History.* Childhood recollections of sex and parental attitudes toward it, masturbation, menstruation, premarital and marital sex relations, marriage, children, unconscious material, such as dreams and fantasies.

The examination regarding the offender's sex life probably demands the greatest amount of discretion on the part of the examiner. He must exercise extreme care in interrogating the offender if a reliable account is to be given. Even then the account may be distorted. If the offender is reluctant to discuss sex, the examiner may first start by asking him general questions concerning his attitudes toward marriage and children. If he is married, did he at any time feel jealous, or were there any problems of infidelity? Did he have pre-marital sex relations, and what was his attitude toward this? Were his sex relations satisfactory? Any signs of impotence or frigidity? If the offender is unmarried, the examiner may start by asking his attitude toward sex, noting his reactions carefully. Does he blush, or does he elaborate calmly on the questions? What does he remember about his puberty? Did he masturbate, and how did he feel about it? Was he concerned about his manliness? What was his attitude toward women? Did he have dreams or nightmares? Similar questions should be asked of a female offender. How did she react to her physical development—breasts, puberty, menstruation? Did she masturbate? Did she feel feminine or masculine?

Progress in taking the sexual history depends upon the case. Principally, the examiner should concentrate on obtaining pertinent information about the offender's sexual behavior. In the case of a sex offender, questions regarding sex are of prime importance. However, here too the topic of sex should be left for the latter part of the examination unless the sex offender feels so guilty that he is compelled to talk about it at once.

(7) *Criminal History.* Age of offender at time of first offense, type and number of crimes committed, presence or absence of criminal tendencies in family, criminal pattern.

If during the examination good contact—positive transference —has been established with the offender, at this stage the examiner should have secured a clear historical picture. Only when the examiner approaches the criminal history may the offender feel apprehensive, defensive, or even become uncooperative. If he does, it is better to avoid further questioning than try to force the issue. Important parts of the examination still remain, and it is well to maintain the good will of the offender as long as possible. Nothing is gained by antagonizing him.

At times the offender may lack information about familial criminality, or if he knows anything about it, does not want to reveal it. Here the examiner should be careful in his questioning and not assume immediately that the offender is deliberately lying. If there has been criminal activity in the family, it may have been concealed from him as is often the case. If the court record indicates the presence of familial crime of which the offender is unaware, no information to this effect should be given to him. It would probably not only hurt his feelings and his pride, but might also lead him to a fatalistic frame of mind, greatly hindering further treatment.

A good way of beginning an examination of the offender's criminal activities is to try to assess his precriminal personality. Although material may have been elicited previously which gave the examiner a fair estimate of this, certain questions might be asked of the offender or repeated to him, e.g., Did he ever display any hostility toward his parents or brothers or sisters? Was he overly attached to them in a dependent sort of way, or had he assumed a degree of independence, for example, by moving away? Was he sensitive to criticism? Did he like to have a good time? Did he manifest any anxieties or fears about his attitudes or his health? What were his aims and ambitions? Did his life change radically at a certain time?

To discover the transition between the precriminal and criminal personality is frequently quite difficult, since the development toward antisocial and criminal activities is most often gradual. If the offender is accused of stealing, for example, the examiner should try to learn whether this was his first offense and also the circumstances surrounding it. Did it originate with a background of truancy and was it deliberate stealing, or was it an expression of kleptomania?

In this part of the interview the offender's story is checked against the court record, and if discrepancies arise, the examiner should try to uncover the reasons for them. The offender's reasons for the crime should also be elicited. In cases where sexual elements are involved—exhibitionism, homosexuality, etc.—questioning along psychoanalytical lines is necessary. But regardless of the type of case, it is advantageous to record the offender's answers in his own words whenever possible. They often accurately express how the crime happened, and they may provide insight to the deeper motivations behind the crime. If necessary, the offender's statements should be corroborated by that of others who know him—friends, parents, wife or husband, teachers. At this point the examiner may be able to understand the offender's reactions to his childhood experiences and to the situation in which he has lived and may also have an inkling of how the crime fits into the formula $C = \dfrac{T + S}{R}$.

II. Physiological Data

1. *Physical Examination.* A thorough routine physical examination should be made also, indicating the general appearance of the offender—his face, physique, and manner.

The experienced psychiatrist will recognize the empty and silly look of the mental defective, the stiff expression of the person suffering from paralytic agitans, the euphoric and smiling appearance of the general paretic, the monotonous, unmovable look, with drooping expression to the lips, of the depressed or melancholic, the upward curling of the lips of the manic, and the distant and blank or grimacing face of the schizophrenic. He looks for scars resulting from head injuries, syphilis, or bullet wounds. He records and compares the offender's height and weight; he notes also the muscular development, which may be indicative of the offender's ability to commit a crime requiring considerable strength. Slightness of build may suggest a feeling of inferiority which prompted criminal activities. Any developmental anomaly of the genitals and hirsutism or irregularities in distribution of hair growth should be observed. They may be supportive evidence of possible disturbances of the sex drive. The blood pressure range should be recorded; this is particularly important with respect to older offenders and those suffering from hemorrhagic diathesis.

The skeletal system should then be examined and notations made concerning deformities of the skull or head, such as oxycephaly, dysostosis, cranio-facialis (Cruozon), and microcephalis, and bony abnormalities on other parts of the skeletal system.

In the routine physical examination of one young man, I discovered a bony outgrowth on the dorsum of his hand, which also was swollen. Questioning revealed he had hurt his hand five years before and had been unable to work at his job. Unemployed for some time, he had finally obtained a job as an office clerk but eventually was laid off and soon became involved in stealing. The configuration of his hand indicated tuberculosis, which was confirmed by subsequent examination of his lungs and abdomen, the latter showing ascites. The X-ray revealed tuberculosis, and his case was disposed of properly.

Finally, as complete a laboratory examination as possible should be made. The urine should be tested for the presence of albuminurie, glycosurie, or other abnormalities. These may indicate organic disease and must be given due consideration in the report. Serology or other special or extralaboratory procedures should be carried out in all cases where it is deemed necessary.

2) *Neurological Examination.* After the physical examination comes the neurological examination. For a neurological examination to be adequate, it must be done in detail. In the same way that the neurological examination cannot be complete without a psychiatric one, or at least without an examination of the offender's mental condition, so also a psychiatric examination cannot be complete without a neurological one.

Since a neurological examination is time-consuming, a psychiatrist will, under usual circumstances, be unable to do this. Here, however, he must use his judgement. Thus if he finds in the course of examination that the offender's speech is hesitating and blurred, with omissions of one or more syllables, he may suspect dementia paralytica. If pupils are unequal and if knee jerks are increased, absent, or weak, this confirms such a diagnosis, and a complete neurological examination with serology is necessary. As it is impossible to go into detail here about how to conduct a complete neurological examination, I refer the reader to the excellent book written by my former teacher, G. H. Monrad-Krohn, *The Clinical Examination of the Nervous System.*[3] Only a few outstanding signs which the psychiatrist may encounter while examining an offender will be stressed here.

It is a good procedure to start by examining the cranial nerves, first the olfactory nerve and then the other eleven cranial nerves. Acuity of vision and field of vision (Donder's test) should be determined, and an ophthalmoscopic examination (color, border, swelling of the disc, vessels, hemorrhages) made. If testing of the pupils reveals no abnormality, the case will hardly be of a syphilitic nature. It is not to be inferred, however, that unequal and nonreacting pupils mean the offender suffers from syphilis because in the absence of other signs and with a negative serology, it only indicates that he has gone through a syphilitic infection, which at present may not be active and may not be related to his criminal activities. Even if Argyll-Robertson's sign—absence of light reflex and unaltered accommodation reflex—is present, it must be remembered that it can be seen sometimes in epidemic encephalitis and in tumors at the base of the cerebrum. However, it should be pointed out that Argyll-Robertson's sign is considered practically conclusive evidence of syphilis of the central nervous system, which disease can escape detection for a long time. Once, after years of incarceration, a prisoner was referred to me because of "nervousness." I discovered Argyll-Robertson's sign, uneven or loss of deep reflexes, loss of deep sensibility, unsteady gait—all symptoms indicative of a tabes (syphilis of the central nervous system), which was later confirmed by serology.

While it is true that marked disturbances of the nervous system, such as exaggerated deep reflexes, tremors of the hands, and dysarthry, may be indicative of organic lesions of the central nervous system, nevertheless these same manifestations may be seen in persons displaying great anxieties, particularly when they are examined for the first time by the physician. Tremor of the eyelids may also be seen in psychoneurotics. It is therefore necessary that proper value be placed upon these findings. Hypersomnic symptoms, such as drowsiness and slowness of intellectual function;

hyperkinetic phenomena (due to basal ganglia envolvement) such as tremors, athetoid or choreiform movements, and myoclonias with mask face; hypokinetic phenomena (due to lesions in the substantia nigra); and disturbances of eye movements such as nystagmus, double vision, oculogyric crises, or restricted upward movements of the eyeballs, must be noted. These symptoms, particularly restricted upward movements of the eyeballs, may be seen a long time after even a slight attack of encephalitis has subsided. If these symptoms are present, or if there is any unexplained fever in the offender's history, the examiner should carefully try to determine if he is afflicted with encephalitis because the disease may in many cases cause a change of personality traits which might have a bearing upon the crime committed.

The motor system is then examined and notations made regarding any deformity, atrophy, hypertrophy, or involuntary movements, such as tremors, tics, myoclonus, athetotic, choreatic, or similar movements, spasms or epileptic seizures (Jacksonian or cryptogenetic). Since criminal behavior sometimes has its roots in a poorly developed or deformed body, the examiner should look for paresis or deformity. Coordination tests, such as finger-nose or knee-heel tests and Romberg's test, should be made.

The sensory system is examined next. There is no need for the examiner to go into detail here unless something suspicious awakens his attention. Sensation of pain, tactile sensation, and sense of temperature should be tested. (Note that a decreased or lost sensation of pain on the tip of the nose and in the ulnar area of the cubital region may be an early sign of tabes incipiens.) Examination of deep sensation and of sense of position and of movements should be made, followed by examination of deep pressure pain. The last one is particularly important in cases where alcoholism is suspected. An increased deep pressure pain (deep hyperesthesia) of the muscles would confirm the suspicion.

It may be necessary to test the stereognostic sense if manifestations of aphasia are present.

If in the course of the examination the offender states that he has suffered a disease of the nervous system of an organic type, signs of it may frequently be detected from changes of the reflexes. Since testing of the reflexes is one of the most objective examinations, being independent of the offender's mood and intelligence, it is of the utmost importance that they be examined. Furthermore, the offender rarely knows how to simulate reflex changes, and, if he does, it is usually easy to detect. The deep reflexes, radialis, biceps, triceps, knee jerks, and ankle jerks, are tested on both sides and compared with each other. The examiner should keep in mind that knee jerks may be absent not only as one of the three cardinal signs of tabes (the other two being Argyll-Robertson's pupils and Romberg's sign), but also after severe bodily exertion, as Monrad-Krohn found.[4] He should remember too that loss of ankle jerks and increased deep pressure pain may also be signs of a polyneuritis of an alcoholic nature.

The presence of ankle clonus is usually indicative of a pyramidal lesion, but it should be borne in mind that it can be present in a psychoneurotic person who has no lesion whatsoever. It is important that the examiner be aware of this. When due to an organic lesion, ankle clonus is stopped when the big toe is plantar reflected, while a clonus due to a functional disorder will usually continue even when this is done.

Then the superficial reflexes must be tested. Of those, the plantar reflex is one which is usually tested, the pathological response being most easily elicited from the lateral border of the sole. A positive Babinski's phenomenon may be elicited in persons who for some time have been addicted to drugs. Record a normal plantar reflex downward: plantar reflex ↓ ; and the pathological plantar reflex upward: plantar reflex ↑ ; if no response, then record: plantar reflex o.

If there are changes in the plantar reflexes, this will be reflected in the response of the abdominal reflexes, which may also reveal signs of pyramidal lesion. In some malingering offenders, however, the examiner may notice that the abdominal reflexes change in accordance with a change of superficial sensibility. In that case the cremaster reflex may be of some value in determining organic or functional symptoms. Testing of corneal and pharyngeal reflexes may also have the same value. The absence of pharyngeal reflexes has been asserted to be a sign of hysteria, which I consider doubtful, however.

Finally, the standing position should be examined. Romberg's test is performed, the offender being asked to put his feet close together and to close his eyes. If he sways, the test is positive. This test is often positive in psychoneurotic persons.

The gait must be observed but should be evaluated together with other findings. Are the arm movements normal while walking? (Movements of arms are absent when pyramidal and extrapyramidal lesions are present.) Is there steppage or hyperextension of the knee? The former condition is seen in foot-drop, the latter in tabes. Does the offender drag one foot along the ground, or does he swing it, as seen in hemiplegia, instead of lifting the leg? Is his gait staggering or propulsive, as seen in drunkenness or paralysis agitans, respectively? While observing the gait, the examiner should watch for such hysterical phenomena as astasia-abasia, during which the offender, performing all kinds of sudden and uncoordinated movements, is always on the verge of falling and tries to find support.

If the examination reveals organic signs indicating an organic brain disorder, additional procedures, such as X-rays of the brain, lumbar puncture, and pneumoencephalogram and electroencephalogram, may be required. The electroencephalogram is always indicated where there is a suspicion of epilepsy or where a murder, assault, or some other crime has been committed without any apparent motivation. Anton has emphasized the importance of making electroencephalographic studies of persons manifesting disturbed consciousness in latent epilepsy.[5]

Frequently the offender and his attorney claim insanity because of epilepsy or an epileptic equivalent, such as psychomotor epilepsy, which has been described as automatic behavior. If an offender claims that he committed his crime during an epileptic attack or in the form of an automatism, the examiner must corroborate the story of the offender with other sources. Does the offender have a history of epilepsy with distinct epileptic attacks during which he has lost consciousness? Was there any tongue-bite during these attacks? Had there been any incontinence of urine or feces during the attacks? Had the offender been examined regularly by a medical doctor, and has he been under medication for his epilepsy? Is there history of epilepsy in the family?

It is necessary to differentiate between genetic and acquired epilepsy, although in most persons suffering from this disease, there are both genetic and acquired factors present.[6] A person who experiences a genuine epileptic attack will always have amnesia regarding what occurred during the attack. As a rule the amnesia is complete (although at rare times there is a slight trace of memory). Frequently offenders claim that they "blacked out" while carrying out their crime. This "blacking out" is often actually a suppression (conscious effort to overcome unacceptable thoughts or desires) or repression (unconscious mental mechanism involuntarily relegating unbearable ideas and impulses into the unconscious) of what took place, rather than a true amnesia.

An electroencephalogram is a good means of determining whether an offender suffers from genuine epilepsy, although it is not conclusive evidence, for only 85 percent of persons afflicted with the disease show positive electroencephalograms. If the encephalogram is normal, even though the offender claims epilepsy and loss of memory during his crime, we can say, as did Dr. William G. Lennox, that "a normal electroencephalogram is presumptive evidence against a plea of epileptic amnesia." [7]

After the neurological examination has been completed, all positive findings should be summarized.

III. Psychiatric Data

When the examiner begins the psychiatric examination, he has already received an impression, though superficial, of the offender's mental make-up. He has observed his attitudes and manner, specifically, whether he is shy or bold, alert or withdrawn, whether he has bitten fingernails, whether his stream of conversation is coherent or irrelevant, whether he is emotionally accessible, and so on—in all, symptoms that may lead the examiner's attention in a certain direction.

The following type of psychiatric examination serves to broaden and deepen the psychiatric knowledge of the offender.[8] However, it should be borne in mind that this outline for the procedure of the examination comprises only suggestions, which the examiner may modify or abbreviate according to the individual criminal. It is rarely practicable to follow any guide to the letter, but the recording and organization of the data should be adhered to strictly.

(1) General Observations. Situation: The situation or situations at the time of the interview should be described. Where was the offender interviewed? Was he alone or with others? Was his behavior unusual or not?

Appearance: The general personal appearance of the offender should be described. Is he quiet, restless, anxious, shy, lively, evasive? Is a particular facial expression notable? Are unusual mannerisms present? Is he dressed neatly or carelessly? The psychiatrist should give little emphasis to the appearance of the offender's clothing if he is seen in a hospital or a jail and he should also recognize the offender whose lawyer, wanting his client to make the best impression possible, sees to it that he is suitably attired, whereas ordinarily he would not be.

Accessibility: The offender's attitude toward the examiner should be described. Does he welcome the interview or refuse it? Is his manner of speaking frank or hesitating, coherent or irrelevant, circumstantial or meager?

Voice: Is the offender's voice loud, strained, or well modulated? Are there abnormalities in his speech?

(2) Perception. Alertness: Does the offender give the examiner his attention? Is he dull, or is he able to follow the examiner's questions? The degree of his alertness should be rated in terms of "very dull," "dull," "average alertness," "hypersensitivity."

Orientation: Is the offender oriented as to time, place, and identity? For example, does he know the day, date, and year? Does he know where and who he is? It is necessary to ask these questions because in a great number of instances the offender may appear oriented according to his conversation, while in reality he may not be so. Only direct questioning will reveal this.

Recent memory: The offender should be asked about events in the immediate past. What did he have for dinner the day before yesterday? How did he arrive at the examiner's place? What new acquaintances has he made?

Paresthesias: The offender should be asked about his physical health. Does he have any queer sensations of the body? How does he feel generally about his physical health? His own opinion should be checked against medical records.

Illusions (an illusion is a perception arising from misinterpretation of an external stimulus): If the offender has displayed some false perceptions, it is necessary to determine their identity. If in doubt, the examiner may ask such questions as: Is there anybody here you have known before? (when actually the examiner knows there is not). It should also be noted whether the offender has heard any nonexistent voices.

Hallucinations (hallucinations are perceptions which have no cause in any external stimulus): Discerning hallucinations in the offender is not a simple matter. Many offenders who do not comprehend what hallucinations are may deny having them, while other offenders will readily admit it. In any event considerable discretion must be used in bringing to light their existence as well as their type and character.

It is well to start by asking a question like this: Have you heard any noises or voices from people you did not see? What did they sound like? What did they say? Did they talk about you? In some instances if an offender who is accused of murder, for instance, is psychotic or in the mood, he might begin by saying: "A voice told me to kill the man." It is essential that the psychiatrist make every effort toward detecting any auditory hallucinations because great emphasis is placed upon them in determining the presence of a psychosis. Closely related to auditory hallucinations are visual ones. The psychiatrist may continue: Did you see anything bright or colored? Did you think they had something to tell you? Did they threaten you?

While asking about auditory and visual hallucinations, test possible olfactory hallucinations by asking: Have you ever smelled bad odors or poisonous gases? These are often associated with the gustatory ones. An appropriate question is: Did you ever feel that your food or your cigarettes or pipe had a queer taste? If the answer is in the affirmative, then the examiner should ask: Do you think any harmful drugs had been put into them? If he thinks so, follow with: Who do you think placed them there? Finally, inquire about tactile hallucinations. Have you at any time had any peculiar sensation throughout your body? If he says yes, ask: Would you know any cause for it?

It is also important to determine how long the offender has had these experiences, what his idea is as to their origin and cause, and whether he committed the crime as a result of them. If hallucinations are present, try to determine whether or not there is any organic basis for them. Some visual hallucinations, for example those of the hemianopic type, may be due to a one-sided occipital irritation of the brain, usually caused by a tumor of the occipital lobe. Complex hemianopic hallucinations may be due to a lesion in the temporal lobe of the brain. Olfactory or gustatory hallucinations may be caused by so-called uncinate attacks, which may be indicative of a lesion, such as a tumor or a scar arising from a trauma around the uncinate lobe. An offender subject to these attacks will be in a dazed condition, having the feeling of reliving some past experience.

5. *Intellect.* Thought content: The offender is asked to give a brief summary of his previous life and of his crime. This has been done in the preceding examination, but important information might still be elicited from further questioning.

Remote memory: This can be ascertained from the offender's account of his life history.

Delusions: At this point the presence of delusions will in all probability have been detected. If the examiner has any suspicion that they exist, he may ask: Have you had any special difficulty in obtaining companionship? Do you think people have treated you nicely, or do you think that somebody is fabricating stories about you? If the examiner is still in doubt, he may go further and ask directly: Has anybody tried to harm you? Do you feel people are against you?

At times the character of the delusions is so absurd that it is impossible to reason with the offender. On the other hand, the offender's answers may seem so logical and sensible that his relatives have to be questioned in order to decide whether his ideas really are of a delusional nature.

It is important to ascertain here whether the offender has conscious feelings of guilt. In persons with a neurotic make-up, strong guilt feelings may be perceived permeating their whole personality. An appropriate question is: Do you think you have done anything which in your opinion was seriously wrong? Do you have a feeling of having sinned at any time? If he answers affirmatively, try to detect the nature of the "sins" so that the proper value may be placed upon them.

Obsessions: It is important to determine whether obsessions exist in offenders because neurotic phenomena, often in the form of obsessions, may be expressed through antisocial or criminal activities. An obsession is a persistent and inescapable preoccupation with an idea or emotion apparently without any external stimulus prompting it. In attempting to ascertain the presence of obsessions, the examiner should ask: Have you ever had thoughts that recur to you? Have you ever had a feeling that the same thoughts have been going through your mind for some time? These questions will usually bring to light any obsessional ideas the offender might have.

Closely related to obsessions are compulsions. A compulsion may be defined as the motor counterpart of an obsession. It is, so to speak, an obsessive acting out, and its presence should be noted.

If the offender suffers from obsessions, their nature and the situation which precipitates them should be described. Obsessive handwashing, dressing, door closing, and any other compulsions should be recorded. In many offenders, such as pyromaniacs and kleptomaniacs, obsessions and compulsions go hand in hand. Sometimes it may be difficult to establish a borderline between normal and abnormal behavior regarding these manifestations because some obsessions exist to a certain extent in every person. That a man locks a door, leaves it, and returns to make certain it is locked may be because he is cautious. But if he locks a door and returns again and again and again to assure himself that it is locked, he is a pathological case. Varying degrees of this behavior are found in offenders. A person may have a strong tendency toward setting a fire, but if he does not do it, it is only an obsession, taking on no criminal character. When these obsessions are transformed into action, they become criminal.

Fantasies: It may be difficult to descry fantasies in the offender, but an effort should be made because much of his wishes are contained in them. A question such as "Do you know what you would do if you had money?" may elicit some highlights in his personality. Closely associated with fantasies are dreams, which are also of value in determining the structure of his personality. The offender should also be queried about any nightmares he may have had.

Knowledge: By this time the psychiatrist has received an impression of the offender's intelligence and his ability to use it. Besides the information previously obtained, the examiner should ask the offender about current events, history, literature, etc.

Judgment and insight: Here the examiner must try to evaluate the offender's opinion and interpretation of matters of an objective nature in order to gain an impression of whether or not his judgment is impaired. The examiner continues then to appraise the offender's evaluation of subjective matters. Does he feel guilty? If he admits to this, he has partial insight. He may not admit being sick, in which case he does not have insight. Or he may be brought to realize that there is something wrong with him, showing that he has some insight into his mental condition. Estimation of intelligence should then follow.

4) *Emotion.* Trend: Sadness, depression, fear, or anxiety is recorded. At times several of these moods may seem to exist simultaneously or alternately. This should also be noted. It must be added that the term "emotion" is used to describe both a subjective and an objective expression. The term "affect" may be considered a better expression for these objective experiences.

Degree: The intensity of the different trends should be specified.

Suitability or disharmony: A disharmony between verbal and emotional expression may be uncovered. Such an intrapsychic ataxia is seen frequently in schizophrenia and should be noted.

5. *Behavior (Action).* Type: The activities spontaneously started by the examiner should be recorded.

Impulsiveness: Describe sudden or unexpected behavior.

Range: The circumstances under which the offender's activities are carried out must be noted.

Suggestibility: The fact that the offender is particularly exposed to suggestion or is impervious to it should be noted, giving specific examples.

Mannerisms: These have been observed during the general examination of the offender and may be repeated here, if they are of an extreme nature.

Negativism: Describe whether the offender manifests stubbornness or perversity and, if so, against whom these actions are displayed. The degree of such behavior must also be recorded.

Here the reader should be reminded of the simulation that offenders sometimes display when awaiting trial or when detained in prison. They may feign all types of symptoms indicative of either physical or mental disturbances. The character of these simulated symptoms depends to a large extent upon emotional conflicts; the stronger the conflict, the more acute and violent the symptoms. Their type revolves around the advantages that may be achieved by simulating either physical or mental disability.

The physical manifestations may be of a motor, sensory, or visceral type. Rather simple is the situation where the offender pretends to be weak or paretic, in the arms, for instance, hoping his case may be deferred for physical reasons. This deception is easily detected by asking the offender to squeeze a dynamomcter as hard as possible at even intervals. Normally the strength of the hand becomes gradually weaker and weaker, but where the offender is simulating symptoms, the strength usually remains the same, from which the examiner may assume that at the beginning of the test he did not use his total strength. Should he claim to be paralytic in one leg, he should be asked to raise it and then let it sink slowly. If he is really paralytic, the leg will fall down; if he is not, it will move down slowly, as he keeps it back. A claim of sensory changes may be confirmed by remembering that an hysterical anesthesia does not follow the distribution of the nerve. Thus the simulator may claim to be anesthetic in half of his body, including loss of hearing, sight, smell, or taste on the same side, symptoms which may be extended by the examiner's suggestion. If an offender states that he has lost his vision or that it is impaired and this is an hysterical manifestation, then his pupils will react to light and accommodation while the visual field will be centrally narrowed. Should he claim muteness, he should be asked to write some words. He will be unable to do so if he has aphasia.

The mental disturbances of an hysterical nature which may be encountered in dealing with offenders, particularly those awaiting trial, are those of the Ganser syndrome. In this syndrome the defendant begins to behave strangely. Actions that were familiar to him he now does in an absurd and ridiculous manner. He is unable to answer simple questions correctly. He gives the approximate date, says 4 x 5 are 18 or thereabouts—replies which may show that he realizes the meaning of the questions but that they are all beside the point. His whole behavior is a union of instinctive, rational, and deceiving elements, a kind of double-dealing. Sometimes the person may lose his identity, his consciousness may be clouded, and he may have amnesia, with confusion or fugue symptoms. Sometimes he may even have visual or auditory hallucinations. The Ganser syndrome arises from the offender's unconscious wish to appear irresponsible, with the result, however, that he actually becomes mentally sick without being aware of it. To the examiner it may look like malingering. In reality this is an hysterical phenomenon prompted by the offender's belief that he will gain more through a mental illness than through a physical one.

The psychiatrist must keep this syndrome in mind to avoid running the risk of incorrectly concluding that the offender is suffering from a real psychosis. The condition will subside after a while, and then the offender himself may offer an explanation for his actions. Although on the surface a person suffering from a Ganser syndrome may appear to be psychotic, in actuality he is somewhat able to control his situation. Weiner and Braiman believe, however, that patients suffering from this syndrome actually are psychotic.[9] In all the cases I have seen, the "psychosis" has cleared up once the stress situation ceased to exist.

Following the routine psychiatric examination, it may be necessary to employ special investigatory procedures. These must be used if the material elicited is scant or considered insufficient to formulate an opinion. Poor material may be the result of the offender having been uncooperative or hesitant in relating details of his life story and his offense. The examiner may also use the following methods if he has the impression that valuable material is still concealed.

First is the previously mentioned method of free associative anamnesis. By encouraging the offender to speak about subjects not previously disclosed in the interview, the examiner may succeed in reaching facts which were not available before. The examination may also be furthered by means of hypnosis to detect preconscious or unconscious trends.

Play technique is a method of obtaining an impression of the offender's attitude, behavior, and reaction to certain situations through play. The technique is commonly used with children, but it is also helpful at times with adults. This technique has been outlined by Anna Freud, Melanie Klein, Homburger-Ericson, David M. Levy, and others. Finger-painting and clay modeling are closely connected with play technique. They may be used when there is a suspicion of certain unconscious trends, such as a destructive trait, not previously detected.

Sodium amytal, metrozal, or other suitable drugs—narcoanalysis —may be used during the examination to reduce or eliminate the offender's resistance. This procedure may render valuable information regarding unconscious elements in the offender's behavior. However, much skill must be exercised in obtaining the information. The question has been raised as to whether it is ethical to utilize the results obtained under narcoanalysis as evidence during court proceedings. Such an authority as Lange [10] maintains that it is completely improper. However, even he agrees that where a question of credibility arises, narcoanalysis is preferable over merely a few psychiatric interviews.[11] According to the law narcoanalysis can be used only with the consent of the offender and only after he has been told that the findings from this medical procedure might be used against him. It has become a more and more accepted procedure by the courts, especially when the question of insanity and legal irresponsibility is raised.

iv. Psychological Tests

The time has passed when the main function of the psychologist is to determine the intelligence quotient. Actually at this point the psychiatrist will already have received an impression of the offender's intelligence. If he has not, it may be due to faulty technique or poor observation on his part. Of course, cases exist where an offender represents a borderline case of mental defectiveness, which may be difficult to determine accurately without tests. However, the strong emphasis placed on measuring the intelligence has to a large extent hampered the development of testing the total personality. The important thing to determine is the psychology of the individual's thinking, instead of the logic of it, which intelligence tests measure. The psychiatrist's essential concern is the person's emotional attitude and the motivations behind his actions.

Even today reports from institutions, agencies, prisons, and parole boards dealing with criminals contain mainly the rating of their intelligence. It is far more important, however, to ascertain whether the offender suffers from emotional or mental disturbances, such as anxieties, phobias, paranoid ideas, or delusions, which, if only vaguely manifest and difficult to uncover, might have escaped the psychiatrist's attention, than it is to focus interest on whether the offender has an I.Q. of 100 or 110. This does not mean that the examiner should put aside the measurement of the intelligence. It means only that the proper value be placed upon the proper matter. The psychiatric examination is one of essentials and must therefore be carried out accordingly.

The following tests are to be performed by the psychologist but should be reviewed by the psychiatrist.

1. Standardized Intelligence Tests. The following tests are used: the Wechsler Adult Intelligence Scale (previously called the Wechsler-Bellevue), the Merrill-Terman, and the Babcock.

An estimation of the offender's intelligence is arrived at while ascertaining the amount of emotions affecting his intellectual ability. Thus there is often a discordance between the score on the intelligence test and the person's actual intellectual ability.

2. *Concept Formation Tests.* The following tests are used: the Hanfmann-Kasanin and the B.R.I. Sorting.

These tests reveal the offender's behavior and reactions in certain situations, thus giving information about his behavior patterns.

3. *Projective Personality Tests.* The following tests are used: the Rorschach, the Szondi, and the Thematic Apperception.

These tests may be valuable in disclosing personality traits which indicate a special trend. Evaluation of the different tests, particularly the Rorschach, is difficult, since it depends so much on the individual psychologist's interpretations, based on his training and experience. The diagnostic personality test may reveal the basis for a mental retardation. If, for instance, the mental retardation is on a neurotic basis, the retardation may not be regarded as innate and therefore constant but as a condition which may improve considerably with psychiatric treatment of the individual's emotional problems.

Another test which has created considerable interest is the *House-Tree-Person* (*H-T-P*) test, on which Buck, Landisberg, and Hammer have worked a great deal. Dr. Hammer, one of my former associates who has been interested in this test, states: "The projective drawing phase of the H-T-P is nonverbal, creative, and almost completely unstructured. Since the medium of expression is a relatively primitive one—drawing—it is, in comparison with other projective techniques, an especially useful and productive device with those of (1) low intelligence, (2) concrete orientation, or (3) relatively barren and underprivileged sociocultural background. Since the majority of a prison population meets one or more of these criteria, in addition to the previously mentioned factor of guarded evasiveness, the H-T-P would appear to be a projective technique especially suited for the purpose of obtaining data concerning the sensitivity, maturity, degree of an inmate's personality intactness and integration, and interaction of that personality with its environment." [12] This test seems to bear out the general psychiatric impression that the drawings of offenders reflect their emotional and mental age. The test confirms psychoanalysts' previous findings that the main motivations for the sexual behavior of the sex offender who seeks out small children, for example, is a psychosexual fixation or regression to an infantile level.

4. *Miscellaneous Tests.* In addition to these tests measurement standards for behavior traits have been formulated. One of these tests, by Hawthorne, measures cruelty-compassion.[13] The degree of the presence of each of these traits in an individual can be measured on a psychometric scale according to the person's responses. Hawthorne feels that the results of this test in many cases would enable us to detect potential offenders.

Another test involves measuring the reaction to ethical standards—friendship or hatred, generosity or selfishness, altruism or egoism, honesty or deceit, truthfulness or lying. By testing these traits, it may be possible to detect the difference between those showing social and those showing antisocial behavior and thus also to detect potential transgressors. It is desirable, of course, that these types of personality traits be singled out in order to ascertain the cause of aggressive behavior. However, these tests do not get to the bottom of the problem; they may show that an aggressive trend is present in an individual, but they do not explain the reason for its presence.

In trying to establish a pattern of behavior traits which differentiates between first-time offenders and recidivists, Tolman [14] found that the latter group showed a greater degree of hostility toward their fathers, a more reserved attitude toward both parents, and a greater amount of antagonism toward authority on the whole, indicating the lack of a proper relationship to love objects.[15]

The Mira Myokinetic Depression Test has been used in cases of depression and is considered to have diagnostic and prognostic value, especially for the prison psychiatrist who is trying to determine the presence of suicidal tendencies.

Certain tests aimed at finding out how the offender handles frustration situations are also employed. They show whether his personality structure is a versatile or a rigid one. Finally tests for educational and vocational ability, such as Brainard's test, may be used for guidance purposes if indicated.

However, as helpful as these psychological tests are, they should be regarded only as tools, and the offender must never be judged merely on the basis of their results. Nothing can replace the clinical acumen and experience of the competent psychiatrist and psychoanalyst. Here too, as in the psychiatric examination, the procedure may vary. Not every existing test need be given. It is up to the keen sense of the psychiatrist to select the appropriate tests which should be administered. Nevertheless, he should always try to stress the essential points, even though the examination may vary from offender to offender.

When a psychiatric-psychological examination is carried out on a juvenile offender, the approach is somewhat modified to take into consideration factors peculiar to that age group. For example, pediatric diseases such as scarlatina, measles, mumps, and whooping cough may lead to character disorders because the child has been overly pampered. So may convulsive or encephalitic conditions or limited mental capacity due to mental deficiency or to an inner conflict having its root in a neurosis. Of course, all these childhood difficulties may also be the root of an adult's problems too. Furthermore, eye or ear diseases which are common to childhood (the latter may produce paranoid trends) interfere with the child's normal development in school and may call forth reading difficulty, truancy, etc. Often too the problem does not rest with a physical ailment, but a social one. It may be the result of a poor adjustment to the opposite sex, which even though temporary, may wreak havoc at the time.

Above all, the child should not receive the impression that he is undergoing a psychiatric examination. It must be conducted subtly, and it is of utmost importance that good rapport be established between the examiner and the child. A valuable contribution to the psychiatric examination of children has been made by David M. Levy in his survey.[16]

v. Conclusion of Examination

In concluding the examination, the psychiatrist should reconstruct the life history and crime of the offender and try to arrive at a diagnosis. No specific rules can be laid down for making a successful psychiatric examination, but the following method for arranging and collecting data has been found to be very effective:

1. Congenital and Early Traumata. Here conditions under which the offender was born and has lived up to the time of his offense should be noted, with emphasis on familial and social history, such as poverty, his position in the family (only child, twin, or tenth sibling), environment, criminal pattern, and so on.

2. Precipitating Events. Here may be listed briefly those events which in the eyes of the examiner have contributed to the development of the personality and which finally became traumatic, acting as precipitating factors prompting the crime. Such precipitating events may be bodily or mental disease, a broken home, neglectful or overprotective parents, threatened loss of security, or alcoholism, for example.

3. Crime. Its type should be briefly described.

4. Maladjustment Structure. Certain trends such as dependency, narcissism, oral orientation, aimless life pattern, inability to identify with constructive figures, reactive alcoholism, etc. should be noted.

5. Personality Structure. The offender's personality structure and his reactions to his environment are to be outlined. Psychodynamic synthesis—a short summary of the etiological factors in childhood, adolescence, and adulthood which might have led to the crime—should be given.

6. Descriptive Diagnosis. This should cover medical and surgical, characterological, psychiatric syndrome, social, symptomatic material.

7. Determination of Responsibility. This is decided according to the findings. If the offender is considered not psychotic at the time of the crime, he is responsible for his act; if he is psychotic, he is not responsible. The law also disregards a crime committed by an idiot or by a child under the age of fourteen.

8. Recommendations. Treatment: changing the personality, changing the environment, and prognosis.

In giving recommendations, it must first be stressed that the court has jurisdiction over the offender. The psychiatrist's position is merely an advisory one. Whether or not the court will follow it, however, the psychiatrist should give his advice according to his view of the case. These recommendations may in many cases not be effected because of restrictions on the part of the law, but these limitations should not keep the psychiatrist from making the recommendations he deems advisable. The purpose is to direct the court's attention to the best possible solution to the case both from the offender's point of view and society's. In most cases this can be accomplished by taking a long-range view of the problem and treating the offender on an etiological basis rather than a symptomatic one.

Thus an offender charged for the first time with kleptomania, for example, should be referred to a psychoanalyst rather than be imprisoned. However, such a recommendation depends upon the type of case. If the offender is dangerous and his personality make-up is that of a high-grade neurotic character disorder which may not be amenable to treatment, the psychiatrist may suggest a particular institution for his treatment; or if no such special institution is available, he should be sent to a maximum security prison. If the case concerns a child whose home situation may be said to be the main cause for delinquency, treatment regarding the environment should be referred to a psychiatric social worker while psychotherapy is given the child. If the child offender has difficulty in school, a child psychiatrist should do the therapy.

At times the court may ask the psychiatrist to make an examination merely to give the court an impression of the offender's mental condition, thus forcing the examiner to conduct only a superficial investigation. At other times the court may want the offender to be observed for a prolonged period of time, which will allow the psychiatrist to use the psychiatric examination as outlined to advantage. In still other instances the court wants the offender examined between trial and sentencing, as is true in the Court of General Sessions of New York City. Here the psychiatrist may be given the opportunity to see the offender several times.

In this day and age the state of the offender's mind (certainly whether he is psychotic or not) has to some extent come to be recognized as important in dealing with him. Because this is so, a greater responsibility than ever before has been placed upon the psychiatrist and psychoanalyst, whose testimony may have a bearing upon the verdict and the sentencing. Therefore, we can readily see the intimate relationship between the psychiatrist, the criminal, and the law.

CHAPTER XII

Criminal Law and Psychiatry

In the past few decades psychiatry has directly and indirectly influenced the evolution of the law, so much so that today we cannot conceive of their being separated. Although the psychiatrist's forte is human behavior, and thus also criminal behavior, to be useful in court he must also have knowledge of criminal law. He cannot dictate the law, but like every other law-abiding citizen, he must endeavor to uphold it, even though at times he may feel that it has not kept pace with what he considers psychiatrically best. However, just as the law must take into consideration not only protecting the rights of the defendant but also the safety of society, so must the psychiatrist.

Here a conflict often arises. The psychiatrist may be said to be basically interested in the person and his behavior—in the motivations, treatment, and prognosis—whereas the court is primarily interested in seeing that justice is done and that the proper punishment is meted out to the guilty. Often the psychiatrist will agree with the court that an offender is too dangerous to be left free in society, but he will usually not stop here. He looks into the future, and his chief aim is to see that the offender is not only isolated from society but that he is treated, thus giving him an opportunity to be rehabilitated and become a useful member of society when released. Many keen-thinking judges feel the same way. And it is only when the law is broadened to include psychiatric aspects and when more psychiatrists become familiar with the problems facing the court that progress will be made.

It is not so strange that throughout history people have basically accepted the law, for law is an order of nature which human beings themselves have produced. The first duty of the law is to control antisocial and criminal aggressions so that society will be protected and its members able to work and create a foundation for an orderly life. Although there have been conflicts between what the law has considered ethical and what individual human beings have considered ethical, law, as it exists on the statute books, is the product of years of considered judgments and evaluations by many thoughtful men, while an individual's ethics are the result of his thinking and feeling only during his lifetime, and are only as broad as his own experience.

The outstanding feature of criminal law in America is that we have two sources of laws—state and federal—which at times may conflict. It is a human trait that people, and this applies also to sovereign states, want to be their own boss, for which reason the federal government may at times have difficulty in enforcing its laws. The states have made laws regarding the regulation of important elements; e.g., banking, business, food, and liquor. The federal government has expanded its jurisdiction and thereby given a greater conformity to the administration of criminal law. The White Slave Act of 1910, the Extortion Act of 1932, the Kidnapping Act of 1934, and the National Firearms Act of the same year indicate that our authorities, generally speaking, are aware of the great need to regulate certain laws on a national basis in order to maintain stability in society.

Because of the tradition of retaliation, there is a widespread and deep-rooted belief within most human beings that every offender must serve a sentence. People fail to consider that in prison the offender will come in contact with dangerous or malicious criminals who may influence him so greatly that after his release he may turn still further into antisocial paths. Lately, there has been considerable interest in the abolition of the death penalty still maintained in many Southern and other states such as New York, New Jersey, and California although several states have abolished it. All lawmakers should bear in mind that the threat of a severe sentence such as the death penalty does not eradicate crime. The most obvious proof occurred in England during the eighteenth and early nineteenth centuries, when picking pockets was punishable by death. Even during a hanging of one of these criminals, pickpockets were operating among the spectators, the threat of a death penalty deterring them not in the slightest. That capital punishment is still in use in the United States shows clearly our failure. The death penalty should be abolished.

Criminal law has come a long way in humanizing its procedures. Yet needless to say, the law has too often been rather tardy in revising its rules when confronted with new scientific evidence. However, it must be remembered that law exists for the purpose of maintaining the established order. It is easy to criticize a judge who metes out a punishment which might be regarded as unwarranted. But in stating such objections, we must not forget that he is bound by the law and must render his decision and pronounce sentence in accordance with the rules governing the particular case; otherwise, he would be derelict in his duty, that of interpreting the law.

THE M'NAGHTEN AND DURHAM RULINGS AND THEIR IMPLICATIONS

At times there have been judges who have expressed opinions that ran counter to the existing law. This happened in the case of Daniel M'Naghten, who stood trial in 1843. A principle was laid down in this case that has had great bearing on British and American criminal jurisprudence.

Daniel M'Naghten suffered from the delusion that certain people wanted to kill him, and that one of these was Sir Robert Peel. One day, in attempting to assassinate Peel, he killed Peel's secretary by mistake. He was charged with murder but acquitted by the jury on grounds of insanity. The case caused a great sensation. The House of Lords formulated five questions for England's judges which concerned the proposing of a concise test for criminal responsibility in cases of delusional and ordinary insanity.

In response to these questions, in 1843 Lord Chief Justice Tindal proposed a test for criminal irresponsibility in cases of ordinary insanity. He said: "To establish a defense on the ground of insanity, it must be clearly proved that at the time of the act the accused was laboring under such a defect of reasoning as not to know the nature and quality of his act, or, if he did, that he did not know that what he was doing was wrong." In explaining what was meant by "wrong," he said that if the accused was conscious that the act was one he should not have committed, and if the act was at the same time contrary to the law of the land, it would be punishable.[1] Regarding the delusions, it was said: "If the accused labors under partial delusions only and is not in other respects insane . . . he must be considered in the same situation as to responsibility as if the facts with respect to which the delusion exists were real."[2]

It was in this way that the concept of legal insanity was formed. In principle, it had been present in the writings of Sir Matthew Hale (1609–1676), and Blackstone also had said: "If a man in his own memory commits a capital offense and before arraignment for it becomes mad, he ought not to be arraigned because he is not able to plead to it with the advice and caution that he ought. And if, after he has pleaded, the prisoner becomes mad, he shall not be tried, for how can he make his defense?"[3]

In the next few years an attempt was made to establish the rule of "irresistible impulse" as an excuse for crime, but this attempt was defeated in England. The "irresistible impulse test" takes into account certain mental conditions, but here too only specific symptoms are stressed rather than the total personality.

In America early law was based upon the principles laid down in English cases, as seen in the writings of such men as Isaac Ray in 1838 (*A Treatise on the Medical Jurisprudence of Insanity*), Francis Wharton in 1846 (*A Treatise on the Criminal Law of the United States*), and others of the time.

The first important case on insanity in America was *Commonwealth v. Rogers* in 1844, in which the judge repeated the rule of

M'Naghten's case in his instructions and also held for the rule of "irresistible impulse." The next outstanding case was *State v. Spencer* in 1846, in which the rule of M'Naghten's case was also accepted, but the rule of "irresistible impulse" was disregarded. Up to about 1900 the courts of the different states adhered either to the rule laid down in the *Commonwealth v. Rogers* case (knowing the difference between right and wrong plus "irresistible impulse") or to that laid down in the *State v. Spencer* case (only knowing the difference between right and wrong).

We know that when the law deals with a mentally ill person, it takes precautions to give him adequate consideration and protection. However, in spite of this, there is a deplorable discrepancy between criminal law as it exists on the statute books and the science of psychiatry with regard to these offenders.

There is no doubt, for example, that for many years, there has been great dissatisfaction with the M'Naghten Rule both here and in England. For that reason, in about seventeen states and in both our military and our federal law, the M'Naghten Rule has been modified or other statutes have been substituted which give the criminal some leeway even though he may know the nature and wrongness of his behavior if he is otherwise deprived of the capacity for self-control as the result of a mental disease. In many states, such as New York, the question of revising the M'Naghten Rule has received considerable attention. I quote from the 1958 Interim Report of the Study Committee appointed in 1957 by Governor Harriman of New York (and extended by Governor Rockefeller) to study the definition of criminal insanity used in the New York courts:

"In this state, speaking ex-judicially, Judge Cardozo said thirty years ago of our statute: 'Everyone concedes that the present definition of insanity has little relation to the truths of mental life. There are times, of course, when a killing has occurred without knowledge by the killer of the nature of the act. A classic instance is the case of Mary Lamb, the sister of Charles Lamb, who killed her mother in delirium. There are times when there is no knowledge that the act is wrong, as when a mother offers up her child as a sacrifice to God. But after all, these are rare instances of the workings of a mind deranged. They exclude many instances of the commission of an act under the compulsion of disease, the countless instances, for example, of crimes by paranoiacs under the impulse of a fixed idea. . . . If insanity is not to be a defense, let us say so frankly and even brutally, but let us not mock ourselves with a definition that palters with reality. Such a method is neither good morals nor good science nor good law.' " [4]

The report also said: "Mental disease, even in its extreme forms, may not destroy the minimal awareness called for by M'Naghten while destroying power to employ such knowledge in determining behavior, the capacity that rational human beings have to guide their conduct in the light of knowledge. The point is a related one to that which we have made respecting the impairment of capacity to know. Capacity to know the nature and wrongfulness of conduct may not have been discernibly destroyed, and yet the transformations in ability to cope with the external world, worked by severe psychosis, may have otherwise destroyed the individual's capacity for self-control. In cases such as this M'Naghten decrees legal responsibility. But since it is precisely the destruction of capacity for self-control, in consequence of mental disease or defect, which from the point of view of morals and of legal policy warrants the special treatment of the irresponsible, the statute forces a discrimination which is neither logical nor just."

Jerome Hall, an astute student of law, has steadily advocated the retention of the M'Naghten Rule.[5] He finds support in psychiatrists such as Percival Bailey who, notwithstanding his ability as a neurologist, does not seem to have specialized experience in the field of criminal psychopathology. It is unfortunate that Hall, in his otherwise interesting paper, does not cite opinions of psychiatrists who constantly deal with these specific problems, such as Dr. Overholser, for instance, and others, including myself. If he had been more aware that the M'Naghten Rule takes in only the cognitive capacity of the offender and disregards the emotional one, he might possibly have come to some other conclusions.

In order to surmount the shortcomings of the M'Naghten Rule, Judge Bazelon presented the following ruling in the case of

Durham v. U.S.[6] for the United States Court of Appeals in the District of Columbia: "An accused is not criminally responsible if his unlawful act was the *product* of mental disease or mental defect." No doubt, this ruling is a great improvement over both the M'Naghten Rule and the "irresistible impulse test," since it does not specifically mention knowledge of the nature, quality, and wrongfulness of the act or "irresistible impulse," thereby being even broader in scope.

The Durham Rule involves two questions: 1) Was the defendant at the time of the act in question suffering from a mental illness or defect? and 2) Was his act the product of this mental illness or defect? Thus in determining legal sanity, the element of causation is brought in. It is still uncertain whether or not this causation must have been a compulsive one.[7]

It should be noted that the Durham Rule does not clarify sufficiently the causal connection between the mental condition and the act. For instance, how much a product of mental illness must the criminal act have been? Can we say that but for the mental illness the criminal act would not have been committed?

Although I am very much in sympathy with the Durham Rule, it must nevertheless be stated that to establish the connection between a criminal act and a person's mental condition is extremely difficult, if not impossible, in many cases. This difficulty is magnified when presented to a jury or when the judge must instruct the jury that the criminal act was the exclusive product of the defendant's mental illness or emotional disturbance.

Since its inception, the Durham Rule has received much criticism. With the exceptions of Justices Douglas and Fortas, who have found it to be good and to the point, there is a great deal of resistance to it on the part of the courts. Drs. Overholser and Cody have stated that in at least six jurisdictions the formulation has been rejected without even a consideration of its merits.[8] The New York Committee for the Definition of Legal Insanity has said that while the Durham Rule has more value than the strict M'Naghten Rule, it cannot be accepted because its own formulation is more specific.[9]

When the Durham Rule was established in the District of Columbia, one criticism was that if an offender was considered insane, he would be committed to St. Elizabeths Hospital from which he could quite easily get himself discharged shortly thereafter by declaring himself sane. However, in most cases, as in the following, this has not been so, and even if it were, in all fairness it is not a criticism of the ruling itself as much as it is of other aspects of the law. John D. Leach was a man suffering from a mild mental disease who managed to convince a jury in Washington, D.C. that he was not mentally responsible for his crimes. At the time, his lawyer and he talked of "walking out of St. Elizabeths within a couple of months." Six months later he was still in the hospital, even though he had already spent as much time in court trying to get out as he had trying to get in. The following chart from the galleys of the Washington *Post & Times Herald* shows the practical results of the application of the Durham Rule and covers all criminal cases since July 1, 1954.

"Column 1 shows those acquitted of crimes by reason of insanity. Columns 2, 3 and 4 show their status at St. Elizabeths Hospital. Columns 5, 6, and 7 show what has happened to those finally released. Metropolitan police records only are the basis of Columns 5, 6, and 7."

Crime	Acquitted	Still in Hospital	Condi- tionally Released	Perma- nently Released	Arrested on Release	Con- victed Minor Crime	Con- victed Serious Crime
Murder	16	13	2	1	0	0	0
Assault	9	4	0	5	0	0	0
Housebreaking	13*	7	0	5	0	2	0
Robbery	13*	9	0	3	1	0	1
Theft	8	4**	1	2	0	1	0
Forgery	10	5	0	5	2	0	1
Other felonies	9	6	1	2	0	0	1
Municipal Court	12	10	0	2	0	1	0
	90	58	4	25	3	4	3

* One person in each category not committed to hospital.
** One died in hospital.

When we know more about the functioning of the human mind than we do at present and it is possible in each case to establish beyond a reasonable doubt a firm connection between the mental condition and the act, the Durham Rule will be satisfactory. Judge David Bazelon's decision—the Durham Rule—is a bold step and deserves much commendation, as was expressed by the fact that the American Psychiatric Association gave him the Isaac Ray Award for 1960.

Keeping the M'Naghten and Durham rulings in mind, let us see how the courts in general deal with the question of insanity as a defense in criminal trials. The psychiatrist must be aware of the legal aspects of insanity as a defense under the existing laws. To be sure, the psychiatrist is called into court only as an expert, but he will do well to be cognizant of the law's attitude toward an offender's emotional and mental capacity to commit the crime and his responsibility therefor.

Let us also see how the insanity of an offender affects his criminal responsibility for his crime under our present laws. It is essential to determine *at what time* the offender became insane and the effect of the insanity upon him. We shall consider the consequences of insanity during the following four periods in relation to the crime: 1) at the time the criminal act was committed; 2) after the crime was committed and before the time of trial; 3) during the trial; and 4) after the trial and during the completion of sentencing.

1. The consequences of insanity at the time the criminal act was committed. Even before any legislation was passed on the subject, it had been an old unwritten law that a person who was insane at the time of his crime could not be punished or be considered criminally responsible for his act. Yet only recently in a case in one of our states, the court asserted that there are forms of mental deficiency or derangement which will not excuse the perpetrator of a crime. In its own words: "If the mental derangement shall excuse the crime, it must be of such an extent that the offender was unable to form a criminal intent." In an opinion expressed by an Illinois court in the case of *People v. Marquer,* it was held that "if the mentality of a person is of such a subnormal character as to render him incapable of distinguishing between right and wrong, it undoubtedly constitutes a legitimate defense." [10] It is clear that in these situations the problem of insanity has a bearing upon the criminal responsibility of the defendant. It is agreed that if he was insane at the time of the commission of the act, he is not criminally responsible. However, legal insanity and psychiatric derangement are unfortunately often not one and the same, and also the line of demarcation between sanity and insanity is so fine that many times even psychiatrists will differ in their opinions. Is it any wonder that it sometimes happens that an offender is judged criminally responsible by the court although in the opinion of the psychiatrist he is psychotic?

2. *The consequences of insanity after the crime was committed and before the time of trial.* Under common law and by statute in several jurisdictions, an insane person cannot be tried, sentenced, or executed. If during the criminal procedure the defendant shows signs of insanity, the court will have to consider this problem before further proceedings take place. Sometimes a situation arises whereby an offender is inadvertently tried while insane, and the question of how to remedy the situation arises. If a defendant has been convicted and afterwards evidence is produced to show that he was insane during the trial, courts have recognized the right of the defendant to move for a new trial. In Michigan a writ of habeas corpus may be obtained by the defendant or by another person in his behalf. In other jurisdictions an application for a writ of error *coram nobis* is proper.[11]

3. *The consequences of insanity during the trial.* In this situation the trial is interrupted until the problem of sanity has been taken up and the offender has been judged sane or insane.

4. *The consequences of insanity after the trial and during the completion of sentencing.* If an offender was sane at the time of the criminal act, at the trial, and at the time he was sentenced and then claims to have become insane during his incarceration, he is not entitled to a new trial to determine his present condition. The criterion is whether or not at the time of the psychiatric examination the defendant thoroughly realized the nature of the charge against him, the aim of the trial, and the implication of the punishment. However, if the question of sanity arises in the

case of a person who is awaiting the death penalty, a psychiatric examination of the defendant is made if the court is in doubt as to the person's current mental condition.

The prime question is what does the word "insanity" mean in legal terms? Insanity in its legal sense means only intellectual insanity, not emotional insanity. Thus the legal term refers only to the cognitive faculties, and not to the emotional or affective ones. It seems then that the law labors under the impression that mental functioning can be divided into different "departments" —intellectual, emotional, perceptional, and volitional faculties. It is impossible to divide the mind in this fashion. Yet even today such a test as the "partial insanity test" which was taken over from the classical medicine of Hippocrates and Galen is still in effect.[12]

Obviously, a psychiatrist testifying in court is faced with the conception—or misconception—of "legal insanity." If we scrutinize the questions asked by the court—did the defendant know the nature and quality of the act, and if he did not, did he know that what he was doing was wrong?—we shall see that the law revolves around the word "know." Psychiatry and current law have different concepts of this word. To the psychiatrist to know means to understand, that is, it is an *emotional* understanding, involving the ability to use knowledge and reasoning whereby a person can emotionally discriminate the essentials of the matter. Our psychological knowledge of today makes understanding a much more encompassing process than the law implied in the word "know" over one hundred years ago.

Depending upon the individual case, an offender suffering from a deep-seated chronic mental condition with psychotic features is often unable to understand emotionally the nature and quality of his act, even if he is able to express the right answer to a question. The "Mad Bomber" is a case in point. He had been psychotic for many years, suffering from paranoid delusions, which made it impossible for him to understand emotionally his actions and their consequences; yet in court he was able to say that he understood what he was doing. Whenever he had placed a bomb in Grand Central Station, for example, he always went home to listen to the news broadcasts for any reports of a bomb explosion. He tuned in on a radio station in New Jersey which broadcast news every afternoon about any bombing incidents related to him. During the trial, which was held at the hospital because the defendant had a case of tuberculosis, the question as to whether he was able to stand trial and confer with counsel was posed. The defense attorney and the defense psychiatrist strongly maintained that the man had no emotional understanding of his criminal actions and their consequences, a point with which I, as the psychiatrist for the State, concurred. The case appeared before Judge Leibowitz, who acted on the advice of the psychiatric experts and had the "Mad Bomber" transferred to Matteawan State Hospital.

Interestingly enough, during the trial it was stated by the defense psychiatrist that because of the defendant's medical condition, he might die in a half year's time, a point which was used as an apparently mitigating circumstance. In my statement to the court I said that the acute relapse of tuberculosis the patient had suffered was a psychosomatic reaction to his being discovered, and that as soon as this reaction had passed, he would in all probability survive the acute attack. Four years later the defendant is still very much alive.

Even when an offender has shown guilt feelings by trying to conceal his crime or by fleeing from the scene, it may not always mean that he knew his act was wrong. When we examine the psychotic person, we often find that the way he knows things is quite different from the normal person's understanding of those same things. His sense of an act is almost like that of a child, his emotional understanding usually being separated from his knowledge, thereby rendering him incapable of fully comprehending the situation. Usually though, as a rule it may be stated that when a person conceals his crime by, for instance, throwing away his murder weapon, as happened in a recent case where I was retained as a psychiatric expert, one can safely conclude he understood fully that his act was wrong.

We must remember that there is no distinct line between normal and abnormal behavior. Criminal law insists that the mentally ill person shall know the difference between right and wrong, a matter upon which the civil law does not insist. Furthermore, since the "right and wrong test" does not embrace motivations for behavior, conscious or unconscious drives (hatred and love, need for punishment, aggressive tendencies and feelings) are not included in the M'Naghten Rule's definition of a person's sanity or insanity.

There is no doubt that we must maintain insanity as a defense; however, we must try to overcome the defects of the M'Naghten Rule. But in trying to amend an old law, we must replace it with a better one. Unless we can effect an improvement, we will accomplish nothing by abolishing the M'Naghten Rule.

After much deliberation, the members of the New York Commission for the Definition of Criminal Insanity recommended that: "Section 1120 of the Penal Law be modified to read substantially as follows:

"1) A person may not be convicted of a crime for conduct for which he is not responsible.

"2) A person is not responsible for criminal conduct if at the time of such conduct as a result of mental disease or defect he lacks substantial capacity:

(a) to know or to appreciate the wrongfulness of his conduct; or

(b) to conform his conduct to the requirements of law."

Such a law would replace the present statute referring to a person who is "an idiot, imbecile, lunatic, or insane." Furthermore, the courts would be bent upon asking not only whether the criminal lacked knowledge of the wrongfulness of his behavior but also whether he had the capacity to *appreciate* its wrongfulness. The reason why "appreciate" has been added to the requirements is that the courts would thereby grant some leeway for an explication of the distinction between mere verbalizing and a deeper comprehension of the act. If an offender lacks the capacity to know and to appreciate the nature and quality of his act, then, of course, he is also unable to know and appreciate its wrongfulness.

In addition the proposed new statute indicates that it is not only a question of whether an offender lacks the capacity to know and to appreciate or lacks the capacity to conform but whether he lacks this capacity *substantially*. By "substantial" capacity the

Committee has in mind the "quantum of capacity that represents a fair appraisal of the wide range which in our culture excludes a diagnosis of severe mental disease or defect. The scope of that range is essentially a problem for the psychiatric sciences, to be reflected in the testimony of the expert witness but sifted and evaluated by the court and jury in the light of common sense."

The Committee recommended a further definition, in the form of an added paragraph under Section 1120 of the Penal Law as follows: "3) The terms 'mental disease or defect' do not include an abnormality manifested principally by repeated criminal or otherwise antisocial conduct." Such a paragraph would "exclude from the concept of 'mental disease or defect,' and thus from the standard of irresponsibility, so-called psychopathic or sociopathic personalities."

As mentioned before, so-called psychopathic persons, that is, those suffering from a character disorder or character disturbance, are people who cannot conform to social or moral standards and therefore repeat their antisocial or criminal behavior. Only when they lack substantial capacity to know and to appreciate the wrongfulness of their conduct or lack substantial capacity to conform to the requirements of the law can insanity be used as a defense. It is my hope that the New York state legislature will see to it that the suggested changes in the M'Naghten Rule are incorporated into law.

This proposed change of the M'Naghten Rule involves a more realistic view of the concept of mental disease as related to criminality. However, it also leads to a special problem of what to do with those offenders who will be adjudged insane and therefore not responsible for their acts. As things stand now, it is more or less up to the judge to determine the further disposition of the case. To be effective, the law should be more specific, and when an acquittal takes place on the ground of irresponsibility because of mental disease or defect, a legal statute should make commitment to a mental hospital mandatory. British criminal law has long had such a provision, and the District of Columbia has just adopted one.

How long this commitment should last is an open question. The problem is: How dangerous is the offender to himself and to society? Ideally he should be committed from one day to life, depending upon the seriousness of his crime, the number of crimes committed, his mental condition, and the amount of improvement effected by treatment. Only psychiatrists are capable of determining the latter two, and it would therefore be reasonable to believe that they should determine when an offender is to be released. This solution would give the offender a chance for rehabilitation and would also raise safeguards whereby the public would be protected.

THE LAW AND THE YOUTHFUL OFFENDER

It is interesting to note that our children's and juvenile courts have aimed at keeping children and juveniles away from the adult offenders, not only during the court proceedings but also later, by sentencing them to state training schools and reformatories.

In New York correctional and penological authorities had for some time felt that elimination of early criminal records and convictions should be brought about by new legislation. In the belief that those adolescents between sixteen and nineteen who, after careful investigation and psychiatric examination, are found to be capable of becoming law-abiding citizens should be handled as youthful offenders, not as criminals, the Wayward Minor Act was initiated. This provides that any person between sixteen and twenty-one who habitually associates with dissolute or disorderly persons, is disobedient to the commands of parents or guardians, or is in danger of becoming morally depraved, can be handled as a wayward minor and not as a criminal.

After the Wayward Minor Act had been used in the Court of General Sessions for several years, it became apparent that while it filled the gap, it was not the best means of proceeding against youthful offenders because in too many instances parents were forced to testify that their children had been habitually disobedient or wayward when, in truth, they had only been involved in a minor offense. Because of this difficulty, the conviction grew that there was a compelling need for a new way to categorize offenders. Finally the legislature passed a new law which authorized courts dealing with felonies and misdemeanors to treat young people between the ages of sixteen and nineteen as "youthful offenders" instead of as convicted criminals. The Youthful Offender Act, which became effective on September 1, 1943, provides that youth courts shall be "youth parts" for the arraignment of such offenders.

Under this law the grand jury or the district attorney may recommend to the court, or the court itself may determine, that a defendant accused of a felony shall be regarded as a youthful offender if he himself consents to such a procedure. If he does, the indictment is not filed by the grand jury, and the defendant is not placed in the criminal category. Fulfilling this aim, the youthful offenders are treated separately and apart from the sessions of the court reserved for adult trials. Also, the law provides that the defendant may be paroled to await the determination of the court. If he is to be incarcerated during the period of his examination, treatment, or investigation, he must be segregated from all persons over nineteen years of age who are charged with crime. The law provides further that the maximum probation period for this type of offender shall be three years. In case the defendant is not fit for probation, the court can commit him for a term of not more than three years to any religious, charitable, or other reformative institution authorized by law to receive persons over the age of sixteen. The law states specifically that the record of a youth considered as a youthful offender shall be sealed and not open to inspection and that his being a youthful offender is no disqualification to public office or to employment or any other privilege.[13]

The law, applying an individualized approach, represents an important contribution to progressive penology. It is implied that the authorities who deal with a young defendant must know the personal, social, and educational background of the offender. These elements can be determined only after careful psychiatric and psychological examinations.

California's Youth Authority Act is similar in its objective to the Youthful Offender Act. It provides that a youth between sixteen and twenty-one shall be dealt with by a State Authority consisting of three persons, that he be detained in a proper place before trial, and that a simplified procedure be used during the trial. Further, the power of sentence is taken away from the judge, except in such serious cases as homicide. The offender is kept under supervision and treated and is released only when this is compatible with the security of society. Such an act repudiates the tradition of punishment and aims at preventing offenders from repeating their crimes.

THE PSYCHIATRIST IN COURT

For centuries the testimony of physicians has been used in criminal prosecutions. The evidence of expert medical witnesses was certainly utilized as early as the sixteenth century, and probably as early as the fourteenth century. At any rate in the famous law of Emperor Charles V, *Constitutio Criminalis Carolina* (1532), the assistance of a physician was demanded in cases involving homicide, poisoning, manslaughter, infanticide, and, what is of great interest to us, the question of whether or not an offender was insane. It is noteworthy that the physician was called to give his testimony as *amicus curiae* (friend of court). He was respected, and he did not take any sides. Later, probably in the eighteenth century, when the power of the jury increased, the court itself ceased to request an expert, and when needed, he had to be called in by the parties involved. The survival of this custom is seen today, where the right of a party to call upon an expert in a case exists by statute or under the common law.

There is no doubt that this change in the expert's position in the court has affected the importance of his role and the value of his testimony in that he is forced to speak in terms of the law as well as in medical terms and in that in the minds of the jury he is on a particular "side." Because he testifies for only one party, it is therefore unfortunately assumed that he testifies against the other one. "So ingrained is this attitude of partisanship that the Supreme Court of Delaware in passing on a statute which permitted the court appointment of an expert stated that as soon as that expert took the stand at the summons of one of the parties, he became that party's witness, thus implying that such a thing as a neutral witness is impossible and unthinkable." [14]

This current method, whereby there is a psychiatrist for the State and one for the defense, serves only to confuse the jury, as one expert may give one opinion, while another gives a different one. The jury is forced to sift through the information and draw its own conclusions on the sanity of the defendant. Thus the jury of laymen becomes the "expert." With all due respect to the average man and woman in this country, the lay member of a jury is not capable of deciding this any more than he is capable of deciding whether a person is physically ill.

Psychiatric experts should be used in the courts to pass on questions of insanity. A distressing fact is that in calling upon an expert, the courts have not always required a *qualified* one. Today in many states there is nothing to prevent practically any licensed physician from testifying as an expert on any condition, be it a mental or an organic one. The damage done to the defendant, the court, the profession, and society, is too obvious to detail. Fortunately, there are many states which have passed laws empowering the courts to appoint experts in the true sense of the word in criminal cases. I shall briefly discuss the requirements in New York.

Prior to September, 1939, persons charged with felonies were examined by a lunacy commission when there was any doubt about their mental condition. This commission consisted of a physician, a lawyer, and a layman, but the physician was not required to have any psychiatric knowledge, until in 1936 this defect was remedied. Today in order to qualify as an expert in a court case, a psychiatrist must be certified by the Board of Psychiatric Examiners, which means that he must have had at least five years' actual practice devoted to the care and treatment of persons suffering from nervous or mental diseases or defects, of which two years must have been spent in an institution having at least fifty patients suffering from mental diseases or defects, or he must have had three years' experience in a clinic approved by the Board dealing with the diagnosis and care of mental disorders. His competence is certified by two duly qualified psychiatrists.

The Board further requires that the expert shall have had at least eight hundred hours' experience in an out-patient clinic.

A beneficial method of choosing these psychiatric experts would be for the Commissioner of the Department of Mental Hygiene in each state to recommend psychiatrists who are thoroughly trained and experienced in psychiatric criminology. A list of such psychiatrists should be available to the courts, and two or three could be chosen from the list in rotation. They would examine the defendant, and utilizing all the data on him, would put their joint psychiatric-psychological report before the court. It is advisable that the rules of evidence be administered in such a way as to permit the psychiatrists to submit all their findings in their report.

This service should be paid for by the state. The court should then instruct the jury that the findings of the psychiatrists are impartial evidence on the question of whether or not the defendant was insane at the time the crime was committed.

After submission of the report, the opinion of the psychiatrists could either be maintained or questioned by the counsel for the defense. This procedure would not exclude the possibility of the defendant's attorney calling in other expert witnesses to advance a different view for the defendant. The impartial psychiatric panel would also be subject to cross-examination on the material they had presented in their official report. If such a procedure were to be followed in the criminal courts, the knowledge of mental illnesses which medical science has today would be utilized advantageously in the interests of the true administration of justice.[15]

In New York the law provides that when the court has a reasonable basis for believing a person charged with a felony is in a state of idiocy, imbecility, or insanity which makes him incapable of understanding the proceedings or of making his defense, or if the defendant pleads insanity, the court may order an examination of the defendant to determine his sanity. The psychiatrist must report on the defendant's sanity at the time he was examined but not necessarily at the time the crime was committed, although the latter, of course, is desirable.

In some cases the court may release a defendant either on bail or on probation when a qualified psychiatrist finds him not harmful to public peace and safety, even though he is incapable of understanding the charge against him. If and when, however, he is no longer in such a state of insanity as to be unable to understand the charge, the court shall require that the defendant be brought again into custody and the proceedings against him resumed. It should be added that if a defendant is found mentally defective or psychotic, in the vast majority of cases the judge will commit him to a proper institution.[16]

Since we have maintained that much of criminal behavior is closely related to some type of pathology in the personality makeup, we can see that it is important for the law to consider the clinical manifestations that involve the state of the offender's mind. The incidence of recognizable types of mental diseases or defects leads us to the conclusion that some of the individuals accused of criminal acts must be considered abnormal. The large number of offenders who are not recognized either by courts or by prison authorities as mentally abnormal are, for the most part, those who have been sentenced without having been psychiatrically examined.

In this connection we should mention the Briggs Law in Massachusetts, which went into effect in September, 1921, and has since been slightly amended. The act states, under Chapter 123, General Laws, Section 100A: "Whenever a person is indicted by a grand jury for a capital offense or whenever a person who is known to have been indicted for any other offense more than once or to have been previously convicted of a felony is indicted by a grand jury or bound over for trial in the superior court, the clerk of the court in which the indictment is returned, or the clerk of the district court, or the trial justice, as the case may be, shall give notice to the department of mental diseases, and the department shall cause such person to be examined with a view to determine his mental condition and the existence of any mental disease or defect which would affect his criminal responsibility. . . . The department shall file a report of its investigation with the clerk of the court in which the trial is to be held, and the report shall be accessible to the court, the probation officer, the district attorney and to the attorney for the accused."

It should be noted that the Briggs Law provides that certain classes of offenders are to be examined before trial by the State Department of Mental Diseases. If it is recommended that the defendant be committed for observation, the court so disposes. If a psychosis is present, the court arranges for the commitment of the offender to a mental institution until his recovery. In case no mental illness is present, the jury accepts the findings of the impartial experts.

In 1953 Dr. Peter B. Hagopian, Assistant Commissioner of the Massachusetts Department of Mental Health, stated that since 1921, when the Briggs Law was implemented, 14,570 cases had been reported for examination. He studied opinions expressed in 6,591 cases, including murder cases, as well as various other types of crimes. His findings were: "In 81 percent of the cases there was no mental disease or defect affecting criminal responsibility. The remaining 19 percent were classified as follows: definitely psychotic, 1.2 percent; observation recommended, 5.5 percent; borderline, 5.4 percent; and other conditions (psychopathic, sexual) 6.8 percent." He went on to say: "Those accused of crimes showed a greater percentage of mental deviation, defect, abnormality, and mental illness than the general population," and he stated further: "These findings must be taken as minimal, since the examiners are not required to make a diagnosis, only to pass on criminal responsibility." [17] Cohen, Sears, and Ewalt suggest that more positive dynamic psychiatric reports be submitted under the provisions of the Briggs Law, rather than negative reports, which discuss only the absence of certain signs and symptoms.[18] Despite this, the Briggs Law has been, without doubt, a most effective step toward solving the problem of expert psychiatric testimony in criminal cases.

LAW AND THE SEX OFFENDER

With only a few exceptions the states continue to recognize criminal responsibility in individuals who are mentally abnormal without being insane. New York is one of these exceptions where the courts have held that "feebleness of mind or will, even though not so extreme as to justify finding that the defendant is irresponsible, may properly be considered . . . and thus may be effective to reduce the grade of the offense." [19] It has been difficult for the law to deal adequately with borderline cases, i.e., those who are mentally abnormal without being legally insane, and not much progress has been made. However, during the past twenty years the law has singled out what it has called sexual psychopaths for special consideration.

Progress in the field of sex offenders had been rather slow until 1950 when New York enacted a law which was probably this country's first important move toward an enlightened penology regarding sex offenders.[20] Here for the first time the definition of psychopathic personality was given in psychiatric terms, and an indeterminate confinement (by which was meant from one day to life) with psychiatric treatment was made part of a law.

Prior to this development, Michigan had passed a special law in 1937, but it was declared unconstitutional. In 1938 and 1939 Illinois and Minnesota had passed laws about sexual psychopaths providing for the commitment of sexually aggressive offenders to hospitals, rather than undertaking criminal procedures against them.[21] This was a big step forward at that time, but their definition of sexual psychopaths was more legal than psychiatric. The Illinois criminal law regarding sex offenders provided for an indeterminate commitment (by which was meant, for example, from five to ten years) of persons indicted for a sex crime when they were found by qualified psychiatrists to be suffering from a mental disorder and yet not insane or feebleminded. The mental disorder, combined with propensities to commit sex offenses, must have existed for a period of not less than one year.[22]

In 1953 Minnesota revised its law according to the law of Wisconsin, the latter of which "provides for the offender whose crime, except for homicide or attempted homicide, 'was probably directly motivated by a desire for sexual excitement' in its commission. The law requires a presentence social, physical, and mental examination of persons convicted of rape, related crimes, and offenses against children. Psychiatric treatment is mandatory for convicted sex offenders judged able to benefit from it." The Minnesota law, however, did not make any mandatory provisions, and it is regrettable that of the fifty persons examined under the law, none have been recommended for treatment or custody as a sexually deviated person, apparently because there were no additional funds available and the limited force of examiners did not believe that sex offenders could profit from psychiatric treatment.

At the present time twenty-seven states and the District of Columbia have introduced new laws dealing with sex offenders. West Virginia passed a law in March, 1957, which is outstanding. The main points are given here.

"1. Commitment required for persons convicted of 'Incest and Crimes against Nature,' and at court discretion for other convicted sex offenders, presentence medical and social examinations; with 2 purposes: a) protection of public; b) prevention of future offenses.

"2. Specialized treatment in suitable cases, under the department of mental health board, with either inpatient or outpatient treatment.

"3. Discharge or parole at board judgment as to 'reasonable probability' of success, with consent of the committing court in all felony cases, and within the maximum legal term of the offense *unless:*

"4. The board deems the person still dangerous to the public and, at least 90 days beforehand, orders his continued treatment and applies for a review, wherein the convict has a full hearing, except for jury trial.

"5. The board's order, if confirmed, may continue thereafter indefinitely, except that a new order must be similarly confirmed every 5 years thereafter.

"6. The law also provides for voluntary admission and either inpatient or outpatient treatment of anyone who thinks himself liable to commit a dangerous sexual action.

"7. The law does not exclude or otherwise interfere with the convict's legal rights of habeas corpus, appeal to a superior court, or other civil rights. It does, however, in what are judged to be suitable cases, substitute treatment and rehabilitation for penal service.

"8. No mention of the word sex psychopath, but only of a person's 'mental or physical aberrations.' "

California's new treatment and classification program for sexual psychopaths is well known. In 1955 its law was amended to provide that "a person found to be a sexual psychopath, but not amenable to state hospital treatment, may be recertified for a hearing and be committed to the Department of Mental Hygiene, institutional unit, at a state prison. This change was made to take care of persons convicted of a misdemeanor sex offense whose indeterminate commitment is necessary protection to society, or persons committed as sex psychopaths who are not treatable. Hospitals cannot be turned into maximum security prisons." [23]

Other states, such as Nebraska, Massachusetts, and Wisconsin, along with Illinois, have tried to define dangerous sex offenders in psychiatric terms and have completely omitted the unscientific term "sexual psychopath," following to a great extent ideas adopted by the New York state law of 1950.

True progress in criminology would be the enactment of a law expanding the most progressive of the sex offender laws to other types of dangerous offenses. Ohio, revising its code in 1953, was on the right track in not making any distinction between sex crimes and other types of dangerous offenses. Massachusetts, Oregon, Wisconsin, and Wyoming have also extended their laws affecting sex offenders to apply to other persons convicted of serious crimes, and Massachusetts has greatly expanded its psychiatric facilities to give treatment to all types of offenders sentenced by the courts or the Department of Correction.

Finally, it should be mentioned that some states, such as California, West Virginia, and Maryland, provide for voluntary commitment of persons who believe they may cause difficulties as sex offenders.

As to treatment facilities for sex offenders, I have already briefly discussed the state of New York. The District of Columbia has a ward in St. Elizabeths Hospital where treatment is given to sex offenders; California extends such service through its state hospitals. In 1955 Maryland opened an institution for diagnosis and treatment where sex offenders receive various types of therapy, particularly group, educational, and occupational therapy. In 1955 Massachusetts repealed its old sexual psychopath law and instead passed an act whereby treatment for sex offenders in its local hospitals was authorized. Sex offenders are now being taken care of there as a part of the general psychiatric services available to the Department of Courts. Although New Hampshire and Vermont do not seem to have any special treatment facilities, New Jersey's diagnostic center commits its sex offenders to one of four state hospitals, where mental hospital care in the form of group therapy is given. Sometimes individual treatment is also extended. As Brancale and Bixby comment: "The handling of sex crimes under the New Jersey law is an awkward but practical combination of legal rights and clinical evaluation and treatment." [24] Even though we cannot avoid combining legal aspects with the psychiatric in dealing with the sex offender, this survey indicates that the states have been accepting more and more responsibility for dealing with offenders given indeterminate sentences and that great progress has been made.

LAW AND THE MENTALLY ABNORMAL OFFENDER

The problem of differentiating between criminals who are mentally abnormal but not legally insane and those who are legally insane is at times difficult. However, both psychiatry and the law are faced with this predicament. I recall the case of a thirty-year-old offender who had been admitted to various state hospitals eight times during his lifetime, the first being when he was only fifteen. Each time he perpetrated a criminal act, he was observed at a state mental hospital, where he was kept for varying periods of time. It seemed to have been the consensus that this man was a psychopath. After he had had a history of fourteen years of severe maladjustment, he was released from a Midwestern hospital and was permitted to resume life on the outside, where he lived in a slum until four years later, when he committed still another, and this time very serious, offense. When the case came up in court and a thorough psychiatric examination was made, it was decided that the offender was not a psychopath with some serious deviations in his make-up as previously thought, but that he was psychotic.

Not only is the psychiatric examination of these borderline cases difficult, but so also is the disposition of them. We are dealing here, by and large, with criminals considered by many courts throughout the world as having a diminished sense of responsibility. A point of view taken by Kurt Schneider [25] is that if the insight or the ability to act according to it was diminished, then the penalty may be diminished, as it is with an attempted crime. Because of their abnormality, in all probability these people will continue their criminal activities, but they should not be punished as other persons are. Instead, they should receive a more beneficial type of treatment and, if necessary, should be sent to a psychiatric institution for an indefinite time, where they would receive medical care.

In 1929 a law was passed in Norway which was concerned with the special treatment of mentally abnormal offenders who were not legally insane, those that the law defines as having a "weakened mind" (not mentally defective). This is the famous Paragraph 39, which states: "If a crime subject to punishment was committed by a person mentally weakened in his development or by a person with a permanently weakened mind and there was a danger that the person would repeat such a crime, the court could decide that the person be placed in custody by one of the following means: a) that he live at a certain place; b) that he report regularly to probation officers; c) that he abstain from the use of alcohol; d) that he be given or secure private care; or e) that he be confined in an institution, such as a farming colony or a prison."

The apparent advantage of this law is that it takes care of those who are mentally abnormal but not legally insane. But there are other advantages. When the offender is transferred to an institution, the original report of the psychiatrist is sent with him so that the authorities have the opportunity to know his mental make-up and will therefore be more competent to treat him and make a more accurate prognosis. Furthermore, when he is considered for release into custody, the Department of Justice considers this report and the information compiled on the offender in the institution, enabling it better to estimate what type of custody should be chosen. This law is more concerned with prevention than punishment and thus ignores the centuries-old concept of retaliation.

The idea of segregating the different types of criminals into three large groups—legally insane offenders, mentally abnormal but not legally insane offenders, and those offenders with no apparent mental pathology—is aimed not only at dealing properly with them, but also at depopulating the prisons. Social considerations are also taken into account, and a great many of the offenders are kept in institutions other than prisons, even in private custody.

Although the development of the law to include psychiatric and psychological findings has been rather tardy, the administration of criminal law has improved considerably. And despite slow progress, the development is in the right direction.

CHAPTER XIII

Rebuilding and Rehabilitating the Offender

Rebuilding an offender requires not only knowledge of criminal law, but also a certain knowledge of the psychiatric aspects of his personality. It would be well for schools teaching those who are going to deal with criminals in any way to emphasize both in their curriculum. Thus we would have more informed judges and lawyers, probation and parole officers, psychiatric social workers, and policemen.

Rebuilding an offender means rehabilitating him so that he can function reasonably well in society and become a useful and valuable person to himself, his family, and the community. However, since all offenders differ from each other in their personality make-ups, in whether or not they show mental abnormalities and to what degree, in whether they are acute or chronic offenders, and in the amount of danger they might present to themselves and to society, it is self-evident that we must deal with each of them as an individual. Only then will we be able to cope with these offenders on a rational basis.

However, because there is such a vast number of criminals, we are often prevented from handling them individually. Not only is there a shortage of trained personnel, but also, and possibly even more important, there exists the conscious or unconscious attitude of the retaliatory principle, "an eye for an eye; a tooth for a tooth," which is held by many law-abiding citizens who constitute our governing society. As I have said before, many of these people who call the loudest for retaliation would unconsciously like to carry out, but do not dare try, many of the same antisocial or criminal acts that the offenders have. They want transgressors punished to alleviate their own feelings of guilt. This is human nature, and so is the feeling that for the criminal's own sake and for society's he should not be permitted to escape the penalty of his crime. Justifiably society feels that if it is to function in an orderly fashion, its members must be protected. Otherwise, chaos would ensue.

In rebuilding an offender, we must remember that the nature of man is both constructive and destructive. When a person becomes a criminal, it does not necessarily follow that he always will remain destructive or that destructiveness permeates him. We, that is, society, have the responsibility of bringing out the good in everyone, including the offender.

We shall more readily be able to follow through on such an approach if we remember that all antisocial or criminal behavior and, in fact, any abnormal manifestation, is only a deviation from, or an exaggeration of, the norm, rather than a completely different phenomenon. Thus behavior is different in degree, not in type. We must never lose sight of this in handling the offender. It helps us to be constructive and positive in dealing with him, for we develop the mental attitude of "There but for the grace of God go I." It also makes us realize that factors outside the criminal often trigger criminal acts. According to our formula $C = \dfrac{T + S}{R}$, we know that a crime can be elicited by a specific situation which lowers a person's resistance. Therefore, it is society's duty to help the offender not only to increase his resistance to criminal behavior, but also to minimize the situations he encounters which may mobilize his antisocial or criminal inclinations.

Every offender, with the possible exception of the genuine psychopath (although he too on rare occasions may show some constructive personality traits) has within him some positive quality, be it kindness, industriousness, unselfishness, or love and protectiveness toward his family. The aim of rehabilitation is to bring out and develop any constructive tendencies and talents that the offender possesses.

In our current, so-called enlightened era, during which psychiatry and psychoanalysis have introduced not only new concepts on the relationship of mental aberrations and illnesses to criminal behavior, but also new techniques for the examination and treatment of offenders, it should have been a matter of course that our handling of criminals would change accordingly. Although some changes for the better have taken place, indicating a more tolerant attitude toward criminals, we still have a long way to go. Even in cases where we have a constructive law on the statute books, e.g., New York State's law dealing with sex offenders, still it is not implemented properly. In some cases this is so because our legal authorities follow the retaliatory principle in meting out punishment. In other cases we hear the argument that it is impossible to carry out a "one day to life sentence with psychiatric treatment," for example, because there are not enough psychiatrists available or because there are not sufficient facilities. This may be true, but if psychiatrists were given sufficient compensation and more attractive working conditions and if some of the money used to keep persons in prisons was directed toward the more constructive purpose of building more psychiatric institutions for these offenders instead of just incarcerating them, the arguments would not hold water.

In all fairness, however, statistics prove that in recent years fewer people are being sent to state and federal prisons than ever before in spite of the rise in population and the rise in crime, which obviously reflects a more enlightened view on the part of many of our judges. Still, in many cases when we don't know how to deal with an offender, we tend to put him in prison simply to get him out of the way.

To be blunt, our prisons are failures. This is obvious when we take note of the large number of recidivists among offenders who have been imprisoned. According to Sellin's study for the American Law Institute, 50.5 percent of males committed to prisons in certain selected areas had been institutionalized before in penal institutions.[1] Then too Glueck's study of 1,000 juvenile delinquents during the first five years after they were released from a penal institution indicated that 85.4 percent manifested recidivism.[2] James V. Bennett, Director of the Federal Bureau of Prisons, made a statement in 1949 that approximately 60 percent of all the men released from prisons throughout the country returned again within a period of five years.[3] Nathaniel Showstack stated that in 1955 84 percent of the men in California state prisons had been sentenced to prison or jail previously and that 70 percent of the men executed at San Quentin were recidivists.[4]

Of course, prison incarceration to some extent is a deterrent to crime in that it keeps the offender out of society for the time being. However, as conditions now are, this is probably its only virtue. The threat of punishment does not prevent a man from killing, robbing, raping, or committing any other crime. When a person commits a crime, he does not think of the consequences. The offender commits a crime because criminality is his particular outlet, just as the seriously mentally ill person's outlet is a psychosis. This is why the argument for the maintenance of capital punishment on the grounds that fear of the death penalty will keep a potential murderer from committing his crime is invalid, and it is unfortunate that as late as March 4, 1959, the New York State Assembly defeated the Kapelman bill, which would have permitted a life term for first-degree murderers.[5]

The principal considerations in dealing with an offender must be his particular personality make-up and the degree of danger he represents to himself and to society. Quite some time ago Julius Wagner Von Jauregg recommended that the period of retention of psychopathic personalities be determined on the basis of their potential danger to the public. However, he also said that it should not depend upon their mental condition, which I believe was a short-sighted view.[6] Both of these factors should determine the court's disposition of the case.

Instead, what actually happens is that all types of offenders—murderers, robbers, kleptomaniacs, embezzlers, exhibitionists, rapists, etc.—are indiscriminately thrown together in the same prison. This would not be so serious if they were given individualized treatment. But they are not. In fact, often no treatment at all is given. Only when the offender is obviously psychotic is he transferred to another institution to receive psychiatric help.

According to Warren S. Wille as recently as 1954 there were only 43 psychiatrists working full-time and 39 part-time in the 167 prisons and reformatories of the United States and its possessions. In addition to this small group there were 51 working in a consultant capacity. However, some of these rendered only token services to the prisons by making visits less frequently than once a month. Twenty-five states, including Hawaii had no psychiatric facilities in their prisons or else had no services except for occasional visits by psychiatric consultants. Wille found that the level of care rendered to the mentally ill person in the prisons of many states was at no higher a level than was common in the average asylum of one hundred years ago.[7] Although it strikes us as senseless and cruel to put a patient suffering from infantile paralysis in a hospital and then let him lie there without treatment, somehow it does not strike us as quite so illogical to do the same with a person who needs help just as desperately but on an emotional level.

Psychiatric-psychological studies indicate that a large number of prisoners are emotionally or mentally disturbed. In fact, many of them commit crimes because of unconscious guilt feelings, which lead them to strive for punishment. Imprisonment without psychiatric treatment fulfills this very aim; thereby the law is unwittingly helping the offender obtain gratification for his unhealthy needs. It becomes a pattern, and when this type of offender is released, he does something wrong again, for which he has guilt feelings, so he commits another crime, back to prison and punishment—a vicious circle.

Back in 1888, at the first meeting of the International Association of Criminal Law, it was maintained that punishment had to be adapted according to the type of offender. The aim of this new idea was to fight the principle of retaliation and to satisfy the demand for an effective prevention of crime. The Association also asserted that the protection of society from crime lay in determining how dangerous the offender was rather than the seriousness of his crime. It went further by saying that with this in mind, stronger penalties would be inflicted on habitual and dangerous offenders than on the great number of occasional and less dangerous ones. (The more dangerous offenders would thereby be restricted from committing new crimes, while the less dangerous would be enabled to return to society and receive treatment outside of prison.) The basis for classifying offenders according to the degree of their danger to society would rest on an evaluation of both their ingrained criminalistic tendencies and the social conditions under which their offenses were committed. This revolutionary view of the criminal law, which embodied a new scientific concept of crime, had healthy repercussions in penal codes throughout Europe and later in America. Examination of the records of prisoners shows that only about 20 to 25 percent are dangerous and therefore in need of confinement in a maximum security prison. It seems a gross injustice to keep the large remaining number of nondangerous offenders there merely to retain these 25 percent within walls. If all prisoners were psychiatrically examined and classified, the remaining 75 percent might very well be placed in a rehabilitation center instead, where they would be treated and re-educated by individual and group therapy, according to their specific needs, until they could be returned to society.

Of course, implementing this new plan would require a thorough psychiatric-psychological examination of every offender in order to know his personality make-up and to determine the degree of danger he represents. The latter should not be determined, nor can it really be, without a thorough study of the personality make-up, for the two are intimately entwined. For example, to determine how dangerous an offender is, we must not only know the type of crime he already committed, even though this is of utmost importance, but also the type of crime he might commit in the future due to uncontrollable, and often unconscious, factors in his personality. A judge is hardly able to decide these things, since he frequently has not had time to acquaint himself with the offender's family background, his economic and social conditions, and above all, his personality make-up. Only in cases where the judge has a full probation report and has had a psychiatric examination made of the offender can he accurately evaluate the criminal's situation in relation to the law.

Logic would thus seem to tell us that our present system of definite sentences without treatment should be replaced by an indefinite term, with rehabilitation as the aim. As our system is today, an offender serves a certain length of time in prison without treatment and then is released and put into society, where he can commit more crimes, often of a worse nature. Many times he comes out a more hardened criminal than when he went in because he has an "ax to grind" at having been caught and incarcerated. More bitterness is therefore added to his other personality difficulties.

The public in general turns its back upon men and women in prisons, and it only focuses its attention there when there are black headlines in the newspapers about a prison break or riot. But those of us who have spent time working with offenders in prisons are shocked by the waste of human material and human happiness. Not to speak of the mismanagement and neglect we see in many institutions here and abroad, how can one human being see another rotting in prison and, practically speaking, do nothing about it? So ingrained are the retaliatory principles that man not only demands that the offender be imprisoned, but also forgets about him once he is there.

But the prisoners themselves do not for one moment forget where they are. Foremost on their minds are parole and the day when they will be free again to lead a normal life with normal sex relations. Since this is unattainable in prison, they frequently have dreams about these and other aspects of life. Often they dream about being on the outside with their loved ones. Sometimes they dream they are being chased, cornered, or fenced in. All these dreams reflect their unconscious state of mind, their tenseness and anxieties, their wishes and fears.

Certainly there are some offenders who are so socially ill and maladjusted that they are unable to adapt to society at all and must be kept within walls for everyone's protection. These are the incorrigibles, those who are beyond correction. But this should not keep us from trying to help offenders who in our considered judgment might be improved by being kept for a certain time in an institution for re-education and psychiatric treatment or by being put on probation with psychiatric treatment if the case warrants it. I admit that this is a difficult task and that there will be many disappointments, but "Joy shall be in Heaven over one sinner that repenteth more than over ninety and nine just persons which need no repentence." [8]

The famous Leopold-Loeb case comes to my mind at this point. Nathan F. Leopold, who was imprisoned from 1924 until 1958 for the serious crime of murder, was able to obtain parole mostly through his own constructive traits and efforts, which convinced the Parole Board in Illinois that he had been rehabilitated. It was most difficult for all involved to determine whether or not he should be released in view of the seriousness of his crime, and I can best express my own opinion by paraphrasing parts of my report presented to the Parole Board:

The basic point in deciding whether or not Nathan F. Leopold can be paroled is the following: Will Nathan F. Leopold present a danger to society if paroled?

In order to reach a sound conclusion, it is necessary to recall that in accordance with the testimony given at the trial in 1924 and in accordance with the psychological make-up of Nathan Leopold, the instigator of the crime was in all probability Richard Loeb. This, of course, does not at all imply that Nathan F. Leopold shall be excused for his participation in it. It only indicates the degree of danger presented by him to society at that time. That Leopold was more or less led on to the crime by Loeb indicates that there does not seem to be present any danger of his committing another crime.

At the time of the trial I believe it was fair to consider both defendants, the one more than the other, dangerous to society. Society's protection was assured by their imprisonment. Until three years ago it was my belief that Nathan Leopold should not be paroled. Today I have changed that opinion.

One basic reason for my current viewpoint is that the chief motivation for the crime no longer exists. Nathan Leopold is now at an age where his biological drive has decreased considerably. This is an essential point because it was in the main this drive which drew him close to and made him dependent upon Loeb and which propelled him into the crime. Since this drive has decreased, it seems highly probable that he will not repeat his crime or associate himself with anyone else in carrying out any other criminal act. My experiences from cases dealing with both sex offenders and other types of offenders at Sing Sing Prison and in other prisons both here and in Europe indicate that after a person has passed his forties, his biological drive becomes diminished. Such decreased biological activity, as applies in Nathan Leopold's case, reduces considerably the motivation and the power for the basis of an antisocial or criminal act.

A second reason which may indicate that, if paroled, Nathan Leopold will not present a danger to the community is the constructive behavior he has manifested throughout his stay in prison, which reflects the positive and constructive traits within him. I am confident that if he is paroled from prison, he will build his future based upon such constructive traits.

A third reason why, if paroled, he will not present a danger to society is that these same constructive traits which he manifested in prison have taken precedence, so to say, over his negative ones and have thereby increased his ability to restrain himself from committing another crime.

In accordance with enlightened views of modern penology, imprisonment has served its purpose when the prisoner is rehabilitated. To the best of my knowledge, I find that Nathan Leopold is rehabilitated and that in all probability it can be considered safe if he is granted parole now. I am quite certain that if Nathan Leopold is granted parole, he will be able to benefit society by continuing to put his mind into constructive endeavors.

It might be argued that the principle of imprisonment collides with the principle of psychotherapy, which is the treatment of people under conditions of freedom and responsibility, except

where they are psychotic, and I myself have previously been opposed to psychiatric treatment in prisons because of this lack of
freedom, the strict discipline maintained, and the limited psychiatric facilities available.[9] However, my point of view in this
respect has changed somewhat. Additional experiences with prisoners have shown me that many of them need discipline, and
therefore it would not be a deterrent to psychiatric treatment. In
fact, in order to maintain discipline, not to encourage the offender's "secondary neurotic gains," and in order to make treatment more beneficial to the offender in general, it would be most
advantageous if some arrangement could be made with the prison
authorities whereby an offender would be permitted to pay for
at least part of his psychiatric treatment. It is my belief that if it is
possible to establish good psychiatric facilities and obtain good
psychiatrists, treatment in prison would be of definite advantage,
especially with regard to the treatment of sex offenders.

The decisive factor in mental health is the dynamic interrelationship between the id, the ego, and the superego. In all cases,
including the neurotic and the psychotic, as well as the criminal,
it is the outcome of the struggle between instinct and ego which
determines whether or not a person will be able to function adequately. The specific aim of treatment is to settle permanently
the conflicts between the instinct, the ego, and the superego. Psychiatrists try to bring the forces from the id into the realm of the
conscious ego so that they become influenced by other parts of
the ego. In this manner, they are usually able to bring about at
least a modification of these conflicts and reduce personality abnormalities to a minimum—be they aggressions, inhibitions, or
fears—so that the individual can function adequately.

From a general point of view we know that the results of treatment depend upon the constitutional strength of the instinct and
the possibility of strengthening the ego. One of the most strenuous
treatment situations arises when the offender's instinctual drives
are constitutionally strong, making it difficult to alter his distorted
or crippled ego. We can also safely say that when the cause of a
neurosis is traumatic, psychoanalysis has a better prognosis.

Psychiatric treatment of prisoners then aims at changing their

antisocial attitudes to constructive ones. To this end the psychiatrist tries to effect emotional growth so that the offender will be
able to understand himself and others better, that is, understand
his emotional needs and the reasons why he has committed his
crime. When he has reached this understanding, emotionally, as
well as intellectually, he will in most instances not have any desire
to commit another crime, since he is aware of his motivations and
the consequences and has usually been able to rechannel his destructive drives toward some constructive effort.

However, there are two prerequisites for successful psychiatric
treatment: a thorough examination (psychiatric-psychological and
medical examinations as well as psychological evaluations by the
psychologist and the psychiatric social worker) and a positive emotional relationship between the psychiatrist or psychotherapist
and the patient. Here the initial interview can be of crucial importance, and it is essential for the psychiatrist not to probe into the
details of the crime at this time unless the offender himself brings
up the subject. The transference situation in a prison is difficult to
maintain because the inmate's original aggressiveness and hostility
are increased by the restrictive regulations imposed upon him in
the artificial environment of the prison. They are further stimulated in cases where the offender blames society for his crime
and considers himself innocent. Often the psychiatrist's endeavors
to change an offender's antisocial tendencies into constructive
ones arouses his resistance, and therefore, I always point out and
interpret resistance to the patient whenever possible. These added
emotional elements add to the difficulties of psychiatric treatment and are partly responsible for the negative transference—
countertransference—often encountered by the psychiatrist during psychiatric treatment of either an adult or a youthful offender.
Where this occurs, the psychiatrist must remain firm but friendly,
yet must not avoid the issue.

Successful treatment also depends in good part upon the offender's ability to identify himself with the psychiatrist. Because
of the offender's inability to identify with his parents, his teachers,
or the law—that is, with any type of authority—he has already
developed an unhealthy emotional attitude. In addition he often

has a personality reaction of rejection (the world hates me, and I hate the world), which has tended to make him defensive.

A positive emotional relationship between the psychiatrist and the patient can only be established when the patient is willing to receive help. In fact, treatment can only be successful when the patient honestly desires it; it cannot be imposed upon him, for he will not cooperate or accept it. If an inmate is compelled to see the psychiatrist against his will, antagonism is created from the very beginning. Even when a prisoner seeks psychiatric help, the psychiatrist must be aware that he may not necessarily feel a true desire for it. Sometimes he does it in order to ingratiate himself with the psychiatrist so that he will receive a good report for the Parole Board. In spite of this, however, in our research project on sex offenders at Sing Sing Prison, even where the prisoner was hostile at the start, as he gained more insight into himself, his resistance lessened, and some offenders came to have a very positive attitude toward psychiatric help. Many came to us outside of their regular sessions, out of loneliness, just to talk or discuss a particular problem which was causing them anxiety at the time. By allowing them to verbalize their fears, their tensions and anxieties were reduced. However, the psychiatrist may serve not only as an outlet for the prisoners, but also as an arbiter in fights between prisoners and as a mediating factor, so to speak, between the prison authorities and the prisoner when the latter commits some infraction of the prison rules. The results we achieved in the period of time we were at Sing Sing were very favorable.

In Nathaniel Showstack's study of prisoners at the California Medical Facility, he found that of the 765 disciplinary infractions during the four years covered by his report, patients attending group therapy were involved in only 220, whereas those who had never received any therapy were responsible for the remaining 545.[10]

For the practical purpose of treatment we can group all types of prisoners according to the same classification we made of sex offenders in an earlier chapter:

1. Offenders who, because of their predisposition to crimes of

violence, are likely to commit new crimes if released and are not treatable by present known methods.

2. Offenders who, because of their personality make-up, age, drug addiction, or alcoholism, are not suitable for treatment at present and who are likely after release to continue as a danger to the public.

3. Offenders who, because of their treatability, could be placed in a treatment center with good prospects of improvement before release.

4. Offenders who, because of their treatability, could be released on parole and treated on an out-patient basis.[11]

We cannot go into any great detail here about the treatment process of the chronic offenders. Only a bare outline can be given.

TREATMENT OF THE NEUROTIC OFFENDER

The first prerequisite in treating a neurotic offender is a psychiatric study in order to find out more about his personality make-up and the motivation which prompted his crime. Depending upon the conclusions, either psychoanalysis, individual psychotherapy, or group therapy should be given. If a person has a few neurotic traits, then possibly a method such as suggestion or persuasion might suffice, but where very involved disturbances are present, indicating a neurosis of a deep-seated nature, psychoanalysis is necessary.

The classical method of psychoanalysis is not feasible in a prison setting because there are too many emotional resistances stemming from the prison atmosphere itself. However, when the psychoanalytic method is modified by having the psychoanalyst play a more active part, this method should be the first choice in dealing with an offender whose general psychological make-up would make psychiatric treatment feasible.

One striking point in the psychoanalytic treatment of prisoners is the repeated discovery that many of their unconscious motivations are very near the surface. Often only a part of a dream or a new insight is very apt to bring out relevant unconscious features of the personality.

A frequent kind of psychoneurosis which can be successfully

treated only by psychoanalysis is the obsessive-compulsory type, such as kleptomania and pyromania. A case in which obsessive-compulsory traits are combined with displaced sexual desires is one which I have mentioned before in passing. It involves a nineteen-year-old boy who was sent to prison for tying up and robbing a young girl.

A history of his background will be helpful in understanding the case. His relationship with his parents was not good. Although he was close to his mother, he felt rejected by her, and he had hostile feelings toward his father, who was a rather dominating, aggressive, and punitive person who restricted his sexual activities and punished him severely when he caught him masturbating. Not only did the boy become rebellious toward his father, but also toward all authority, and he became inhibited both socially and sexually. He felt that these inhibitions were imposed upon him by an outside force, and because of this, he became suspicious of everyone. He started hating women when a young boy, and after he grew up, he was too shy to ask a girl for a date. He was a good student in school but lost interest when he started on his path of crime.

During the psychoanalytic sessions it became clear that the boy's marked hostility toward his father was not only due to his father's strictness, but also to the boy's own unresolved Oedipal feelings. He attributed the rejection he felt from his mother to his own inadequacy. Therefore, he developed the idea that he could not win the love of a woman on his own merits but could only obtain sexual gratification by force.

Graduation from high school to him meant freedom from authority, and time to carry on his criminal activities. He would follow girls into their apartments, tie them up, and then leave. It was his vicarious way of obtaining some sort of sexual gratification. By tying up the girl, he frustrated himself but at the same time made her helpless or powerless; in a sense he thereby castrated her. Unconsciously he really wanted to tie up his own mother.

Because he somehow felt "this whole thing was crazy" and because he found a pistol in one of these apartments, he got the idea of holding up the women as well before leaving. He would take money from their pocketbooks in order to cover up his original motive for entering the apartment. Once, he stated, he tied up a woman and took her out of town, where they spent the entire night together without his molesting her. The next morning he walked her back to town and released her.

During treatment he showed symptoms of withdrawal and suspicion. He admitted that he had difficulty in talking about himself because he feared that people would find him ridiculous. He was anxious to know the reason for his strange behavior toward women. The answer is obvious to the psychoanalyst who has had this patient in treatment. He obtained complete satisfaction by tying women up and walking away from them, thus denying them the satisfaction of what he felt were their own wishes (their unconscious wish to be raped) and thereby revealing his utter contempt for them.

His psychoanalysis in prison brought him to some understanding of the motivations for his attacks on women and also of his need to submit to authority. His feelings of inferiority lessened, and he was more at peace with himself, which was substantiated by new psychological tests, showing that he had a better conscious control of his motor impulses than before. It was interesting to see that while the original Rorschach tests indicated that he was emotionally immature and narcissistic, later psychiatric examinations, coupled with psychological tests, revealed that his feelings had matured and that he had a better understanding of himself.

During psychoanalysis his dreams reflected his strong desire for parole and his feeling of rejection and dejection when the Parole Board at first refused him. Toward the end of his stay in prison, the idea of being incarcerated became almost unbearable, and he had frequent nightmares which indicated his feeling of being passed by and of being unjustly treated. When he was given notice that he was to be paroled, I asked him to write down what he felt and thought. He wrote the following:

"Frankly, I feel kind of happy and tired—happy because I will soon be going home and because a turning point in my life has been reached where I believe the future years will be much more pleasant and happy than the past ones and tired because for a long number of years I have been waging quite a battle to understand and conquer the deficiencies and fears which for too many years became an integral part of my personality and led to much unhappiness and ultimately to jail. I am very grateful . . . I myself feel quite sure that by continuing the process of self-understanding when I return to a normal physical environment—that is, when I get out of jail—I will be able to lead a happy life and in some small way be useful in this world."

He was paroled a few months later in the custody of his parents upon the strict condition that he continue psychiatric treatment. I do not know whether he did or not, for his parents lived in a distant part of the country, and it was difficult to keep track of the case. When his parole was up five years later, he moved to another state and unfortunately reverted to his old custom of tying up women, except that, tragically, this time he killed them. He had murdered three women before he was apprehended and sentenced to death. It is a pity that this offender could not have received more psychiatric treatment in a suitable institution. Perhaps his victims—and he—could have been saved.

A method of treatment not too far removed from psychoanalysis is individual psychotherapy. It differs from psychoanalysis chiefly in that it treats on a more conscious level and handles more situational difficulties than deeper problems. For example, dreams are usually not the essence of an individual psychotherapeutic session, whereas they are vital in psychoanalysis, which invades the unconscious mind. Psychotherapy is less likely to bring about a change of feelings and attitudes than psychoanalysis is because of this. The therapist uses both directive and nondirective therapy in that he lets the patient talk out his problems but endeavors to channelize his mode of thinking. A drawback to psychotherapy is that the patient is apt to intellectualize his behavior and actions rather than understand them emotionally. However, its greatest asset is that it tries to solve the immediate situational problems, which often is the only thing the patient wants or even needs in some cases, and thus allows him to continue functioning for a while free of this pressing strain.

Another form of treatment is group therapy, which was used in prison for the first time by my associates and me at Sing Sing in 1948. Since then, this method has become quite common. Although group therapy cannot do as much for a person as psychoanalysis or individual psychotherapy it has definite advantages. For one thing, more prisoners per hour can be treated than either of the other two methods allow. During our treatment of prisoners in Sing Sing, we made many observations of this method. At that time for comparison purposes we had four groups of offenders, two consisting of sex offenders only, and two consisting of both sex offenders and offenders whose crimes were those other than directly sexual.

When initial contact was made with the men, they were suspicious and either openly aggressive or obviously withdrawn. Eventually this distrustful attitude disappeared, if not wholly, at least to the extent to which they could be reached. All of the men in the group came to agree that their crimes, if nothing else, were impractical; that is, they caused needless suffering to other people and themselves.

At the outset the men in all groups complained about prison and its conditions. At times these complaints were accompanied by small, inconsequential outbursts in the shop, the cell, the mess hall, etc. Once this negativism subsided, however, they began to concentrate upon themselves and their own problems. In general, after receiving group therapy, all of these men made better adjustments to prison than they had previously—their work record improved, their school marks went up, and there were fewer rebellions.

The following observations of a group therapy session which I conducted are quite interesting. This particular session centered around gambling. After one inmate, B., had stated that gambling belonged to life and that there was gambling in every situation in life from the time you were born, D. stated that many people liked to gamble, but they did not know the reason for it. I had pointed out in a previous meeting that there were two reasons which induced people to gamble. One was sexual in nature (masturbation), and the other was the gambler's enjoyment of putting things in the hands of fate; he liked to leave things up to destiny, to place them in "the lap of the gods." B. and D. agreed that there could be a sexual thrill in gambling, but that that was not the whole story.

G. said that he wanted money because he had always been poor. " 'No money, no food,' " my mother used to say, "and I was always hungry." The discussion then centered around money and what one could get for it. "You can buy all things in the world," F. said. He continued, "When you have money, you can get everything." H. interrupted and said, "You must have a personality to handle money."

At the end of the hour D. began to speak again. He admitted that he had gambled away $7,000. He had not had a job since 1936. When asked why he had not spoken earlier about his gambling, he said that he had wanted to listen rather than speak. "Society is against you," he said bitterly. H. said that when I had last told them the story of the gambler who was on the verge of shooting himself, he had stated that women were greater gamblers than men. Then he went on to say that everything we did was a gamble. B. concurred and said that when you sat in a bar and flipped a coin for who was going to pay for the drink or when you bet in any situation, it all showed that there was gambling in every part of life.

During this latter part of the hour, there was a certain amount of regression in some of the members. A few of them acted out their hostility by becoming threatening, but it passed over. A catharsis had taken place, as has been observed in many other groups during therapy sessions.[12]

During group therapy sessions the members frequently acted out their conflicts, which in this type of treatment is healthy and important in that it provides clues to unconscious material. At times a prisoner stopped therapy abruptly, refusing to attend the sessions. He was then called in for an individual session to explain his absence if he wished. Sometimes he was advised to attend the sessions even if he did not say anything. At other times it was felt that the prisoner was so hostile and rebellious that in his present state of mind it would have been to his disadvantage and also to the group's for him to participate.

As a result of group therapy we found that a process of maturation took place. Most of the offenders gained more insight into themselves, felt more at ease, and had fewer anxieties. How deep this process of maturation went was difficult to assess at the time therapy was over.[13] However, during treatment in a prison setting, or in any other setting, for that matter, it is always advantageous to utilize psychological tests in order to gauge any progress the offender makes in treatment.

The goals of group therapy are essentially the same as all other socially oriented plans of treatment—to help the patients express their more positive emotions and constructive traits. Here is a partial listing of the changes in the group as a whole over a period of fourteen months. Initially some of the negative factors expressed included overt hostility toward the project, the therapist, and prison in the form of negativism, suspiciousness, tardiness, absence without apparent cause, defensiveness, use of vile language, and expressions of cynicism, disgust, and futility. It is reasonable to assume that the same kind of behavior was manifested by the inmate before he entered prison and before therapy and that most likely it would have continued when he left prison, were he not treated. Subsequent changes toward positive emotions and behavior included assertiveness, humor and laughter, expressions of warmth, love, and sympathy, emphasis on helping others as well as self, and expressions of trust and of feelings of worthiness.

TREATMENT OF OFFENDERS WITH NEUROTIC CHARACTER DISORDERS AND GENUINE PSYCHOPATHIC OFFENDERS

Treatment of offenders with neurotic character disorders and genuine psychopathic offenders presents the most difficult problem to the psychiatrist and to prison authorities. Such offenders are usually the prison troublemakers, since they act out their impulses and try to exploit their environment. There is hardly another group in which therapy and prognosis is of so much significance because of the seriousness of the crimes committed by such criminals. Although punishment ,most often is without success, nevertheless in many cases incarceration is the only protection society has against these offenders. This is especially true of offenders with genuine psychopathic personalities, who are not amenable to treatment.

Individual psychiatric treatment of the offender manifesting a character disorder is difficult because, as Dr. Edward Glover says, the offender tries "to test the analyst's capacity to stand the strain and disappointment caused by his behavior. Indeed, unless the analyst is capable of meeting this situation without either a negative response or a calculated restraint of negative reactions, he should not undertake the analysis of a delinquent psychopath, who will not be long in penetrating the analyst's armor and so bring about, either actively or passively, the end of his analysis." [14]

In view of this difficulty the question arises as to whether many of these people are not better off in an institution for rehabilitation and training, where the authorities have due consideration for the individual capacity of the offenders. Provided that no mental defect or organic brain lesion is present, the offenders will have a chance to mature and to adjust socially. Such training, in addition to some type of psychotherapy when indicated, is then a matter of re-education. During the past twenty years a training and re-educational program has been inaugurated in certain institutions with the aim of repairing the offender's character defect. Such a program can only be successfully carried out, however, when the prisoners are under a consistently disciplined yet friendly regime.

Many homosexuals suffer from a neurosis, a neurotic character disorder, or even a psychosis. The choice treatment for homosexuality, and any other type of sexual perversion, is psychoanalysis. The result of the treatment depends largely upon the offender's desire to change his own personality so that he can take up a heterosexual life. The outlook for a homosexual or other type of sexual deviate is better when his distorted drive is related to a neurosis than when it is part of his neurotic character, although even in the latter instance the treatment is not hopeless. If the sexual deviation is not connected with any neurosis, psychosis, or any character defect, the patient does not seek help because the pleasure he receives from his perversion is too pronounced. Also some homosexuals, like other offenders, have an unconscious desire to be punished, which makes them avoid psychoanalysis so that they can be imprisoned.[15]

But if prison can do obvious harm to any type of offender, it is most likely to be the homosexual, for not only is there very little or no psychiatric treatment available here for him, but also he is exposed to nothing but men and to an atmosphere where, because of the lack of opportunity for normal sex relations, homosexuality is likely to exist even among persons who do not practice it on the outside. The rather severe punishment to which homosexuals are subjected in comparison with the short sentences given to other sex offenders who have committed more serious acts is out of order in an organized society. It is not unusual to see sex offenders who impair the morals of minors given shorter sentences than homosexuals, although the former are considered more dangerous to the security of society because it is in that group that we find many murderers. It is my fervent belief and hope that the time will come when society regards those persons suffering from homosexuality in a more enlightened manner.

A program for criminal psychopaths (offenders suffering from neurotic character disorders) with special emphasis on sex offenders was instituted in Herstedvester, Denmark, in 1935 under the directorship of Dr. Georg K. Stürup. It was set up in a special detention institution under the direction of psychiatrists, and because its growth necessitated constant expansion, another similar, but temporary, institution, which is independent of it, was established at Horsens in 1952. When I visited Dr. Stürup at Herstedvester a few years ago, he told me that the most important types of treatment at his institution were work therapy (which was sometimes supplemented by psychotherapy) and castration.

He said that of the 120 sex offenders who had been admitted to his hospital, 80 had been castrated, and up to that time, only 2 of these 80 had committed new sex offenses after their release. It is also interesting to note that Dr. C. C. Hawke of the State School of Mental Defectives in Winfield, Kansas, issued a report on about

300 sex offenders, most of whom were mentally defective, who had been castrated. He feels that the remedy for the confirmed sex criminal is castration, which they have used at the school since 1894.

Aftereffects of castration in the form of mental or emotional disturbances are often present, but the depressive emotional phenomena, which are so frequently observed in noncriminal castrates, occur very rarely after the castration of a sex offender. Castration brings about an inner tranquility in the sex offender which he did not possess before. However, it must be admitted that suicide has occasionally taken place following castration. Of 190 operations of this type performed, 5 of the castrates committed suicide.

Dr. Stürup reports that of 16 men committed for the rape of adult women, 13 have been released and 3 are still institutionalized but have not been castrated. All 13 are getting along well on the outside, 11 of whom were castrated. Of 49 offenders who had committed indecent assaults upon boys and who had been released after castration, there was no recidivism among 38 of them. This is in contrast to only 9 out of 22 offenders showing no recidivism who were charged with the same offense but were released without castration.[16]

In comparing these results, it can be seen that those persons released after castration showed a better prognosis than those released without it. However, comparative studies of sex offenders who were castrated and those who received a deeper kind of treatment, such as psychoanalysis, have never been made on a large scale to my knowledge. Although some countries, particularly the Scandinavian countries, have passed castration acts, in my opinion castration is a very drastic measure and should not be the ultimate therapy. When a person has an infection of the body, we try to cure that infection rather than remove any vital tissue unless absolutely necessary, even though removal would in a sense be a type of cure. The same should hold for a psychological disease. Moreover, in my extensive experience with sex offenders, I have found that basically they are more or less impotent anyway, be the cause physical, psychological, or both, and it is not sexual potency which stimulates the offense.

Lobotomy is another method which has been tried in the treatment of sex offenders. However, its results in this connection have been unsuccessful. Drs. Julius Levine and Harold Albert [17] report that they interviewed 40 patients after lobotomy in order to determine changes in their sexual behavior. One patient became not only psychotic but also promiscuous after the operation. His relatives reported that there seemed to be a lessening of guilt and modesty in association with sexual activity. In 4 patients the operation could be said to have been in some way responsible for involving them in social difficulties. In this connection Dr. Ørnulv Ødegård has stated that persons suffering from psychopathy can expect a good result from lobotomy when the basis for the psychopathy is constitutional and when increased emotional tension is present. He believes that an enemy of society, or a particularly aggressive antisocial person, has a good chance of being helped by this method.[18]

Narcotic addicts represent a great number of persons in the neurotic character disorder group. They are always unable to deal with their own problem, which necessitates therapy for rehabilitative purposes. Our federal government has two hospitals where this type of offender can receive treatment, but in view of the great number of addicts, each state should establish its own. In this connection Michigan has enacted a law compelling the drug addict to undergo therapy and rehabilitation, which is an encouraging step. Here a narcotics clinic has been established as part of the Detroit Department of Health. In contrast to the many out-patient narcotics clinics which were in existence in the 1920s, this clinic does not follow the ambiguous practice of maintaining that the sale of such drugs is illegal on the one hand and on the other providing the offender with them so that he need not obtain them illegally at black market prices, a procedure that only helps to maintain the addiction, thus defeating its own purpose in a sense. The Michigan clinic does not provide drugs to the addicts but endeavors to treat them so that they can overcome their addiction.

A very close relationship exists among the Detroit Department of Health, the psychiatric division of the Detroit Receiving Hospital, and the Department of Psychiatry of Wayne University. All three facilities work jointly under clinical, therapeutic, and administrative control. This type of program, however, requires highly specialized treatment facilities, where the staff is particularly trained to deal with all phases of acute withdrawal, physiological and physical rehabilitation, and psychological and social reorientation. Dr. Raskin and his associates indicate that there must be compulsory contact with the patient after his release from the hospital so that he can continue treatment on an out-patient basis.[19]

It is my considered opinion that our coping with drug addicts, whether or not they have committed any crime, has been a failure. Although psychiatric treatment would be the choice method of handling them, this method, including hospitalization, has failed in a great majority of cases. Addicts are going in and out of psychiatric hospitals, jails, and prisons year in and year out with little or no improvement in sight. What we forget is that the drug addict most often suffers from a deep-seated emotional and mental disturbance which can be cured or alleviated only under persistent psychiatric care and only if he is willing to accept such treatment. Often he accepts treatment only because the court orders him to do so, which means his participation is involuntary.

It is high time to reorient ourselves in dealing with drug addicts. We must establish institutions and work camps where addicts can be confined for a long period of time and where they are given constructive work according to their individual ability and in conjunction with individual and group psychotherapy. Remember that most drug addicts are extremely self-centered and somehow must be drawn out of their shells. This may possibly be achieved by putting them to team or group work where some of their individual ambitions may be gratified.

A detailed, carefully worked-out plan ought to be instituted both by federal and state agencies where research projects are included. In this respect it is gratifying that the State Department of Mental Hygiene of New York, under the able direction of Commissioner Paul H. Hoch, has started research on drug addicts at Manhattan State Hospital, New York City.

But research is not enough in dealing with the many-sided problem of drug addiction. We first have to change our attitude toward the drug addict. Basically he is not a criminal although, of course, his craving may lead him into criminal activity. Rather we should consider him a mentally ill person in need of treatment. For this reason we must establish a program of medical supervision in which rehabilitation is stressed.

Last but not least, drug addiction may possibly be eased by taking the great profit out of the illegal drug traffic. England, which has instituted distribution of drugs to addicts in established clinics, does not have an addiction problem of the dimensions we have here, although, of course, our population in the United States is quite different from that in England. If the enormous profit that the illegal drug traffic pours into the pockets of racketeers could be eliminated, a reduction in the number of drug addicts would be an indirect result. Although we may not find any ideal solution for this constant problem, medical and correctional rehabilitation will have to go hand in hand.

Many offenders suffering from character disorders are alcoholics. Alcoholics are usually socially sensitive persons who do not feel that they are part of society, that is, that they do not belong. They are unhappy people, escaping from reality, causing untold anxiety to their families, and creating danger to society, since much of criminal behavior receives its impetus from alcoholic intoxication.

The basis for the alcoholic's maladaptation is fundamentally sexual. By and large, psychoanalysis is essential for his rehabilitation, although individual psychotherapy and group therapy have been successful in a certain number of cases. Once in a while we see alcoholics cured through prolonged, determined abstinence from alcohol. In a study made by Dr. Frederick Lemere, it was found that 7 percent of alcoholics who quit drinking did so on their own without outside help.[20] However, often in these cases there are unhealthy side effects; e.g., some of these persons come out of the cure becoming ascetics or fanatics of another sort. In these cases the manifestation of the problem has changed, but the problem itself still remains. Then too Alcoholics Anonymous has

done much good work with alcoholics, and the Danish drug antabuse has served as a deterrent. But sobriety should not be the chief
aim. The ultimate achievement is an emotionally healthy person,
and we can only attain this when we get to the root of the
problem.

By the same token probation or imprisonment without any
therapy is useless. And if therapy is given, it should be continued
after the alcoholic has been released from prison—when he is on
parole—which, by the way, is a good rule to follow for any type
of offender.

A relatively new development in dealing with offenders is probation combined with psychiatric treatment. For the past twenty-
five years many offenders, such as kleptomaniacs, burglars, and
some types of sex offenders—exhibitionists and homosexuals, for
example—have been put on probation and given psychiatric treatment. There is no doubt that in suitable cases more progress can
be made by giving psychiatric treatment to an offender while
under probation than by incarcerating him, and it is particularly
true with young offenders. This system eliminates the blot of a
prison record, as well as the deleterious effects of prison, while it
endeavors to help the offender change and adjust to society.

However, it should be noted that not all offenders are suitable
for probation even with psychiatric treatment. Therefore, each
one should be carefully screened, particularly taking into consideration his personality make-up, including the ego strength of
his personality, his constructive traits, and his desire to reform,
which to a large extent determines his ability to identify with the
psychiatrist and his rapport with him, so essential for successful
treatment. Also important are the offender's family situation in
general and the strength of his family ties in particular, his prospects for getting a job, and his susceptibility to alcohol and drugs.

An effective system of probation requires probation officers of
a high caliber. The probation officer must have integrity and a
sound motivation for choosing his field of work. And above all,
he must have a full understanding of himself in order to handle
the offender adequately and to build a good rapport with him.
Although it is not a necessary prerequisite, it would be of great

advantage if the probation officer himself has undergone psycho-analysis. It would help him understand the many different personality types with whom he has to deal, and, of course, it would be helpful because by knowing his conscious and unconscious self, he would be better able to establish a good emotional relationship with the offender, which is necessary for the profitable outcome of probation. The probation officer's best therapeutic tool in handling offenders is his personality, just as it is the psychiatrist's.

In an excellent study which was carried out at Oxford, Dr. M. Grünhut went through 104 case histories of probationers, of which 62.5 percent were marked as successes and 37.5 percent as failures. Since a total of 104 cases was insufficient, 96 case studies were added so he had a total of 200 probationers. One drawback to this study is that it was not a true sampling; that is, of the 200 persons 119 were male and 81 female, an unusually high proportion of women—2 out of every 5 probationers compared with 1 woman out of every 5 offenders put on probation in England and Wales during the years 1948 to 1951.

In evaluating successes and failures, Dr. Grünhut is aware of the fact that it requires some time for the probationer to attain social maturity, overcome his criminalistic tendencies, and adjust himself to life. Thus in discussing the outcome of probation, he states: "An offender who, within a specified period, has not been brought before the court, may in the end turn out to be a failure, while an early relapse will not exclude a final success. As a working hypothesis, it has been assumed that persons for whom at least two years after the termination of treatment no symptoms of maladjustment were on record could be regarded as early successes. Correspondingly, those with a bad record within the first two years after their penal and corrective treatment have been assessed as early failures. There are, further, cases with a long history of criminal offences and repeated experiences of penal and corrective treatment. Some of these show a definite improvement, manifested over a period of at least two years without further recidivism. This sub-group has been classified as late successes. The rest must be regarded as late failures." Dr. Grünhut classified the 200 as follows: 71 early and 61 late successes; 21 early and 47 late failures. "The general success-rate of the whole unselected group is therefore 66 percent." [21]

A case of successful probation with psychoanalysis is that of a young married man who embezzled $35,000. For five years he had been involved with another woman, for whom he had bought expensive clothes, jewelry, and furs. Since she unconsciously represented a mother to him, he was never sexually intimate with her. He only wanted from her the attention which he had not received from his parents, who had lavished it all upon his younger brother. His upbringing had been strict, with a complete lack of sex education. When he was twenty-four years old, he married but felt that he did not receive enough affection and attention from his wife and so sought another woman.

After untangling the facts of this case, particularly taking into consideration the offender's neurotic make-up and the fact that this was his first crime, I recommended probation with psychiatric treatment—in this case psychoanalysis—rather than prison, and the offender was to make restitution for the embezzled money. When the judge had finished reading my lengthy report, he called me into his chambers and asked: "Can you guarantee that if this man is given treatment he will get well?"

"No," I told him. "I cannot guarantee that he will get well, but I will guarantee you this: if he is sent to prison, he will become a hardened offender." The judge, recognizing the particular aspects of this case, put him on probation with the understanding that he pay back the money and undergo psychiatric treatment.

Thanks to the extensive cooperation of the Probation Department and the probationer, psychiatric treatment was initiated. The road was long and bumpy, but after a few years of psychoanalysis, most of the probationer's conflicts were solved. He got a good job, became reunited with his wife, and bought a house, all the while paying back the money which he had embezzled. Six years after he had received probation, his old firm took him back, and he has been working there ever since. He has written me regularly, telling how happy he is and expressing his gratitude. Indeed, this is gratifying.

TREATMENT OF MENTALLY DEFECTIVE
AND PSYCHOTIC OFFENDERS

The procedure for handling mentally defective and psychotic offenders, including epileptics, is clear if they are insane or mentally defective according to the law. However, the cases where these persons are mentally abnormal without being legally insane are of serious concern to the psychiatrist, the judge, the probation officer, and all other authorities who will have to deal with them.

The case of a man who was sentenced to the Michigan penitentiary for three-and-a-half to four years for attempted rape will demonstrate this. He was kept out of society as long as the law permitted, but because his term of punishment expired and he was not insane in the legal sense, he could not be held any longer by the prison authorities. Hence he was released in spite of the fact that the prison psychiatrist stated in the following words that his release would be definitely dangerous to society: "Frankly, he is not psychotic, not committable to an institution for the insane, but he is definitely assaultive and potentially homicidal." Within two weeks he had murdered three people.[22] Cases like this are too numerous to be listed, and it is clear that the criterion should be whether such persons are able to get along in society without being a menace to it.

The same standard should apply to mental defectives. The test should actually be whether or not they are socially defective. I remember one man who had been kept in an institution for mental defectives throughout his childhood and who later led a disorganized life full of antisocial and criminal activities. Psychometric tests indicated an I.Q. of borderline intelligence, but in view of his personality make-up and his antisocial and criminal activities, I raised the question as to whether this man would be able to adjust to society at all. It was my opinion that he would be a source of constant trouble and that it was imperative he be given adequate care. The judge sentenced him to prison, in accordance with the law, but there is little doubt that when he is released he will resume his criminal activities.

On the other hand, there are those offenders who are found to be mentally defective by psychometric tests but who are not really socially defective. In fact, they are able to adjust themselves socially. The case of a twenty-five-year-old man comes to my mind. He was mentally defective, but up to the time of the minor offense for which he was imprisoned, he had been able to make a good adjustment, so good that even his friends, neighbors, and employers gave him the best recommendations. One may readily doubt whether such a man, even though he was mentally defective and for this reason committable, should be institutionalized.

The fact that some mentally defective people are able to adjust socially indicates that intelligence tests do not necessarily reflect a person's emotional behavior or ability to get along in society. Thus we may assume that there are nonintellectual, as well as intellectual, factors which determine the behavior of a person. These nonintellectual factors too would therefore have to be tested if one is to obtain a proper appreciation of the person's endowment and social adjustments. An approach to such determination has already been made by Wechsler and by Doll in his Social Maturity Scale. These are excellent tools, but no psychological test can replace the clinical acumen of an experienced psychiatrist.

OTHER PSYCHOTHERAPEUTIC METHODS

Besides the psychotherapeutic methods of individual psychotherapy and group therapy already described, other techniques and tools for treatment of offenders are also available to the psychiatrist—work therapy, shock therapy, psychosurgery, hypnosis, and narcosynthesis. Work therapy can be especially beneficial to offenders not in institutions.

In the summer of 1959, Philadelphia inaugurated a program of healthful, outdoor work in order to rehabilitate its delinquent boys. Boys between sixteen and eighteen years of age who had had brushes with the police and the courts were hired to keep the city's noted Fairmount Park clean. They performed such tasks as clearing away fallen trees, thinning underbrush, maintaining paths and bridle paths and improving picnic areas. Philadelphia's

Welfare Commissioner, Randolph E. Wise, in describing the purpose of the project, said: "One of the possible approaches to the complex problem of juvenile delinquency is to offer boys in their late teens practical work experience of a constructive nature and to teach them skills and habits of a discipline that will help them to become useful citizens." [23]

Work therapy, shock therapy, psychosurgery, hypnosis, and narcosynthesis are particularly useful in the case of the mentally defective offender. If a mentally defective offender is institutionalized, the type of therapy of course depends upon the degree of defectiveness. If the offender is not too far from borderline intelligence, often a combination of individual or group psychotherapy and work therapy are effective in helping him adjust to the institution and perhaps even to society if he is released. In many cases the defectiveness is so great that no benefit can be derived from any type of therapy, with the possible exception of work therapy on a simple level. If the defectiveness is due to hereditary factors or to an acquired brain injury, the chance of improving the defective's condition is practically nil. However, we have found that the intellectual capacity of a person can be raised if emotional factors are responsible for a low I.Q. In these cases, psychiatric treatment is of utmost importance in rehabilitating the offender.

In general, prisoners who show a schizophrenic-like mechanism or who manifest a depressive or paranoid condition may be treated by shock therapy, psychosurgery, psychoanalysis, individual psychotherapy, or group therapy, or a combination of any of these. Hypnosis and narcosynthesis have been used a good deal in recent years, especially in connection with acutely deep-seated disturbances. Dr. H. M. Buchanan, of New Zealand, reported at the annual conference of Justice Department psychologists that he used hypnosis on 16 difficult prisoners and that it was a better method of helping muddled and hysterical prisoners than the use of tranquilizing drugs, although the use of tranquilizers has not been abandoned. He described the case of a young man with hysterical paralysis of the leg. Hypnosis helped him to walk without crutches and to make a complete recovery. Another prisoner was a twenty-two-year-old girl who was aggressive, insolent, and required tranquilizers in large doses. After hypnosis the dosage of the drug was reduced and finally eliminated. When she was released, she was well enough to enter nurse's training.[24]

The last few years have seen the introduction of tranquilizing drugs in the treatment of passing anxieties or depressions. Although it is too early to say how extensively these drugs will be used in the future, there is no doubt that they have increased our therapeutic armaments, especially when used in conjunction with some form of psychotherapy. If some of these chemical therapies prove successful, then we shall have to adapt psychotherapy accordingly. In the words of Paul H. Hoch: "If it is possible to reduce an individual's anxiety or to increase his ego strength with drugs, the psychotherapeutic procedure with such an individual will be different than it has been in the past." [25]

To summarize, the aim of psychiatric treatment of the offender is to integrate his ego and superego so that they can function at the same time in both an independent and an interdependent way. While realizing his assets, at the same time the offender also learns to estimate his limitations correctly. Since ego identification takes place and his egocentricity diminishes, he is better able to learn from his surroundings, bringing his superego into accord with the demands of society and himself. Previously his criminal type of ego made it possible for him to manipulate others and obtain gratification often free of guilt, but he has now learned to receive gratification on a healthy basis.

During the emotional maturation process the offender's inner tensions lessen, enabling him to withstand and endure painful experiences so that he does not need to act out all of his impulses, particularly his antisocial ones. Thus his superego becomes more integrated with his ego, and he functions consistently, not intermittently, as he did when he carried out criminal acts. It is this emotional maturation of the offender which the psychiatrist can foster.

CHAPTER XIV

The Prevention of Crime

Volumes have been written about the prevention of crime, all more or less overlooking the basic facts—the variations between human beings and the overwhelming part the mind plays in the commission of a crime. The theory of retaliation as a basis for punishment has been proven inadequate in preventing criminal acts. Although there are a few human beings who are restrained by the knowledge that they will be punished if they transgress the law, there are two types of criminals who are not at all influenced by any threat of punishment. These are the habitual criminals, who, because of a faulty development of their superego, adhere only to their own criminal code, and those persons generally manifesting pronounced neurotic symptoms, who, because of strong unconscious conflicts, are unable to resist their inner drives.

Since criminal behavior begins basically in childhood or adolescence as an emotional and social maladjustment, the elimination of crime depends principally upon the eradication of juvenile delinquency and its causes. Adult offenders usually started out as young ones, and once they have begun following an antisocial or criminal path, it is difficult to turn them from it. In trying to exterminate juvenile delinquency, however, we must realize that individual psychotherapy or psychoanalysis will not succeed in all cases, even if we did have a sufficient number of psychiatrists to handle all of our delinquent children.

Bearing in mind that the roots of crime are both mental and social, our approach to the problem must be both a psychological and a sociological one. It is of the utmost importance to distinguish between those children whose delinquency problem is predominantly a sociological one and those who manifest personality disturbances. Where both of these causative factors are present, both approaches have to be used; each case must be evaluated to determine what proportion of the problem is rooted in a psychological disturbance and what proportion has sociological causes.

How, then, are we going to prevent, control, or counteract emotional, mental, biological, or sociological deficiencies?—by directing our attention and applying our knowledge to their causes, much as a physician treats a physical or mental disease. Our treatment must be causative and manifold but of course, more highly individualized than for most physical ailments. In many cases a cure will depend upon how easy it is to modify the personality structure of the individual. Treatment of an offender will thus vary with each individual and each situation.

In creating a program for the prevention of crime, we must be aware that the psychological and sociological factors which contribute to the making of a criminal do not operate singly. Rather they intermingle, resulting in an interplay where sometimes psychological, and at other times sociological, forces predominate. It must be stressed here that environmental factors, generally speaking, do not in themselves produce criminal behavior in youngsters. Practically all cases of juvenile delinquency will therefore require some type of psychiatric treatment. But this is not enough. The social situation of the young offender has to be investigated carefully and possibly remedied. This means examining his entire socio-economic situation—his family, school, neighborhood, etc.—and then charting a course for action.

I have found that the most beneficial time for treating youngsters is around the period of their puberty—from the age of ten or eleven to fifteen or sixteen—as Dr. Melitta Schmideberg concurs.[1] But if a youngster is quite disturbed or manifests persistent antisocial behavior, there is no doubt that he must be treated at once. If we are able to catch and cope with a child's problem at an early stage, we might prevent his pathological development to such an extent that the child in many cases would not need psychoanalysis.[2] Therefore, I cannot emphasize enough how important early detection is.

Fortunately, not all juvenile delinquents or criminals are neurotic; some are only slightly emotionally disturbed. However, it is the neurotic ones who always seem to get caught. In Edith Buxbaum's words: "Those who are neurotic constitute the unsuccessful delinquents who are easily caught and never learn from experience."[3] I would like to add that the reason is that they unconsciously prefer to be caught and punished in order to rid themselves of their guilt feelings.

The sometimes baffling thing to many people is that since all of us have criminal desires and wishes within ourselves, why do some act them out while others do not, even where the situation seems to be identical? Here the strength or weakness of "T" and "R" in our formula $C = \dfrac{T + S}{R}$ comes into play. Actual acting out of antisocial impulses seems to stem from a definite stimulus arising from either or both of two main sources: conscious or unconscious environmental sanction of antisocial or criminal behavior by parents, peers, etc., and the offender's defective superego and ego.

When we say that an offender's superego and ego are defective we do not necessarily mean consistent malfunctioning. The superego and ego may sometimes be weak or defective, and sometimes even apparently normal. Although we need not point to a specific case history of this vicariously working superego and ego, it may be clear when we think of the child who steals but never acts out other antisocial or criminal impulses or the offender who unlawfully acts out his sexual impulses but in other respects is quite law-abiding. Since he is specific in his selection, he may choose his particular crime because his superego and ego are weak in that area, permitting him to act out impulses so that tension can be relieved.

THE ROLE OF PARENTS

Giving psychiatric treatment to an offender who always acts out his impulses is difficult. In fact, a patient who constantly acts out cannot be psychoanalyzed. How then can we proceed? Such offenders have to be treated in a controlled environment where they are continually supervised and where a psychiatrist is available for treatment. With the juvenile delinquent who only acts out his impulses at times, frequently not only the child but also the parents must be treated. For example, hostility by parents is often expressed in the form of a threat of desertion. Parents too often say to a child: "If you don't like it here, you can leave. We can get along without you." I am sure that many who say these things are consciously not aware of the effect it has on a child—instilling him with a feeling of complete rejection.

Often we find that only one child out of several in a family becomes delinquent, and we ask why. The answer may lie in unconscious parental hostility toward a particular child or favoritism toward another. The psychiatrist can often determine this when he sees the type of communication which exists between parents and child. Then too, tension within a family, whether it be overt or covert, often plays a strong part in a child's delinquency. The psychiatrist must make every effort to uncover it, however difficult.

I remember Bob, a twelve-year-old whose parents were divorced when he was eight. Prior to that time, he had witnessed many quarrels between them, always with the end result of being sent to his room, which filled him with resentment. In a sense he was being punished for something beyond his control. Bob had also been strongly attached to his mother until his brother was born. Then he became resentful toward her and jealous of the baby, expressing these feelings in aggressiveness, lying, and petty stealing. The problem grew progressively worse. One day Bob beat his little brother severely, and when his mother interfered, he protested that his brother had started the fight. His mother became infuriated and shouted at Bob, "You'll *never* be any good! You'll always be a troublemaker!" Thus, unwittingly Bob's mother instilled in his mind the idea that he would always be in trouble, and because of her own neurotic make-up, she actually, though unconsciously, expected only failure from him and also unconsciously wished for it. Her prediction was not long in coming true. Shortly thereafter, it was discovered that Bob had been truant from school quite often, and when some money disappeared from the house, his mother became suspicious that Bob had taken it, despite his denials. One day he was caught stealing five dollars, and that same night he dreamed his mother gave him water instead of the chocolate milk she usually served. He awakened the entire family with his screaming and could be quieted down only after great effort on everyone's part.

In my first interview with Bob I did not ask him anything about his truancy or stealing. I let him talk about himself freely. He mentioned that his father no longer lived with them and that he had a younger brother. As the interviews continued, it became apparent that he felt a lack of attention and love from his mother. He had therefore invented another way, however indirect, of gaining attention by stealing money and "playing hooky." His desire for attention was intimately connected with his feeling of being unwanted, which had come more to the fore when his younger brother was born.

It was obvious that Bob's mother also had to be seen by a psychotherapist. At first she insisted that Bob received enough attention from her, but as treatment progressed she realized that she did favor the younger child, and attention was directed toward uncovering the reasons for this. One day she revealed that her younger sister and she had quarreled frequently as children. Yet after her parents died she had taken care of her sister and supported her through college, though she resented doing so. After disclosing this, she was able to recognize her hostility toward her sister and the way it had carried over to Bob. In truth Bob's mother was hostile toward both of her children. Her seeming favoritism toward the younger boy was shown to be overprotectiveness, which was an unconscious mask for feeling guilty about her hostility toward him.

Further sessions revealed that her father had objected to her marriage because her intended husband was "no good," and that she had postponed it until after her father died. Her marriage was unsuccessful, and when her husband finally left her, she took out on Bob the hostility she felt toward her husband, thus achieving some gratification for her hostile feelings. This also reflected how poorly integrated a personality she had. Within herself were unconscious forbidden impulses which she could not act out but found it a strain to control. When Bob acted out his antisocial impulses, she received vicarious gratification, and in scolding and punishing Bob for his misbehavior, she was providing him with the attention he sought and thus propelling him toward further antisocial acts. Simultaneously she was also punishing herself, for consciously she was unhappy and disturbed about her child's behavior.

Bob's case shows how a child can be started on the wrong path through family tension at home and through a feeling of being unloved and unwanted. It also shows that sometimes the problem is not so simple that it can be solved merely by giving treatment to the child but often requires treatment of a strategically dominant member of the family as well.

It goes without saying that the mother's attitude toward her child and the atmosphere she creates in the home are of utmost importance to the child in psychoanalysis, particularly if he has not yet reached the latency period. And possibly one of the most difficult problems for the psychiatrist during a child's psychoanalysis is that of handling the mother, i.e., establishing a positive relationship with her. Since the psychoanalyst tries to reduce the child's dependence upon the mother and to develop his ego functioning so that he does not revert to his infantile fantasies and regressions, thus in a sense liberating the child from his dependence upon his mother and helping him develop as normally as possible, we can see where this might play upon the antagonisms of a mother whose very neurosis is that she must dominate her child and thereby keep him dependent. If the mother's problem is very deep-seated, she would probably need psychoanalysis herself, and often it is better for her to go to a different analyst than her child's, since the child's emotional problems are so intimately tied up with hers.

However, often it is unnecessary for a mother to undergo psychoanalysis. She may merely need to consult a psychiatrist at certain times, or if she cannot do so for some reason, then a competent psychologist or psychiatric social worker who work under the supervision of a psychiatrist or psychoanalyst. In her contacts with the consultant her problems concerning her child are worked through, and she is given insight into them and her own actions, often resulting in a change of attitude and behavior toward her child. By giving the mother some form of psychiatric help, her jealousy of her child which may have arisen because he is given analysis is lessened. Such jealousy or hostility may arise because in a sense the mother considers herself a failure because her child needs analysis, because of the added expense placed on the budget, because her child has a closeness toward someone other than herself, or because her child is receiving something which she has not received, thereby feeling a narcissistic hurt. She becomes placated and even gratified in knowing that she is doing something to help work out her child's problem.

Group therapy is of value in treating the child if it is combined with individual therapy because it affords an interpersonal and intercommunicative action.[4] Group therapy at times is often of much benefit to the child's parents as well in that it may ease their resistance and the psychoanalyst or psychiatrist may not have to be the one to point out the neurotic traits exhibited by the parent which he, the psychiatrist, feels are responsible for the child's behavior; the group members frequently do this for him so that the risk of interrupting his own rapport with the parent is lessened.

Some people believe that parents are always at fault when their child becomes a juvenile delinquent or has difficulties at home, with other children, or with school. This is not so. There are many reasons why parents, in and of themselves, may not be completely responsible for their child's misbehavior. Sometimes a child develops antisocial and hostile feelings because of situations beyond the parents' control. He may feel resentful and jealous of the attention his mother must necessarily give to the younger children, or an incident in school which he does not confide to his parents may seriously upset him. All too often parents become the scapegoat of children who, because of their own immaturity (and perhaps partially that of the parents), cannot accept the responsibility for their behavior and blame their actions on having been "rejected" by their parents. True, as we saw in Bob's case, there are mothers and fathers who consciously or unconsciously reject their children, but not every parent does. A great deal depends on the situation and the child's interpretation and reaction to it.

Regardless of whether it is their fault or not, what can parents do when they discover that their child is antisocial? With passing symptoms, such as occasional lying or stealing, a factual talk with the child may help, but it can be beneficial only if the parents make a definite attempt to understand the child.

We cannot establish a blanket rule for all cases. Each parent must know his own child. Is he hostile or fearful? Is he shy or aggressive? Does he let his aggressiveness out by being unduly destructive or by committing antisocial or even criminal acts? What lies underneath his hostility or hatred? It is probably fear because a child who is emotionally secure will not hate.

Parents can avoid or reduce rebelliousness in children by setting a good example, for children identify with their parents and tend to mimic them. When parents tell their children "Do as I say, but not as I do," it only confuses them, while being a good model for the child to follow keeps discipline at a minimum.

For example, how many mothers have not unwittingly encouraged stealing by saying something like this to their daughter: "You can take your sister's blouse. She hardly ever wears it, and I'm sure she won't miss it." If a child is too young to understand and such incidents occur often enough in her home, she may well extend this attitude to other areas. Seeing a department store counter filled with merchandise and distorting her mother's statement somewhat, she may simply help herself here too. Or a father may say to his son: "I'll give you a dollar, but don't tell your mother."

This gives the boy the impression that things can be obtained by sneakiness or by undercover methods.

Let us take the case of Marie, for example, a sixteen-year-old girl whose antisocial and criminal inclinations were rechanneled into healthy directions and who was rehabilitated emotionally through extensive psychiatric treatment but who came upon dishonesty in her job. Marie became a salesgirl after she was discharged from an institution. One day she was showing a sweater to a customer, who commented that the size was too small and was about to leave the store because Marie told her the sweater was not available in the size she wanted. At that moment the proprietor appeared on the scene. When Marie explained the situation, he asked the customer to wait while he located her size, and he took Marie with him into the stockroom. There he merely replaced the size tag on the original sweater with a tag stamped the size the customer had requested. Marie was faced with the difficult choice of doing something dishonest or running the risk of losing her job by refusing to sell the mismarked item.

A basic move in our fight against juvenile delinquency would be to change our fundamental method of child-rearing. Although every child must be brought up with a certain degree of freedom in order to express himself, there must also be some discipline, for with freedom comes responsibility. Too many well-meaning parents and so-called "lay professionals" have misconstrued progressivism. Complete and absolute freedom does not mean that the child will have no emotional problems. Quite the contrary is true. Children need to know that there is a guiding hand which will not let them run wild and will be there as a symbol of strength in times of trouble. Furthermore, a child must learn that in this world he must give as well as take; otherwise, he will grow up to be an immature, selfish, egocentric, and unloving, as well as an unloved, human being.

Even a somewhat emotionally disturbed child can withstand and tolerate discipline, and only in cases where the child is obviously psychotic or otherwise severely disturbed emotionally will disciplinary measures be harmful. But punishment or any other form of discipline must be consistent or the child will be confused about acceptable and unacceptable behavior. What was wrong yesterday is wrong today and will be wrong tomorrow and should not depend upon the mood of the parent. Only by proper guidance and discipline can a child learn to discipline himself later in life.

If a child feels that he is genuinely loved and that punishment is justified, his hostility toward his parents or those who administer discipline will be shortlived. It is of tremendous importance for parents to establish a good emotional relationship with their child so that there is a feeling of rapport between them. They must let him know that they are his friends and that he is a person they would like to understand. Only when they have gained his confidence will he talk to them and reveal what is on his mind. If, however, his antisocial behavior persists or he reveals many negative traits over a certain period of time, the parents must seek outside professional help—a child guidance clinic, a psychiatrist, or a psychoanalyst.

THE IMPORTANCE OF THE SCHOOLS

The conquest of juvenile delinquency does not rest only in the home, however. It requires a broad mental hygiene plan embodying the concept of guidance and discipline and including the schools, one of the most important means of preventing juvenile delinquency. When parents or the general environment have failed the child, the schools must carry an even greater burden. It is impossible to go into all aspects of the schools' handling of youngsters, but a few main points need to be stressed.

In a national survey I made a few years ago of almost 2¾ million children in public and private schools throughout the United States, it was found that about 10 percent of our children in public schools are emotionally disturbed;[5] the percentage in private schools is 11.7.[6] To meet this need, there was only one psychiatrist for every 50,000 children, one psychologist for every 10,964 children, and one psychiatric social worker for every 38,461 children in the public schools. This is highly inadequate, since we know that ideally a school system should have one psychiatrist for every

8,000 children, one psychologist for every 2,000 children, and one psychiatric social worker for every 3,000 children.[7]

The lack of professional psychiatric help in our schools, and in fact, in child guidance and mental hygiene clinics outside of our schools, is a serious situation, especially in the light of the close connection between mental abnormality and crime. Even if we could concentrate our help on only one group of disturbed youngsters—the habitually truant—it would be a giant step in the right direction. In examining adult criminals, a high proportion were truant from school as children and teen-agers. Truancy, therefore, is one danger signal which should put us on the alert if we are to effectively prevent the ever-growing increase in crime. Here is one area in which the schools can be of utmost help.

To solve the problem somewhat, the New York City school system has developed the "600 Schools" for children who are truant or who have committed antisocial acts. These are children who manifest serious emotional and behavioral problems and for whom the present procedures in grade and junior high schools have not been successful. The purpose of the "600 Schools" is to separate disturbed youngsters from the more normal pupils, for a disturbed child can be a handicap in a classroom, disrupting the learning process for others and constituting an actual hazard for the safety of all in the school. The "600 Schools" accomplishes this, and it is one of their greatest advantages. However, the benefit is much more one of isolation than of correction.

It has been estimated that between 10 and 15 percent of the youngsters sent to the "600 Schools" are so disturbed that they need a different type of treatment and a different setting from that provided by the "600 Schools," which lack psychiatric facilities and sufficient or proper teaching and psychiatric personnel so direly needed for these children. Other criticisms of this type of school is the haphazard selection of those sent there, the fact that selection is made by the school principals rather than by professional persons in the Bureau of Child Guidance, and the physical condition of the schools (most are ancient and unaesthetic in appearance, to say the least).

In view of the new outbreaks of delinquency in schools during

1957 and the beginning of 1958, the New York City Board of Education made provisions for the opening of what it calls "700 Schools," all of which, with the exception of one, are for boys. They were established for pupils who manifest consistent and even more serious behavior problems in school, e.g., those convicted in court but returned to school because of lack of room in an appropriate institution, those who had been returned from institutions perhaps prematurely, and those who had been charged with violence or insubordination. The same criticisms which apply to the "600 Schools" also are valid for this type of school. However, here too the benefit of isolation of these children from the others must not be minimized.

Attempts have been made both outside and within schools to improve conditions. For example, mental health legislation has been passed in many states, including New York, which allows the expansion of mental hygiene facilities by providing additional funds. The state promises to match, dollar for dollar, funds given by the city or the community to establish mental hygiene clinics. Although we have recently seen a good deal of expansion by the state, all of the states ought to take part in this growth program. New York can take care of children in Rockland State Hospital, Creedmore State Hospital, and in other institutions upstate, as well as at the Psychiatric Institute. New York City has facilities at Bellevue Hospital. Throughout the country a great many private institutions providing child guidance have been established and expanded, such as the Ittleson Center and the Jewish Board of Guardians in New York City, the Southard School in Topeka, Kansas (connected with the Menninger Clinic), and the Devereux Schools in Pennsylvania and in California.

Additional help in combating and preventing juvenile delinquency could be gained through setting up public nursery schools, especially for children of working parents, where they could remain most of the day, with teachers trained as specialists in child guidance. Many public schools have instituted divisions which keep track of children who are truant or who need remedial reading or other types of treatment services, and a number of school systems have attempted to meet the need by employing guidance counselors or counseling teachers. They are of utmost value in detecting emotional upsets in children and referring them to a clinic and in helping to implement a program of therapy. However, ordinary teachers are usually not sufficiently trained to cope with the more serious problems which often present themselves, and they may often have their own unresolved conflicts, which are serious barriers to accomplishing an adequate job in this connection with children.

Whether or not a teacher is aware of mental hygiene principles determines whether his classroom will be a place where children are encouraged to work out the problems of their day-to-day lives and to test out their concepts of social living or whether it will be a place where disturbances go unnoticed and symptoms are left to develop, frequently creating permanent scars, maladjustments, or delinquency.[8]

Teachers bear the greatest responsibility in this sphere, for they are in constant contact with their pupils, and it is they who must impart knowledge with a view toward creating emotionally mature children. Since they are often in a position to either "make or break" a child, we can readily see that they themselves must be sufficiently mature so that almost automatically they set a good example which the children can follow.

A prime requisite for a good teacher is that he know himself, because only then will he be able to understand his students— their emotional needs, desires, aims, and behavior. And only then will he be able to take an objective, though not unsympathetic, view of his children and their problems. Of course, in addition to knowing himself, he must know his pupils. He must be able to recognize the early signs of emotional disturbance and delinquency which children manifest in order to assist in preventing these problems from developing further. Since major difficulties grow out of small ones, it is logical that the earlier we discover antisocial signs and mental or emotional difficulties, the better chance we have of combating them actively.

In this connection it would be important to find criteria by which to distinguish children who are emotionally disturbed only from those who show tendencies toward persistent delinquency and criminal behavior. The question is: who of the children are going to be chronic offenders? This question leads to another: can as yet unmanifested delinquent behavior be predicted? Among those in the forefront of such research have been Drs. Sheldon and Eleanor Glueck.[9]

The difficulty in establishing criteria for predicting a child's future behavior is that we are basically dealing with at least three unknown factors: first, the psychological-psychiatric make-up of the youngster; second, the personality make-ups of his parents; thirdly, the situation he may enter into when he grows up. Unless these factors are taken into consideration, the prediction tables will not be able to depict accurately those personality traits and social situations that lead to either emotional disturbances or juvenile delinquency. In summing up prediction tables, researchers must keep in mind the aggressive and social traits children have and under what circumstances those traits are mobilized resulting in antisocial or criminal acts.

It should be added that much of the prognostic value of a specific prediction table will depend upon what type of treatment the delinquent receives, whether it is intensive psychiatric treatment —individual psychotherapy, group therapy, or both—or whether the delinquent is given any treatment at all.

What program of action, then, can the United States public school system take in order to achieve fusion of the learning process with emotional adjustment of both child and teacher? The National College of Education in Illinois, a training center for teachers, has already instituted pilot courses with this aim in mind. A psychoanalyst, psychiatrist, and psychologist meet weekly with the enrollees to study the reactions of the teachers to the problems presented and their interaction with each other. In 1955 at the request of the Metropolitan School Council, an affiliate of Teachers College, Columbia University, I directed a fifteen-week course for schoolteachers entitled Therapeutic Approach to Emotional Problems in the Classroom. Designed to promote in the teacher understanding of himself, his students, and their mutual interaction, the experiment proved quite promising. There is no doubt that more such courses dealing with the dynamics of psychology would greatly enrich the teacher-training program and afford present and prospective teachers with particular insight into transference and countertransference between themselves and the children.

Should these courses not be possible, the teachers' entrance examination requirements should at least include more extensive personality screening. Today, for example, prospective teachers must pass the most scrutinizing speech tests. It would seem to be more important to have a psychological screening with comprehensive psychological tests. This problem, of course, is extremely complex and needs the most careful scrutiny.

Frequent consultation with the school clinician would help the teacher appraise the social-emotional climate in the classroom. Also valuable would be discussions with parent groups, assembled according to the problems presented by their children, such as bed-wetting, nail-biting, stuttering, etc.

Thus mental health practices would be gradually woven into the fabrics of the school day. The teacher would certainly have a tremendous task in her role as academician and group-leader therapist, in which she would try to establish a full rapport with each pupil in her class. However, by necessity, this presupposes that the number of pupils in each class would be far, far fewer than exist in the average public school classroom in the United States today.

It is high time for us to add a fourth R—Relationship, that is, emotional relationship—to the school curriculum. Only through an integrated synthesis of the atmosphere of mental hygiene with the curriculum of the three R's can the educational process, as well as the personality growth of the pupils, be enhanced.

Planning for the emotional satisfaction of the child includes establishing useful extra-curricular activities within the school but outside the classroom. It must be stressed that youngsters need and like to be active. They have a great deal of energy which has to be channeled constructively. When they do not have a proper outlet for their energy, they may well resort to undesirable activities to satisfy their fantasies and ambitions. This does not mean, of course, that all young people who do not have enough constructive activities for their surplus energy will automatically become antisocial or emotionally maladjusted. There are many other factors involved, as we have already discussed.

NATIONAL PROPOSALS

The problem of preventing juvenile delinquency has aroused not only a general national concern, but several members of Congress have given serious thought to this question. A measure sponsored by Senators Hill and Clark and Representative Elliott would provide $5 million a year for five years to pay part of the costs of projects demonstrating better ways of preventing or reducing juvenile delinquency. Among the projects the program might help finance are: demonstrating what can be done working through the schools; a detailed study of one area of city to try to identify predelinquent children; identifying personality ingredients in adults who are able to influence youths to "go straight"; and changing certain training schools to therapeutic communities with high-grade social workers to try to work changes among those committed.[10]

Senator Hennings is the author of bills to provide grants to states for research and for training of specialized personnel to deal with youth crime. Senator Kefauver has introduced bills providing grants to states and municipalities for minimum-security rehabilitation institutions. Senator Humphrey was joined by Representative Pfost in a proposal for a Youth Conservation Corps and by Representative Addonizio in other juvenile delinquency proposals including grants to states for planning programs to reduce delinquency, for training specialized personnel, and for research and special projects to be conducted by nonprofit institutions. An Advisory Council on Juvenile Delinquency would also be set up in the Department of Health, Education, and Welfare under the Humphrey-Addonizio bills.

TELEVISION, MOTION PICTURES, AND COMIC BOOKS

There has been a wide divergence of opinion as to the causative or influential effects of television, motion pictures, and comic books in producing criminal behavior among our youth today. For example, Dr. Frederick Wertham attributes a major portion of juvenile delinquency to the reading of comic books. He advocates curbing the widespread sale of crime and horror comics, maintaining that it is primarily the "normal" child upon whom these comics have had the greatest detrimental effects and that it is this type of child who is tempted and seduced into imitating the crime portrayed in the story.[11] Professor Frederic M. Thrasher has taken exception to Dr. Wertham's view, claiming that an alleged weakness of the latter's study is that his conclusions are not supported by adequate research data.[12] According to the Subcommittee to Investigate Juvenile Delinquency, the majority opinion seems inclined toward the view that it is unlikely that reading of crime and horror comics would lead to delinquency in the well-adjusted and normally law-abiding child.[13]

More study on the subject is needed in order to determine whether these comics are as harmful as some suggest. However, if we are trying to establish a good emotional climate in which our children can develop their feelings and intellect in the most harmonious way, all possible crime-reducing factors must be employed, in comic books or any other medium reaching the attention of our youngsters. Specific techniques depicted for committing crimes could be eliminated, the heroes need not be superhuman beings, but rather officers of the law, and the "crime does not pay" principle could be clearly stressed. However, that many delinquent children are preoccupied with reading comics or watching television does not bring us any nearer the answer, since there are also many nondelinquents who do the same every day. A youngster who reads or watches constantly is exhibiting an attachment to his childhood, which may reflect emotional disturbance, but this disturbance is not the result of the habit; the habit is rather a symptom of the disturbance.

There is no doubt that there is much emphasis on "horror stories" in all three media. But, in my opinion, it is doubtful whether any of these in and of themselves are sufficient to produce criminal behavior in a normal, well-adjusted person. In fact, in a sense they may even deter crime by providing emotionally healthy children and adults with a vicarious outlet for their aggressive feelings. Of course, we must remember that children who become antisocial or criminal have so much of a criminal pattern within them that any stimulus will affect them, and we must also keep in mind that there are some instances in which these media might trigger off criminal behavior among mentally disturbed persons.

In the light of what I have said above, I do not want the reader to believe for a moment that I think it healthy for children to constantly keep their eyes glued to the television set, go to the movies three times a week, or keep their noses buried in comic books. I do not. It utilizes too much of their time which could be used for much more constructive activities. I am merely discussing these media in their relationship to crime.

AN OVERALL PLANNING AGENCY

Preventing juvenile delinquency and crime is the responsibility of the entire country. Ideally, an overall planning agency should be established in each community, whether it be a city, suburb, or rural community, with complete facilities to handle all those people in need of help. However, I realize that this is not a practicable solution in that it would involve a tremendous expense and perhaps more professional people than are available. The second best solution would be the establishment of such an agency in the largest city within a certain area. But this course of action must be based upon close cooperation between the city and all its environs within that area, including suburbs and small localities, so that even the tiniest community is not left uncovered. It could even be arranged whereby one or two persons could be directed to each community so that there would be on-the-spot coverage, even if only to refer people to the proper source for help.

The overall planning agency should have complete authority. I know this will be difficult in the light of the numerous agencies already existing on different levels, each having a certain degree of authority of its own which it is reluctant to relinquish. For example, in New York the Youth Board, a central agency under the able leadership of Judge Nathaniel Kaplan, suffers from this very drawback, i.e., its authority is curbed by other agencies. Nevertheless, such a complete reorganization is vital to prevent the development of piecemeal plans, which not only produce waste, but also, and even more important, impede the central agency's progress in combating juvenile delinquency.

This proposed authority, which I shall call the Youth Crime Authority, should, at its inception, set out to do two things: appraise already existing facilities and recommend the abolition, improvement, or creation of agencies when necessary. From a broad viewpoint its chief goal would be to develop a mental and social hygiene-oriented community which would employ all the tools available to provide therapeutic treatment for individuals and families and to create a climate conducive to emotional well-being and social comfort. It would devote the greatest part of its time to the problem of juvenile delinquency and would require the help of all social and civic agencies, including schools, churches, the courts, correctional institutions, clubs, and business organizations—in fact, all community resources.

To this end, the chief emphasis of the Youth Crime Authority should be on the establishment, supervision, and proper maintenance of professionally staffed mental hygiene and guidance clinics (under the leadership of a qualified psychiatrist) for children, adolescents, and parents in need of advice or treatment. These clinics could give guidance to children who do not know what career to follow, could give work guidance, could help a parent with a particular problem he may be having with his child at a certain time, and could carry out the necessary diagnostic and psychotherapeutic procedures for those who need it. Among the Authority's duties would be to examine an adolescent who had been arrested in order to determine such things as his personality make-up and the degree of danger he presents to society and to recommend the proper disposition of the case to the court. One of its more important functions would be to find these children before they become criminals and come before the law, that is, when they first manifest signs of antisocial behavior.

It would be important in this respect to have a mobile psychiatric unit attached to a mental hygiene clinic consisting of psychiatric personnel which could be made available to communities where no such clinics exist. Upon the arrest of an adolescent, this mobile clinic would examine him and determine his personality make-up and whether he was dangerous or whether he could be returned to his family.

In addition to all this, the Youth Crime Authority would have to take the initiative in a community, for very often those who need help most will not seek it, either because they are not aware it exists or because of financial hardships or lack of psychiatric orientation. The Authority could register as many families as possible, preferably those which are trouble spots because they have already produced a juvenile delinquent, because there is much family tension (broken families should always be included), or because of a poor financial situation requiring support from the community. These are very often the "hard core" families, which are breeding grounds for crime and which show excessive resistance to reform or improvement. Each of these families should be carefully evaluated as to social and ethnical background, economic status, the number of members in the family and their earning capacity, their emotional and physical health, their emotional attitudes toward one another, and, last but not least, the presence of family tension. If treatment of a family member should be required, contact with these families should not terminate when treatment is over, but should continue over a long period and take into consideration the entire family.

With respect to families who require economic support, the attitude of the community needs to be changed. Instead of trying to meet their needs without expecting them to support themselves partially, the community should see to it that as soon as these families have been able to progress, they should not depend upon the community for the same degree of support as was necessary initially. The community should be educated to understand that prolonged and complete support of such families increases their dependency and perpetuates their helplessness. They must therefore be helped to mobilize their resources from the first moment on so that they can stand on their own feet as early as possible. In this connection, liaison work with housing and slum clearance authorities should be instituted to make better housing more readily available for socially deprived families.

Close contact must also be maintained with the police and law enforcement authorities so that the Youth Crime Authority would have a good picture of the efficiency of law enforcement and perhaps aid in effecting possible improvements. For example, our juvenile courts have not been able to cope with the complex situation of juvenile delinquency because there are insufficient resources—facilities and available personnel are extremely inadequate. Also although many judges have made and are making major contributions to these courts, in a study made by the New York City Children's Court,[14] it was found that many do not function in a fashion consistent with the philosophy of the juvenile courts. It must be remembered that cases coming into these courts, generally speaking, are quite involved, both socially and mentally. To illustrate, it was found that of 31 cases brought into the Children's Court of New York City, 15 were severely disturbed, 12 moderately disturbed, and only 4 showed little, if any, discernible pathology.[15] Thus of these 31 cases 27 showed a need for more intensive study, a specialized treatment, or both.

In order to render adequate service in handling juvenile delinquents, a juvenile court judge must request and receive support from the fields of psychiatry, psychology, social work, and probation. It is part of the task of the Youth Crime Authority to promote a closer cooperation between these juvenile courts and the mental hygiene agencies in the community. In addition to this cooperation if we had more and better examination and treatment facilities and more qualified personnel, hearings and investigations would be expedited whereby more cases could be studied and processed. Also since children's problems are often intimately tied to their emotional relationship with their parents and to the problems of their parents, it would be a good idea to make the juvenile court part of a broader family court system.

A RESEARCH INSTITUTE

In close cooperation with the Youth Crime Authority should be an established Institute for Research on the diagnosis and treatment of juvenile delinquents and adult criminals, which I advocated in 1944 [16] and again in 1952 [17] and which has never existed for offenders. Some topics for research might be: How can the schools contribute further in helping to deal with misbehavior problems in children? How can the services of a training school for young offenders be improved? What are the relative merits of the Borstal System in England and ours? Can the Scout movement be brought more actively into the anticrime program by providing more and better recreational activities? Could the fight against delinquency be aided substantially by assigning more workers and professionally trained personnel to the job of eliminating gangs?

Additional questions for investigation could be: How can an individual's resistance to criminal behavior be increased? How are antisocial impulses transformed into criminal action? (What is the role of brain metabolism?) What are the warning signs in persons potentially capable of committing violent crimes? (This would involve finding the origin of intense aggressiveness, working out methods of detecting it in its early stages, and determining its treatability in all stages. Since the tendency to commit violent acts is intimately connected with strong aggressiveness and the inability to restrain or suppress motor impulses, this study should look for specific personality traits and the way they function in the offender as contrasted with the nonoffender.) Is there a relationship between the functioning or malfunctioning of endocrine glands and a sex crime? Some of these projects could be carried out in conjunction with special schools, such as medical schools, for example.

In addition, this institute would act as a repository for research material and could also provide courses on the subject for doctors, lawyers, law students, judges, psychiatrists, psychologists, psychiatric social workers, clergymen, child guidance counselors, anthropologists, sociologists, teachers, probation officers, prison personnel, etc. In these ways it would disseminate its research information to professional people and the public, and especially to the Youth Crime Authority, so that there could be practical application of the results of its research.

CONCLUSION

Although there will always be a lag between what we know and the application of that knowledge, still we must apply this new-found information as early as possible in order to convert possibilities into actualities so that they become useful to society. If we fail to do this, research has no legitimate or ethical value. Only by experimenting—trial and error—will we know whether we are on the right road.

It is regrettable that the great strides we have made in psycho-analysis, psychiatry, sociology, anthropology, education, and social work have been applied in such small measure to the actual treatment practices in the field of juvenile delinquency and crime, particularly with regard to correction. This is evidenced by the slow progress in the fields of rehabilitation and correction and by the reluctance to appropriate funds for these purposes.

Unfortunately, certain of our newspapers encourage the principle of retaliation by playing up to the public's morbid interest in sensational crimes for commercial purposes. This is not to say that the public is not entitled to the truth. People want the news as it happens, and newspapers are responsible for furnishing adequate coverage, but it should be news which is not only "fit to print," as is the rule followed by one of our most outstanding newspapers, the New York *Times,* but also "fit to educate." It is indeed a sad commentary on the American scene when, in competing with one another for sales, newspapers print large pictures, headlines, and gory details of sordid crimes. The general public usually comprehends little of what is behind the offender's criminal behavior, and it knows probably even less of his suffering afterwards or the intense unhappiness he has brought to his family. Nor is it aware that many a criminal, especially a young offender, craves precisely the publicity given him by tabloid newspapers in order to win the recognition of adults and the admiration of his fellow criminals. Thus it serves only to arouse and incite the public to a feeling of hatred and retaliation, rather than to positive thinking and feeling.

Prevention and elimination of crime is truly a problem of education—educating each man and woman to find within himself worth-while values by which he can live. It is by bringing out the best in the individual, by blending both his intellectual and emotional wisdom into healthy reasoning, that he will be able to get along with himself and others, thereby maintaining his own worth and dignity as an individual and as a useful member of society. Only as a healthy individual can he integrate his own personal goals with those of a healthy society, and only when society tries to keep all mental and social deviations or abnormalities to a minimum can a high social order be reached. On man's character depends man's greatness, and on society's character depends its primacy and prestige.

Notes

INTRODUCTION

1. Edward Westermarck, *Origin and Development of Moral Ideas* (London: 1906–8), I, 162. See also Westermarck's, *The Goodness of Gods.*
2. Bronislaw Malinowski, *Crime and Custom in Savage Society* (New York: Harcourt Brace, 1926), p. 24.
3. Cesare Bonesana Beccaria, *An Essay on Crimes and Punishment* (Dublin: 1777), p. 133.
4. Malcolm Guthne, *Spencer's Formula of Evolution* (London: 1879).
5. Hooton, *The American Criminal: An Anthropological Study,* Vol. I, *The Native White Criminal of Native Parentage.*
6. Sheldon, *Varieties of Delinquent Youth.*
7. Hurwitz, *Criminology,* p. 40.
8. Franz Boas, "Race and Progress," *Science* (1931), p. 74.
9. Abrahamsen, *Crime and the Human Mind,* p. 10.
10. K. V. Lilienthal, "Frantz von Liszt," *Zeitschrift für die gesamte Strafrechtswissenschaft,* Vol. XL (1919), p. 535.
11. Von Liszt, "Zur Vorbereitung des Strafgesetzentwurfs," *Strafrechtliche Aufsätze und Vorträge,* II, 412.
12. Von Liszt, *Lehrbuch des Deutschen Strafrechts* (Berlin, 1891).
13. Benjamin Rush, *Sixteen Introductory Lectures to Courses of Lectures upon the Institute and Practice of Medicine* (Philadelphia: Bradford and Innskeep, 1811), p. 380.
14. Isaac Ray, *A Treatise on the Medical Jurisprudence of Insanity* (Boston: Little, Brown, 1838), p. 52.
15. Charles K. Mill, "Arrested and Aberrant Development of Fissures and Gyres in the Brains of Paranoics, Criminals, Idiots, and Negroes," *Journal of Nervous and Mental Disease,* Vol. XIII (1886), pp. 523–50.

16. Hamilton D. Wey, "Criminal Anthropology," *Proceedings of the National Prison Association* (1890), pp. 274–91.

17. George Ellsworth Dawson, "A Study in Youthful Degeneracy," *Pedagogical Seminary* (1896), pp. 232–33.

18. Eugene L. Talbot, *Degeneracy, Its Causes, Signs and Results* (London: 1898), p. 18.

19. Hall, *Adolescence*, pp. 335–37.

20. Healy and Bronner, *Delinquents and Criminals, Their Making and UnMaking;* Healy, *New Light on Delinquency and Its Treatment.*

21. Aichhorn, *Wayward Youth.*

22. Glueck, *Unraveling Juvenile Delinquency.*

23. Abrahamsen, *Crime and the Human Mind.*

24. Alexander and Staub, *The Criminal, the Judge, and the Public;* Alexander and Healy, *Roots of Crime.*

25. Many journals, other than predominantly psychiatric or sociological ones, ought to be cited, such as the *Journal of Criminal Psychopathology* (which, unfortunately, has ceased publication), the *Journal of Criminal Law and Criminology,* and *Federal Probation,* edited by Victor Evjen. Two new journals, *Archives of Criminal Psychodynamics,* edited by Benjamin Karpman, and the *British Journal of Delinquency,* have recently appeared.

26. Gregory Zilboorg, "Contribution of Psychoanalysis to Forensic Psychiatry," *International Journal of Psychoanalysis,* Vol. 37, Parts IV–V (July–October, 1956), pp. 318–24.

27. "Psycho-Analysis and the Ascertaining of Truth in Courts of Law." Lecture delivered to Professor Loffler's seminar in June, 1906. Reprinted in Freud, *Collected Papers,* II, 13–24.

28. Freud, *Collected Papers,* IV, 342.

I. SOCIAL PATHOLOGY AND CRIME

1. F. Heinemann, *Neue Wege der Philosophie* (Leipzig, 1929), p. 283. About the functional method see also K. Mannheim, *Mensch und Gesellschaft im Zeitalter des Umbaus* (Leiden, 1935).

2. T. M. French, "Some Psychoanalytic Applications of the Psychological Field Concept," *Psychoanalytic Quarterly,* Vol. XII, No. 1 (1942), pp. 17–32.

3. U.S. Department of Justice, *Uniform Crime Reports,* Vol. XII, No. 4 (1941), p. 165.

4. U.S. Department of Justice, *Uniform Crime Reports,* Vol. XVII, No. 2 (1946), p. 77.

5. U.S. Department of Justice, *Uniform Crime Reports,* Vol. XXIII, No. 2 (1952), p. 71.

6. U.S. Department of Justice, *Uniform Crime Reports,* Vol. XXVIII, No. 2 (1957), p. 69.

7. U.S. Department of Justice, *Uniform Crime Reports,* Vol. XXVIII, No. 2 (1957), p. 72.

8. Emanuel Perlmutter, "Major Crimes Up 8 percent in 1958," *The New York Times,* Monday, March 2, 1959, p. 29.

9. M. Grünhut, "Statistics in Criminology," *Journal of the Royal Statistical Society,* Series A (General), Vol. CXIV, Part II (1951), pp. 147–48.

10. "Brottslighetens Utveckling: Aren 1913–1947, av Statistiska Central-byran," Statistiska Meddelanden, Series A, Vol. VI, No. 3 (Stockholm: Norstedt, 1949), pp. 14–15.

11. Abrahamsen, *Who Are the Guilty?*, p. 4.

12. Taft, *Criminology*, p. 223.

13. Abrahamsen, *Who Are the Guilty?*, p. 6.

14. Shaw and McKay, *Juvenile Delinquency and Urban Areas*, pp. 17–18. See also Lander, *Towards an Understanding of Juvenile Delinquency, A Study of 8,464 Cases of Juvenile Delinquency in Baltimore*, p. 5.

II. THE FORMULA OF CRIMINAL BEHAVIOR

1. Hurwitz, *Criminology*, p. 45.

2. World Health Organization Technical Report Series No. 9 (Geneva: 1950), p. 25.

3. Abrahamsen, *Crime and the Human Mind*, p. 36.

4. E. R. Spaulding and William Healy, "Inheritance as a Factor in Criminality," *Bulletin of the American Academy of Medicine*, Vol. XV (February, 1914), pp. 4–27.

5. Sheldon, *Varieties of Delinquent Youth*.

6. Stourzh-Anderle, *Sexuelle Konstitution. Psychopathie, Kriminalitat, Genie*.

7. Eduardo Weiss, "Emotional Memories and Acting Out," *Psychiatric Quarterly*, Vol. XI (1942), pp. 477–92.

8. Ben Karpman, "Aggression," *American Journal of Orthopsychiatry*, Vol. XX (October, 1950), pp. 694–718.

9. Abrahamsen, *Who Are the Guilty?*, p. 66.

10. Jerome E. Bates, "Abrahamsen's Theory of the Etiology of Criminal Acts," *Journal of Criminal Law and Criminology of Northwestern University*, Vol. 40, No. 4 (November–December, 1949), pp. 474–75.

IV. JUVENILE DELINQUENCY

1. C. K. Simon, "A New Chance for Youth," *Survey Midmonthly* (November, 1943), p. 297.

2. U.S. Department of Justice, *Uniform Crime Reports*, Vol. XXVIII, No. 2 (1957), p. 70.

3. Bess Furman, "Hearing Tuesday on Youth Crimes," *The New York Times*, Sunday, March 15, 1959, p. 128.

4. Emanuel Perlmutter, "Major Crimes up 8 Per Cent in 1958," *The New York Times*, Monday, March 2, 1959, p. 29.

5. Bess Furman, "Hearing Tuesday on Youth Crimes," *The New York Times*, Sunday, March 15, 1959, p. 128.

6. Thomas J. McHugh, Commissioner of Correction, "Major Crime Trends in New York State, Calendar Year 1957 and December 1957," p. 1.

7. Bess Furman, "Hearing Tuesday on Youth Crimes," *The New York Times*, Sunday, March 15, 1959, p. 128.

8. See report by John M. Beckmann, Commissioner of Police, Mineola, Long Island.

9. Figures released by New York City Police Department, February, 1958

10. "Juvenile Delinquency Reported as Major Police Problem in England," *Correction Sidelights*, Jan.–Feb., 1959, p. 12.

11. "Concern in Britain," *The New York Times*, April 24, 1958.

12. Paul Hoffmann, "Juvenile Crime on Rise in Italy," *The New York Times*, Sunday, July 12, 1959, p. 27.

13. Ninetta Jucker, "Italians Find Delinquency Is Increasing," *New York Herald Tribune*, Sunday, September 13, 1959, p. 7.

14. Winfred Overholser, "Some Psychiatric Aspects of Delinquency," *Transactions and Studies of the College of Physicians of Philadelphia*, 4th Series, Vol. XVIII, No. 1 (April, 1950), p. 24.

15. Julian P. Price, S. C. Florence, Russell A. Nelson, and W. Clarke Wescoe, "Changing Characteristics of Society," *Journal of the American Medical Association*, Vol. 167, No. 1 (May 3, 1958), p. 49.

16. Maurice E. Linden, "Relationship Between Social Attitudes Toward Aging and the Delinquencies of Youth," *American Journal of Psychiatry*, Vol. 114, No. 5 (November, 1957), p. 444.

17. Wheelis, *The Quest for Identity*.

18. Abrahamsen, *Who Are the Guilty?*, p. 37.

19. Walter Bonime, "The Psychic Energy of Freud and Jung," *American Journal of Psychiatry*, Vol. 112, No. 5 (November, 1955), p. 373.

20. Abrahamsen, *The Road to Emotional Maturity*, p. 107.

21. Glueck and Glueck, *Unraveling Juvenile Delinquency*, p. 181. See also Joseph J. Michaels and Arthur Steinberg, "Persistent Enuresis and Juvenile Delinquency," *British Journal of Delinquency*, Vol. 3 (October, 1952).

22. Glueck and Glueck, *Unraveling Juvenile Delinquency*, p. 239.

23. Glueck and Glueck, *Unraveling Juvenile Delinquency*, p. 234.

24. Glueck and Glueck, *Unraveling Juvenile Delinquency*, p. 247.

25. Glueck and Glueck, *Unraveling Juvenile Delinquency*, p. 239.

26. Healy and Bronner, *New Light on Delinquency and Its Treatment*, p. 122.

27. *Facts About Mental Illness* (New York, National Association for Mental Health, January, 1959), pp. 1–2.

28. *Joint Information Service: Fact Sheet No. 9* (Washington, D.C., American Psychiatric Association and the National Association for Mental Health, May, 1959), p. 2.

29. *Facts About Mental Illness* (New York, National Association for Mental Health, January, 1959), p. 1.

30. Winfred Overholser, "Psychiatry and Crime," *Year Book of the National Probation Association* (1930), p. 5.

31. An excellent account of teen-age gang activities has been written in the New York *Times* by Harrison E. Salisbury (March 24–March 31, 1958). See also *The Gang: A Study in Adolescent Behavior*, by Herbert A. Block and Arthur Niederhoffer.

32. Paley, *Rumble on the Docks*.

V. PSYCHOSOMATIC DISORDERS AND CRIME

1. Felix Deutsch, "The Associative Anamnesis," *Psychoanalytic Quarterly*, Vol. 8 (1939), p. 354. See also Deutsch and Murphy, *The Clinical Interview*.

2. David Abrahamsen, "Psychosomatic Disorders and Their Significance in Antisocial Behavior," *Journal of Nervous and Mental Disease,* Vol. 107, No. 1 (January, 1948), pp. 11–24.

3. Abrahamsen, "Psychosomatic Disorders and Their Significance in Antisocial Behavior," *Journal of Nervous and Mental Disease,* Vol. 107, No. 1 (January, 1948), p. 21. (See also Flanders Dunbar, "Homeostasis During Puberty," *American Journal of Psychiatry,* Vol. 114, No. 8 (February, 1958), p. 675.)

4. Abrahamsen, "Psychosomatic Disorders and Their Significance in Antisocial Behavior," *Journal of Nervous and Mental Disease,* Vol. 107, No. 1 (January, 1948), p. 14.

5. It is noteworthy that August Aichorn in *Wayward Youth* also describes a state of mind termed "latent delinquency."

6. Abrahamsen, "Personality Reaction to Crime and Disease," *Journal of Nervous and Mental Disease,* Vol. 104, No. 1 (July, 1946), p. 81.

7. Abrahamsen, "Personality Reaction to Crime and Disease," *Journal of Nervous and Mental Disease,* Vol. 104, No. 1 (July, 1946), p. 81.

VI. THE OFFENDER AND THE EMOTIONALLY DISTURBED NONOFFENDER

1. Abrahamsen, *Report on Study of 102 Sex Offenders at Sing Sing Prison,* pp. 15–16.

2. Maurice Kaplan, John F. Ryan, Edward Nathan, and Marion Bairos, "The Control of Acting Out in the Psychotherapy of Delinquents," *American Journal of Psychiatry,* Vol. 113, No. 12 (June, 1957), p. 1109.

VII. THE CLASSIFICATION OF CRIMINALS

1. Abrahamsen, *Crime and the Human Mind,* p. 34.

2. Ferri, *Criminal Sociology,* pp. 23–43.

3. Liszt, *Strafrechtliche Aufsätze und Vorträge,* II, 174–82.

4. Goring, *The English Convict,* p. 370.

5. Kretschmer, *Physique and Character.*

6. Olaf Kinberg, *Der Biopsykologisha Konstitutionsproblemet, Människokunskap och Människobehandling* (Stockholm, 1941), p. 327.

7. Kinberg, *Biopsykologiska Konstitutionsproblemet,* p. 340.

8. Hurwitz, *Criminology,* p. 138.

9. Friedlander, *The Psychoanalytical Approach to Juvenile Delinquency,* pp. 186–87.

10. Burt, *The Young Delinquent.*

11. Healy, *The Individual Delinquent.*

12. Alexander and Staub, *The Criminal, The Judge, and The Public.*

13. Thomas A. Szasz, "The Problem of Psychiatric Nosology," *Journal of American Psychiatry,* Vol. 114, No. 5 (November, 1957), p. 406.

14. Hurwitz, *Criminology,* p. 400.

VIII. THE ACUTE AND THE CHRONIC OFFENDER

1. Abrahamsen, *The Mind and Death of a Genius,* pp. 104–22. See also Abrahamsen, *The Road to Emotional Maturity,* pp. 131–54.

2. W. L. Neustatter, "The Psychology of Shoplifting," *Medico-Legal Journal*, Vol. 22 (1954), pp. 118–30.

3. Abrahamsen, *Who Are the Guilty?*, pp. 83–87.

4. G. E. Partridge, "Current Conceptions of Psychopathic Personality," *American Journal of Psychiatry*, Vol. X (July, 1930), pp. 53–99. See also, "Psychotic Reactions in the Psychopath," *American Journal of Psychiatry*, Vol. VIII, No. 3 (November, 1928), p. 493, and "Psychopathic Personality and Personality Investigation," *American Journal of Psychiatry*, Vol. VIII, No. 6 (May, 1929), p. 1053.

5. Kahn, *Psychopathic Personalities.*

6. Henderson, *Psychopathic States*, p. 43.

7. Henderson, *Psychopathic States*, p. 18.

8. English and Finch, *Introduction to Psychiatry*, p. 260.

9. J. J. Michaels, *Disorders of Character, Persistent Enuresis, Juvenile Delinquency, Psychopathic Personality* (Springfield: Charles C. Thomas, 1955), p. 59.

10. Daniel Silverman, "Clinical and Electroencephalographic Studies on Criminal Psychopaths," *Archives of Neurology and Psychiatry*, Vol. L, No. 1 (July, 1943), pp. 18, 19, 20, 30, and 31.

11. J. J. Michaels, "The Relationship of Anti-Social Traits to the Electroencephalogram in Children with Behavior Disorders," *Psychosomatic Medicine,* Vol. VII, No. 1 (January, 1945), pp. 43 and 44.

12. R. L. Jenkins and B. L. Pacella, "Electroencephalographic Studies of Delinquent Boys," *American Journal of Orthopsychiatry,* Vol. 13 (1943), pp. 107–20.

13. As quoted from Frederic A. Gibbs, B. K. Bagchi, and Wilfred Bloomberg, "Electroencephalographic Study of Criminals," *American Journal of Psychiatry*, Vol. 102, No. 3 (November, 1945), p. 297.

14. Gibbs, Bagchi, and Bloomberg, "Electroencephalographic Study of Criminals," *American Journal of Psychiatry*, Vol. 102, No. 3 (November, 1945), p. 297.

15. M. G. Gray and Merrill Moore, "Incidence and Significance of Alcoholism in the History of Criminals," *Journal of Criminal Psychopathology*, Vol. III, No. 2 (October, 1941), pp. 347, 348, and 349.

16. Hurwitz, *Criminology*, p. 110.

17. Gray and Moore, "Incidence and Significance of Alcoholism in the History of Criminals," *Journal of Criminal Psychopathology*, Vol. III, No. 2 (October, 1941), pp. 347, 348, and 349.

18. Eugene I. Falstein, "Juvenile Alcoholism: A Psychodynamic Case Study of Addiction," *American Journal of Orthopsychiatry*, Vol. XXIII, No. 3 (July, 1953), pp. 530–51.

19. Granville W. Larimore and Henry Brill, "The British Narcotic System, Report of Study," *New York State Journal of Medicine* (January 1, 1960), p. 111.

20. Larimore and Brill, "The British Narcotic System, Report of Study," *New York State Journal of Medicine* (January 1, 1960), p. 112.

21. C. B. Thompson, "Some New Aspects of the Psychiatric Approach to Crime," *Mental Hygiene*, Vol. XX, No. 4 (October, 1936), p. 533.

22. Winfred Overholser, "Some Possible Contributions of Psychiatry to a More Effective Administration of the Criminal Law," *Canadian Bar Review* (November, 1939), pp. 645–61.

23. Hurwitz, *Criminology*, p. 171.

24. Peter F. Bowman, "The Defective Delinquent," *The American Journal of Psychiatry*, Vol. 114, No. 2 (August, 1957).

IX. THE SEX OFFENDER

1. Jack Frosch and Walter Bromberg, "The Sex Offender—A Psychiatric Study," *American Journal of Orthopsychiatry*, Vol. IX, No. 4 (October, 1939), p. 766.

2. Benjamin Apfelberg, Carl Sugar, and A. Z. Pfeffer, "A Psychiatric Study of 250 Sex Offenders from the Psychiatric Division, Bellevue Hospital, New York City, and the Department of Psychiatry of the New York University College of Medicine," *American Journal of Psychiatry*, Vol. C, No. 1 (May, 1944), pp. 762–70.

3. Thomas J. McHugh, Commissioner of Correction, Major Crime Trends in New York State Calendar Year 1957 and December 1957. State of New York Department of Correction, Alfred E. Smith Office Building, Albany, New York. Table A.

4. U.S. Department of Justice, *Uniform Crime Reports*, Vol. XXI, No. 2 (1950), p. 74.

5. U.S. Department of Justice, *Uniform Crime Reports*, Vol. XXVIII, No. 2 (1957), p. 71.

6. U.S. Department of Justice, *Uniform Crime Reports*, Vol. XXVIII, No. 2 (1957), p. 72.

7. M. Grünhut, "Statistics in Criminology," *The Journal of the Royal Statistical Society*, Vol. CXIV, Part II (1951), Series A (General), pp. 139–62.

8. Abrahamsen, *Report on Study of 102 Sex Offenders at Sing Sing Prison*, Appendix Table I, p. 64.

9. Apfelberg, Sugar, and Pfeffer, "A Psychiatric Study of 250 Sex Offenders from the Psychiatric Division, Bellevue Hospital, New York City, and the Department of Psychiatry of the New York University College of Medicine," *American Journal of Psychiatry*, Vol. C, No. 1 (May, 1944), pp. 762–70.

10. Johan Scharffenberg, Pamphlet containing his discussion before the Norwegian Association of Criminology, *The Norwegian Society of Crime*, (Oslo, 1935), p. 110.

11. Aschaffenburg, *Crime and its Repression*, p. 191.

12. Guttmacher, *Sex Offenses—The Problem, Causes and Prevention*, pp. 60, 61, 63, and 72.

13. Abrahamsen, *Report on Study of 102 Sex Offenders at Sing Sing Prison*, p. 20. The case of Otto is taken from the same study.

14. The material on family testing is from Palm and Abrahamsen, "A Rorschach Study of the Wives of Sex Offenders," *Journal of Nervous and Mental Disease*, Vol. 119, No. 2 (February, 1954), p. 167–72.

15. Sandor Ferenczi, *Contributions to Psychoanalysis* (Boston: Badger, 1916).

16. Felix Boehm, "Ueber zwei Typen von maennlichen Homosexuellen," *Internationale Zeitschrift fuer Psychoanalyse*, Vol. XIX (1933).

17. Otto Fenichel, *The Psychoanalytic Theory of Neurosis* (New York: Norton, 1945), p. 332.

18. Kinsey, Pomeroy, and Martin, *Sexual Behavior in the Human Male*, p. 623.

19. Abrahamsen, *Crime and the Human Mind*, pp. 118, 119.

20. Fenichel, *The Psychoanalytic Theory of Neurosis*, p. 348.

21. Edward Glover, *The Psycho-Pathology of Prostitution* (London: Institute for the Study and Treatment of Delinquency), p. 6.

22. Elizabeth O'Kelly, "Some Observations on Relationships between Delinquent Girls and their Parents," *British Journal of Medical Psychology*, Vol. 28 (1955), pp. 59–66.

23. *Report of the Governor's Study Commission on the Deviated Criminal Sex Offender*. State of Michigan, 1951.

24. Daniel Lieberman and Benjamin A. Siegel, "A Program for 'Sexual Psychopaths' in a State Mental Hospital," *American Journal of Psychiatry*, Vol. 113, No. 9 (March, 1957), pp. 801–7.

25. The material on offenders at Sing Sing and the recommendations of the committee are taken from Abrahamsen, *Report on Study of 102 Sex Offenders at Sing Sing Prison*, pp. 24, 25, 27–29, 44, 45.

X. THE PERSONALITY OF THE MURDERER

1. U.S. Department of Justice, *Uniform Crime Reports*, Vol. XXVII, No. 2 (1957), p. 71.

2. U.S. Department of Justice, *Uniform Crime Reports*, Vol. XII, No. 4 (1941), pp. 185, 188.

3. U.S. Department of Justice, *Uniform Crime Reports*, Vol. XXVIII, No. 2 (1957), pp. 99, 103.

4. U.S. Department of Justice, *Uniform Crime Reports*, Vol. XII, No. 4 (1941), p. 172.

5. U.S. Department of Justice, *Uniform Crime Reports*, Vol. XXVIII, No. 2 (1957), p. 92.

6. *Criminal Statistics, England and Wales, 1939–1945* (London: H.M.S.O.), Table A, p. 26.

7. *Criminal Statistics, England and Wales, 1957* (London: H.M.S.O.), Table A, p. 2.

8. "Brottslighetens Utveckling Åren 1913–1947 av Statistiska Centralbyrån," *Statistika Meddelanden*, Ser. A. Band VI:3 (Stockholm: Norstedt, 1949), p. 14.

9. U.S. Department of Justice, FBI, *Uniform Crime Reports*, Vol. XXVIII, No. 2 (1957), p. 93.

10. David Abrahamsen, "Mass-Psychosis and Its Effects," *Journal of Nervous and Mental Disease*, Vol. XCIII, No. 1 (January, 1941), pp. 63–72.

11. John Holland Cassity, "Personality Study of 200 Murderers," *Journal of Criminal Psychopathology*, Vol. II, No. 3 (1942), p. 297.

12. U.S. Department of Justice, *Uniform Crime Reports*, Vol. XIII, No. 4 (1941), p. 209.

13. U.S. Department of Justice, *Uniform Crime Reports,* Vol. XXVIII, No. 2 (1957), p. 118.

14. For further details see Winfred Overholser, "Psychiatry and the Law—Cooperators or Antagonists?", *Psychiatric Quarterly,* Vol. XIII (October, 1939), pp. 622–38.

15. Gregory Zilboorg, "Some Sidelights on Psychology of Murder," *Journal of Nervous and Mental Disease,* Vol. 18 (April, 1935), p. 442.

16. See Neustatter, *The Mind of the Murderer.*

17. Philip R. Lehrman, "Some Unconscious Determinants in Homicide," *Psychiatric Quarterly,* Vol. XIII, No. 4 (October, 1939), pp. 605–21.

18. D. Stafford-Clark and F. H. Taylor, "Clinical and Electro-Encephalographic Studies of Prisoners Charged with Murder," *Journal of Neurology, Neurosurgery, and Psychiatry,* Vol. 12 (November, 1949), pp. 325–30.

19. Menninger, *Man Against Himself,* p. 22.

20. Alexander and Staub have described a case where the infantile Oedipus situation plays the fatal part in *The Criminal, the Judge and the Public,* pp. 190–206.

21. Indirect suicide, as seen throughout human history, may very well take such a form. In the seventeenth and eighteenth centuries there was an epidemic of indirect suicides in Norway and Denmark. Depressed people committed murder so that they themselves might be put to death.

22. Warren Stearns, "Murder by Adolescents with Obscure Motivation," *American Journal of Psychiatry,* Vol. 114, No. 4 (October, 1957), pp. 303–5.

23. Glueck and Glueck, *500 Criminal Careers,* p. 86.

24. Hartvig Nissen, *Alkohol og Forbrydelse* (Oslo: 1933), p. 20.

25. John Holland Cassity, "Personality Study of 200 Murderers," *Journal of Criminal Psychopathology,* Vol. II, No. 3 (1942), pp. 296–304.

26. Luton Ackerson, "Inferiority Attitudes and Their Correlations among Children Examined in a Behavior Clinic," *The Pedagogical Seminary and Journal of Genetic Psychology,* Vol. 62, First half (March, 1943), pp. 85–96.

27. Information in the main from the Senate Crime Investigating Committee, headed by Senator Kefauver.

28. Bjerre, *The Psychology of Murder,* p. 73.

XI. PSYCHIATRIC-PSYCHOLOGICAL EXAMINATION OF THE OFFENDER

1. Harald Petersen, "Mentalitetserklaeringer i Straffesager," *Annuaire des Associations de Criminalistes Nordiques* (Stockholm, 1940), p. 95.

2. "Automatism and Hypoglycemia," *The Journal of the American Medical Association,* Vol. 165, No. 15 (December 14, 1957), p. 1991.

3. See also, Wechsler, *A Textbook of Clinical Neurology.*

4. Monrad-Krohn, *The Clinical Examination of the Nervous System,* p. 130.

5. Anton, "Deutsche Gesund," *Zeitschrift für Medizine,* 10:1504 (November 17, 1955).

6. William G. Lennox, "The Genetics of Epilepsy," *American Journal of Psychiatry,* Vol. 103, No. 4 (January, 1947), p. 462.

7. William G. Lennox, "Amnesia Real and Feigned," *American Journal of Psychiatry,* Vol. 99, No. 4 (January, 1943), p. 741.

8. It is impossible to mention by name all authors who have served as sources for the outlining of this part of the examination. Much credit, however, should be given to Arthur B. Noyes, Adolph Meyer, Nolan D. C. Lewis, G. H. Monrad-Krohn, Karl A. Menninger, E. B. Strecher, William Malamud, Johan Scharffenberg, and others.

9. Herbert Weiner and Alex Braiman, "The Ganser Syndrome—A Review and Addition of Some Unusual Cases," *American Journal of Psychiatry*, 111: 767–73 (April, 1955).

10. Johannes Lange, *Deutsche Zeitschrift für Gerichtliche Medizine*, 43:552 (1955).

11. *North Carolina Law Review*, 35:515 (June, 1957).

12. Emmanuel F. Hammer, "A Comparison of H-T-P's of Rapists and Pedophiles," *Journal of Projective Techniques*, Vol. 18, No. 3 (1954), p. 347.

13. Joseph Hawthorne, "Group Test for the Measurement of Cruelty-Compassion," *Journal of Social Psychology*, III (May, 1932), 189–211.

14. R. S. Tolman, "Differences Between Two Groups of Adult Criminals," *Genetic Psychological Monographs*, III (August, 1938), No. 20, 408.

15. Our present knowledge of the foundation for emotions does not allow any specific conclusions. The following seems to have been established: The hypothalamus represents the center of autonomic and somatic integration of the motor expression of emotions, and emotion is characterized by sympathetic and parasympathetic excitatory and parasympathetic inhibitory discharges. It should be stressed that rage, shame rage, and fright are accompanied by a sympathetic (adrenalin) discharge and may also involve the excitation of the vago-insulin system. See Gellhorn, *Autonomic Regulations: The Significance for Physiology, Psychology and Neuropsychiatry*, pp. 202–3.

16. David M. Levy, "A Method of Integrating Physical and Psychiatric Examination," *American Journal of Psychiatry*, IX, No. 1 (July, 1929), 121–94.

XII. CRIMINAL LAW AND PSYCHIATRY

1. Regina v. Oxford, 9 C. & P. 525, 173 Eng. L. & Eq. R. 941 (1840); Offord's Case, 5 C. & P. 168, 172 Eng. L. & Eq. R. 924 (1831).

2. Weihofen, *Insanity as a Defense in Criminal Law*, pp. 28–29.

3. *The American Students' Blackstone*, IV, 24.

4. Cardozo, *Law and Literature*, pp. 106–8.

5. Jerome Hall, "Mental Disease and Criminal Responsibility, etc.," *Indiana Law Journal*, Vol. 33, No. 2 (Winter, 1958), pp. 219–20.

6. Durham v. U.S. (1954), 94 U.S. App. D.C. 228.

7. Case of Wright v. United States, *Harvard Law Record* (April 3, 1958).

8. Winfred Overholser and William J. T. Cody, "Forensic Psychiatry," *Review of Psychiatric Progress 1957* (January, 1958), pp. 642–44.

9. See also "Insanity as a Defense in Criminal Cases: The Durham Rule or the M'Naghten Rule in Illinois," *Journal of the American Medical Association*, Vol. 165, No. 11 (November 16, 1957), pp. 1490–91.

10. 344 Ill. 261, 176 N.E. 314 (1931).

11. Hawie v. State, 121 Mo. 197, 83 So. 158 (1919).

12. Gregory Zilboorg, "Misconceptions of Legal Insanity," *American Journal of Orthopsychiatry*, IX, No. 9 (July, 1939), p. 349.

13. C. K. Simon, "A New Chance for Youth," *Survey Midmonthly,* (November, 1943), p. 297.

14. Overholser, "Psychiatry and the Law—Cooperators or Antagonists?", *The Psychiatric Quarterly,* XIII (October, 1939), pp. 622–38, 656.

15. W. Hubert Smith has proposed that the court appoint expert referees from authorized lists in which the qualifications of the experts are beyond doubt. These referees would then have the power of acting as an "auditing" committee, whereby all medical data concerning the case could be properly considered and put before the court in a detailed scientific report. Such a committee could act as an advisory body not only to the jury but to the judge and counsels themselves. "Scientific Proof and the Relations of Law and Medicine," *Boston University Law Review,* XXIII (April, 1943), pp. 143–82.

16. B. Apfelberg, "Experiences with the New Criminal Code in New York State," *American Journal of Psychiatry,* XCVIII (November, 1941), pp. 415–21.

17. Peter B. Hagopian, "Mental Abnormalities in Criminals Based on Briggs Law Cases," *American Journal of Psychiatry,* 109:486–490 (January, 1953).

18. *Massachusetts Law Quarterly,* 41:30 (December, 1956).

19. People v. Moran, 249 N.Y. 179.

20. "New York's New Indeterminate Sentence Law for Sex Offenders," *Yale Law Journal,* 60:350 (February, 1951).

21. D. A. Thom, "Irresponsibility of Juvenile Delinquents," *American Journal of Psychiatry,* XCIX, No. 2 (September, 1942).

22. Smith-Hurd, *Ill. Annot. Stat.,* Chap. 38, Criminal Code, Div. XVI (1938).

23. The preceding information on Minnesota, West Virginia, and California has been adapted from Karl M. Bowman and Bernice Engle, "Certain Aspects of Sex Psychopath Laws," *American Journal of Psychiatry,* Vol. 114, No. 8 (February, 1958), pp. 690–97.

24. Ralph Brancale and F. Lovell Bixby, *Nation,* 184:293 (April 6, 1957).

25. Schneider, *Die Beurteilung der Zurechnungsfähigkeit: Ein Vortrag.*

XIII. REBUILDING AND REHABILITATING THE OFFENDER

1. Sellin, *The Criminality of Youth.*

2. Sheldon and Eleanor Glueck, "Toward Rehabilitation of Criminals: Appraisal of Statutory Treatment of Mentally Disordered Recidivists," *Yale Law Journal,* 57:6 (April, 1948), p. 1085.

3. James V. Bennett, "A Sponsorship Program for Adult Offenders," *Federal Probation,* Vol. XIII, No. 1 (March, 1949), p. 19.

4. Nathaniel Showstack, "Preliminary Report on the Psychiatric Treatment of Prisoners at the California Medical Facility," *American Journal of Psychiatry,* Vol. 112, No. 10 (April, 1956), p. 821.

5. Warren Weaver, Jr., "Capital Penalty Upheld in Albany—Assembly Defeats Bill that Permits a Life Term in First-Degree Murder," *New York Times,* (March 5, 1959), p. 20.

6. Maximilian Silbermann, "Julius Wagner Von Jauregg," *American Journal of Psychiatry,* Vol. 113, No. 12 (June, 1957), p. 1057.

7. Warren S. Wille, "Psychiatric Facilities in Prisons and Correctional Institutions in the United States," *American Journal of Psychiatry,* Vol. 4, No. 116 (December, 1957), pp. 481–87. (See also Winfred Overholser, "Forensic Psy-

chiatry," *American Journal of Psychiatry,* Vol. 115, No. 7 (January, 1959), p. 646.)

8. Luke: 15.7.

9. Abrahamsen, "Evaluation of the Treatment of Criminals," *Failures in Psychiatric Treatment,* p. 58.

10. Nathaniel Showstack, "Preliminary Report on the Psychiatric Treatment of Prisoners at the California Medical Facility," *American Journal of Psychiatry,* Vol. 112, No. 10 (April, 1956), p. 824.

11. Abrahamsen, *Report on Study of 102 Sex Offenders at Sing Sing Prison,* p. 24.

12. S. R. Slavson, "Catharsis in Group Psychotherapy," *Psychoanalytic Review,* Vol. 38 (January, 1951), pp. 39–52.

13. Martin Grotjahn, "The Process of Maturation in Group Psychotherapy and in the Group Therapist," *Psychiatry,* Vol. 13 (February, 1950), pp. 63–67.

14. Edward Glover, "Observations on Treating the Psychopathic Delinquent," *Journal of the Association for Psychiatric Treatment of Offenders,* Vol. I, No. 3 (October, 1957), p. 3.

15. E. Bergler, "Suppositions about the Mechanism of Criminosis," *Journal of Criminal Psychopathology,* Vol. V, No. 2 (October, 1943), p. 239.

16. Georg K. Stürup, "Sexual Offenders and their Treatment in Denmark and the other Scandinavian Countries," *International Review of Criminal Policy,* No. 4 (July, 1953), pp. 1–16.

17. Julius Levine and Harold Albert, "Sexual Behavior after Lobotomy," *Journal of Nervous and Mental Disease,* Vol. 113, No. 4 (April, 1951), pp. 332–41.

18. Ørnulv Ødegård, "Psykokirurgi I, Indikasjoner, Psykologiske Undersøkelser of Resultater," *Nordisk Psykiatrisk Medlemsblad,* Bd. III, Ekstranummer, pp. 67 and 68.

19. Herbert A. Raskin, Thomas A. Petty, and Max Warren, "A Suggested Approach to the Problem of Narcotic Addiction," *American Journal of Psychiatry,* Vol. 113, No. 12 (June, 1957), pp. 1089 and 1094.

20. Frederick Lemere, "What Happens to Alcoholics?", *American Journal of Psychiatry,* Vol. 109, No. 9 (March, 1953), p. 675. Entire article, pp. 674–76.

21. M. Grünhut, "Probation as a Research Field—a Pilot Survey," *British Journal of Delinquency,* II (1953), pp. 288, 290 and 291.

22. J. B. Waite, "The Prevention of Repeated Crime," Associated Press Dispatch (April 3, 1942), p. 32.

23. New York *Times,* March 15, 1959.

24. "Hypnosis of Prisoners," *Journal of the American Medical Association,* Vol. 167, No. 4 (May 24, 1958), p. 494.

25. Paul H. Hoch, "Progress in Psychiatric Therapies," *American Journal of Psychiatry,* Vol. 112, No. 4 (October, 1955), p. 243.

XIV. THE PREVENTION OF CRIME

1. Melitta Schmideberg, "Psychodynamics of Child Delinquency; Round Table, 1952," *American Journal of Orthopsychiatry,* Vol. XXIII, No. 7 (January, 1953), p. 14.

2. David Abrahamsen, "Emotionally Maladjusted Children with or without Delinquency," *Quarterly Journal of Child Behavior*, Vol. IV, No. 4 (October, 1952), pp. 446–47.

3. Edith Buxbaum, Symposium 1954, "Antisocial Acting Out," *American Journal of Orthopsychiatry*, Vol. XXIV, No. 4 (October, 1954), p. 690.

4. Emanuel K. Schwartz and Alexander Wolfe, "Psychoanalysis in Groups: Three Primary Parameters," *The American Imago*, Vol. XIV, No. 3 (1957), p. 295.

5. David Abrahamsen, "Status of Mental Hygiene and Child Guidance Facilities in Public Schools in the United States," *Journal of Pediatrics*, Vol. XLVI, No. 1 (January, 1955), p. 107.

6. David Abrahamsen, "Mental Hygiene Services in Private Schools," *Mental Hygiene*, Vol. 43, No. 2 (April, 1959), p. 282.

7. David Abrahamsen, "Status of Mental Hygiene and Child Guidance Facilities in Public Schools in the United States," *Journal of Pediatrics*, Vol. XLVI, No. 1 (January, 1955), p. 111.

8. David Abrahamsen, "Mental Hygiene and Child Guidance Facilities," *Journal of Pediatrics*, Vol. XLVI, No. 1 (January, 1955), pp. 115–16.

9. Sheldon and Eleanor Glueck, *Unraveling Juvenile Delinquency*, Chapter 20.

10. New York *Times*, March 15, 1959.

11. Wertham, *Seduction of the Innocent*.

12. Frederic M. Thrasher, "The Comics and Delinquency: Cause or Scapegoat," *Journal of Educational Sociology* (December, 1949), pp. 195–205.

13. "Comic Books and Juvenile Delinquency," Interim Report of the Subcommittee to Investigate Juvenile Delinquency (Washington, D.C.: Government Printing Office, 1955).

14. Alfred J. Kahn, *A Court for Children: A Study of the New York City Children's Court*.

15. Mildred B. Beck, Carmi Hariri, and Harris B. Peck, "Roundtable Discussion about Mental Health Problems Confronting a Children's Court," *American Journal of Psychiatry*, Vol. XXV, No. 1 (January, 1955), p. 39.

16. Abrahamsen, *Crime and the Human Mind*, p. 218.

17. Abrahamsen, *Who Are the Guilty?* p. 307.

Bibliography

Abrahamsen, David. *Crime and the Human Mind*. New York, Columbia University Press, 1944 and 1945.

—— *The Mind and Death of a Genius*. New York, Columbia University Press, 1946.

—— *Report on Study of 102 Sex Offenders at Sing Sing Prison*. Utica, N.Y., State Hospitals Press, 1950.

—— *The Road to Emotional Maturity*. New York, Prentice-Hall, 1958.

—— *Who Are the Guilty? A Study of Education and Crime*. New York and Toronto, Rinehart, 1952.

—— "Emotionally Maladjusted Children With or Without Delinquency," *Quarterly Journal of Child Behavior*, Vol. IV, No. 4 (October, 1952).

—— "Evaluation of the Treatment of Criminals," in *Failures in Psychiatric Treatment*, Paul Hoch, ed. New York, Grune and Stratton, 1948.

—— "Mass-Psychosis and Its Effects," *Journal of Nervous and Mental Disease*, Vol. 93, No. 1 (January, 1941).

—— "Mental Hygiene Services in Private Schools," *Mental Hygiene*, Vol. 43, No. 2 (April, 1959).

—— "Personality Reaction to Crime and Disease," *Journal of Nervous and Mental Disease*, Vol. 104, No. 1 (July, 1946).

—— "Psychosomatic Disorders and Their Significance in Antisocial Behavior," *Journal of Nervous and Mental Disease*, Vol. 107, No. 1 (January, 1948).

—— "Status of Mental Hygiene and Child Guidance Facilities in Public Schools in the United States," *Journal of Pediatrics*, Vol. XLVI, No. 1 (January, 1955).

Aichorn, August. *Wayward Youth*, Vienna, 1925; New York, Viking, 1935.

Alexander, Franz and William Healy. *The Roots of Crime*. New York, Knopf, 1935.

Alexander, Franz and Hugo Staub. *The Criminal, the Judge, and the Public.* New York, Macmillan, 1931.

Aschaffenburg, Gustav. *Crime and Its Repression.* Boston, Little, Brown, 1913.

Bjerre, Andreas. *The Psychology of Murder.* London, Longmans, 1927.

Blackstone, Sir William. *The American Students' Blackstone.* 4th ed. Edited by George Chase. New York, Banks Law Publishing Co., 1914.

Bloch, Herbert A. and Arthur Niederhoffer. *The Gang: A Study in Adolescent Behavior.* New York, Philosophical Library, 1958.

Burt, Cyril. *The Young Delinquent.* London, University of London Press, 1938.

Cardozo, Benjamin. *Law and Literature.* New York, Harcourt, 1931.

Cassity, John Hullard. "Personality Study of 200 Murderers," *Journal of Criminal Psychopathology,* Vol. II, No. 3 (1942).

Deutsch, Felix and F. William Murphy. *The Clinical Interview.* New York, International Universities Press, 1955.

English, Spurgeon and Stuart M. Finch. *Introduction to Psychiatry.* New York, Norton, 1957.

Ferri, Enrico. *Criminal Sociology.* London, Appleton, 1895.

Freud, Sigmund. *Collected Papers.* London, Hogarth, 1946.

Friedlander, Kate. *The Psychoanalytical Approach to Juvenile Delinquency.* London, International Universities Press, 1947.

Gellhorn, Ernst. *Autonomic Regulations: The Significance for Physiology, Psychology, and Neuropsychiatry.* New York, Inter Science, 1943.

Glueck, Sheldon and Eleanor Glueck. *500 Criminal Careers.* New York, Knopf, 1930.

—— *Unraveling Juvenile Delinquency.* New York, The Commonwealth Fund, 1950.

—— "Toward Rehabilitation of Criminals: Appraisal of Statutory Treatment of Mentally Disordered Recidivists," *Yale Law Journal,* Vol. 57, No. 6 (April, 1948).

Goring, Charles. *The English Convict.* London, 1913.

Guttmacher, Manfred S. *Sex Offenses: The Problems, Causes, and Prevention.* New York, Norton, 1951.

Hall, G. Stanley. *Adolescence.* 2 vols. New York, Appleton, 1904.

Healy, William. *The Individual Delinquent.* London, Little, 1915.

Healy, William and Augusta Bronner. *Delinquents and Criminals, Their Making and Unmaking.* New York, Macmillan, 1926.

—— *New Light on Delinquency and Its Treatment.* New Haven, Yale University Press, 1936.

Henderson, D. K. *Psychopathic States.* New York, Norton, 1939.

Hooton, Ernest Albert. *The American Criminal: An Anthropological Study.* 3 vols. Cambridge, Harvard University Press, 1939.

Hurwitz, Stephan. *Criminology.* London, Allen & Unwin, 1952; Copenhagen, Gad, 1952.

Kahn, Alfred J. *A Court for Children: A Study of the New York City Children's Court.* New York, Columbia University Press, 1953.

Kahn, Eugen. *Psychopathic Personalities.* Translated by Flanders Dunbar. New Haven, Yale University Press, 1931.

Kinsey, Alfred C., Wardell B. Pomeroy, and Clyde E. Martin. *Sexual Behavior in the Human Male*. Philadelphia and London, Saunders, 1958.

Kretschmer, Ernst. *Physique and Character*. New York, Harcourt, Brace, 1925.

Lander, Bernard. *Towards an Understanding of Juvenile Delinquency: A Study of 8,464 Cases of Juvenile Delinquency in Baltimore*. New York, Columbia University Press, 1954–55.

Liszt, Franz von. "Zur Vorbereitung des Strafgesetzentwurfs," *Strafrechtliche Aufsätze und Vorträge*, Berlin, 1905.

Menninger, Karl A. *Man Against Himself*. New York, Harcourt, Brace, 1938.

Monrad-Krohn, G. H. *The Clinical Examination of the Nervous System*. New York, Harpers, 1938.

Neustatter, W. Lindesay. *The Mind of the Murderer*. London, Johnson, 1957.

Overholser, Winfred. "Forensic Psychiatry," *American Journal of Psychiatry*, Vol. 115, No. 7 (January, 1959).

—— "Psychiatry and the Law—Cooperators or Antagonists?" *Psychiatric Quarterly*, Vol. XIII (October, 1939).

Paley, Frank. *Rumble on the Docks*. New York, Crown, 1953.

Palm, Rose and David Abrahamsen. "A Rorschach Study of the Wives of Sex Offenders," *Journal of Nervous and Mental Disease*, Vol. 119, No. 2 (February, 1954).

Schneider, Kurt. *Die Beurteilung der Zurechnungsfähigkeit: Ein Vortrag*. Stuttgart, Verlag, 1956.

Sellin, Thorsten. *The Criminality of Youth*. Philadelphia, The American Law Institute, 1940.

Shaw, Clifford R. and Henry D. McKay. *Juvenile Delinquency and Urban Areas*. Chicago, University of Chicago Press, 1942.

Sheldon, W. H. *Varieties of Delinquent Youth*. New York, Harper, 1949.

Stourzh-Anderle, Helene. *Sexuelle Konstitution: Psychopathie, Kriminalitat, Genie*. Vienna, Mandrich, 1955.

Taft, Donald R. *Criminology*. New York, Macmillan, 1942.

U.S. Department of Justice, Federal Bureau of Investigation, *Uniform Crime Reports*.

Wechsler, Israel S. *A Textbook of Clinical Neurology*. Philadelphia, Saunders, 1939.

Weihofen, H. *Insanity As a Defense in Criminal Law*. New York, The Commonwealth Fund, 1933.

Wertham, Frederic. *Seduction of the Innocent*. New York, Rinehart, 1954.

Wheelis, Allen. *The Quest for Identity*. New York, Norton, 1958.

Wille, Warren S. "Psychiatric Facilities in Prisons and Correctional Institutions in the United States," *American Journal of Psychiatry*, Vol. 4, No. 116 (December, 1957).

Zilboorg, Gregory. "Misconceptions of Legal Insanity," *American Journal of Orthopsychiatry*, IX (July, 1939), No. 9.

—— "Some Sidelights on Psychology of Murder," *Journal of Nervous and Mental Disease*, Vol. 18 (April, 1935).

Index

Abnormal, and normal, 209, 255 f.

Abrahamsen, David: research in criminal behavior, 11 f.; research project on offenders and their families, 42 f.; *Who Are the Guilty?* 90; research project at Columbia University, 91 ff.; study of "psychopathic" offenders, 135; research project at Sing Sing, 153, 156, 173 ff., 282; report on Leopold and Loeb to Parole Board, 278 f.; survey of children in public and private schools, 312; course at Teachers College, 316

Accidental offender, 123

Accident proneness, 93 ff.

Ackerson, Luton, study of inferiority, 204

Acting out: of desires and fantasies, 33 f.; of antisocial impulses, 81, 305; release through, 96; in group therapy, 288 f.

Acute offender: alcoholism and, 122, 123-26, 141

Adjustment: emotional, and behavior, 24, 33, 101; and learning process, 316 f.

Adjustment, social, of mental defective, 300

Adolescence: inner tensions, 65; and puberty, 74

Adolescents: criminal activities, 57 f.; car thief, 102; incidence of murder by, 201; *see also* Juvenile Delinquency

Adonis, Joe, 205

Advisory Council on Juvenile Delinquency, 318

Aggressiveness: and criminal behavior, 33; handling of, 36; constructive and destructive, 36; indirect, 40; nature of acts of, 41; projection of, 109; cause of, 121; sexual, submission and rejection in, 163 f.; and symptomatic murder, 197; relation with sex drive, 202; vicarious outlet for, 319

Aichhorn, August, 11

Alcoholics: self-aggressiveness of, 40; character disturbance, 139 f.; crimes committed by, 140 f.; and sex offenses, 158 f.; and homicide, 202; and pain, 225; psychoanalysis for, 295 f.

Alcoholics Anonymous, 295 f.

Alexander, Franz, 136; and Hugo Staub, 12, 120

Ambivalence, 40, 68

Ambulatory schizophrenia, 148

American culture: crime as product of, 18; and homicide, 180

Amicus curiae, 260

Amnesia, 228

Anal phase, of child development, 71 f.
Anamnesis, free associative, 92, 215, 236
Anastasia, Albert, 206
Anethopathy, 136
Ankle clonus, 226
Antabuse, drug, 296
Anthropology, and psychiatry, 6
Antisocial act: compared to crime, 14 f.; psychosomatic disorders substituted for, 95; *see also* Crime
Antisocial tendencies: as factor in criminal behavior, 33; universality of, 35
Anxiety: discharge of, 65, 81, 96; and criminal behavior, 110; handling of, and murder, 207; use of tranquilizers for, 302
Appearance: physical, and mental condition, 119 f.; of offender, 222, 229
Argyll-Robertson's sign, 224
Arrests, of young people in New York City, 58
Arson, criminogenic factors, 109
Aschaffenburg, Gustav, 8 f.; study of sex offenders, 155
Assault: by alcoholics, 202; in hypoglycemia case, 219
Associational offender, 123
Attention-getting, 95
Attitude, unrealistic, of criminals, 21; *see also* Reality
Authority: loss of respect for, 64; child and, 73; attitude of sex offenders toward, 158
Autism, 145
Automobile thefts, 57, 60, 102

Babinski's phenomenon, 226
Bazelon, David (judge), ruling, 249 f.
Beccaria, Cesare, on inhuman punishment, 4
Behavior: scientific investigations, 4 f.; four roots of, 15; conflict of forces and, 34 f.; formula of, 37 f.; and type of inner conflict, 101 f.; psychobiological concepts for understanding of, 103 f.; effect of disease on, 219; traits, measurement standards for, 239; motivations, and right and wrong test, 256; nonintellectual factors, 300
—— *criminal:* reorientation of understanding of, 1; and anatomical type, 6; and social pathology, 14-28; factors in, 23 f., 25 f.; formula of, 29-41; predis-

posing factors, 30, 108 f.; genesis of, 74; and symptoms of emotional disturbance, 76; receptivity to, 91 ff., 98; acting out of aggressions, 106; history of, and classification, 117; and symbolism, 114 f.; electroencephalographic findings, 138 f.; and narcotic addiction, 142; of offender's family, 221; and pathology, 263; normal behavior and, 272; and juvenile delinquency, 303 f.; interrelationship of psychological and sociological factors, 304 f.; warning signs of, 324
Bellevue Hospital, Psychiatric Division, 213
Blackstone, Sir William, on legal insanity, 247
Board of Psychiatric Examiners, 261
Body, deformed, and criminal behavior, 225
Body structure: and crime, 6 f., 31 f.; classification by, 119 f.
Borderline cases, difficulties re, 269
Borstal System, England, 324
Boys: background of family tension, 43 ff.; identification with strong male figure, 62 f.; hostility to mother, 67; development into homosexual, 168 f.; feeble-minded, case, 184 f.; tying up and robbing, case, 284 ff.; *see also* Adolescents; Gangs
Brain: knowledge of structure of, 15; damage, 138; disorder, signs of, 227
Briggs Law, 149, 263 f.
Bronner, Augusta, *see* Healy, William
Burt, Cyril, classification of criminals, 120

California, 314; incidence of sex crimes, 152; treatment of sex offenders, 173; Youth Authority Act, 259 f.; program for sexual psychopaths, 267 f.; Medical Facility, 282
Capital punishment: prisoner's attitude toward, 193; abolition of, 246; and insanity, 254
Capone, Al, 18
Cardozo, Benjamin N., on criminal insanity, 248 f.
Case histories: Arnold, effect of family tension, 43 ff.; Diana Addison, poor family relationship, 46 ff.; Nevin, effect on, of unconscious family ten-

Law, criminal: development of, 1, 8; age of legal responsibility (*q.v.*), 56 f.; classification of crimes, 118; statutory rape, 154 f.; recommended, for sex offenses, 176 f.; re narcoanalysis, 236; and psychiatry, 244-70; and the sex offender, 264-68; International Association, 275f.; and the youthful offender, 258-60
Law enforcement authorities, 323
Law No. 1, in etiology of crime, 30-37
Law No. 2, 37-41, 64, 103, 222, 272, 305
Leibowitz, Samuel (judge), case of the "Mad Bomber," 255
Leopold, Nathan: background and personality make-up, 199 ff.; parole, 278 f.
Leopold-Loeb case, 11, 134, 171, 198 ff., 278
Lesbianism, 167
Libido, 69, 98
Liszt, Franz von, 8; classification of criminals, 119
Lobotomy, of sex offenders, 293
Loeb, Richard: background and personality make-up, 198 ff.; *see also* Leopold-Loeb case
Lombroso, Cesare, 5; on criminal types, 118 f.
Love: deprivation of, and hostility, 52; unconscious substitutes for, 96; food as, 100; acceptance of punishment and, 312
Luck, and gambling, 130 f.
Lunacy commission, re felony, 261
Lydstone, G. Frank, and Eugene Talbot, *The Diseases of Society,* 10
Lynching, 182 f.
Lyon school, 7

"Mad Bomber," case, 254 f.
Manic-depressive psychosis, 149
Manifest (essential) murder, 205-7
Manslaughter, 183
Marriage: and sex offenses, 162 f.; background of murder, 190
Maryland, treatment for sex offenders, 768
Masochism: aggression and, 65 ff., 164; juvenile, 82; and sadism, 161 f.
Massachussetts: State Prison, 140; Briggs Law in, 149, 263 f.; treatment for sex offenders, 268
Masturbation, and gambling, 131

Materialism, 66, 99; and crime, 19
Maturity, emotional: Oedipus-Electra stage in, 39; family tensions and, 44 ff.; inhibiting factors, 54; *see also* Adjustment
Medical history of offender, 218 f.
Memory, recent, of offender, 229 f.
Menninger, Karl A., 12, 191
Mental defectives, 109, 126; and crime, 144-50; in murder case, 213 f.; commitment of, 263; treatment of, 299 f.; socially adjusted, 300; therapy for, 301
Mental hospitals: and treatment of sexual psychopaths, 173; commitment for psychiatric examination, 213; mandatory commitment to, 257 f.
Mental hygiene: state departments of, recommendation of psychiatrists, 262; clinics, 313, 321; state legislation, 314
Mental illness: incidence of, 83 f.; and crime, 61, 106 ff., 121, 188 f., 248 f.; and personality make-up, 103; of sex offenders, 155; and guilt feelings, 196; Ganser syndrome, 235; and legal protection, 248; and responsibility, 264 f.; the law and, 268-70; without legal insanity, 299
Michaels, J. J.: re enuresis, 136 f.; electroencephalographic study, 138 f.
Michigan, 265; writ of habeas corpus, 253; law re drug addicts, 293
Migration: to cities, 62; family, effect of, 137
Mind, state of: and crime, 10, 108, 250; and physical appearance, 119 f.; of offender, 242 f.
Mind and body, interrelationship of, 90 f., 204 f.; *see also* Psychosomatic disorders
Minnesota, law re sex offenders, 265 f.
Mira Myokonetic Depression Test, 239
M'Naghten, Daniel, Rule, 246-58
Monrad-Krohn, G. H., 226; *The Clinical Examination of the Nervous System,* 224
Moral standards: weakening of, 64; *see also* Ethical standards
Mother: immature attachment to, 26 f.; dream of killing, 35; wish for separation from, 97; hostility toward, 100; of sex offender, 160; identification with, 163; homosexual identification with, 170; exhibitionist's relationship

with, 171; effect of attitude toward, on marriage, 197 f.; murder of, 207; attachment to, and rejection by, 307 f.

Motion pictures, and juvenile delinquency, 318-20

Motivation: of criminal act, 2; in biological drives, 5; of offender and nonoffender, 14 f.; and crime, 35; criminal, homosexuality and, 171; determination of, 185; unconscious, 186, 189 ff., 283; unrecognized, 205, 206

Motor system, examination of, 225

Murder: universal condemnation of, 2; dreams and, 35; homosexuality and, 171; psychological and sociological background, 180 f.; legal definition, 183; by whites and Negroes, 183; surrogate, 186, 198; multiple, case, 191 ff.; symptomatic, 196-205; indirect form of suicide, 200; under the influence of alcohol, 202; abnormalities and, 203 f.

Murderers: investigations of brains of, 10; personality make-up, 179-207; psychiatric examination of, 213; potential, 299

Murder Incorporated, 205 f.

Narcissism, 115, 129; of drug addicts, 142; homosexual, 168; and exhibitionism, 171

Narcoanalysis, use of, 236

Negativism: in anal phase, 72 f.; effect of treatment on, 289

Negroes: sex offenses, 152; incidence of murder among, 183

Neoclassical school of penology, 4, 9

Neurological abnormalities, 138

Neurological examination, 223 ff.

Neurosis, 106 f.; traumatically caused, 280; related to sexual deviation, 290 f.

Neurotic character disorders, 134-44; treatment of offenders with, 289-98

Neurotic offenders, 127-34; treatment of, 283-89

Neurotic person, compared with criminal, 12, 109-14, 114-16; family tension and, 53; different from psychotic, 106 f.

New Jersey, treatment for sex offenders, 268

Newspapers, crime coverage, 325

New York City: increase in youth crime, 58; truancy, 75 f.; street gangs, 85; narcotic addicts, 141; homicides, 179; Court of General Sessions, 212, 242, 258; Manhattan State Hospital, 294; "600 Schools," 313; "700 Schools," 314; Youth Board, 320 f.; Children's Court, cases, 323

New York state: legal age of juvenile delinquent, 56 f.; Joint Legislative Committee on Narcotics Study, 141; sex offenses, 152; Department of Correction, statistics on rape, 154; law re sex offenders, 177, 273; appointment of psychiatrist, 212; Committee for the Definition of Legal Insanity, 212, 250, 256 f.; discussion of the M'Naghten Rule, 248 f.; suggested modification of Penal Law, 256; Wayward Minor Act, 258; qualifications for expert psychiatrist, 261 f.; responsibility of mentally abnormal, 264 f.; Kapelman bill, 274; Department of Mental Hygiene, 294; state hospitals, 314

Nonoffender, emotionally disturbed, 105-16

Normal, and abnormal, borderline between, 209, 255 f.

Norway, study of sex offenses, 155; study of alcohol and crime, 202; treatment of mentally abnormal offenders, 269

Obedience, in childhood, 78

Object relationship, 137

Obsession, 232 f.; defined, 127

Obsessive-compulsory neurotic, 111 f., 127 ff., 166 f.; case, 284 ff.

Oedipus-Electra stage of development, 39, 73, 166

Oedipus situation, 197; unsolved, 83, 147, 284; legend, 115; homosexuality and, 169

Offenders: and families, research project re, 91 ff.; and emotionally disturbed nonoffender, 105-16; type of, and psychiatric examination, 213; educational and vocational history of, 217 f.; social history of, 218; orientation of, 229; physical examination of, 222 f.; behavior during examination, 233 ff.; desire for treatment, 282; suitable for probation, 296; mentally defective, 299 f.; see also Criminals; Prisoners

Ohio, law re dangerous offenses, 267

Protest reactions, indirect aggression as, 40

Psychiatric examination: in research project, 92 f.; of sex offenders, 156 f.; of murderer, 185, 206; and psychological examination, 208-43; procedure, 211; and type of offender, 213; data, concerning offender, 228-36; of juvenile offender, 240; conclusion of, 240-43; Briggs Law and, 264; of borderline cases, 269

Psychiatric Institute, New York, 92

Psychiatric-psychological studies, 275

Psychiatric treatment: for sex offenders, 178; with indeterminate sentence, 273; of prisoners, 280; prerequisites for, 281; during probation, 296 ff.; offender's family, 306 ff.

Psychiatric unit, Mobile, 321 f.

Psychiatrists: studies of criminal behavior, 10; abstention from moral pronouncements, 207; notes and observations during examination, 211; court-appointed, 212; recommendations to the court, 241 f.; as expert in court, 260-64; qualifications as expert, 261 f.; use of report by, 269; number of, in penological services, 275; role of, with prisoners, 282; ratio of, to number of schoolchildren, 312 f.

Psychiatry: use of, for sex offenders, 176 f.; defined, 210 f.; and criminal law, 244-70

Psychoanalysis: applied to delinquency, 11; change in problems of, 64; application of, 91; of juvenile delinquent, 97 ff.; of prisoners, 283 f.; treatment for homosexuality, 290 f.; of alcoholics, 295 f.; child in, 308

Psychobiotics, 32, 90

Psychological tests: of offenders, 43; of sex offenders, 174 f.; in psychiatric examination, 237-40

Psychometric tests, of mental defectives, 299 f.

Psychoneurosis: and ankle clonus, 226; susceptibility to psychoanalysis, 283 ff.

Psychopaths, 39 f., 135, 265; and feelings of guilt, 134; categories of, 136 ff.; neurotic character disorder, of, 137; diagnosis of, 143 f.; term, 143, 156; genuine, 143 f., 289; sexual, program for, 173; repetition of behavior, 257;

criminal, prison term, 274; criminal, program for, 291 ff.

Psychosis, 106 f.; homicide committed in, 187 f.; and personality, 209 f.; Ganser syndrome, 235

Psychosomatic disorders: and crime, 11 f., 90-104; and family tension, 53; emotional problems and, 76; of delinquent group, 93; based on character deformation, 101 f.; among criminals, 114

Psychotherapy: individual, 286; group, 287, 309; see also Psychiatric treatment

Psychotic: family tension and, 53; offender, 144-50, 299 f.; knowledge and emotional understanding of, 255; commitment of, 263; case diagnoses as psychopath, 268 f.

Puberty, 74 f.; and hostility to mother, 97; therapy at period of, 304 f.

Publicity, offender's craving for, 325

Public morals, sex offenders as threat to, 174 f.

Punishment: as retaliation, 2 f., 245, 272, 303; unconscious desire for, 33, 133 f., 186 f., 291; self-, 40, 93; harsh, of child, 43; wish for, 195, 200 f.; as deterrent, 246, 274; adapted to type of offender, 275 f.; and guilt feelings, 305; justified, 312

Pyromania, 127 ff., 284; relation to sexual desires, 129

Racketeer, income of, 18; see also Murder Incorporated

Rape, 38; number of cases in the U.S., 152; and robbery, 153; incidence of, 153 f.; statutory, 154 f.; study of wives of offenders, 162; age of victim, 166; case of mental abnormality without legal insanity, 299

Reality: lack of, 106 f.; in environment and life situation, 76 f.; among delinquents, 83; in schizophrenia, 148

Rebellion against authority, 46, 73; manifestations of, 74 f.

Recidivism, 274; of the mentally retarded, 150; of sex offenders, 153; of alcoholics, 202 f.; of psychopathic person, 257; lack of treatment and, 277; of castrates, 292

Reflexes, testing of, 224 ff.

Regression, see Fixation

Rehabilitation, 271-302

penal codes re murder, 184; criminal law, 245; death penalty, 246; M'Naghten Rule, 248; laws re sex offenders, 265 ff.; treatment facilities for sex offenders, 267; psychiatric services, 275; mental health legislation, 314

Stealing, 307; for immediate gratification, 27; personality structure and, 33 f.; environmental stress and, 38; and background of emotional disturbance, 47 ff.; pattern of, 65; as attention-getting device, 95; and sexual excitement, 128 f.; and gambling, 131; *see also* Robbery

Subcommittee to investigate Juvenile Delinquency, 319

Sublimation, of instincts, 69

Suicide: as self-aggression, 40; in Japan, 181; murder as indirect form of, 200; of castrates, 292

Superego: and criminal tendencies, 24; and ego, 34 f.; and resistance to crime, 39; structure, 53, 105 f.; and moral standards, 64; defective, 77, 305 f.; healthy, and identification, 96; overdeveloped, 110 f.; external, 137 f.; in obsessive-compulsory offenders, 167; dynamic relationship with id and ego, 280

Suppression, and emotional growth, 61 f.

Symbolism: in neurosis and criminal behavior, 114 f.; in criminal acts, 128 f.

Symptoms, simulated by offender, 234 f.

Syndicates, crime, and cost of crime, 17 f.

Syphilis, evidence of, 224

Tabes incipiens, 225

Teachers: counseling, 315; requisite for aid to emotionally disturbed children, 315; entrance examination requirements, 317

Teachers College, Columbia University, 316

Technology, effect of, 19 f.

Television, and juvenile delinquency, 318-20

Tendencies, criminalistic, 37 f.; in abnormal personality make-up, 188 f.; released by alcohol, 202

Theft, *see* Stealing

Toilet training, 68, 71 f.

Tranquilizers, 301 f.

Transference: positive, 92, 110, 281; in

psychiatric examination, 215; in psychiatric interview, 220

Treatment: for sex offenders, 174 f., 267 f.; of borderline cases, 269; *see also* Psychiatric treatment

Trial: examination of criminal prior to, 213; insanity plea in relation to time of, 253 f.

Truancy, 66 f., 158, 217, 307, 313; acting out of hostility, 51; habitual, 75 f.

Tuberculosis, sensitivity to, 22 f.; and configuration of hand, 223; as psychosomatic reaction, 255

Tying up and robbing, case, 284 ff.

Understanding, and emotional awareness, 249, 254

United Nations: Social Commission of the Economic and Social Council, 17; Expert Committee, 31; Conference on Juvenile Crime, 59

United States: increase in crime, 17; increase in juvenile crime, 58; heterogeneous population and juvenile delinquency, 64; mental illness in, 83 f.; incidence of rape in, 152; homicide in, 179 f.; regional homicide rates, 182; early criminal law in, 247 f.; drug traffic in, 295

Victim: criminal's choice of, 161; substitute, 185

Vocabulary, of street gangs, 85 ff.

Voyeurism, 171 f.

Wayne University, Department of Psychiatry, 294

Wayward Minor Act, 258

Wealth, greed for, and crime, 19

West Virginia, law re sex offenders, 266 f.

White Slave Act of 1910, 245

Wife: relationship with sex-offender husband, 161 ff.; of rapist, similar to his mother, 164; unconscious motivation for murder of, 187 f.; murder of, 189 ff.

Wisconsin, law re sex offenders, 265 f.

Withdrawal, psychotic, 107

Women: increase of crime among, 17; victimized as substitute for mother, 100 f.; type of crimes committed by, 126; case of kleptomania, 128 f.; and